Fundamental Philosophy
Vol. 2

by

Jaime Luciano Balmes

Fundamental Philosophy
Vol. 2
by Jaime Luciano Balmes

ISBN: 978-93-60466-18-3

Published by

DOUBLE 9 BOOKS
2/13-B, Ansari Road
Daryaganj, New Delhi – 110002
info@double9books.com
www.double9books.com
Tel. 011-40042856

ABOUT THE AUTHOR

Spain's Jaime Luciano Balmes y Urpiá was a philosopher, theologian, Catholic defender, sociologist, and political writer who lived from August 28, 1810, to July 9, 1848. Balmes was an original philosopher who did not follow any particular school or line. He knew about the ideas of Saint Thomas Aquinas and was known as the Prince of Modern Apologetics by Pope Pius XII. He was born in Vic, Spain, in the Catalonia region. On the same day he was born, Balmes was baptized in the church of that city with the name Jaime Luciano Antonio. He passed away in the same place. Starting in 1817, Balmes went to the college in Vic to study. He took three years of Latin grammar, three years of rhetoric, and starting in 1822, three years of philosophy. In Solsona in 1825, the Bishop of that city, Manuel Benito Tabernero, gave him the tonsure. Balmes also took courses in theology at Vic Seminary from 1825 to 1826. It was free for him to take four courses in theology at the University of Cervera's College of San Carlos. Because the University of Cervera had to close in 1830, Balmes continued to study on his own in Vic for two years. He got his degree in religion on June 8, 1833.

CONTENTS

BOOK FOURTH
ON IDEAS

CHAPTER I
CURSORY VIEW OF SENSISM

1. Having spoken of sensations, we come now to ideas. We must, however, before making this transition, inquire if there be in our mind ought else than sensation, if all the inward phenomena which we experience be ought else than sensations transformed.

Man, when he rises from the sphere of sensations, from those phenomena which place him in relation with the external world, meets a new order of phenomena, of whose presence he is equally conscious. He cannot reflect upon sensations without being conscious of something more than sensation; nor on the recollection or the inward representation of sensations, without discovering something distinct both from the recollection and from the representation.

2. According to Aristotle, there is nothing in the understanding which has not first been in the senses; and the schools have for long ages re-echoed this thought of the philosopher: *nihil est in intellectu quod prius non fuerit in sensu*. The order, therefore, of human knowledge, is from the external to the internal. Descartes pretended that we ought to invert this order, and proceed from the internal to the external. Malebranche, his disciple, went farther, and was of opinion that the understanding, enfolded in itself, should hold only the least possible intercourse with the external world. According to him, no atmosphere is so fatal to intellectual health as that of the world of the senses; sensations are an inexhaustible fountain of error, and the imagination is an enchantress only the more dangerous because she has fixed her dwelling at the very portal of the intellect, which, with her seductive beauty and gorgeous ornaments, she hopes to rule at her pleasure.

3. Locke strove to rehabilitate the old Aristotelian maxim, joined, however, to the criterion of observation: besides sensation he admitted only

reflection, but he taught that the mind was endowed with innate faculties. His disciple, Condillac, not satisfied with this, taught that all the actions of our mind were simply sensations transformed: instead of distinguishing with Locke two sources of our ideas, the senses and reflection, he thought it more exact to admit only one, as well because reflection is in its root only sensation, as because it is rather the channel by which ideas originating in the senses pass, than their source.

Judgment, reflection, desires, and passions are in Condillac's estimation nothing else than sensation transformed in various modes. It seemed to him, therefore, very idle to suppose the mind to have received immediately from nature the faculties with which it is endowed. Nature has given us organs which show us by pleasure or pain what we ought to seek or to avoid; but here she stops, and leaves to experience the task of leading us to contract habits and finish the work she has commenced.[1]

4. In view of this system, in which not even natural faculties are conceded to the soul, and those which it does possess are considered as only simple effects of sensation, it is worthy of remark how soon its author contradicts himself; for, almost in the same breath, he professes to be an occasionalist, and pretends that the impressions of our organization are nothing more than the occasion of our sensations. Can there be a natural faculty more inexplicable than that of placing one's self in relation with objects which do not produce sensations, but are only the occasion of their production. If such a faculty as this be conceded to the mind, why may we not admit others? Is not that a very singular natural faculty which perceives by means of causes operating only occasionally? In this case, is there not attributed to the mind a natural faculty of producing sensations on occasion of organic impressions, or is it not supposed to be an immediate relation with another and superior being which produces them? Why may not this internal activity, this receptivity, apply itself to ideas? Why must not other innate faculties be conceded to the mind? And why does he pretend not to suppose them, when his whole argument is based upon the supposition of their existence?

Hostile as he professes to be to hypotheses and systems, Condillac is eminently addicted both to systems and hypotheses. He imagines an origin and a nature of ideas of his own, and to them he insists that every thing must conform. To give a better idea of Condillac's opinions, and to combat them at once successfully and loyally, we will briefly analyze the groundwork of his *Treatise on Sensations*, the book on which he most prides himself, and in which he flatters himself to have given to his doctrine its highest degree of clearness and certainty.

CHAPTER II
CONDILLAC'S STATUE

5. Condillac supposes a statue, which he animates successively with each of the senses: then beginning with the sense of smell, he says; "So long as our statue is limited to the sense of smell, its knowledge cannot go beyond odors; it can neither have any idea of extension, of space, or of any thing beyond itself, nor of other sensations, such as color, sound, taste." [2] If, according to the conditions of the supposition, all activity and every faculty be denied to this statue, it certainly can have no other idea or sensation, and it may be added that even its sensation of smell will be for it no idea.

"If we present it a rose," continues Condillac, "to us it will be a statue which smells a rose; but for itself it will be only the smell of a rose. It will then be the smell of the rose, the pink, the jasmine, or the violet, according to the objects which operate upon its organ; in a word, with respect to it, these odors are only its own modifications and manners of being, and it cannot believe itself any thing else, since these are the only sensations of which it is susceptible."

6. It is very obvious that at the first step, the statue must take a great leap. Close upon the apparent simplicity of the sensible phenomenon, *reflection*, one of those acts which suppose the intellect already well developed, is introduced. First the statue believes itself something; it believes itself the odor; next consciousness of itself in relation to the impression it has just received, is attributed to it; then it is made to form a kind of judgment, whereby it affirms the identity of itself with the sensation. This, however, is impossible, unless we have something besides bare sensation; but we neither have nor can have at this stage any thing beyond this purely passive impression, an isolated phenomenon, upon which there can be no reflection of any kind whatever; and the statue can have no other reflection of itself than this sensation, which in the reflective order has no title to be so called. Condillac's hypothesis rigorously applied, presents only a phenomenon leading to nothing; and the moment he leaves sensation to develop it, he admits an activity in the mind distinct and very different from sensation, which destroys his whole system.

The statue confined to the sensation of smell will never believe itself smell; such a belief is a judgment, and supposes comparison, no trace of which can be discovered in the sensible phenomenon, considered in all its purity, as Condillac requires in his hypothesis. He begins his analytical investigations by introducing conditions which he at the same time supposes to be eliminated. He undertakes to explain every thing by sensation alone, and his first step is to amalgamate sensation with operations of a very different order.

7. Condillac calls the capacity of feeling, when applied to the impression received, attention. So if there be but one sensation, there can be but one attention. If various sensations succeeding each other leave some trace in the memory of the statue, the attention will, when a new sensation is presented, be divided between the present and the past. The attention directed at one and the same time to two sensations becomes comparison. Similarities and differences are perceived by comparison, and this perception is a judgment. All this is done with sensations alone; therefore attention, memory, comparison, and judgment are nothing but sensations transformed. In appearance nothing clearer, more simple, or more ingenuous; in reality nothing more confused or false.

8. First of all, this definition of attention is not exact. The capacity of feeling, by the very fact of being in exercise, is applied to the impression. It does not feel when the sensitive faculty is not in exercise, and this is not in exercise except when applied to the impression. Consequently, attention would be nothing but the act of feeling; all sensation would be attention, and all attention sensation; a meaning which no one ever yet gave to these words.

9. Attention is the application of the mind to something; and this application supposes the exercise of an activity concentrated upon its object. Properly speaking, when the mind holds itself entirely passive, it is not attentive; and with respect to sensations it is attentive when by a reflex act we know that we feel. Without this cognition there can be no attention, but only sensation more or less active, according to the degree in which it affects our sensibility. If Condillac means to call the more vivid sensation attention, the word is improperly used; for it ordinarily happens that they who feel with the greatest vividness are precisely those who are distinguished for their want of attention. Sensation is the affection of a passive faculty; attention is the exercise of an activity; and hence it is that brutes do not participate of it except inasmuch as they possess a principle of activity to direct their sensitive faculties to a determinate object.

10. Is the perception of the difference of the smell of the rose and that of the pink a sensation? If we are answered that it is not, we infer that the judgment is not the sensation transformed; for it is not even a sensation. If we are told that it is one sensation, we then observe that if it be either that of the rose or that of the pink, it follows that with one alone of these sensations we shall have comparative perception, which is absurd. If we are answered that it is both together, we must either interpret this expression rigorously, and then we shall have a sensation which will at once be that of the pink and that of the rose, the one remaining distinct from the other so as to satisfy the conditions of comparison; or we must interpret it so as to mean that the two sensations are united; in which case we gain nothing, for the difficulty will be to show how co-existence produces comparison, and judgment, or the perception of the difference.

The sensation of the pink is only that of the pink, and that of the rose only that of the rose. The instant you attempt to compare them, you suppose in the mind an act by which it perceives the difference; and if you attribute to it any thing more than pure sensation, you add a faculty distinct from sensation, namely that of comparing sensations, and appreciating their similarities and differences.

11. This comparison, this intellectual force, which calls the two extremes into a common arena, without confounding them, discovers the points in which they are alike or unlike each other, and, as it were, comes in and decides between them, is distinct from the sensation; it is the effect of an activity of a different order, and its development must depend on sensations as exciting causes, as a condition *sine qua non*; but this is all it has to do with sensations themselves; it is essentially distinct from them, and cannot be confounded with them without destroying the idea of comparison, and rendering it impossible.

No judgment is possible without the ideas of identity or similarity, and these ideas are not sensations. Sensations are particular facts which never leave their own sphere, nor can be applied from one thing to another. The ideas of similarity and identity have something in common applicable to many facts.

12. What next happens to a being limited to the faculty of experiencing various sensations? It will receive without comparing them. It is certain that when it feels in one manner it will not feel in another, that one sensation is not another; but this sensitive being will take no notice of the variety. Sensations will succeed sensations, but will not be compared with each other. Even supposing them to be remembered, the memory of them will be nothing more than a less intense repetition of the same sensations. If it

be admitted that this sensitive being compares them, and perceives their relations of identity or distinction, of similarity or difference, a series of reflex acts are admitted which are not sensations.

13. Nor can the memory, properly so called, of sensations, be explained by them alone; and here again Condillac is wrong. The statue may recollect to-day the sensation of the smell of the rose which it received yesterday, and this recollection may exist in two ways: first, by the internal reproduction of the sensation without any external cause, or relation to time past, and consequently without any relation to the prior existence of a similar sensation; and then this recollection is not for the statue a recollection properly so called, but only a sensation more or less vivid: secondly, by an internal reproduction with relation to the existence of the same or another similar sensation at a preceding time, in which recollection essentially consists; and here there is something more than sensation; here are the ideas of succession, time, priority, and identity, or similarity, all distinct and separable from sensation.

Two entirely distinct sensations may be referred to the same time in the memory; and then the time will be identical, and the sensations distinct. The sensation may exist without any recollection of the time it before existed, or even without any recollection of having ever existed; consequently, sensation involves no relation of time; they are distinct and very different matters, and Condillac deceives himself when he undertakes to explain the memory of sensations by mere sensations.

14. These reflections utterly refute Condillac's system. Either he admits something besides sensation or he does not; if he does, he violates his own original supposition; if he does not, he cannot explain any abstract idea, nor even the sensitive memory: he will therefore be obliged to admit with Locke reflection upon sensations, and for the same reason, other faculties of the soul.

15. It is easy to comprehend why certain philosophers have maintained that all our ideas come from the senses, if we understand them to mean that sensations awaken our internal activity, and, so to speak, supply the intellect with materials: but it is not so easy to see how it can be advanced as a certain, clear, and exceedingly simple truth that there is in our mind nothing but these materials, these sensations. We have only to fix our attention for a moment upon what passes within us to discover many phenomena distinct from sensation, and various faculties which have nothing to do with sensation. If Condillac had been satisfied with maintaining that these faculties needed sensation as a kind of excitement in order to be developed, he would have advanced nothing contrary to sound philosophy: but for him to pretend

that all that is excited and all that is developed is only the principle which excites, and to insist that this is confirmed by actual observation, is openly to contradict observation itself, and to render it absolutely impossible for him to make the least progress in the explanation of intellectual activity, unless he abandons the supposition upon which his whole system is founded. Nevertheless, the author of the *Treatise on Sensations* seems to be perfectly satisfied with his system: the actual impression is the sensation; the recollection of the sensation is the intellectual idea. If this is not sound, it is at least deceptive: with the appearance of nice observation he stops at the surface of things, and does not fatigue the pupil. Every thing comes from sensation; but this is because Condillac makes his statue talk as he pleases, without paying the least attention to his hypothesis of sensation alone.

16. This system, by reason of its philosophical meagerness, is fatal to all moral ideas. What becomes of morality if there are no ideas, except sensations? What becomes of duty if every thing is reduced to sensible necessity, to pleasure or pain? And what becomes of God, and of all man's relations to God?

CHAPTER III
DIFFERENCE BETWEEN GEOMETRICAL IDEAS AND THE SENSIBLE REPRESENTATIONS WHICH ACCOMPANY THEM

17. Sensible representations always accompany our intellectual ideas. This is why in reflecting upon the latter we are apt to confound them with the former. We say, in reflecting upon them, not in making use of them. We none of us, have any trouble in making use of ideas according to circumstances; the error lies in the reflex, not in the direct act. It will be well to bear this last observation in mind.

18. It is next to impossible for the geometrician to meditate upon the triangle without revolving in his imagination, the image of a triangle as he has seen it drawn a thousand times; and he will, for this reason, be disposed to believe that the idea of the triangle is nothing else than this sensible representation. Were it thus, Condillac's assertion that the idea is only the recollection of the sensation would be verified in the idea of the triangle. In fact, this representation is the sensation repeated: the only difference between the two affections of the mind is that the actual sensation is caused by the actual presence of its object, wherefore it is more fixed and vivid. To prove that the difference is not essential, but consists only in degree, it is sufficient to observe, that if the imaginary representation attain a high degree of vividness we cannot distinguish it from sensation, as it happens to the visionary, and as we have all experienced in our dreams.

19. By noticing the following facts, we shall readily perceive how different the idea of the triangle is from its imaginary representation.

I. The idea of the triangle is one, and is common to all triangles of every size and kind; the representation of it is multiple, and varies in size and form.

II. When we reason upon the properties of the triangle, we proceed from a fixed and necessary idea; the representation changes at every instant, not so, however, the unity of the idea.

III. The idea of a triangle of any kind in particular is clear and evident; we see its properties in the clearest manner; the representation on the contrary is vague and confused, thus it is difficult to distinguish a right-angled from an acute-angled triangle, or even a slightly inclined obtuse-angled triangle. The idea corrects these errors or rather abstracts them; it makes use of the imaginary figure only as an auxiliary, in the same manner as we give our demonstrations when we draw figures upon paper, abstracting their exactness or inexactness, often when we know that they are not exact, which they cannot always be.

IV. The idea of the triangle is the same to the man born blind and to him who has sight; and the proof of this is that both, in their arguments and geometrical uses, develop it in precisely the same manner. The representation is different, for us it is a picture, which it cannot be for the blind man. When he meditates upon the triangle he neither has, nor can have, in his imagination, the same sensible representation as we, since he wants all that can relate to the sensation of sight. If the blind man experiences any accompanying representation of the idea, he can have received it only from the sense of touch; and in the case of large triangles, the three sides of which cannot be touched at the same time, the representation must be a successive series of sensations of touch, just as the recollection of a piece of music is essentially a successive representation. With us the representation of the triangle is almost always simultaneous, excepting the case of exceedingly large triangles, much larger than we usually see, in which case, especially when we are unaccustomed to consider such, it seems necessary to go on extending the lines successively.

20. What has been said of the triangle, the simplest of all figures, may with still greater reason be said of all others, many of which cannot be distinctly represented by the imagination, as we see in many-sided figures; and even the circle, which for facility of representation rivals the triangle, we cannot so perfectly imagine as to distinguish it from an ellipse whose foci are only at a trifling distance from each other.

CHAPTER IV
THE IDEA AND THE INTELLECTUAL ACT

21. Having shown that geometrical ideas are not sensible representations, we can safely conclude that no kind of ideas are. Could there be a difficulty concerning any, it would be concerning geometrical ideas, for the objects of the latter can be sensibly represented. When objects have no figure, they cannot be perceived by any of the senses; to speak in such a case of sensible representations is to fall into a contradiction.

22. These considerations draw a dividing line between the intellect and the imagination; a line which all the scholastics drew, which Descartes and Malebranche respected and made still more prominent, but which Locke began to efface, and Condillac entirely obliterated. All the scholastics recognized this line; but they, like many others, used a language which, unless well understood, was of a character to obscure it. They called every idea an image of the object, and explained the act of the understanding as if there were a kind of form in the understanding which expressed the object, just as a picture presented to the eyes offers them the image of the thing pictured. This language arose from the continual comparison which is very naturally made between seeing and understanding. When objects are not present we make use of their pictures, and thus, since objects themselves cannot be present to our understanding, we conceive an interior form which performs the part of a picture. On the other hand, sensible things are the only ones which are strictly susceptible of representation; we never discover within ourselves the form in which the objects are portrayed, except in the case of imaginary representations; and therefore it was rash to call this an idea, and every idea an imaginary representation, in which the whole system of Condillac consists.

23. St. Thomas calls the representations of the imagination *phantasmata*, and says that so long as the soul is united to the body we cannot understand except *per conversionem ad phantasmata*; that is, unless the representation of the imagination, which serves as material for the formation of the idea, and assists in clearing it up, and heightening its colors, precedes and accompanies the intellectual act. Experience teaches that whenever we understand, certain sensible forms relative to the object which occupies us,

exist in our imagination. Now, they are the images of the figure and color of the object, if it have any; now, the images of those with which they are compared, or the words which denote them in the language we habitually speak. Thus, even when thinking of God, the very act by which we affirm that he is most pure spirit, offers a kind of representation to the imagination under a sensible form. When we speak of eternity, we see the *Ancient of days*, as we have often seen him represented in our churches; when we speak of the infinite intelligence, we imagine perhaps a sea of light; infinite mercy, we picture to ourselves as a pitying likeness; justice, with angry countenance. To force ourselves to form some conception of the creation, we fancy a spring whence light and life both flow, and thus also we endeavor to render immensity sensible by imagining unlimited extension.

The imagination always accompanies the idea, but is not itself the idea; and we perceive the evident and unimpeachable proof of the distinction between the two, if we ask ourselves, while in the very act of imagining a sea of light, an old man, an angry or placid countenance, a fountain or extension, if God is any one of these, or any thing resembling them; for, we very promptly answer, no, that this would be impossible. All this demonstrates the existence of an idea which has no connection with these representations, but essentially excludes what is contained in them.

24. What we have said of the idea of God, may be said of many other ideas. Rarely do we understand any thing into which the idea of relation does not enter as an indispensable element. How then is relation represented? In the imagination, in a thousand different manners; as the point of contact of two objects; as the link which unites them. But is relation any one of these? No! When we inquire in what it does consist, is there the slightest shadow of doubt that it is no one of these? Certainly not.

25. It is an error to call every idea an image, if you mean to consider ideas as something distinct from the intellectual act, which places itself before the understanding when it is in the exercise of its functions. An image is that which represents, as a likeness: and how, I ask, do we know that this representation or likeness exists? And how do we know that in order to reason we need an internal form, which is, as it were, a picture of the object? What is a picture beyond the sensible order? There are, it is true, similarities in the intellectual order, but not in the sense in which we perceive them in the material order. I think; so does my neighbor: here is a similarity, since the same thing is found in both one and the other, identical in species, but not in number. But this similarity is of a different order from that of sensible similarities.

26. When we understand, we know that which is in the object understood; but whether this be understood by a simple act of the intellect, or a medium be required to represent the similarity, we do not know. We understand the thing, not the idea; and it is as difficult to say how the intellect perceives without the idea, as it is to say how the supposed representation refers to its object. How does our idea refer to an object? If by itself, then by itself alone, since it is purely internal, it refers to the external, and requires no intermediary to place the subject in relation with external objects. What it does, the intellectual act of itself alone can also do. If we perceive the relation of the idea with the object by means of another idea, this intermediate idea presents the same difficulty as the preceding idea; and so at last we must come to a case in which there is a transition from the intellect to the object without any intermediary.

If we see an object which is the image of another not known, we shall see the object in itself, but we shall not know that it has the relation of image, unless informed that it has: we shall know its reality, but not its representation. The same will happen in ideas which are images; these, therefore, do not at all explain how the transition from the internal act to the object is made; for this would require them to do for the understanding that which we find them unable to do for themselves.

27. There is something mysterious in the intellectual act, which men seek to explain in a thousand different ways, by rendering sensible what they inwardly experience. Hence so many metaphorical expressions, useful only so long as they serve merely to call and fix the attention, and give an account of the phenomenon, but hurtful to science if they go beyond these limits, if it be forgotten that they are metaphors, and are never to be confounded with the reality.

By intelligence we see what there is in things, we experience the act of perception; but when we reflect upon it we grope in the dark, as if there were a dense cloud about the very source of light, preventing us from seeing it with clearness. Thus the firmament is at times flooded with the light of the sun, although the sun is encircled with clouds and hidden from our view, so that we cannot even determine its position upon the horizon.

28. One cause of obscurity in this matter is the very effort to clear it up. The act of the understanding is, in its objective part, exceedingly luminous, since by it we see what there is in objects; but in its subjective nature, or in itself, it is an internal fact, simple indeed, but incapable of being explained by words. This is not a peculiarity of the intellectual act, it is common to all internal phenomena. What is it to see, to taste, to hear? What is a sensation, or feeling of any kind whatsoever? It is an inward phenomenon, of which

we are conscious, but which we cannot decompose into parts; nor can we explain with words the combination of these parts. A word is enough to indicate the phenomenon, but this word has no meaning for him who does not now experience this phenomenon, or has not oat some former time experienced it. No possible explanations would ever enable a man born blind to understand color, or a deaf man sound.

The act of understanding belongs to this class; it is a simple fact which we can point out, but not explain. An explanation supposes various notions, the combination of which may be expressed by language; in the intellectual act there are none of these. When we have said, I think, or, I understand, we have said all. This simplicity is not destroyed by objective multiplicity; the act by which we compare two or more objects is just as simple as the act by which we perceive a single object. If one act be not enough, more will follow; and finally one act will unite or sum them all up; but it will not be a composite act.

CHAPTER V
COMPARISON OF GEOMETRICAL WITH NON-GEOMETRICAL IDEAS

29. The idea is a very different thing from the sensible representation, but it has certain necessary relations with it which it will be well to examine. When we say *necessary*, we speak only of the manner in which our mind, in its actual state, understands, abstracting the intelligence of other spirits, and even that of the human mind when subject to other conditions than those imposed by its present union with the body. So soon as we quit the sphere in which our experience operates, we must be very cautious how we lay down general propositions, and take care not to extend to all intelligences qualities which are possibly peculiar to our own, and which, even with respect to it, will perhaps be entirely changed in another life. Having made these previous observations, which will be found of great utility to mark the limits of things there is danger of confounding, we now proceed to examine the relations of our ideas with sensible representations.

30. A classification of our ideas into geometrical and non-geometrical naturally occurs when we fix our attention upon the difference of objects to which our ideas may refer. The former embrace the whole sensible world so far as it can be perceived in the representation of space; the latter include every kind of being, whether sensible or not, and suppose a primitive element which is the representation of extension. In their divisions and subdivisions the latter present simply the idea of extension, limited and combined in different ways; but they offer nothing in relation to the representation of space, and even when they refer to it, they only consider it inasmuch as numbered by the various parts into which it may be divided. Hence the line which in mathematics separates geometry from universal arithmetic; the former is founded upon the idea of extension, whereas the latter considers only numbers, whether determinate, as in arithmetic properly so called, or indeterminate, as in algebra.

31. Here we have to note the superiority of non-geometrical to geometrical ideas,—a superiority plainly visible in the two branches of mathematics, universal arithmetic and geometry. Arithmetic never requires

the aid of geometry, but geometry at every step needs that of arithmetic. Arithmetic and algebra may both be studied from their simplest elementary notions to their highest complications without ever once involving the idea of extension, and consequently without making use of one single geometrical idea. Even infinitesimal calculus, in a manner originating in geometrical considerations, has been emancipated from them and formed into a science perfectly independent of the idea of extension. On the contrary, geometry cannot take a single step without the aid of arithmetic. The comparison of angles is a fundamental point in the science of geometry, but it cannot be made except by measuring them; and their measure is an arc of the circumference divided into a certain number of degrees, which must be counted; and thus we come to the idea of number, the operation of counting, that is, into the field of arithmetic.

The very proof by superposition, notwithstanding its eminently geometrical character, stands in need of numeration, inasmuch as the superposition is repeated. We do not require the idea of number to demonstrate by means of superposition the equality of two arcs perfectly equal; but in order to appreciate the relation of their quantity we compare two unequal arcs and follow the method of placing the less upon the greater several times, *we count*, we make use of the idea of *number*, and find we have entered upon the ground of arithmetic. We discover the equality of two radii of a circle, when we compare them by superposition, abstracting the idea of number; but if we would know the relation of the diameter to the radii, we employ the idea of *two*; we say the diameter is twice the radius, and again enter the domains of arithmetic. As we proceed in the combination of geometrical ideas, we make use of more and more arithmetical ideas. Thus the idea of the number *three* necessarily enters into the triangle; and the *sum of three* and the *sum of two* both enter into one of its most essential properties; the *sum* of the *three* angles of a triangle is equal to *two* right angles.

32. The idea of number cannot be replaced by the sensible intuition of the figure whose properties and relations are under discussion. In many cases this intuition is impossible, as, for example, in many-sided figures. We have little difficulty in representing to our imagination a triangle, or even a quadrilateral figure, but the difficulty is greater in the case of the pentagon, and greater still in the hexagon and heptagon; and when the figure attains a great number of sides, one after another escapes the sensible intuition, until it becomes utterly impossible to appreciate it by mere intuition. Who can distinctly imagine a thousand-sided figure?

33. This superiority of non-geometrical over geometrical ideas is very remarkable, since it shows that the sphere of intellectual activity expands in proportion as it rises above sensible intuition. Extension, as we have before

seen, [3] serves as the basis not only of geometry, but also of the natural sciences, inasmuch as it represents in a sensible manner the intensity of certain phenomena; but it can by no means enable us to penetrate their inmost nature, and guide us from that which appears to that which is. This and other subordinate ideas are, so to speak, inert, and from them springs no vital principle to fecundate our understanding, and still less the reality; they are an unfathomable depth in which our intellectual activity may toil, perfectly certain of never finding any thing in it which we ourselves have not placed there; they are a lifeless object which lends itself to all imaginable combinations without ever being capable of producing any thing, or of containing any thing not given to it. The naturalists in considering inertness as a property of matter, have perhaps regarded more than they are aware the idea of extension, which presents the inertness most completely.

34. The ideas of number, cause, and substance abound in results, and are applicable to all branches of science. We can scarcely speak without expressing them; it might almost be said that they are constituent elements of intelligence, since without them it vanishes like a passing illusion. They extend to every thing, apply to every thing, and are necessary, whenever objects are offered to the intellectual activity, in order that the intellect can perceive and combine them. It makes no difference whether the objects be sensible or insensible, whether there be question of our intelligence or of others subject to different laws; whenever we conceive the act of understanding we conceive also these primitive ideas as elements indispensable to the realization of the intellectual act. They exist and are combined independently of the existence, and even of the possibility, of the sensible world; and they would also exist in a world of pure intelligences, even if the sensible universe were nothing but an illusion or an absurd chimera.

On the other hand, take geometrical ideas and remove them from the sensible sphere; and all that you base upon them will be only unmeaning words. The ideas of substance, cause, and relation do not flow from geometrical ideas; if we regard them alone, we see an immense field extending into regions of unbounded space; but the coldness and silence of death reign there. If we would introduce beings, life, and motion into this field we must seek them elsewhere; we must use other ideas, and combine them, so that life, activity, and motion may result from their combination, in order that geometrical ideas may contain something besides this inert, immovable, and vacant mass, such as we imagine the regions of space to be beyond the confines of the world.

35. Geometrical ideas, properly so called, as distinguished from sensible representations, are not simple ideas, since they necessarily involve the

ideas of relation and number. Geometry cannot advance one step without comparing them; and this comparison almost always takes place by the intervention of the idea of number. Hence it is that geometrical ideas, apparently so unlike purely arithmetical ideas, are really identical with them so far as their form or purely ideal character is concerned; and are only distinguishable from them when they refer to a determinate matter, such as extension as presented in its sensible representation. The inferiority therefore of geometrical ideas already mentioned, only refers to their matter, or to their sensible representations, which are presupposed to be an indispensable element.

36. Another consequence of this doctrine, is the unity of the pure understanding, and its distinction from the sensitive faculties. For, the very fact that the same ideas apply alike to sensible and to insensible objects, with no other difference than that arising from the diversity of the matter perceived, proves that above the sensitive faculties there is another faculty with an activity of its own, and elements distinct from sensible representations. This is the centre where all intellectual perceptions unite, and where that intrinsic force resides, which, although excited by sensible representations, develops itself by its own power, makes itself master of these impressions, and converts them, so to speak, by a mysterious assimilation, into its own substance.

37. Here we repeat what we have already remarked, concerning the profound ideological meaning involved in the *acting intellect* of the Aristotelians, so ridiculed because not understood. But we leave this point and proceed to the careful analysis of geometrical ideas, to discover, if possible, a glimpse of some ray of light amid the profound darkness which envelops the nature and origin of our ideas.

CHAPTER VI
IN WHAT THE GEOMETRICAL IDEA
CONSISTS; AND WHAT ARE ITS
RELATIONS WITH SENSIBLE INTUITION

38. In the preceding chapters we have distinguished between pure ideas and sensible representations, and we seem to have sufficiently demonstrated the difference between them, although we limited ourselves to the geometrical order. But we have not explained the idea in itself; we have said what it is not, but not what it is; and although we have shown the impossibility of explaining simple ideas, and the necessity of our being satisfied with indicating them, we do not wish to be confined to this observation, which may seem to elude the difficulty rather than to solve it. Only after due investigations, by which we shall be better able to understand what is meant by *designate*, will it be allowable to confine ourselves to their designation, for it will then be seen that we have not eluded the difficulty. Let us begin with geometrical ideas.

39. Is a geometrical idea, without any accompanying or preceding sensible representation, possible? It would seem that we can have none. What meaning has the idea of the triangle if not referred to lines forming angles and enclosing a space? And what do lines, angles, and space mean, without sensible intuition? A line is a series of points, but it represents nothing determinate, nothing susceptible of geometrical combinations, except it be referred to that sensible intuition in which the point appears to us as an element generating by its movement that continuity which we call a line. What would become of angles without the real or possible representation of these lines? What would become of the area of the triangle were we to abstract a space, a surface which is or may be represented? We might challenge all the ideologists in the world to assign any sense to the words used in geometry if absolute abstraction be made all sensible representation.

40. Geometrical ideas, such as we conceive them, have a necessary relation to sensible intuition. In order the better to understand this relation, let us define the triangle to be the figure enclosed by three right lines. This

definition involves the following ideas: space, enclosed, three, lines. With a space and three lines which do not enclose the figure, we have no triangle; the word *enclosed* cannot therefore be omitted. If you enclose a space, but with more than three lines, the result will not be a triangle; and if you take less than three lines you can have no enclosure. The idea of *three* is therefore necessary to the idea of the triangle. It is useless to add that the idea of *line* is as necessary as the others, since without it no triangle can be conceived. Different and distinct ideas, it is true, are here combined, but they are all referred to one sensible intuition, although in an indeterminate manner. We here abstract the longness or shortness of the lines and their forming larger or smaller angles. But we cannot thus abstract in the case of determinate intuitions; for every determinate intuition has its own peculiar qualities; otherwise it would not be a determinate representation, and consequently not sensible as it is supposed to be. But although the reference be to an indeterminate intuition, it always supposes some intuition either actual or possible, since otherwise the material of combination would be wanting to the understanding; and the four ideas involved in the triangle would be empty and unmeaning forms, and their combination extravagant if not absurd.

41. The idea then of the triangle seems to be simply the intellectual perception of the relation between the lines presented to the sensible intuition, considered in all its generality, without any determining circumstance limiting it to particular cases or species. This explanation admits nothing intermediate between the sensible representation and the intellectual act, which, exercising its activity upon the materials presented by sensible intuition, perceives their relations, and this pure and simple perception constitutes the idea.

42. We shall understand this better if, instead of the triangle, we take a many-sided figure, such as a polygon of a million sides, which cannot be clearly presented to the sensible intuition. The idea of this figure is as simple as that of the triangle; we perceive it by an intellectual act, express it by a single word, and can calculate its properties and relations with the same exactness and certainty as we can those of the triangle, although it is absolutely impossible to represent it distinctly to our imagination. When we reflect upon what it offers to the intellectual act, we notice the same elements as in the idea of the triangle, with this single difference that the number three is changed into *million*. We can have no sensible representation of all these lines; but the understanding has sufficiently combined the idea of line with that of number to perceive its object, a million. Here, then, we perceive the same elements as in the triangle; but it is upon these elements, considered in general without any other determination than results from the fixed number, that the perceptive act operates.

43. The idea of a polygon in general, abstracting the number of its sides, offers in its sensible representation, nothing determinate to the mind, nothing but the abstract idea of a right line, the general idea of an enclosed space. The relation which these objects of the intellectual, act even in the midst of their indeterminateness, have amongst themselves, is perceived by the intellectual act. This perceptive act is the idea. Every thing beyond this is useless, and not only useless but affirmed without reason.

44. It will perhaps be asked how the understanding can perceive what passes without it, since sensible intuition is a function of a faculty distinct from the understanding? In reply, we shall abstract the questions discussed in the schools concerning the powers of the mind, and be content to remark that whether these be really distinct among themselves, or only one power exercising its activity upon different objects and in different manners, it will be alike necessary to admit a consciousness common to all the faculties. The soul which feels, thinks, recollects, desires, is one and the same, and is alike conscious of all these acts. Whatever be the nature of the faculties by which she performs these acts, she it is that performs them and knows that she performs them. There is then in the soul a single consciousness, the common centre where dwells the inward sense of every activity exercised, and of every affection received, to whatever order they may belong. However, supposing the case the most unfavorable to our theory, that the faculty to which sensible intuition corresponds, is really distinct from the faculty which perceives the relations of the objects offered by sensible intuition; does it therefore follow that the understanding cannot without something intermediate exercise its activity upon objects presented by this intuition? Certainly not. The act of pure understanding and that of sensible intuition, are indeed different, but they meet in consciousness, as in a common field; and there they come in contact, the one exercising its perceptive activity upon the material supplied by the other.

CHAPTER VII
THE ACTING INTELLECT OF
THE ARISTOTELIANS

45. I shall now briefly explain the scholastic theory of the manner in which the understanding knows material things. This explanation will show how much reason we had to assert that this doctrine of the schools can be ridiculed only when not understood, and that, whatever its foundation, it cannot be denied to possess an ideological importance.

46. The schoolmen began with this principle of Aristotle, *nihil est in intellectu quod prius non fuerit in sensu;* "There is nothing in the understanding which has not previously been in the senses." Conformably to this principle they maintained that before the soul received impressions from the senses, the understanding was like a clean table upon which nothing had been written: *sicut tabula rasa in qua nihil est scriptum.* According to this doctrine all our knowledge flows from the senses; and at first sight the system of the schools might seem to be very similar to, if not identical with, that of Condillac. Both seek the origin of our cognitions in sensation; both teach that there is no idea in our understanding prior to sensation. But the two systems are, notwithstanding these apparent similarities, very different, and even diametrically opposed.

47. The fundamental principle of Condillac's theory is, that sensation is the sole operation of the mind; and that whatever exists in our mind is nothing more than the sensation transformed in various ways. Prior to sensible impressions, this philosopher admits no faculty; the development of sensation is all that fecundates the soul, not by exciting its faculties, but by generating them. The school of the Aristotelians took, indeed, sensations for the starting-point, but did not consider them as producing intelligence; on the contrary, they were very careful to mark the limits of the sensitive faculties, and of the understanding in which they recognized a peculiar and innate activity altogether superior to the faculties of the sensible order. We have only to open any one of the innumerable works of this school, to meet on every page such words as *intellectual force, light of reason, participation in the divine light,* and others in the same style, in which a primary activity

of our mind, not communicated by sensations, but prior to them all, is expressly recognized. The acting intellect, *intellectus agens*, which figures so much in this ideological system, was a standing condemnation of the system of transformed sensation advocated by Condillac.

48. The Aristotelians, governed by their favorite idea of explaining every thing by matter and form, modified the meaning of these words according to the exigencies of the objects to which they applied them, and considered the faculties of the soul as a class of forces incapable of acting unless united to a form which brought them into action. Thus they explained sensations by species, or forms, which placed the sensitive power in act. The imagination was a force which, although it sometimes rose above the external senses, contained nothing but species of the sensible order, subject also to the necessary conditions of this faculty. These species were the forms which placed the imaginative force in act, and without which it could not exercise its functions. The Aristotelians, after having thus explained the phenomena of the external senses, and of the imagination, undertook to explain those of the intellectual order; and in this they displayed their genius by inventing an auxiliary which they named the *acting intellect*. The necessity of making two principles in seeming contradiction accord, was the reason of this invention.

On the one hand the Aristotelians held that our cognitions all flowed from the senses; and on the other they asserted that there was an essential and intrinsic difference between feeling and understanding. Having drawn this dividing line, the sensitive and intellectual orders were separated; but as it was on the other side requisite to establish some communication between these two orders, it was necessary for them, if they wished to save the principle, that all our ideas come from the senses, to discover some point where the two channels might unite.

The cognition of material things could not be denied to the pure understanding; but as this was not an innate cognition and could not be acquired by it, they were under the necessity of establishing some communication by means of which the understanding might comprehend objects without soiling its purity by sensible species. The imagination contained them, already purified from the grossness of the external senses; in it they existed more aerial, purer, and less remote from immateriality; but they were still at an immense distance from the intellectual order, and had themselves to support the burden of those material conditions which never allowed them to attain the altitude necessary to be put in communication with the pure understanding. In order to know, the understanding requires forms to unite themselves to it intimately; and although it be true that it discerned them far down in the lower regions of the sensitive faculties, yet it could descend to them without compromising its dignity, and denying its own nature. In this conflict they required a mediator; it was the acting intellect. We will now proceed to explain the attributes of this faculty.

49. The sensible species contained in the imagination, the true picture of the external world, were not of themselves intelligible, because enveloped, not with matter properly so called, but with material forms, to which the intellectual act could only indirectly refer. If they could have discovered a faculty capable of rendering intelligible what is not intelligible, this difficult problem would have been satisfactorily solved; as in this case the mysterious transformer by applying its activity to the sensible species, would elevate them from the category of imaginary species, *phantasmata*, to that of pure ideas or sensible species, and thus make them serve the intellectual act. This faculty is the acting intellect; a real magician which possesses the wonderful secret of stripping sensible species of their material conditions, of smoothing every roughness which prevents them from coming in contact with the pure understanding, and transforms the gross food of the sensitive faculties into the purest ambrosia, fit to be served at the repast of spirits.

50. This invention merits to be called ingenious rather than extravagant, poetical rather than ridiculous. But its most remarkable feature is, that it involves a profound philosophical sense, as well because it marks an ideological fact of the highest importance, as because it indicates the true way of explaining the phenomena of intelligence in their relations to the sensible world. This remarkable fact is the difference, even with respect to material objects, between sensible representations and pure ideas. The indication of the true way consists in presenting the intellectual activity as operating upon sensible species, and converting them into food for the mind.

Let us leave the poetical part to the explanation of the schools, and see if what it involves be worth as much, to say the least, as what Kant advanced when, combating sensism, he distinguished between the pure understanding and sensible intuitions.

CHAPTER VIII
KANT AND THE ARISTOTELIANS

51. Lest I be accused of levity in comparing Kant's philosophy with that of the schools, in what relates to the distinction between the sensitive and intellectual faculties, I shall give a rapid examination of this philosopher's doctrine so far as the present matter is concerned.

Since the German philosopher is in the habit of expressing himself with great obscurity, and of using an obsolete language liable to different interpretations, I shall insert his own words, so that the reader may judge for himself, and rectify any inaccuracies into which I may fall, in comparing Kant's doctrine with that of the Aristotelians.

"In whatever manner," says Kant, "and by whatever means a cognition may be referred to objects, that which makes the cognition refer immediately to things, and to which all thought is a means, is *intuition*. This intuition exists only inasmuch as the object is given us, which is not possible, at least for us men, except so far as it affects the mind in some way. The capacity of receiving impressions by the manner in which objects affect us is called *sensibility*. By means of sensibility objects are given to us: it alone supplies us with *intuitions*: but they are thought by the understanding, and from it arise *conceptions*. All thought must ultimately be referred, either directly, or indirectly by means of certain signs, to intuitions, and consequently to sensibility, since no object can be given to us in any other.

"The action of an object upon the representative faculty, so far as we are affected by it, is *sensation*. The intuition, which is referred to an object by means of sensation, is called *empirical*. The immediate object of an empirical intuition is called a *phenomenon*." [4]

The distinction between the faculty of feeling and that of conceiving is fundamental in Kant's system: and we see that he gives it a hasty exposition before beginning his investigations on Æsthetics or the theory of sensibility. Further on, in treating of the operations of the understanding, he has more fully developed his doctrine: and by the emphasis he puts upon it, it would seem evident that he regarded it as of high importance, and perhaps as a discovery of a region entirely unknown to the philosophical world. Thus he speaks of it in his *Transcendental Logic*:

"Our knowledge proceeds from two intellectual sources; the first is the capacity of receiving representations, (the receptivity of impressions,) the second is the faculty of knowing an object by these representations, (the spontaneity of conceptions.) By the former the object is given to us; by the latter, it is *thought* in relation to this representation (as mere determination of the mind.) Intuition and conception constitute the elements of all our knowledge; so that neither conceptions without an intuition in some manner corresponding to them, nor an intuition without conceptions, can give knowledge.

"We call *sensibility* the capacity (receptivity) of our mind to receive representations, so far as affected in any way whatever: on the contrary, the faculty of producing representations, or the *spontaneity* of knowledge, is called *understanding*. Our nature is such that there can be no intuition not *sensible*, that is to say, which only comprehends the manner in which we are affected by objects. The *understanding* is the faculty of *thinking* the object of sensible intuition. Neither of these properties of the soul is preferable to the other. Without sensibility no object could be given to us; without the understanding none could be thought. Thoughts without contents are empty; intuitions without conceptions are blind. It is, then, just as necessary to make conceptions sensible, — that is, to give them an object in intuition, as to make intuitions intelligible, by subjecting them to conceptions. These two faculties or capacities cannot interchange their functions. The understanding can perceive nothing, [5] and the senses can think nothing. Knowledge results only from their union. Their attributes, therefore, ought not to be confounded; on the contrary, there is every reason to distinguish them, and to separate them with great care. We distinguish then the science of the laws of sensibility in general, that is to say, *Æsthetics*, from the science of the laws of the understanding in general, that is, from *Logic*." [6]

Mark well the meaning of this doctrine. Two facts are established; sensible intuition, and the conception of it; consequently the existence of two faculties, sensibility, and the understanding, is affirmed. To the first correspond sensible representations; to the latter conceptions. These two faculties, though different, are closely interlinked; and they are mutually necessary in order to produce cognitions. But how do they give each other that mutual aid they stand in need of?

"The understanding," Kant elsewhere says, "has been thus far defined only negatively, as a not-sensible faculty of knowing." But as we can have no intuition independently of sensibility, it follows that the understanding is not a faculty of intuition. Excepting intuition, there remains no way of knowing other than by conceptions; wherefore we infer that the knowledge of every intellect, at least every human intellect, is a knowledge by conceptions; not intuitive, but discursive. All intuitions, as sensible, rest upon affections, and consequently, all conceptions upon functions. I understand by functions, the unity of action necessary to arrange different representations under one common representation. Conceptions, then, are grounded on the spontaneity of thought, as sensible intuitions on the receptivity of impressions. The understanding can make no use of these conceptions except to judge by means of them, and as intuition is the only representation which has an immediate object, no conception can ever be immediately referred to an object, but only to some other representation of this object, whether this be an intuition, or even a conception. *Judgment* is the mediate cognition of an object, and consequently the representation of a representation of the object. In every judgment there is a conception applicable to many things, and under this plurality it comprises also a given representation, immediately referable to the object. Thus, in the judgment: *all bodies are divisible*; the conception of *divisible* is common to different conceptions, among which that of body is the one it here particularly refers to. But this conception of body relates to certain phenomena we have in view; these objects are then mediately represented by the conception of divisibility. All judgments are functions of unity in our representations, since instead of one immediate representation, there comes in another more elevated, which includes the first and many others, and conduces to the cognition of the object; and a great number of possible cognitions are reduced to one alone. But we may reduce all the operations of the understanding to judgment; so that the understanding in general may be represented as *a faculty of judging*; because, from what has been said, it is the faculty of thinking. Thought is cognition by conceptions; but conceptions, as predicates of possible judgments, may be referred to any representation whatever of an object, however indeterminate. Thus the conception of body signifies something, for example, a metal, which may be known by this conception. It is then a conception only because it contains in itself other representations by means of which it may be referred to objects. It is then the attribute of a possible judgment, for instance, of this: *every metal is a body*. [7]

52. There are in this doctrine of Kant, two things to be distinguished: first, the facts upon which it is based; and secondly, the manner in which he examines and applies them, and the consequences he deduces from them.

We detect at once a radical difference, as far as the observation of ideological facts is concerned, between Kant's system and that of Condillac. While the latter discovers in the mind no fact but sensation, no immediate faculty more noble than that of feeling, the former upholds as a fundamental principle the distinction between sensibility and the understanding. And here the German triumphs over the French philosopher, for in his support stand both observation and experience. But this triumph over sensism had already been obtained by many philosophers, the scholastics in particular. With Kant and Condillac they admitted that all our cognitions came from the senses; but they had also noted what Kant afterwards saw, but Condillac did not discover that sensations by themselves alone could never suffice to explain all the phenomena of our soul, and that, besides the sensitive faculty, it was necessary to admit another very different, called understanding.

Kant regarded sensations as materials furnished to the understanding, which it combined in various ways, and reduced to conceptions. "Thoughts without contents," he said, "are empty; intuitions without conceptions are blind. It is then just as necessary to make conceptions sensible, that is, to give them an object in intuition, as to make intuitions intelligible by subjecting them to conceptions." Who does not perceive in this passage, the *acting intellect* of the Aristotelians, although expressed in other words? Substitute *sensible species* for *sensible intuition, intelligible species* for *conception* and we recognize a doctrine very like that of the scholastics. Let us see. Kant says: to enable us to acquire knowledge, the action of the senses, or sensible experience is necessary. The scholastics said: there is nothing in the understanding which has not previously been in the senses: *nihil est in intellectu quod prius non fuerit in sensu.*

Kant says: sensible intuitions of themselves are blind. The scholastics said: sensible species, or those of the imagination, also called *phantasmata*, are not intelligible.

Kant says: it is necessary to make conceptions sensible by giving them an object in intuition. The scholastics said: it is impossible to understand, either by acquiring science, or by using that already acquired, unless the understanding directs itself to sensible species, "*sine conversione ad phantasmata.*"

Kant says: it is indispensable to render intuitions intelligible by subjecting them to conceptions. The scholastics said: it is necessary to make sensible species intelligible in order that they may be the object of the understanding.

Kant says: we judge by means of conceptions; and that judgment is the mediate cognition of an object, and consequently its representation. The scholastics said: we know objects by means of an intelligible species, which is derived from the sensible species, and is its intelligible representation.

Kant says, that in every judgment there is a conception applicable to many things, and that under this plurality it comprises also a given representation which is referred immediately to its object. The scholastics said, that the intelligible species was applicable to many things, because universal; that, when separated from a sensible and particular species, it abstracts from all material and *individuating* conditions, and consequently embraces all individual objects in one common representation.

Kant uses the words *conception*, and *to conceive*, to denote the intellectual act, form, or whatever it may be, by which the understanding, making use of sensible intuitions, combines the materials offered by sensibility conformably to the laws of the intellectual order. The scholastics likewise taught that the intelligible species, called also species *impressed*, fecundated the understanding by producing in it an intellectual conception, whence resulted the *word*, internal locution, or species *expressed*, which they also styled *conception*.

Kant says, that the cognition of human intelligence is a cognition by conceptions, not intuitive, but discursive and general, and that out of the sphere of sensibility there is for us no true intuition. The scholastics said: our understanding, in this life, has a necessary relation to the nature of material things, and for this reason it cannot *primo et per se*, know immaterial substances: hence it happens that we know them perfectly only by certain comparisons with material things, and chiefly by way of removal, *per viam remotionis*, in a negative way.

53. The sample we have just given is exceedingly interesting, since it enables us to appreciate as they merit the points of similarity in these two systems, which occupy a prominent place in the history of ideology,—a similarity which has not always hitherto been sufficiently noticed, although apparent upon the simple perusal of the German philosopher. Nor is this extraordinary: the study of the scholastics is exceedingly difficult; one must accommodate one's self to the language, the style, the opinions, and the prejudices of their epoch, and travel over much useless ground to collect a little pure ore. Note well, however, that I do not pretend to discover the *"Critic of Pure Reason"* in the works of the scholastics, I would only mark a fact but little known; it is that whatever is good, fundamental, and conclusive against the sensism of Condillac, in the German philosopher's system, had been said ages before by the scholastics.

Are we hence to infer that Kant took his doctrine from these authors? We cannot say; but we believe it may, with some reason, be asserted, that possibly the German philosopher, a man of vast reading, most retentive memory, and very laborious, may have received certain inspirations, reminiscences of which glimmer through his doctrines. A writer is not a plagiarist, although he make ideas his own which have originated with others. But it is often true that man imagines he creates, when he only recollects.

54. Although the German philosopher agrees with the scholastics in the observation of the primitive faculties of our mind, he differs from them in their application; and whilst they go on preparing a philosophical dogmatism, he marches towards a despairing skepticism. Nothing that all the most eminent philosophers have regarded as indisputable, can stand in the eyes of the German philosopher. True, he has distinguished the sensible from the intelligible order; he has recognized two primitive faculties in our soul; sensibility and the understanding; he has indicated the line which divides them, and carefully remarked that it should never be effaced; but, on the other hand, he has reduced the sensible world to a collection of pure phenomena, and explains space in such a way as to render it extremely difficult to avoid the idealism of Berkeley. He has also, so to speak, walled in the understanding by preventing all communication with it, excepting by sensible experience, and has resolved all the elements that meet in it into empty forms, which lead to nothing when there is question of applying them to the not-sensible, and which can teach us nothing concerning the great ontological, psychological, and cosmological problems which have been the object of the meditations of the profoundest metaphysicians, who, to resolve them, have published a vast amount of sublime doctrines, just cause of a noble pride in the human mind which knows the dignity of its nature, vindicates its lofty origin, and discerns from afar the immensity of its destiny.

CHAPTER IX
HISTORICAL VIEW OF THE
VALUE OF PURE IDEAS

55. Now that we have shown the points of similarity between Kant's system and that of the scholastics, we propose to note their differences chiefly in what concerns the application of these doctrines. To give an idea of the gravity and transcendentalism of these differences, we have only to remark the discrepancy of their results. The Aristotelians built upon their principles a whole system of metaphysical science, which they considered the noblest of sciences, and which, like a rich and brilliant light, fecundates and directs all others; whereas Kant, starting with the same facts, destroys metaphysical science by taking from it all power to know objects in themselves.

56. We here find Kant in opposition not only to the scholastics, properly so called, but also to all the most eminent metaphysicians who had preceded him. On the side of the scholastics in this matter may be cited Plato, Aristotle, Saint Augustine, Saint Anselm, Saint Thomas, Descartes, Malebranche, Fenelon, and Leibnitz.

57. No one can deny the transcendency of these questions, if he be not totally ignorant how vital it is to the human mind to know if a science superior to the purely sensible order be possible, whereby man may extend his activity beyond the phenomena offered by matter. These questions are exceedingly profound, and must not be lightly treated. The difficulty and the great abstruseness of the objects treated, the importance, the transcendency of the consequences to which they lead, according to the road followed, demand that no labor whatever should be spared to penetrate these matters. It is easy to assure one's self that upon these questions depends the conservation of sound ideas of God and of the human mind; man's most important and lofty considerations.

To give this matter a thorough examination, let us go back to the origin of the divergence of these philosophical opinions, and let us investigate the reason why, starting with the same facts, they arrive at contradictory results. This requires a clear exposition of the opposite doctrines.

58. All philosophers agree in admitting the fact of sensibility; concerning it there can be no doubt; it is a phenomenon attested by consciousness in so palpable a manner, that not even skeptics could ever deny the subjective reality of the appearance, however much they called in question its objective reality. Idealists, when they deny the existence of bodies, do not deny their phenomenal appearance, their appearance to the mental eye under a sensible form. Sensibility then, and the phenomena it exhibits, have in all ages been primary data in ideological and psychological problems; there may be a discrepancy with respect to the nature and consequences of these data, but there can be none as to their existence.

59. The history of ideological science shows us two schools; one of which admits nothing but sensation, and explains all the affections and operations of the mind by the transformation of the senses; while the other admits primitive facts distinct from sensation; other faculties than that of feeling, and recognizes in the mind a line dividing the sensible from the intellectual order.

60. This latter school is divided into two others; one of which regards the sensible order as not only distinct, but also separate from the intellectual order, and in some sense at war with it; and it therefore maintains that the intellectual can receive nothing from the sensible order, except malign exhortations which either mislead it, or enervate its activity. Hence the system of innate ideas in all its purity; hence the metaphysics of an intellectual order entirely exempt from sensible impressions, metaphysics which, cultivated by eminent geniuses, has in modern times been professed by the author of the *Investigation of Truth*, with sublime exaggeration. The other ramification of the school also admits the pure intellectual order, but does not hold it to be contaminated by being brought into communication with sensible phenomena; on the contrary, it is rather inclined to believe that the problems of human intelligence, such as it exists in this life, cannot be resolved without fixing the mind upon the aforesaid communication.

61. Experience teaches that this communication exists, conformably to a law of the human mind, and that to contend against the law is to struggle against a truth attested by consciousness: to attempt to destroy it would be a rash undertaking, a kind of mental suicide. For this reason, the school of which we have just spoken, accepts the facts, such as internal experience presents them, and endeavors to explain them by indicating the points where the sensible and intellectual orders may come into communication without being destroyed or confounded.

62. The school that admits the existence of the two orders, the sensible and the intellectual, and at the same time admits the possibility and the

reality of their reciprocal communication and influence, has, for its fundamental principle, that the origin of all cognition is in the senses, these being the exciting causes of intellectual activity, and a kind of laborers who supply it with materials, which it then combines in the manner necessary to raise the scientifical structure.

63. Thus far, Kant and the scholastics agree; but here they separate at a point of the greatest importance, and the result is that they pass on to conflicting consequences. The scholastics believed that there were in the understanding true ideas having true objects, and that they might discuss them, independently of the sensible order, with perfect security. They even admitted the principle that there can be nothing in the understanding which was not previously in the senses; but pretended, nevertheless, that there really was something in the understanding, which might conduce to the knowledge of the truth of immaterial, as well as of material things in themselves. The ideas of the purely intellectual order originate in the senses as movers of the intellectual activity; but this activity, by means of abstraction and other operations, forms to itself ideas of its own, by whose aid it may go beyond the sensible order in its search for truth.

64. In their explanation of the purely intellectual order, metaphysicians, both scholastics and anti-scholastics agree, so far as there is question of giving a real objective value to ideas, and of making them a sure means of discovering truth independently of sensible phenomena. However much these schools disagree as to the origin of ideas, they agree in all that relates to their reality and value.

65. Kant, at the same time that he admits the principle of the scholastics, that all our cognitions come from the senses, and recognizes with them the necessity of acknowledging a purely intellectual order, a series of conceptions different from sensible intuition, maintains that these conceptions are not pure cognitions, but empty forms, which of themselves mean nothing, teach the mind nothing, and cannot, in the least, aid us to know the reality of things. These conceptions mean nothing unless filled, so to speak, with sensible intuitions. If these intuitions are wanting, they correspond to nothing, and can be of none but a purely logical use; that is to say, the understanding will think upon and combine them, without, indeed, falling into contradiction, but also without ever coming to any conclusion.

"That the understanding," Kant says, "can never make a transcendental, but only an empirical use, either of its *a priori* principles, or of its conceptions, is a principle which, if known with conviction, leads to the most important consequences. The transcendental use of a conception in any principle, consists in referring it to things, *in general, and in themselves*; whilst the empirical use is in referring the conception to phenomena alone, that is, to the objects of a possible experience, by which we may easily see that this latter use is the only one that can stand. To every conception is necessary, first of all, a logical form of a conception in general, of the thought: and secondly, the possibility of subjecting to it an object, to which it may refer; but without this object it wants all sense, it contains nothing, although it may involve the logical function necessary to form a conception by means of certain data. The object cannot be given to a conception except in intuition; and although pure intuition may be *a priori* possible before the object, it cannot, however, receive its object, and consequently its objective value, otherwise than by the empirical intuition of which it is the form. All conceptions and with them all principles, although they be possible *a priori*, do, notwithstanding, refer to empirical intuitions, that is, to data of possible experience. *Without this they have no objective value; they are nothing but a mere play, whether of the imagination or of the understanding,* with the respective representations of the one or the other faculty.

"That the same is the case with all the categories and principles formed from them, is apparent from this, that we cannot really define a single one of them; that is to say, we cannot render the possibility of their object intelligible without attending to the conditions of sensibility, and consequently to the form of the appearances; conditions to which these categories must be confined as to their sole objects. If this condition be taken away, all meaning, that is, all relation to the object is destroyed, and by no example can we be made to conceive what is the proper meaning of these conceptions.

"If no account be made of all the conditions of sensibility which denote them (he is speaking of the categories) as conceptions of a possible empirical use, if they be taken to be conceptions of things in general, and consequently, of transcendental use, nothing remains to be done, so far as they are concerned, but to preserve the logical functions in judgments, as the condition of the possibility of the things themselves, without being able to show in what case, their application and their object, and consequently they themselves, may, in the pure understanding, and without the intervention of sensibility, have a meaning and an objective value.

"It incontestably follows from what has been said, that pure conceptions of the understanding can *never have a transcendental use,* but only an empirical use; and that the principles of the pure understanding do not refer to the objects of the senses, except when the senses are in relation with the general conditions of a possible experience; *but never to things in general,* without relation to the way in which we may perceive them." [8]

66. Thus Kant destroys all metaphysical science, and, involved in its deplorable ruins, perish the most fundamental, most precious, and most sacred ideas of the human mind. According to him, transcendental analysis makes us see that the understanding can never pass the limits of sensibility, the only limits within which objects are given to us in intuition. These principles which were regarded as eternal pillars of the scientific edifice sink into empty forms, into words without meaning, so soon as they rise from the sphere of sensibility.

Ontology, with its transcendental doctrines, avails not in the eyes of the German philosopher to explain the nature and origin of things. "These principles," he says, "are simply principles of the exposition of phenomena; and the *proud name of an ontology* which pretends to give an *a priori*, synthetic cognition of things, in a systematic doctrine, for example, *the principle of causality*, ought to be replaced by the modest denomination of simple *analysis of the pure understanding*."

67. It would be hard to find a more noxious doctrine. What is left to the human mind when all means of rising from the sensible sphere are taken away? To what is our understanding reduced, if its most fundamental ideas, and its noblest principles can teach nothing concerning the nature of things? If the corporeal world is for us nothing but a collection of sensible phenomena, beyond which we can know nothing, our cognitions have nothing real, they are all purely subjective; the soul lives on illusions, and vanishes with its imaginary creations, to which there is nothing to correspond in reality. Space is but a subjective form; time is but a subjective form; pure ideas are empty conceptions, and all in us is subjective. We know nothing of objects, we are totally ignorant of what is; we know only what *appears*. This is pure skepticism; assuredly it was not necessary to consume so much time in analytical investigations to get thus far. The doctrine of Kant presents no extravagance so outrageous, no error so hideous, as the works of Fichte, Schelling, and Hegel; but it contains the germ of the greatest extravagance, and of the most fatal errors. He has made a philosophical revolution, which some have incautiously deemed a progress; but doubtless they did not detect the skepticism it contains, which is the more dangerous, the more it is enveloped in analytical forms.

68. Notwithstanding the importance justly attached to the refutation of the German philosopher's errors, I do not deem it necessary to combat his doctrines step by step; this system of refutation labors under the serious objection that it gives little satisfaction to the reader, who seems to see one edifice torn down, but not replaced by another. I consider it more useful carefully to examine questions as they arise in the order of their subjects, to establish my opinion as best I can, and there to refute Kant's errors as I

find them obstructing the march of truth. It is ordinarily very easy to say what a thing is not; but it is not so easy to say what it is; and it is not proper that the advocates of sound doctrine should be charged with impugning false doctrines, and not caring to expose their own. We believe that in these matters sound philosophy may be presented to the light of the day struggling against error, and that it ought not to rest satisfied with being the instrument of war to overthrow its adversary, but that it should aspire to found a noble and enduring edifice upon the very site the other occupied.

The minds of men are not satisfied with simple refutations; they desire to have a doctrine substituted in the place of the one impugned. Whoever impugns, denies; and the understanding is not satisfied with negations; it wants affirmation, for it cannot live without positive truth.

We have permitted ourselves this brief digression, which is indeed far from being useless; for at the sight of the transcendency of the German philosopher's errors I have recollected the necessity of careful, assiduous, and profound labor to oppose this deluge of errors which threatens to inundate the whole field of truth; and we could not do less than insist upon this point, and observe that it is not enough to tear down, but that it is also necessary to build up. Refutations will soon come; but let positive doctrines abound. It is not enough to cover the long line of frontiers where error makes its attacks, with light and active troops which may fall upon the enemy; it is necessary to found colonies, foci of cultivation and civilization, who will defend the country, at the same time that they make it flourish and prosper.

CHAPTER X
SENSIBLE INTUITION

69. Intuition, properly so called, consists in the act of the soul by which it perceives an object that effects it: this the signification of the Latin word derived from the verb *intueri*, to see a thing which is present, indicates.

70. Intuition belongs only to perceptive powers, to those by which the subject affected distinguishes between its affection and the object causing it. We do not pretend to say that this must be a reflex distinction, but simply that the internal act must refer to an object. If we suppose a being to experience various affections, but to neither refer them to any object, nor reflect upon them itself; this being can never with propriety be said to have true intuition, for intuition seems to involve the exercise of an activity occupied with a present object. The object of intuition need not always be an external being; it may be an affection or action of the soul made objective by a reflex act.

71. The sensations which are with the greatest propriety called intuitive, are those of sight and touch; for, since it is impossible for us, when we perceive extension, to regard it as a purely subjective fact, the acts of seeing and feeling necessarily involve relation to an object. The other senses, although they may have a certain relation to extension, do not perceive it directly, so that were they to stand alone, they would partake more of the affective than of the intuitive; that is, the soul would be affected by the sensations, but would be under no necessity of referring them to external objects. If reflection made upon these sensations come to teach, as in effect it would teach that their cause is a being distinct from those that experience them, there would be no true intuition; not for the senses, because they would remain foreign to complex combinations; nor for the understanding, because it would then know the cause of the sensations, not by intuition, but by discursion.

72. We infer from this, that not every sensation is an intuition; and that the imaginary reproductions of past sensations, or the imaginary production of possible sensations, although repeatedly styled intuitions, are, since they do not refer to an object, unworthy of the name. We ought, nevertheless, to

observe that the phenomena of purely internal sensibility do, perhaps, owe to the habit of reflection their non-reference to objects. Reflection perceives the difference of time, the more or less vividness of sensations, their greater or less constant connection, and also other circumstances; and it is enabled by these to distinguish between representations which do really refer to an object, such as external sensations, and those that have only a past or possible object, such as purely internal representations. Thus experience teaches us that the purely internal sensibility, wholly abandoned to itself, transfers whatever is presented to it to the external world, without the aid of reflection, and converts imaginary appearances into realities. This is verified in sleep, or even in our waking hours, when by some cerebral inversion the sensibility works by itself alone, and entirely free of reflection.

73. The reason why the sensibility left to itself, renders all its impressions objective, is to be looked for in the fact, that being a non-reflective faculty, it cannot distinguish between a purely internal affection, and one coming from without. Since comparison, however inconsiderable it may be, always implies reflection, sensibility does not compare. Hence it happens that when the subject does nothing but feel, it cannot appreciate the differences of sensations, by calculating the degrees of their vividness, nor ever perceive the existence or want of order and constancy in their connection.

The faculty of feeling is perfectly blind to all but its determinate object; whatever it does not discover in this so far as it is its object, does in no manner exist for it. We can now see why, when left to itself, it will render its impressions objective, and believe itself intuitive by converting simple appearances into realities.

74. It is worthy of notice, that of the sensitive faculties, some would always be intuitive, that is, would always refer to an external object, if reflection did not accompany them; whilst others would never be intuitive, not even if separated from reflection, or unaccompanied by those which are by their nature intuitive. To the former class belong the representative faculties, properly so called, that is, those which affect the sensitive subject by presenting to it a form, the real or apparent image of an object. Such are those of sight and of touch, which can neither exist nor be conceived without this representation. Other sensations, on the contrary, offer no form to the sensitive subject; they are simple affections of the subject, although they proceed from an external cause; if we refer them to objects, this we do by reflection; and when this warns us that we have in attributing to the object not only the principle of causality, but also the sensation in itself, carried the reference too far, we easily recognize the illusion, and lay it aside. This does not occur in representative sensations; no one, no matter how great efforts he may make, will ever be able to persuade himself that beyond himself

there is nothing real, nothing resembling the sensible representation in which objects are presented as extended.

75. When we say that some sensations would not be intuitive were they not accompanied by reflection, we do not mean to say that man refers them to an object, after explicit reflection, for we cannot forget what we have already said when explaining at length the instinctive way in which our faculties develop themselves prior to all reflection, in their relations with the corporeal world; but only that no necessary relation to an object as represented can be discovered in these sensations considered in themselves, and in perfect isolation; and that, probably, if a confused reflection be not mingled with the instinct which makes us render them objective, there at least enters some influence of other sensations, which are by their proper object representative.

CHAPTER XI
TWO COGNITIONS: INTUITIVE AND DISCURSIVE

76. Now that I have explained sensible, I pass to intellectual intuition. There are two modes of knowing; the one is intuitive, the other discursive. Intuitive cognition is that in which the object is presented to the understanding, such as it is, and upon which the perceptive faculty has to exercise no function but that of contemplation; it is therefore called *intuition*, from *intueri*, to see.

77. This intuition may take place in two ways. It may either present the object itself to the perceptive faculty, and unite them without any intermediacy; or by the intervention of an idea or representation, capable of putting the perceptive faculty in action, so that it may, without the necessity of combination, see the object in this representation. The first requires the object perceived to be intelligible by itself, since otherwise there could be no union of the object understood with the subject understanding; the second needs a representation to supply the place of the object, and consequently it is not indispensable that this should be immediately intelligible. [9]

78. Discursive cognition is that in which the understanding does not have the object itself present, but forms it itself, so to speak, by uniting in one whole conception several partial conceptions, whose connection in one subject it has found out by ratiocination.

In order to render more apparent the difference between intuitive and discursive cognition, I will illustrate it by an example. "We see a man; his physiognomy is presented to us, such as it is; no combinations are necessary, none could possibly make him appear differently. We see his characteristic features, such as they are; but the collection of them is not a thing produced by our combinations; it is an object given to the perceptive faculty which has nothing to do but to perceive it." When an object is offered to our understanding in this way, the cognition we have of it will be intuitive.

We have said that the object of intellectual intuition may be united immediately to the perceptive faculty, or that it may be presented to it by a medium which acts the part of the object. Keeping in view the same example, we might say that these two classes of intuitions correspond to those of the man seen by himself, or in his portrait. There would be in both cases intuition of his physiognomy, but no combination would be necessary, and none could possibly form it.

But suppose some one to tell us of a person whom we have never seen, and whose portrait cannot be shown to us. He would be obliged, in order to give us an idea of his physiognomy, to enumerate one by one his characteristic features, by the union of which we shall form an idea of the likeness he has just described. To this imaginary representation may be compared discursive cognition, by which, although we do not see the object, we in some sense construct it, as it were, from the assemblage of those ideas which we have by means of discursion interlinked, and formed into one whole conception representing the object.

79. Kant, in his *Critic of Pure Reason*, speaks repeatedly of intuitive and discursive cognition; but he does not explain with perfect clearness the distinctive characteristics of these two classes of cognition. Let it not, however, be supposed that the discovery of these two ways of perceiving is due to the German philosopher. Many ages before him, the theologians had known them; nor could it be otherwise, since the distinction between intuition and discursion is intimately connected with one of the fundamental dogmas of Christianity.

It is well known that our religion admits the possibility and reality of a true cognition of God, even in this life. The sacred text tells us that we may know God by his works; that the invisible things of God are manifested to us by his visible creatures; that the heavens narrate his glory, and the firmament announces the works of his hands; that they who have thus known God are inexcusable, because they have not glorified him as they ought; but this same religion teaches us that the Blessed, in the life to come, will know him in a very different manner, will see him as he is, face to face. It was Christianity then that marked the difference between intuitive and discursive cognitions, between the cognition by which the understanding, proceeding from effects to their cause, and uniting in it the ideas of wisdom, omnipotence, goodness, holiness, and infinite perfection, rises to God; and the cognition in which the mind does not need to advance, drawing its conclusions by aid of discursion, from various conceptions, in order to force from them an idea of God, in which the Infinite Being will offer himself clearly to the eyes of the mind, not in a conception elaborated by reason, nor under the sublime mysteries of faith, but such as he is, in himself, as an object given immediately to the perceptive faculty, not as an object discovered by the force of discursion, or presented under august shadows. And here we find another proof of the great profoundness hidden under the dogmas of the Christian religion. This distinction is to be met with in the catechism, and yet who would have suspected that religion had taught us a doctrine so important to ideological science? If the child be asked, who is God, he replies by enumerating his perfections, and showing thereby that he knows him. If you ask this same child, to what end man has been created, he will answer, to *see* God, etc.

Here again is the distinction between discursive cognition, or by conceptions, and intuitive cognitions; with the former one is said, simply to *know*, with the latter to *see*.

CHAPTER XII
THE SENSISM OF KANT

80. Kant maintained that while in the present life, we have only sensible intuition; and he considers the possibility of a purely intellectual intuition, whether for our own or for other minds doubtful. But as we have seen elsewhere (ch. IX.) that he does not attribute any value to conceptions separated from intuition, we infer that he is, notwithstanding his long dissertations upon the pure understanding, a confirmed sensist; and that the authors of the *Critic of Pure Reason*, and of the *Treatise on Sensations*, differ much less than at first sight might be supposed. If our mind has no other intuition than the sensible, and the conceptions of the pure understanding are, if they do not include some one of these intuitions, nothing but empty forms; if when we abstract these intuitions, there are in the understanding only purely logical functions, which mean nothing, and in no sense deserve to be called cognitions; it follows that there is in our mind nothing but sensations, which may be methodically distributed in conceptions, as if packed away in a kind of hut, where they are registered and preserved. According to this philosopher, the understanding is reduced so low, that Condillac himself might admit it.

81. Indeed, in the system of sensations transformed, the mind is supposed to possess a transforming force, since otherwise, it would be impossible to explain all ideological phenomena by mere sensation, and the very title of the system would be a contradiction. This being so, would any sensistic scruple have prevented Condillac from admitting *the synthesis of the imagination*, the relations of all sensible intuitions to the *unity of apperception*, and finally, a variety of logical functions, to classify and compare sensible intuitions? So far is this from being the case, it would seem that the root of all these doctrines might be found in the system of the French philosopher, whose fundamental principles, when summed up, amount to this: that nothing can be seen in the mind besides sensations; but he does not therefore deny it a force capable of transforming, classifying, and generalizing them.

82. Here, then, is another check to the originality of the German philosopher; he has, to combat sensism, said in substance just what, ages before, all the schools repeated; and now when he undertakes to follow a

new road to the explanation of the purely intellectual order, he falls into Condillac's system. His empty conceptions, without meaning, without application, beyond the sensible order, amount to no more than what Condillac taught when analyzing the generation of ideas, and showing how they flowed from sensations by means of successive transformations. Could there be any difficulty, it would be concerning words, not things: no sensist ought to hesitate accepting whole and entire the *Critic of Pure Reason*, when once he has seen what applications the German spiritualist makes of his doctrines. It would be very desirable for those who insist that the spiritualism of Kant is decidedly destructive of Condillac's sensism, to weigh well these observations.

CHAPTER XIII
EXISTENCE OF PURE
INTELLECTUAL INTUITION

83. It is not true that the human mind even in this life has no intuition other than the sensible. There are within us many non-sensible phenomena, of which we are clearly conscious. Reflection, comparison, abstraction, election, and all the acts of the understanding and will, include nothing of the sensible. We should like to know, to what species of sensibility, abstract ideas, and the acts by which we perceive them, belong; these among others: *I desire, I do not desire, I choose this, I prefer this to that.* Not one of these acts can be presented by sensible intuition; they are facts of an order superior to the sphere of sensibility, and yet we have in our mind a clear and lively consciousness of them; we reflect upon them, make them the object of our studies, distinguish them one from another, and classify them in a thousand different ways. These facts are presented to us immediately; we know them, not by discursion, but by intuition; therefore it is false that the intuition of the soul refers to none but sensible phenomena, for it encounters within itself an expanded series of non-sensible phenomena, which are given to it in intuition.

84. It is of no use to say that these internal phenomena are empty forms, and mean nothing, unless referred to a sensible intuition. Whatever they may be, they are something distinct from this same sensible intuition; and we perceive this something, not by discursion, but by intuition; therefore, besides sensible intuition, there is another of the purely intellectual order.

The question is not whether these pure conceptions have, or have not, a certain power to enable us to know objects in themselves; but it is simply to ascertain if they do exist, and if they are sensible. That they exist, is certain; consciousness attests this fact, and all ideologists admit it. That they are sensible, cannot be maintained without destroying their nature; and least of all can Kant maintain this, since he has so carefully distinguished between sensible intuition and these conceptions.

85. This sea of non-sensible phenomena, which we experience within us, is like a mirror wherein the depths of the intellectual world are

reflected. Minds, it is true, are not presented immediately to our perception, and to know them we need a discursive process; but we shall, upon careful examination, find in this intuition of our inward phenomena the representation, imperfect though it be, of what is verified in intelligences of a superior order. Thus we have in a certain mode idea-images, since there can be no better image of one thought than another thought, nor of one act of the will than another act of the will. Thus we know minds distinct from our own, by a kind of mediate, not immediate, intuition, in so far as they are presented to our consciousness as the image in a mirror.

86. The communication of minds by means of speech and other natural or conventional signs, is a fact of experience intimately connected with all intellectual, moral, and physical necessities. When a mind is put into communication with another, the cognition it has of what passes in the other is not by mere general conceptions, but by a kind of intuition, which although mediate, does not therefore fail to be true. The thought, or affection of another communicated to our mind by means of speech, excites in us a thought, or affection, similar to that of the mind communicating them. We do, then, not only know, but *see*, in our own consciousness, the consciousness of another; and so perfect is at times the likeness, that we anticipate all that he is about to tell us, and unroll within ourselves the same series of phenomena that are verified in the mind of him with whom we are in communication. It happens thus when we say: "I understand perfectly what N. thinks, what he wants, what he is trying to express."

87. This observation seems to us of great service to place beyond all doubt that there are in our mind, independently of the sensible order, conceptions, not empty, but referable to a determinate object. The cognition of the phenomena of the purely intellectual order, transmitted to us by means of speech, or other signs, does not destroy the character of the intuition, since we here find all the necessary conditions assembled; internal representation, and its relation to a determinate object affecting us.

88. This analysis of ideological facts, whose existence cannot be doubted, demonstrates the falseness of Kant's doctrine, that there are in our mind none but sensible intuitions; as well as the non-existence of the German philosopher's problem: whether it is possible, or not, for objects to be given to other minds in an intuition other than the sensible. This very problem is found solved within us, since the attentive observation of the internal phenomena, and the reciprocal communication of minds, has given us to know not only the possibility, but also the existence of intuitions different from the sensible.

CHAPTER XIV
VALUE OF INTELLECTUAL CONCEPTIONS.—ABSTRACTION MADE FROM INTELLECTUAL INTUITION

89. Although we should admit that our mind can have no intuition but the sensible, it could not thence be inferred that conceptions of the purely intellectual order are empty forms, and in nowise conducive to the knowledge of objects in themselves. It has always been understood that general ideas are not intuitive, since by the very fact that they are general they cannot be referred *immediately* to a determinate object; and yet no one ever doubted that they could serve to give us true cognitions.

90. It is certain that general ideas, of themselves alone, do not lead to any positive result; or, in other words, they do not make us know existing beings; but if they be joined to other particular ones, a reciprocal influence is established between them, from which cognition results. When we make the general affirmation: "Every contingent being requires a cause;" this proposition, although very true, means nothing in the order of facts, if we abstract the existence of contingent beings and causes of every kind. In such a case, the proposition will express a relation of ideas, not of facts: the cognition which results therefrom will be merely ideal, not positive.

91. This relation of ideas tacitly involves a condition, which gives them, so far as facts are concerned, a hypothetical value; for, when we affirm that every contingent being must have a cause, we are not to be understood to affirm a relation of ideas destitute of all possible application; but rather, on the contrary, to intend that if any contingent being exists, it must have a cause.

92. In order that this hypothetical value of ideas may be converted into a positive value, nothing is necessary but that the condition involved in the general proposition: "Every contingent being must have a cause," be verified. Of itself alone this teaches us nothing concerning the real world; but from the moment that experience shows us a single contingent being, the general proposition, before sterile, becomes exceedingly fruitful. So

soon as experience shows us a contingent being, we know the necessity of its cause; we also infer the necessity of the proportions, which the activity producing must preserve with the thing produced; knowing the qualities of the latter, we infer those which ought to be found in the former. In this manner, resting upon two bases, one of which is ideal truth and the other real truth, or data supplied by experience, we construct a true positive science referred to determinate facts.

93. Since the being that thinks necessarily has consciousness of itself, no thinking being can be limited to the cognition of purely ideal truths. Even if we were to suppose it perfectly isolated from all other beings, in absolute non-communication with every thing not itself, so as neither to exert any influence upon them, nor to be influenced by them, it could not be reduced to the cognition of a purely ideal order; for, by the very fact that it is thinking, it is conscious of itself, and consciousness is essentially a particular fact, a cognition of a determinate being, since without it there could be no consciousness.

94. This observation overturns to its very foundation the system which pretends to bar all communication between the real and ideal orders. It shows also that experience is not only possible, but absolutely necessary to every thinking being, since consciousness is by its very nature an experience, and the clearest and surest experience. The truths of the ideal order are then necessarily interlinked with those of the real order: to suppose all intercommunication between them impossible, is to disown a fundamental fact of ideological and psychological science, consciousness.

95. To render the truth and exactness of the preceding doctrine more evident, let us suppose a man, or rather a human mind, absolutely ignorant of the existence of an external world, of every body, and even of every spirit; one that knows nothing concerning its own origin or destiny, but one that would nevertheless at the same time exercise its intellectual activity, without which it would be a lifeless thing, and could offer no field to observation. Let us suppose him to have general ideas, such as of being and of not-being, of substance and accidents, of the absolute and the conditioned, of the necessary and contingent. Manifestly he may combine them in various ways, and arrive at the same purely ideal results to which we ourselves arrive. There is no supposition more favorable to a series of abstract cognitions independent of experience, and yet not even in this case would the truths known be limited to the purely ideal order; it would even here be impossible for them not to descend to the real order, if the thinking being were not dispossessed of all consciousness of itself.

Indeed, by the very fact that a being is supposed capable of thinking, it is supposed able to say to itself, *I think*. This act is eminently experimental, and it needs only to be united with general truths in a common consciousness, to enable the isolated being to rise above itself, and create for itself a positive science, by which to pass from the world of ideas to that of facts. The instability of its thoughts, and the permanence of the being that experiences them, offer to it a practical case in which the general ideas of substance and accident are particularized. The successive appearance and disappearance of its own conceptions will show to it the ideas of being and of not-being realized; the recollection of the time when its own operations commenced, beyond which the memory of its existence does not extend, will enable it to know the contingency of his own being; and this fact, combined with the general principles which express the relations between contingent and necessary beings, will suggest to the thought that there must be another that communicated to it its existence.

CHAPTER XV
ILLUSTRATIONS OF THE VALUE
OF GENERAL CONCEPTIONS

96. However vague the ideas an isolated being would form of objects distinct from itself, they will never be so vague as not to refer to a real thing. The mind may not know the nature of this reality, but it knows for certain that it exists. A man blind from his birth can form no clear idea of colors, nor of the sensation of seeing; but is he therefore ignorant that sensation exists, and that the words, color, seeing, and others which refer to sight, have a positive and determinate object? Certainly not. The blind man does not know in what these things, of which he hears, consist, but he knows that they are something; those of his conceptions that refer to them may be called imperfect, but they are not vain; the words by which he expresses them, have for him a positive, although incomplete meaning.

97. There is a great difference between incomplete and indeterminate conceptions; the former may refer to a positive thing, although imperfectly known; the latter include nothing but a relation of ideas, meaning nothing in the order of facts. We will render this difference more apparent by explaining the example of the preceding paragraph.

A man blind from his birth has no intuition of colors, nor of any thing that refers to the sense of sight; but he is sure that there exist external facts which correspond to an internal affection called *seeing*. This idea is incomplete, but it has a determinate object. The words of those who possess the sense of sight reveal to him its existence; he knows not, what it is, but, that it is; in other words, he does not know its essence, but its existence. Let us now suppose the possibility of an order of sensations different from ours, and in nowise resembling those which we experience, to be called in question. The conception referred to the new sensations would not only be incomplete, but would have no relation to any real object. The general idea, then, of affection of a sensitive being, will be all that our mind will have; but it will know nothing of its existence, and can form only mere conjectures as to the conditions of its possibility. This example illustrates our idea. We find in the man blind from his birth, who hears of what pertains to the sense of sight, an incomplete conception, but one to which the existence of a series of facts, known to his mind, corresponds. But in ourselves, if we reflect upon a kind of sensations different from our own, we find conceptions, having, indeed, a general object, but of whose realization we know nothing.

98. Thus is it explained how our mind, without having intuition of a thing, can, nevertheless, know it, and be perfectly certain of its existence. We have here demonstrated that conceptions may, although they do not refer to a sensible intuition, have a value, not only in the order of ideas, but also in that of facts.

99. In order to prove the sterility of all conception beyond sensible intuition, Kant adduces one reason, which is, that we cannot define the categories and the principles which flow from them without referring to the objects of sensibility. This is no proof at all; for, in the first place, the impossibility of a definition does not always arise from the fact that the conception to be defined is empty; but it very frequently results from the conception being simple, and consequently not susceptible of a division into parts that may be expressed by words. How will he define the idea of *being*? No matter how he attempts to define it, the thing to be defined will enter into the definition: the words, thing, reality, existence, all signify *being*.

It is very natural, since sensible intuition is the basis of our relations with the external world, and consequently with our fellow-men, that when we purpose to express any relation whatever, we should call to our aid sensible applications; but we are not thence to infer that there is not in our mind, independently of them, a real truth contained in the conception which we wish to explain.

100. This capacity of knowing objects under general ideas, is a characteristic property of our mind, and we cannot, in our inability to penetrate to the essence of things, think without this indispensable auxiliary. In the ordinary course of human affairs, it often happens that we need to know the existence of a thing and of some of its attributes, but do not require a perfect knowledge of it. In such cases, general ideas, aided by some data of experience, put us in mediate communication with the object not presented to our intuition. But why cannot the same thing be verified with respect to non-sensible beings, which alone are the object of intellectual intuitions? I know not what exception can be taken to these observations, founded as they are upon observation of internal phenomena, and confirmed by common sense.

CHAPTER XVI
VALUE OF PRINCIPLES, INDEPENDENTLY
OF SENSIBLE INTUITION

101. The principle of contradiction, indispensable condition of all certainty, of all truth, and without which the external world, and intelligence itself, would become a chaos, offers us a good example of the intrinsic value of purely intellectual conceptions independent of sensible intuition.

No determinate idea is united to the conception of being when we affirm the impossibility of a thing being and not-being at the same time, or the exclusion of not-being by being; and so far we absolutely abstract all sensible intuition. Whatever be its object, whatever its nature and the relations of its existence; be it corporeal or incorporeal, composite or simple, accident or substance, contingent or necessary, finite or infinite, always will it be found true that being excludes not-being; the absolute incompatibility of these two extremes will always be verified, so that the affirmation of the one is always, in all cases, and under all imaginable suppositions, the negation of the other.

This being so, to limit the value of these conceptions to sensible intuition, would be to destroy the principle of contradiction. The limitation of the principle is equivalent to its nullification. Its absolute universality is closely allied to its absolute necessity; if it be curtailed, it is made contingent; for, if the principle of contradiction may fail us in one instance, it fails us in all. To admit the possibility of what is absurd, is to deny its absurdity. If the contradiction of being and not-being does not exist in every supposition, it exists in no supposition.

102. The difficulty is to know how the transition from the principle of contradiction to real truths, is made; because not affirming any thing determinate in it, but solely the repugnance of yes to no, and of no to yes, we assert that it would be impossible to affirm either one of these extremes without denying the other; and as on the other hand, it is impossible, if we confine ourselves to the principle of contradiction, for it to include any thing more than the most general relation between two general ideas, we conclude that it is of itself alone, perfectly sterile and unable to conduct us

to any positive result. This is all true; but it contradicts in no point what we have said concerning the intrinsic value of general conceptions.

We have remarked that truths of the purely ideal order have none but a hypothetical value, and that in order to produce a positive science, they require facts to which they may apply. We have also remarked, that experience furnishes these facts, and that every thinking being possesses one at least, consciousness of itself. Every thinking being will therefore, provided it discover in its own consciousness facts to which it may apply it, make a positive use of the principle of contradiction.

103. Even were we to admit the supposition that there is in our mind no intuition but the sensible, it could not therefore be concluded that general principles, and more particularly that of contradiction, can have no positive value; because, if we suppose these principles combined with sensible intuition to produce a cognition of other beings out of the order of sensibility, it would follow that we really know them, although they were not given to us in immediate intuition. And this is verified in the human mind, when it rises by discursion to the cognition of the non-sensible. On the one hand, the data furnished by experience, and on the other, general and necessary truths, form a connection constituting a positive science, which guides us with perfect security to the cognition of objects not subject to immediate experience.

This theory is so clear, so evident, so rooted in the consciousness of our own acts, so perfectly in accordance with all that we observe in the proceedings of the human mind, that it causes us a strange surprise to meet philosophers, whose erroneous doctrines oblige us to explain and defend it.

104. The transition from the known to the unknown is a proceeding characteristic of our understanding; and this transition is impossible if the reality of every cognition, not referred to an intuition, be denied. Whatever is presented to us in this latter way, is given to us, is present to our sight, and we have no necessity of seeking it. If, therefore, no object be really known, unless offered in intuition, all intellectual progress becomes impossible: all the advances of our mind are reduced to combinations of the forms presented to the sensibility, and even these lead to nothing whenever they cease to be intuitive; that is, when they no longer relate to determinate objects immediately perceived. The *Critic of Pure Reason* is the destruction of all reason: for it examines itself with suicidal intent, or in order to prove that it contains nothing positive.

Science cannot survive the reduction of general principles to one only value relative to sensible intuitions. What we have demonstrated concerning the principle of contradiction, is *a fortiori* applicable to all other principles. If this be not saved, all must perish in the wreck. Moreover, the very basis of the necessity involved in these principles is threatened. We know nothing, save that there is within us a series of phenomena which *seem* necessary. But what use can we make of them beyond the subjective order? None at all. Behold us then in the most perfect skepticism, condemned to simple appearances, with no means of knowing any reality.

105. No! the human mind is not condemned to so despairing a sterility: reason is not an empty word; ratiocination is not a puerile play, only fit to serve as an amusement. In the midst of the prepossessions, errors, and extravagance of human misery, towers on high that force, that admirable activity, by which the mind springs beyond itself, *knows* what it does not *see*, and *foresees* what it will one day *feel*. Nature is veiled to our eyes; impenetrable secrets surround us; whichever way we turn deep shadows hide the reality of objects: but through this darkness we discern from afar some scintillation of light. Notwithstanding the profound silence which reigns over the sea of beings, whose surges toss us about like imperceptible atoms in the immensity of the ocean, we hear at times mysterious voices tell us the course we must keep to reach unknown shores.

CHAPTER XVII
RELATIONS OF INTUITION WITH THE
RANK OF THE PERCEPTIVE BEING

106. The perfection of intelligence involves extension and clearness of its intuitions; the more perfect it is, the more intuitive it will be. The infinite intelligence does not know by discursion, but by intuition: it does not need to seek objects: it sees them all before itself. It sees with intuition of identity what belongs to its own essence, and with intuition of causality every thing that does or can exist outside of itself. Other minds have an intuition so much the more perfect as they are more elevated in the order to which they belong; so that cognition by conceptions indicates an imperfection of intelligence.

107. The relations of one being with other beings will therefore depend upon the rank it holds in the scale of the universe. God, infinite being, and the cause of all that does or can exist, has intimate and immediate relations with the whole universe, considered not only in its entireness but even in its smallest particles. There is consequently in God a most perfect representation of all beings taken not only in their generality, but also in their minutest differences. The Being, cause of all, does not know objects by vague conceptions, by means of representations which only show what all beings have in common, but as he has made their slightest differences, they must be presented to him with perfect clearness. His cognition is founded upon a reality which is himself; his understanding does not fluctuate through an ideal and hypothetical world; but, fixed with clearest intuition upon infinite reality, he sees all that the infinite being is, and all that it can produce with its infinite activity. For God there is no experience proceeding from without, for nothing can exert any influence upon him; all his experience consists in the knowledge and love of himself.

108. Created beings, occupying a determinate place in the scale of the universe, relate to it only under certain aspects. Their relations with their fellow beings are brought to a point of view, to which their perceptive faculties are subordinated. The representativeness, which they contain in themselves, must be proportionate to the cognition that has to produce it.

Hence it follows that every intelligent being will have its representativeness adapted to the functions it has to exercise in the universe. If the being do not pertain to the order of intelligences, its perceptive faculties will be limited to sensible intuitions, in a measure corresponding to the place it is destined to occupy.

109. We have seen that general ideas and the intuition of determinate objects fecundate the intellectual faculties. From this we infer that every intelligence stands in need of intuitions, if its cognitions are not to be limited to a purely hypothetical order.

The human mind, destined to a union with the body, and to a continual communication with the corporeal universe, has received the gift of sensible intuition as the basis of its relations with bodies. The same is the case with brutes. Sensible intuition has been given to them because they must have continual relations with the external world: but, being confined to the functions of animal life, they have no intuitions superior to the sphere of sensibility, nor do they possess the force necessary to convert sensible representations into objects of intellectual combinations.

110. There is an immense difference between brutes and man, in the scale of beings. Since every intelligence is conscious of itself, and can fix its attention upon its acts, the human mind knows its own intuitively, and therefore discovers in itself an intuition superior to the sensible. Besides these intuitions, we have the power of discursion by which we form representations, and by them attain to the cognition of objects not offered immediately to our perception.

Thus, starting with the data furnished by external and internal experience, and aided by those general principles which involve the primary conditions of every intelligence and of every being, we are enabled to penetrate to the world of reality, and to know, although imperfectly, the assemblage of beings which constitute the universe, and the infinite cause which made them all.

CHAPTER XVIII
ASPIRATIONS OF THE HUMAN SOUL

111. A close observation of internal phenomena shows that the human soul aspires to something far beyond all that it actually possesses. Not satisfied with the objects given to it in immediate intuition, it darts forward in pursuit of others of a superior order; and even in those that are offered to it immediately, it is not contented with the aspect under which they *appear*, but seeks to know what they *are*. The purely individual does not satisfy the soul. Nailed to one point in the immense scale of beings, it is unwilling to limit itself to the perception of those that are in its environs, and form, as it were, the atmosphere wherein it must live; it aspires to the cognition of those that precede and follow it, and seeks to know the connection, to discover the law from which results the ineffable harmony that presides over the creation. It finds its purest pleasures in rising from the sphere where the limitation of its faculties holds it confined. Its activity is greater than its strength; its desires superior to its being.

112. We discover the same phenomenon in the sentiment and the will as in the understanding. Man has, to satisfy his necessities, and provide for the preservation of the individual and of the race, sensations and sentiments which direct him to determinate objects; but at the side of these affections, limited to the sphere in which he is circumscribed, he experiences sentiments of a more elevated character, which make him spring beyond his orbit, and absorb, so to speak, his individuality in the ocean of infinity.

When man comes in contact with nature in herself, despoiled of all conditions relating to individuals, he experiences an indefinable sentiment, a kind of foretaste of the infinite. Go into an uninhabited region and sit down by the sea side; hark to the deafening roar of the waves breaking at your feet, and the whistling of the winds which have raised them; with eyes fixed on this immensity, see the azure line where the vault of heaven unites with the waters of the ocean: stand on a vast and desert plain, or in the heart of ancient forests; contemplate in the silence of night the firmament studded with stars, following their course in tranquillity, as they have followed it for ages past, and will follow it for ages to come: without effort, or labor of any kind, abandon yourself to the spontaneous movements of your soul, and you will see how sentiments spring up in it and move it to its very centre; how they elevate it above itself, and absorb it, as it were, in immensity. Its individuality vanishes from its own eyes, as it feels the harmony presiding over that immense creation of which it forms but a most insignificant part. In such solemn moments is it that inspired genius chants the glories of creation, and lifts one corner of the veil that hides the resplendent throne of the supreme Creator from the eye of mortals.

113. That calm, grave, and profound sentiment which masters us on such occasions, has no relation to individual objects; it is an expansion of the soul at a touch of nature, as the flower expands to the rays of the sun in the morning, it is a divine attraction by which the author of all created things raises us above the dust in which we drag out our brief days. Thus the heart and the understanding harmonize; thus the one foretastes what the other knows; thus we are warned in different ways, that the exercise of our faculties is not limited to the narrow orbit conceded to us upon this earth. Let us be on our guard, lest the heart be frozen with the coldness of insensibility, and the torch of the understanding quenched by the devastating blasts of skepticism.

CHAPTER XIX
ELEMENTS AND VARIETY OF
THE CHARACTERS OF SENSIBLE
REPRESENTATION

114. I now come to examine the primitive elements of our mental combinations. I shall begin with their sensible elements. Extension enters into every act of representative sensibility; without it nothing is represented to us, and sensations are reduced to mere affections of the soul, having no relation to any object.

115. Extension, of itself, abstracted from its limitability, is susceptible of no combination; it only offers a vague, indefinite, immense representation, from which nothing distinct of itself results. But if limitability be joined to extension, figurability, that is, the infinite field over which geometrical science extends, will result.

116. *Extension* and *limitability* are then the two elements of sensible intuition. These elements may be offered to us in two ways, either joined to sensations which present to us determinate objects, or as productions of our own internal activity. If we see the disc of the moon, we have an intuition of the former class; and if we study the properties of a circle by producing within ourselves its representation, this will be an intuition of the latter class.

117. This internal activity, by which, at our will or caprice, we produce an indefinite number of representations, with an indefinite variety of forms, is an important phenomenon and one worthy of attention. It shows us that the productive activity is not limited to the purely intellectual order, since we detect it in the sensible order, not in any way whatever, but as unrolled on an infinite scale. Suppose a right line to be produced to infinity, besides it and in the same plane, we may infinite other lines; the variety of angles in which we may consider the position of the different lines will extend to the infinite; so that with right lines alone, the productive activity in the order of sensibility will know no limit. If we substitute curves for right lines, their combinations in form, in nature, in their respective positions and

relations with determinate axes, will likewise be infinite: so that without quitting the sensible order, we discover within ourselves a force productive of infinite representations, and one needing no elements besides terminable or figurable extension.

118. The representative sensible faculty develops itself sometimes by the presence of an object; at other times, spontaneously, without any dependence on the will; and finally, at other times, in consequence of a free act. This is not the place to examine in what way the phenomenon of representation is connected with the affections of the corporeal organs; at present, we propose only to designate and explain facts in the ideological sphere, absolutely abstracting their physiological aspect.

Among the sensible representations just classified, which we may call *passive, spontaneous,* and *free,* there are differences worthy of observation.

119. Passive representation is given to the soul, independently of its activity. If we be placed in presence of an object, with our eyes open, it will be impossible not to see it, or even not to see it in a certain manner, if we do not change the direction of our eyesight or other condition of vision. For this reason, the soul seems, in the exercise of its senses, to be purely passive, since its representations necessarily depend on the conditions to which its corporeal organs in their relation to objects, are subject.

120. Spontaneous representation, or the faculty productive of sensible representations, seems also, since it operates independently of external objects and of the will, to be more or less passive, and its exercise to depend upon organic affections. And the fact that these sensations are wont to exist without any order, or at most, if they are recollections of old sensations, with that only which they had at another time, appears to indicate it. It is also worthy of note that these representations are sometimes offered to us, in spite of all the efforts of the will to dissipate and forget them: some are so tenacious as for a long time to triumph over all the resistance of freewill.

It is not easy to explain this phenomenon without recurring to organic causes, which, on determinate occasions, produce the same effect upon the soul, as the impressions of the external senses. It is certain that the internal representation reaches, in certain cases, so high a point of vividness, that the subject confounds it with the impressions of the senses. This can only be explained by saying that the interior organic affection has become so powerful, as to be equivalent to that which the impression of an object operating upon the external organ, could have caused.

121. In this spontaneous production it is to be remarked that present representations do not always correspond with others previously received; but a power of combination is developed in them from which result

imaginary objects entirely new. This combination is sometimes exercised in a perfectly blind manner, and then follow extravagant results; but, at other times, this activity subjected to certain conditions produces, independently of free will, objects artistically beautiful and sublime.

Genius is nothing else than the spontaneity of the imagination and sentiment, developed in subordination to the conditions of the beautiful. Artists, not gifted with genius, do not lack strength of will to produce works of genius; nor are they wanting in imagination to reproduce a beautiful object if they have once seen it; they do not lack discernment and taste to distinguish and admire beautiful objects, nor are they ignorant of the rules of art or of all that can be said to explain the character of beauty; what they lack is that instinctively fine spontaneity which develops itself in the most recondite sinuosities of the soul, and far from being dependent upon the free will of its possessor, directs and domineers over him, pursues him in sleep as in the hours of waking, in the time of recreation as in that of business, and often consumes the very existence of the privileged man, as a furious fire bursts the sides of the frail cage that holds it.

122. Free production occurs when representations are offered to us by command of our will, and under the conditions it prescribes, as in works of art, and in the combinations of those figures which constitute the object of the science of geometry.

123. This *a priori* construction cannot be referred to a type existing in our imagination; since, as this type would then be the sensible representation itself, it would not need to be constructed. How then is it possible to form a representation of which we have not already the image? It is not enough to possess the elements, that is, figurable extension, since with them infinite figures may be constructed; something else then is needed, something to serve as a rule, in order that the desired representation may result.

For the better understanding of this, I would observe that sensible intuitions are allied to general conceptions, by whose aid they may be reconstructed. Although, in reality, no sensible representation is offered to us, of any figure whatsoever, for example, a regular hexagon; the conception formed of the ideas, *six, line, equality of angles*, is all that we need to produce in our interior the sensible representation of the hexagon, and to construct it within us, if we require it.

This shows us that the free activity producing determinate sensible representations is based upon general conceptions, which, though independent of sensibility, refer to it in an indeterminate manner. Hence, also, it follows, that the understanding may, if it observe the conditions to which the elements furnished by sensibility in their respective cases, are subject, conceive the sensible indeterminately, without the intellectual act being referred to any determinate intuition.

124. If we analyze the object of these general conceptions, referred to sensible intuition, also considered in general, the understanding, while occupied in them, seems to be taken up with things not distinctly offered to it, but retained only by certain signs; confident, however, that it can develop whatever they involve, and contemplate it with perfect clearness.

CHAPTER XX
INTERMEDIATE REPRESENTATIONS
BETWEEN SENSIBLE INTUITION
AND THE INTELLECTUAL ACT

125. The question now occurs, whether the understanding, in order to perceive the geometrical relations offered in sensible intuition, does or does not need some intermediate representations which bring it into contact with the sensible order? [10] Such a necessity would, at first sight, seem to exist, since, as the understanding is a non-sensible faculty, sensible elements cannot be its immediate object. But on maturer examination, it seems more probable that there is no necessity of any thing intermediate, except some sign to connect the sensible elements, and to show the point where they must unite, and the conditions to which they are subject. As this sign may, however, be a word, or something else, susceptible of a sensible representation, its mediation will not at all solve the difficulty; since the question will always recur: How is the understanding placed in communication with the sensible sign?

This difficulty arises from the faculty of the soul being considered, not only as distinct, but also, as separate, and as exercising each one of its faculties in its own peculiar and exclusive sphere, entirely isolated from that of all others. This mode of considering the faculties of the soul, though favorable to the classification of their operations, does not accord with the teachings of experience.

It cannot be denied that we observe within ourselves, affections and operations, very unlike each other, and arising from distinct objects, and producing very different results. This has led to a distinction of faculties, and in some degree, to a separation of their functions, so as to prevent them from mixing together and being confounded. But there can be no doubt that all the affections and operations of the soul are, as consciousness reveals, bound to a common centre. Whatever becomes of the distinction of the faculties among themselves, it is very certain, as consciousness tells us, that it is one and the same being that thinks, feels, desires, acts, or suffers: it is certain that this same consciousness reveals to us the intimate communication of all the operations of the soul. We instantaneously reflect upon the impression received; we instantaneously experience an agreeable or disagreeable sensation in consequence of a reflection which occurs to us: we reflect upon the will; we seek or repudiate the object of our thought; there is, so to speak, within us a boiling spring of phenomena of different kinds, all interlinked, modified, produced, reproduced, and mutually influenced by each other in their incessant communication. We are conscious of all these; we encounter them all in one common field, which is the subject that experiences them. What necessity, then, is there to imagine intermediate beings in order to bring the faculties of the soul into communication with each other? Why may it not with its activity, called understanding, occupy itself immediately with sensible representations and affections and with all that is in its consciousness? Supposing this consciousness in its indivisible unity to comprise all the variety of internal phenomena, it does not therefore follow that the intellectual activity of the soul cannot be referred to whatever it contains of active or receptive, without its being necessary to imagine species to serve as courtiers between the faculties, to announce to one what has taken place in the other.

126. The *acting intellect* of the Aristotelians, admissible in sound philosophy so far as it denotes an activity of the mind applied to sensible representations, does not seem alike admissible, if it be supposed to be the producer of new representations distinct from the intellectual act itself. The understanding is all activity; the receptivity of the soul has nothing to do with it, but to proportion its materials; and the conceptions elaborated in presence of these materials, seem to be nothing else than the exercise of this same activity, subject on the one hand to the conditions required by the thing understood, and subordinated on the other hand to the general conditions of every intelligence.

127. I do not mean to say that the intellectual act does not refer to any object. I replace the idea by other acts of the soul, or by affections or representations of some kind or other, whether active or passive. This being so, if I am asked, for example, what is the immediate object of the intellectual act perceiving of determinate sensible intuition, I reply that it is the intuition itself. If the difficulty of explaining the union of such different things be urged, I answer: first, that this union exists in the unity of consciousness, as the internal sense attests: second, that the same difficulty militates against those who pretend that the understanding elaborates an intelligible species, which it takes from the sensible intuition; and how, I may ask, does the understanding place itself in contact with this intuition when it would

elaborate its intelligible species. If this immediate contact be impossible in the one case, it will be equally so in the other; and if they concede it to be possible in their own case, they cannot deny it to be possible in ours also.

When the understanding refers to no determinate intuition, but only to sensible intuitions in general, its immediate object is their possibility also in general, subject to the conditions of the object considered in general, and to those of every intelligence; among which, the principle of contradiction holds a primary place.

CHAPTER XXI
DETERMINATE AND INDETERMINATE IDEAS

128. We must, under pain of falling into sensism, by limiting the understanding to the perception and combination of objects presented by sensibility, admit other than intellectual acts referable to sensible objects in general. And what, in this case, is the object of the intellectual act, is a question as difficult as it is interesting.

129. The pure understanding can exercise its functions either upon determinate or indeterminate ideas; that is, upon ideas which contain something determinate, something realizable in a being, that is or may be offered to our perception, or upon ideas which represent general relations, without application to any object. Care should be taken not to confound general with indeterminate, or particular with determinate ideas. Every intermediate idea is a general idea, but not *vice versa*. The idea of *being* is general and indeterminate; that of *intelligence* is general but determinate. The particular idea refers to an individual; the determinate to a property, and it does not cease to be determinate although we abstract all relation in it to an existing individual. This distinction opens the way to considerations of the highest importance.

130. When the understanding proceeds by indeterminate conceptions, its principal object seems to be *being* in its greatest universality. This is the radical and fundamental idea, round which all other ideas are grouped. From the idea of being springs the principle of contradiction, with its infinite applications to every class of objects; from it also flow the ideas of substance and accidents, of cause and effect, of the necessary and the contingent, and every thing contained in the science of ontology, called for this very reason *ontology*, or the science of being.

131. There is nothing in those conceptions which express the general relations of all beings, to characterize them until they quit their purely metaphysical sphere and descend into the field of reality.

In order to be able to conceive of a real being, we require it to be presented to us with some property. Being and not-being, substance and accidents, cause and effect, are, when combined with something positive, highly fruitful ideas; but taken in general, with nothing determinate assigned to them, they do not offer us any existing, or even possible object.

132. The idea of being presents us that of a *thing* in the abstract; but if we would conceive of this as existing or as possible, we must imagine this thing to be something with characteristic properties. Whenever we hear an existing thing spoken of, we instinctively ask what it is, and what is its nature. God is essentially being, is infinite being; but nothing would be represented to our mind were we to conceive of him only as of being, and not also as intelligent, active, free being endowed with all the other perfections of his infinite essence.

133. The idea of substance offers us that of a permanent being, which does not, like a modification, inhere in another. This idea, taken in its generality without other determination than that added to the idea of being, by that of subsistence, offers us nothing real or realizable. Permanence in general, subsistence by itself, non-inherence in a subject, do not suffice to enable a substance to exist or to be possible; some characteristic mark, some attribute is also needed, as corporeal, intelligent, free, or any other you please, to determine the general idea of substance.

134. The same may be said of the idea of cause, or productive activity. An active thing, in general, offers us nothing either real or possible. In order to conceive an existing activity, we must refer to a determinate activity; the idea of acting, or of being able to act, in general, does not suffice; we must represent it to ourselves, as exercising itself in one way or another, referring to determinate objects, producing, not beings in general, but beings having their own characteristic attributes. True, we do not need to know what these attributes are; but we do need to know that they exist with their determinateness.

The most universal cause conceivable is God, the first and infinite cause; and although we do not conceive of him as of cause in the abstract, regarding the simple idea of productive activity, but we attach to the general idea of cause the ideas of free will and intelligence. When we say that God is omnipotent, we assign an infinite sphere to his power; we do not know the characteristic attributes of all the beings which can be created by this infinite activity; but we are certain that every existing or possible being must have a determinate nature; and we do not conceive it to be possible for a being to be produced, which, without any determination, would be nothing but being.

135. We do not meet this determination, indispensable as it is to us, if we would conceive of the existence or possibility of a being, in indeterminate ideas, but must take it from experience; wherefore, if our understanding were limited to the combination of those relations offered in indeterminate

conceptions, it would be condemned to a perfectly sterile science. We have already seen (Chap. XIV.) that the absolute non-communication of the real with the ideal order is impossible if the intelligible order be not deprived of all consciousness of itself. It is not enough to know, that such a communication exists, but we must ascertain in what points it is verified, and how far it extends.

136. Before passing to this investigation, we would observe, that the doctrine explained in this chapter is not to be confounded with that of the fourteenth chapter. There, it was shown that general ideas of themselves alone, have only a purely hypothetical value, and lead to nothing because they are not combined with any thing positive, furnished by experience; here, we have proved that indeterminate ideas of being, substance, and cause, do not of themselves alone suffice to enable us to conceive of any thing either existing or possible, if they be not accompanied by some determinate idea, which gives a character to the general ideas. There, a hypothetical value, with respect to their existence, was allotted to general ideas: here, we affirm it to be necessary for these ideas to be accompanied by some property that shall render them capable of constituting an essence, at least in the possible order. These are very different things, and must not be confounded; hence the importance of not forgetting the distinction between general and indeterminate, and between particular and determinate ideas.

CHAPTER XXII
LIMITS OF OUR INTUITION

137. Could we assign limits to the field of experience, and determine exactly how much they inclose, we could also determine the characteristics by which a being may be presented to us as existing or as possible.

138. Passive sensibility, active sensibility, understanding, and will, are, if we be not mistaken, all that our understanding contains; and this is why we cannot conceive of any attribute characteristic of being, except these four. Let us examine these, each in its turn, and with the care required by the importance of the results which will follow this demarcation.

139. By passive sensibility we understand the form under which bodies are presented. As we have already explained it in several places, this form is reducible to figured or bounded extension.

It cannot be denied that this attribute contains a true determination, as there is nothing more determinate than objects presented to our senses, with extension, and figure, and other properties annexed to these fundamental attributes. Motion and impenetrability are determinations which accompany extension, or rather they are relations of extension. To us, motion is the change of the situations of a body in space, or the alteration in the positions of the extension of a body, with respect to the extension of space. Impenetrability is the reciprocal exclusion of two extensions. The idea of solid and liquid, of hard and soft, and other similar ideas, express relations of the extension of a body to their admission, with greater or less resistance, of the extension of another in one and the same place.

Questions upon the nature of extension have no place here. Extension is, so far as we are concerned, a determinate object, presented to us in the clearest intuition. The attribute of passive sensibility has ever been regarded as one of the most characteristic determinations; and this is why it has been made to enter as a fundamental classification in the scale of beings. The distinctions of corporeal and incorporeal, of material and immaterial, of sensible and insensible, are of as frequent use in ordinary language as in that of the schools; and it is obvious that the words, corporeal, material, and sensible, although not perfectly synonymous under some aspects, are usually taken to be such, in so far as they express a kind of beings, whose characteristic properties are those forms under which they are offered to our senses.

140. Active sensibility is the faculty of feeling; and is to us an object of immediate experience, since we have it within us. From the clear presence of sensitive acts, we may easily conceive what feeling is in other subjects than ourselves. We have no consciousness of what passes in another subject when it sees; but we know what it is to see; it is in others the same as in ourselves. In our own consciousness that of others is portrayed. We well know what is spoken of, when we hear a sensitive being mentioned; and this too by a perfectly determinate, not by a vague idea. If the question be raised, whether other senses are possible, the idea of a being endowed with them, loses a certain amount of its determinateness: our understanding has no intuition of what it would be; it discourses upon the reality or possibility by means of general conceptions.

141. Understanding, or the force of conceiving and combining, independently of the sensible order, is another of the data furnished by our own experience. As this is a fact of consciousness, we know it by intuition, not by abstract ideas; it is the exercise of an activity which we feel within ourselves; it is the *me* which we ourselves are. This activity, by reason of its very union, its identity with the subject perceiving it, is present to us in so intimate a manner that we find no difficulty in perceiving it.

The idea of understanding is intuitive to us, not indeterminate, since it presents an object which is immediately given to our perception in our soul itself. When we speak of understanding, we fix our views upon what passes within ourselves, and we see greater or less perfection in the scale of intelligent beings portrayed in the gradation of the cognitions which we experience within ourselves; and when we would conceive of a far higher understanding, we enlarge and perfect the type we have discovered within ourselves; just as we represent to ourselves greater, more perfect, and more beautiful sensible objects, than those we see, without quitting the sphere of sensibility, but making use of the elements it furnishes to us, and enlarging and embellishing them so as to attain to that ideal type already conceived of in our imagination.

142. The will, although an inseparable companion of the understanding, and even necessary to its existence, is nevertheless a very different faculty from it; for the will offers to our intuition a series of phenomena very unlike the phenomena of the understanding. To understand is not to will; a thing may be known, and yet not willed. One and the same act of the understanding may unite at various times, or in diverse subjects, very different if not contradictory acts of the will; to will and to not will; or inclination and aversion.

The cognition of that series of phenomena called *acts of the will*, is not a general but a particular, not an abstract but an intuitive, cognition. What necessity is there of abstraction or discursion to ascertain what we will or do not will, what we love or what we abhor? This cognition is intuitive, so far as the acts of our own will are concerned; and although we have no immediate intuition of what the will of others is, we know perfectly well what passes in them, from seeing it in some degree manifested by what we ourselves experience. When we hear the acts of another's will spoken of, have we, by chance, any difficulty in conceiving the object in question? Are we obliged to proceed discursively by abstract ideas? Certainly not! The same occurs in others as in ourselves. When they will, or do not will, they experience just what we ourselves experience when we will or do not will. The consciousness of our will is the image of all others existing or possible. We conceive that will to be more or less perfect, which unites in a higher or lower degree the actual or possible perfections of our own: and if we would conceive a will of infinite perfection, we must elevate to an infinite degree the actual or possible perfection which we discover in the finite will.

143. When the Sacred Text tells us that man is created to the image and likeness of God, it teaches us a truth highly luminous, whether considered in a purely philosophical or in a supernatural aspect. We discover in our soul, in this image of infinite intelligence, not only a multitude of general ideas which carry us beyond the limits of sensibility, but also an admirable representation wherein we contemplate, as in a mirror, every thing that passes in that infinite sea which cannot be known by immediate intuition so long as we remain in this life. This representation is imperfect, is enigmatical; but it is a true representation: in its minutest particles, infinitely increased, we may contemplate the infinite; its feeblest brilliance reflects back to us the splendor of infinity. The slight spark struck from the flint may lead the imagination to that ocean of fire, discovered by astronomers in the orb of day.

CHAPTER XXIII
OF THE NECESSITY INVOLVED IN IDEAS

144. In all ideas, even in those that relate to contingent facts, there is something of the necessary, something from which science may spring, but something which cannot emanate from experience, however multiplied we suppose it. Every induction resulting from experience is confined to a limited number of facts, — a number, which, even if augmented by all the experience of all men of all ages, would still remain infinitely below universality, which extends to all that is possible.

Moreover, however little we reflect upon the certainty of the truths intimately connected with experience, such as are arithmetical and geometrical truths, we cannot fail to perceive that the confidence with which we build upon them is not founded upon induction, but that we assent to them independently of any particular fact, and consider their truth as absolutely necessary, although we cannot verify it by the touchstone of experience.

145. The verification of ideas by facts is in many cases impossible, because the weakness of our perception and of our senses, and the coarseness of the instruments we use, fail to render us certain that the facts correspond exactly to the ideas. It is sometimes absolutely impossible to establish this proof, since geometrical truth supposes conditions such as cannot be realized in practice.

146. Let us apply these observations to the simplest truths of geometry. Certainly no one will doubt the solidity of the proof called superposition: that is to say, if one of two lines, or surfaces, be placed upon the other, and they exactly correspond, they will be equal. This truth cannot depend upon experience: first, because experience is limited to a certain number of cases, whereas the proposition is general. To say that one serves for all is to say that there is a general principal, independent of experience, since, without recognizing an intrinsic necessity in this truth, the universal could in no other way be deduced from the particular. Secondly, because even where experience avails, it is impossible for us to make it exact, since superposition made in the most delicate manner imaginable, can never attain to geometrical exactness, which repudiates the minutest difference in any point.

It is an elementary theorem, that the three angles of a triangle are equal to two right angles. This truth does not rest upon experience: first, because the universal cannot be deduced from the particular; secondly, because, however delicate be the instruments for measuring angles, they cannot measure them with geometrical exactness; thirdly, because geometry supposes conditions which we cannot realize in practice; lines have no thickness, and the vertices of angles are indivisible points.

147. If general principles depended upon experience they would cease to be general, and would be limited to a certain number of cases. Neither would their enunciation be absolute, even for the cases already observed; for it would of necessity be reduced to what had been observed, that is to say, to a little more or less, but never be perfect exactness. Consequently we could not assert that the three angles of every triangle are equal to two right angles; all that we could say would be, that so far as our experience goes, we have observed that in all triangles the three angles are very nearly equal to two right angles.

This would obviously destroy all necessary truths; and even mathematical truths would be no more certain than the reports of adepts in any profession who recount to us their observations concerning their respective objects.

148. There can be no science without necessary truths; and even the cognition of contingent truths would become exceedingly difficult without them. How do we collect the facts furnished by observation, and adjust them? Is it not by applying certain general truths to them, as, for example, those of numeration? Otherwise we could have no perfect confidence in them, nor in the results of observation.

149. Human reason cannot live, if it abandon this treasure of necessary truths which constitute its common patrimony. Individual reason could take no more than a few short steps, overwhelmed as it constantly would be with the mass of observations; distracted unceasingly by the verifications to which it would always have to recur; in want of some light to serve for all objects; and prohibited ever from simplifying, by uniting the rays of science in a common centre.

General reason would also cease to be, and men would no longer understand each other: every one would be confined to his own experience: and since there would be in the experiences of all men, nothing necessary, nothing to connect them, there would be no unity in them all together: all the sciences would be a field of confusion, to which all restoration of order would be utterly impossible. No language could have been formed; or even if formed could be preserved. We meet in the simplest enunciations of language, as well as in the complication of a long discourse, an abundance of general and necessary truths, which serve as the woof for the weaving-in of contingent truths.

150. To inquire, therefore, if there are necessary truths, is to inquire, if individual, if general reason exists; if what we call reason, and discover in all men, really exists, or is but a fantastical illusion. This reason does exist: to deny it is to deny ourselves: not to wish to admit it, is to reject the testimony of our consciousness, which assures us that it is in the depth of our soul; it is to make impotent efforts to destroy a conviction irresistibly imposed by nature.

151. And here I would remark that this community of reason among all men of all ages and of all climes; this admirable unity, discoverable in the midst of so much variety; this fundamental accord which neither the diversity nor the contradiction of views can destroy, evidently proves that all human souls have one common origin; that thought is not a work of chance; that, besides human intelligences, there is another which serves as their support, illuminates them, and has, from the first moment of their existence, endowed them with all the faculties needed to perceive, and to know what they perceived. The admirable order which reigns throughout the material world, the concert, the unity of plan discoverable in it, are not a more conclusive proof of the existence of God, than are the order, the concert, the unity, offered by reason in its assent to necessary truths.

For our own part, we ingenuously confess, that we can discover no more solid, more conclusive, or more clear proof of the existence of God, than that deduced from the world of intelligences. Beyond this it has another advantage, which is, that it takes for its point of departure the act most immediate to us, the consciousness of our own acts. It is true, the proof best adapted to the capacity of ordinary men, is the one founded on the admirable order reigning over the corporeal world: but this is because they are unaccustomed to meditate upon insensible objects, upon what passes within themselves; wherefore it is that they abound more in direct cognitions than in power of reflection.

The atheist asks how we can be certain of the existence of God, and demands an apparition of the divinity: very well, this apparition exists, not without, but within us: and although it may be pardonable for men of little reflection not to perceive it, most certainly it is not pardonable for those who pretend to be adepts in metaphysical science, not even to endeavor to discover it. The system of Malebranche, which makes men see every thing in God, cannot be sustained, but it shows a very profound thinker.

CHAPTER XXIV
EXISTENCE OF UNIVERSAL REASON

152. General truths have some relation to particular truths; for since they are not a vain illusion, they must of necessity be connected with some object either existing or possible. Whatever exists is particular; not even possible being can be conceived of, if it be not, so to speak, particularized in the regions of possibility. God himself, being by essence, is not a being in abstract, but an infinite reality. In him, the general idea of the plenitude of being, of all perfection, of infinity, is, so to speak, particularized.

General truths would then be vain illusions did they not refer to something particular either existing or possible. Without this relation, cognition would be a purely subjective phenomenon; science would have no object; knowledge would be had, but there would be nothing known.

The appearance of knowing is never offered to us as a purely subjective fact; that is to say, when we think we know, we think we know something either within or without us, according to the matters which occupy us. Supposing, then, the phenomenon of cognition to be purely subjective, and to become objective for itself, we should have what would constantly lead us into error; for the human reason would be infected with a radical vice, which would oblige it to view these phenomena as means of perceiving the truth, whereas they are only eternal sources of deception.

153. There may arise a doubt in this correspondence of general with particular truth, as to which is the principle; that is, whether general truth is truth by means of particular truths, or the contrary. "All the diameters of a circle are equal;" this is a general truth. If we suppose a circle to exist, all its diameters will be equal. We have already seen that the certainty of the general truth neither does nor can reach us through the particular truth; but neither, on the other hand, does the particular stand in need of the general; so that it seems, that even when we abstract all intelligence, capable of perceiving this general truth, the existing circle will not cease to have all its diameters equal.

154. Moreover, if the truth fail in one single instance, it cannot be general; but the particular may be true although it fail in general. The equality of the diameters of an existing circle is, then, a condition necessary to the general truth; but the general truth is not necessary to the equality of the diameters.

It is true in general that all diameters are equal, since this is verified in all either existing or possible, and the general truth is only the expression of this verification; but yet it does not appear that the diameters, in any one particular case, are equal by reason of the general truth. It is true that one particular whole is greater than one of its parts, although considered in itself, abstracted from all general truth; but it would not be true that the whole is greater than one of its parts, if in any one particular whole, the axiom should fail.

155. It would seem that from these observations we could infer that the truth of principles depends upon the truth of facts, and not *vice versa*. Nevertheless, if we reflect more upon this matter, we shall discover that truth is not based upon particular facts, but upon something superior to them.

I. We cannot from a particular fact infer a universal truth; but from universal truth we can infer the truth of all particular existing or possible facts. The reason why this consequence is legitimate is found in the necessary connection of the predicate and subject; and this necessity cannot be discovered in particular facts of their own nature contingent.

II. Neither can the reason of this necessity be found in the simple proposition enunciating it, since this establishes nothing, but only expresses. The enunciation is true, because it expresses the truth; but the existence of the truth does not depend upon its enunciation.

III. Nor can it depend upon our ideas; for these are not productive of things; all imaginable perceptions cannot change one iota of reality. The idea may express a thing, but does not make it. The relation of ideas with each other, in so far avails as it expresses the relation of objects; if for one moment we permit ourselves to doubt this correspondence, our reason becomes reduced to utter impotence, to a vain illusion of that which ought to be of no account. The properties of the triangle are contained in the idea we have of it; but if this idea were purely subjective, if it had no exact or approximate relation to any real or possible object, it and all that is built upon it, would be mere phenomena of our mind, would signify absolutely nothing, and would have no more weight than the ravings of a madman.

IV. The reason of necessary truths can in nowise be discovered in our understanding; every one perceives them, without thinking of others or even of himself. Truth existed before any individual; and when we shall have disappeared, it will continue the same, it will lose nothing.

V. All men, although they neither do nor can agree, perceive certain necessary truths; all individual intelligences, therefore, have drunk at some common fountain; therefore universal reason exists.

CHAPTER XXV
IN WHAT DOES UNIVERSAL REASON CONSIST?

156. What is universal reason? If we consider it as a simple idea, as an abstraction from individual reason, as something separate from them, but not real, we strike upon the very rock we try to shun. We endeavor to assign a cause of the unity of human reason; and appeal to universal reason; and then to explain in what universal reason consists, we recur to an abstraction from individual reason. Evidently, this is a vicious circle; we place the cause of a fact so fruitful in an abstraction, in a generalization of the very thing we have to explain; we assign to a great effect a cause totally insufficient, which has no existence out of our understanding, and which only grows out of the very effect whose origin we are investigating.

157. A real fact must have a real principle; a universal phenomenon must have a universal cause; a phenomenon independent of all finite intelligence must spring from some cause independent of all finite intelligence. There is, then, a universal reason, the origin of all finite reason, the source of all truth, the light of all intelligences, the bond of all beings. There is, then, above all phenomena, above all finite individuals, a being, in which is found the reason of all beings, a great unity, in which is found the bond of all order, and of all the community of other beings.

The unity, therefore, of all human reason affords a complete demonstration of the existence of God. The universal reason is; but universal reason is an unmeaning word, unless it denote an intelligent, active being, a being by essence, the producer of all beings, of all intelligences, the cause of all, and the light of all.

158. *Impersonal reason*, of which some philosophers speak, is an unmeaning word. Either there exists a reason distinct from ours, or there does not: if it does exist, it is not impersonal; if it does not exist, it is impossible to explain the community of human reason: this community would be to us a phenomenon, which we might call impersonal reason, or any thing else we pleased, without it therefore being possible for us to assign it any origin: it would be an effect without a cause; a fact without a sufficient reason.

159. The understanding extends to a world of possibilities, and there discovers a connection of necessary relations, some of dependence, others of contradiction: but if there were no reality whereon to found the possibility, this would be an absurdity; if nothing existed, nothing would be possible.

Upon nothing, nothing can be founded; consequently, not even possibility. The connection of necessary relations which we discover in possible beings, must have a primitive type to which they refer: but in nothing there are no types.

160. The assemblage of human understandings cannot establish possibility. No one of them considered isolately is necessary to general truth; and all together cannot have what no one of them has. We conceive necessary truth, absolutely abstracted from the human understanding: individual understandings appear and disappear, but work no change in the relations of possible beings: on the contrary, the understanding needs, in order to exercise its functions, a collection of pre-existing truths, and without them it cannot work.

What any one individual understanding requires, all require. Their union does not increase the strength of each one: since this union is nothing more than an assemblage formed in our mind, and may not correspond to any thing in reality except the individual understandings, and their respective strength.

161. Necessary truths, therefore, exist before human reason; but their pre-existence is an unmeaning word, if they be not referred to a being, the origin of all reality, and the foundation of all possibility. There is then no impersonal reason properly so called; there is a community of reason in so far as one and the same light illumines all finite intelligences; God the creator of them all.

CHAPTER XXVI
REMARKS ON THE REAL FOUNDATION
OF PURE POSSIBILITY

162. Since the argument proving the necessity of a being in which is laid the foundation of all the relations in the possible order, is one of the most transcendental in all metaphysics, and at the same time one of the most difficult to be perfectly understood, we judge it advisable to enlarge somewhat upon the considerations thrown out in the preceding chapter.

An example, in which we undertake to establish the possibility of things, independently of a being in which is found the reason of all, will serve our purpose better than abstract reflections.

163. "Two circles of equal diameters are equal." This proposition is evidently true. Let us analyze its meaning. The proposition refers to the possible order, and abstracts absolutely the existence of the circles and of the diameters. No case is excepted; all are comprised in the proposition.

164. Neither does the truth refer to our mode of understanding; but on the contrary, we conceive it as independent of our thought. Were we asked, what would become of this truth were we not to exist, we should without hesitation reply that it would be the same, that it acquired nothing by our existence, that it would lose nothing by our extinction. If we believed this truth to depend in any way upon us, it would cease to be what it is, it would no longer be a necessary but a contingent truth.

165. Nor is the corporeal world indispensable to the truth and necessity of the proposition: on the contrary, if we suppose no body to exist, the proposition would lose none of its truth, necessity, or universality.

166. What would happen, if, withdrawing all bodies, all sensible representations, and even all intelligences, we should imagine absolute and universal nothing? We see the truth of the proposition even on this supposition; for it is impossible for us to hold it to be false. On every supposition, our understanding sees a connection which it cannot destroy: the condition once established, the result will infallibly follow.

167. An absolutely necessary connection, founded neither on us, nor on the external world, which exists before any thing we can imagine, and

subsists after we have annihilated all by an effort of our understanding, must be based upon something, it cannot have nothing for its origin: to say this, would be to assert a necessary fact without a sufficient reason.

168. It is true that in the proposition now before us, nothing real is affirmed; but if we reflect carefully, we find even here the greatest difficulty for those who deny a real foundation to pure possibility. What is remarkable in this phenomenon, is precisely this, that our understanding feels itself forced to give its assent to a proposition which affirms an absolutely necessary connection without any relation to an existing object. It is conceivable that an intelligence affected by other beings may know their nature and relations; but it is not so easy of comprehension how it can discover their nature and relations in an absolutely necessary manner, when it abstracts all existence, when the ground upon which the eyes of the understanding are fixed, is the abyss of nothing.

169. We deceive ourselves when we imagine it possible to abstract all existence. Even when we suppose our mind to have lost sight of every thing, a very easy supposition, granting that we find in our consciousness the contingency of our being, the understanding still perceives a possible order, and imagines it to be all occupied with pure possibility, independent of a being on which it is based. We repeat, that this is an illusion, which disappears so soon as we reflect upon it. In pure nothing, nothing is possible; there are no relations, no connections of any kind; in nothing there are no combinations, it is a ground upon which nothing can be pictured.

170. The objectivity of our ideas and the perception of necessary relations in a possible order, reveal a communication of our understanding with a being on which is founded all possibility. This possibility can be explained on no supposition except that which makes the communication consist in the action of God giving to our mind faculties perceptive of the necessary relation of certain ideas, based upon necessary being, and representative of his infinite essence.

171. Without this communication the order of pure possibility means nothing: none of the combinations referable to it contain any truth: and this ruins all science. There can be no necessary relations if there be no necessity upon which they are based, and where they are represented; if this condition be wanting, all cognitions must refer to something actually existing; they are even limited to what *appears*, to what affects us, and they cannot affirm any thing beyond the actual order. Science, in this supposition, is unworthy of the name; it is nothing but a collection of facts, gathered together in the field of experience; we cannot say: "This will be, or will not be; this may be, or may not be;" we are necessarily limited to what is; or, rather, we ought to confine ourselves to that which affects us by simple appearances, and never be able to rise above the sphere of individual phenomena.

CHAPTER XXVII
INDIVIDUAL AND INTELLECTUAL PHENOMENA EXPLAINED BY THE UNIVERSAL SUBSISTING REASON

172. Starting from the phenomena observable in individual reason, we have arrived at universal reason. Let us, so to speak, make the counterproof; taking this universal subsisting reason, let us see if individual reason in itself and in its phenomena can be explained by it.

I. What are necessary truths? They are the relations of beings, such as they are represented in the being which contains the plenitude of being. These necessary truths, then, stand in need of no individual finite reason; their reason is found in an infinite being.

II. The essence of all beings, abstracted from all particular beings, is something real, not in itself, and separately, but in the being which contains the plenitude of every thing.

III. On this supposition science is not full of empty words, nor of mere creations of our reason, but of necessary relations represented in a necessary being, and known by it from all eternity.

IV. Science is possible; there is some necessity in contingent objects; their destruction does not destroy the eternal types of all being, the only object of science.

V. All individual reason, sprung from the same source, participates in one same light, lives one same life, has one and the same patrimony, is indivisible in the creative principle, but divisible in creatures. The unity, then, or rather the uniformity or community of human reason is possible, is necessary.

VI. The reason, then, of all men is united by the infinite intelligence: God then is in us; and the most profound philosophical truth is contained in these words of the Apostle: "In ipso vivimus, movemur, et sumus."

VII. All philosophy, therefore, which seeks to explain reason, by isolating it, considers only particular phenomena unconnected by a general bond, pretends to construct the magnificent fabric of our reason upon particular facts alone, but does not appeal to a common origin, to one source of light whence all lights have sprung, is a false philosophy, is superficial, at war with theory, and in contradiction with facts. When we reflect upon this, we can but pity Locke, and still more Condillac, and their explanations of human reason by sensations alone.

VIII. Thus we understand why we cannot give the reason of many things; we see them; they are thus: they are necessary; more we cannot say. A triangle is not a circle: what reason can we assign for this? None! It is so; this is all. But why? Because there does actually exist an immediate necessity in the relation represented in the infinite being, which is truth by essence. The same infinite intelligence sees no greater reason of itself, than in itself. It finds every thing, and the relations of all things in the plenitude of its being; but beyond them is nothing. He gave to individual reason, when creating it, an intuition of these relations: no discursion proves them; we see them; this is all.

IX. Some even who admit the subjective value of ideas, either doubting or denying their objectivity, lose sight of this fact. They seek an argument, where there is need only of a vision; they demand degrees where there are none. When human reason sees certain truths, it cannot go farther and doubt of them. It is subject to a primitive law of its nature, which it cannot abstract without ceasing to be what it is. By the very act of seeing the object it is sure of it; the difference between subjectivity and objectivity falls within the space of inferences, but not within that of immediate reason, or the understanding of necessary truths.

173. We leave it to the reader's judgment whether the preceding explanation is more satisfactory than that by *impersonal reason*; the theory we have attempted to expound has been held by all the most eminent metaphysicians. With God, all is clear; without God, all is a chaos. This is true in the order of facts, and not less so in the order of ideas. Our perception is also a fact; our ideas likewise are facts; over all presides an admirable order; a chain which cannot be destroyed unites all; but neither this order nor this chain depends upon this. The word *reason* has a profound meaning, for it refers to the infinite intelligence. What is true for the reason of one man cannot be false for the reason of another; there are, independently of all communication among human minds, and of all intuition, truths necessary for all. We must, if we would explain this unity, rise above ourselves, must elevate ourselves to that great unity in which every thing originates, and to which every thing tends.

174. This point of view is high, but it is the only one; if we depart from it we can see nothing, but are forced to use unmeaning words. Sublime and consoling thought! Although man disputes upon God, and perhaps denies him, he has God in his understanding, in his ideas, in all that he is, in all that he thinks; the power of perception communicates God to him; objective truth is founded on God; he cannot affirm a single truth without affirming a thing represented in God. This intimate communication of the finite with the infinite, is one of the most certain truths of metaphysics. Although ideological investigations should produce no other result than the discovery of so important a truth, we ought to consider the time spent in them well improved.

CHAPTER XXVIII
OBSERVATIONS ON THE RELATION
OF LANGUAGE TO IDEAS

175. The relation between thought and language is one of the most important ideological phenomena. When we speak we think; and when we think we speak with an internal language. The understanding needs speech as a kind of guiding thread in the labyrinth of ideas.

176. The connection of ideas by a sign seems necessary. The most universal and most convenient of these signs is language; but we must not forget that it is an arbitrary sign, as is proved by the variety of words used in different languages to express the same idea.

177. The phenomenon of the relation of ideas to language originates in the necessity of perpetuating ideas by determinate signs; and the importance of speech results from its being the most general, most convenient, and most flexible sign. And hence it is that when these circumstances can be united in another sign, the same object is attained. Physically speaking, written language is very different from language spoken; nevertheless, in very many cases it answers equally well.

178. The internal language is, sometimes, rather a reflection in which the idea is enlarged and developed, than an expression of it. True, we do not ordinarily think without speaking inwardly; but as we have already observed, speech is an arbitrary sign, and consequently we cannot establish a perfectly exact parallel between ideas and the internal language.

179. We think with instantaneousness, which defies the succession of words, however rapid we may suppose them to be. It is true that the internal language is far more rapid than the external; but it always involves succession, and requires a greater or less time, according to the words to be spoken.

This observation is important, lest we too greatly exaggerate the relation of ideas to speech. Language is certainly a wonderful channel for the communication of ideas, and a powerful auxiliary of our understanding; but we can, without ignoring these qualities, take care to avoid that exaggeration which seems to pronounce all thought impossible, if some word thought does not correspond to it.

180. We experience often enough the instantaneous occurrence of a multitude of ideas, which we afterwards develop in our discourse. We see this in those quick and lively replies excited by a word, or a gesture, which contradicts our opinions or wounds our feelings. In replying, it is impossible for us to speak inwardly, since the instantaneousness with which we reply forbids it. How often, in listening to an argument, do we instantly detect a fault, which we could not explain with words without a long discourse? How often, in proposing a difficulty to ourselves, do we catch its solution in an instant, although we could not possibly explain it without many words? How often do we at the very first glance discover the flaw in a proof, the force of an argument, or the ease with which it can be retorted upon the proposer of it, and all this without occupying a moiety of the intervals necessary to either external or internal locution? Thus it happens that the sudden thought is not unfrequently expressed by a single gesture, a glance of the eye, a nod of the head, a *yes*, or a *no*, an exclamation, or any other similar sign; all far more rapid than it is possible for the words expressive of our thought to be.

181. Let us illustrate this observation by a few examples. Some one says: "All men are naturally equal." The sense of this proposition cannot be known until the word *equal* is pronounced. How, then, is it that an enlightened and judicious man, will, by an instinctive impulse, answer *no*, will catch the word at the moment, and refute the empty boast of the declaimer with a flow of reasons? Until after the word, naturally the understanding remained in suspense; there was nothing to show the meaning of the proposition, since instead of *equal*, might have been said *weak, mortal, inconstant,* or any other such word; but so soon as the word *equal* is pronounced, the understanding says *no*, without having had the time to use an internal or external locution. The exact parallel which some suppose to exist between ideas and speech is, therefore, impossible; and they who defend it are guilty of an exaggeration incompatible with experience.

Another asserts, "justice to have no bounds but the limit of power." All who have any idea of morality, at once answer *no*: do they, forsooth, need an inward locution? True, in order to explain what is expressed by this *no*, and upon what it is based, many words are required, and that to reflect upon the proposition one must speak in inwardly; but this is all independent of that intellectual act, signified by the *no*, and which would have been still more briefly expressed had it been possible.

Another yet may say: "If this fact be attested by the senses, it will be true; and if it be true, it will be attested by the senses." The hearer assents to the former part, but rests in suspense as to the latter part until the word *attest* is pronounced. Then an instantaneous *no* leaps from his lips, or is expressed by a negative gesture. Does any interior locution precede? None, for none is possible. The following would be the words expressive of this act: "It is not true that every fact must be attested by the senses; since many facts are true, which do not belong to the sphere of sensibility." Let us examine whether or not these words are compatible with the instantaneousness of the *no*.

182. It will, perhaps, be objected, that the negation is one thing, and the reason of the negation another: that the simple *no* suffices for the former, and that it is only for the latter that more words are needed. But this is an equivocation. When the *no* was said, it was said for a reason, and this reason was the sight of the inconsequence then expressed by the words. Otherwise it would be necessary to admit the negative to be a blind judgment, and given without a reason. This being so, this reason founded upon the judgment, although expressed in the most laconical mode possible, would require some words, to form which, either interiorly or exteriorly, there has been no time. There is a question of calculation. He who hears the proposition cannot know the meaning of it, until the word *attest* is pronounced, and the sentence brought to a *full stop*. Before reaching the word attest, the sense of the proposition was unknown; it was not possible to form any judgment, since instead of saying, "If it be true the senses will attest it," he might have said, "If it be true the senses *will not belie it.*"

We have spoken of the *full stop*, in order to show the instantaneousness of the perception and of the judgment, which proves that the understanding does not determine until the last moment. But let us suppose the same word *attest* to have been used indeed, but instead of a full stop, to have been followed by these other words, "if this fact falls under their jurisdiction." The words are the same, and yet they do not provoke a negative judgment; and why? Simply because the speaker continued. If he had ceased speaking, or had used an inflection of voice indicative of a period, the *no* would have risen like a flash. A comma or a period in writing, produce the same effect as a pause or an inflection of the voice in speaking. When we see these signs, we judge instantaneously, with a velocity incomparably greater than any internal or external locution.

It would be easy to multiply examples showing the superiority of thought to speech, so far as rapidity is concerned; but those already adduced seem to us sufficient to prove that there is some exaggeration in saying that "man before speaking his thought, thinks his words," if it be understood that all thought is impossible without a word thought.

CHAPTER XXIX
ORIGIN AND CHARACTER OF THE RELATION
BETWEEN LANGUAGE AND IDEAS

183. Many ideas seem to be like sensations and sentiments; simple facts, incapable of decomposition, for which reason we cannot explain them with words. Words illustrate ideas; but do they not sometimes also confuse them? When we speak of an idea, we reflect upon it, and I have already remarked [11] that the reflective force of our perceptive ideas is much inferior to their direct force.

184. We have sometimes thought that we do, perhaps, know things which we imagine we do not know, and that we are ignorant of things we think we know. It is certain that disputes have been had in all schools of philosophy upon many ideas, without attaining any satisfactory result; and yet these ideas ought to be sufficiently clear to our mind, since we all use them every day without any equivocation. Philosophers have not, as yet, been able to agree upon the ideas of space and time, but the most ignorant men, nevertheless, make use of these words, and whenever the necessity occurs, apply them with exactness. This seems to prove that the difficulty is not in the idea but in its explanation.

185. It has been remarked that there is great truth and exactness in ordinary language, so much so, that the careful observer is astonished at the recondite wisdom hidden in a language; to see how great, how various, and how delicate are the gradations into which the sense of words is distributed. This is not the fruit of reflection; it is the work of reason operating directly, and consequently making use of ideas without reflecting upon them.

186. In ideological investigations some idea of the idea is sought, and it is not noted that if this be necessary to science, another idea of the other idea may be exacted, and that thus an infinite process may be given. It ought to be borne in mind that in treating of simple facts, as well external as internal, no other explanation of them can be demanded than an exposition.

187. *Idea-images* are a font of error, and probably all ideas explicable by words are not less so. An *idea-image* induces the belief that there are in our

mind no ideas but sensible representations, and the supposition that every idea can be expressed by words, makes us imagine that to be composite which is simple, and attribute to the substance what belongs to the form.

188. A composite idea seems to be a union, or rather a connected series of ideas, which are either excited simultaneously, or follow each other with great rapidity. Our understanding requires words to bind this collection, to retain the thread which connects them; and hence it is, that when the idea is simple, language is not indispensable. It is said that speech is necessary in order to think, it might sometimes be said with more propriety, that it is necessary in order to *recollect*.

189. When the object occupying our attention is offered to the sensible intuition, we have no need of speech. We can, when we reflect upon a right line, an angle, a triangle, observe that their imaginary representation is all that we require, and that we do not need to bind these objects together by words. The same thing happens in thinking of unity, or on the numbers two, three, and four, which we easily represent to ourselves sensibly. The necessity for speech begins when the imagination loses the distinct representation of objects, and needs to combine various ideas. Did we not assign to a word the idea of a many-sided polygon, we should be in the greatest confusion, and it would be impossible for us to reason upon it.

190. Since, on the one hand, our perceptive faculties do not create their objects, but are limited to the combining of them; and, on the other hand, our perception is not capable of embracing many at one time, it results that the exercise of our faculties is necessarily successive; the unity of consciousness serving as the bond of union to our perceptions. But consciousness has no other means of knowing what passes within it, than to fix its operations by determinate signs, whence flows the necessity of arbitrary signs, which must be sensible, by reason of the relation uniting our intelligence with the sensitive faculties: and it is to be observed, that for this reason, every sign to which we assign an idea, may be the object of one of the senses. The great number and variety of ideas and their combinations, require an exceedingly variable and flexible sign, and this variety and flexibility require certain characters to simplify it, and thus render its retention in the memory more easy, whence the advantages of language: in the midst of its astonishing variety it lays these characters in radical syllables. The conjugation of a single verb alone offers us a considerable number of very different ideas, the retention of which would be excessively difficult, were they not joined by some tie such as the radical syllable: as in the verb to speak, the syllable speak. We see this by the greater labor the irregular verbs cost us than do the regular verbs when learning a language: and it may be remarked in children also, who blunder on the irregularities. We might compare

language to the catalogue of a library, which is the more perfect, the more it unites simplicity with variety, so as to designate exactly the classes of the books and the shelves whereon they are to be found.

191. *Succession of ideas and operations*; here, then, originates the necessity of a sign by which to connect and recollect them: *relation of our understanding with the sensitive faculties,* is the reason why the signs must be sensible; *variety and simplicity of language* constitutes its merit so far as the sign of ideas. [12]

CHAPTER XXX
INNATE IDEAS

192. Among the adversaries of innate ideas there exist profound differences. The materialists maintain that man has received every thing through the senses, in such a way as to make our understanding nothing more than the product of an organism which has been advancing in perfection, just as a machine acquires, by use, a greater facility and delicacy of movement. They suppose nothing but the faculty of sensation to pre-exist in the mind; or, to speak more correctly, they admit no mind, but only a corporeal being, whose functions naturally produce what is called the intellectual development.

The sensists who do not attribute to matter the faculty of thinking, do not admit innate ideas; they confess the existence of the mind, but concede to it non-sensitive faculties; all that it owns must have come to it through the senses, and it can be nothing else than a transformed sensation.

Innate ideas counted other adversaries who were neither materialists nor sensists: such were the scholastics, who on the one hand defended the principle that there is nothing in the understanding which has not previously been in the senses; but, on the other hand, combated both materialism and sensism. The difference between the scholastics and the friends of innate ideas would not perhaps have been so great as it was supposed to be, had the question been proposed in another manner.

193. The scholastics regarded ideas as accidental forms, in such a way that an understanding with ideas may be compared to a piece of canvas covered with figures. The defenders of innate ideas said; "The figures already exist upon the canvas; to see them we have only to raise the veil which covers them." This explanation is somewhat forced, since it openly contradicts experience, which testifies: first, the necessity of the understanding being excited by sensations; secondly, the intellectual elaboration which we experience in thinking, and which teaches us that there is within us a kind of production of ideas.

"The canvas," say the adversaries of innate ideas, is all white, "and in proof witness the unceasing labor of the artist to cover it with figures." But does their doctrine, forsooth, suppose that nothing exists before experience? Do they admit man to be the simple work of instruction, of education? Do they maintain that our interior world is nothing more than a series of phenomena caused by impressions, and that it would have been other than what it is, had it had other impressions? Most certainly not. They admit: first, an inward activity excited and improved by sensible experience: secondly, the necessity of first principles as well intellectual as moral: thirdly, an interior light, to enable us to see them when presented, and to assent to them by an irresistible necessity. We find the words, "Signatum est super nos lumen vultus tui Domine," cited upon every page of those authors.

194. Saint Thomas says that first principles, as well speculative as practical, must be naturally communicated to us: "Oportet igitur *naturaliter nobis esse indita*, sicut principia speculabilium, ita et principia operabilium." [13] In another place, inquiring whether the soul knows immaterial things in their eternal reasons, (in rationibus æternis,) he says that the intellectual light which is within us, is nothing else than a certain participated likeness of the uncreated life, in which the eternal reasons are contained: "Ipsum enim lumen intellectuale, quod est in nobis nihil est aliud, quam quædam participata similitudo luminis increati, in quo continentur rationes æternæ." [14]

195. We find it, in these passages, expressly taught that there is within us something besides what we have acquired by experience, in which point the scholastics all agree with the defenders of innate ideas. The difference between them is this: the former do not consider the intellectual light to suffice for knowledge, if the forms or *species* upon which it may reflect are wanting; the latter distinguish the light from the colors, and them they make originate in the light itself.

196. The question of innate ideas, so warmly contested in the schools of philosophy, would never have presented so great difficulties, had it been stated with proper clearness. To do this it was necessary to classify the inward phenomena called ideas in a corresponding manner, and to determine with accuracy the sense of the word *innate*.

197. According to what we have already said, we hold that there are in our mind sensible representations; intellectual action upon them, or geometrical ideas; ideas purely intellectual, either intuitive or non-intuitive; and general determinate and indeterminate ideas. I will give examples of these cases that they may the better be understood. A particular triangle is represented in our imagination; here, then, is a sensible representation: intellectual act perceiving the nature of the triangle considered in general; here is a geometrical idea, an idea relating to the sensible order: cognition

of one of our acts of understanding or will; here is a pure and intuitive idea: intelligence, will, conceived in general; here is a general determinate idea: substance; here finally is a general indeterminate idea. [15]

198. What is understood by innate? That which is not born, which the mind possesses, not acquired by its own labor, nor by impressions coming from the exterior, but by the immediate gift of the author of its nature; the innate is opposed to the acquired, and to inquire if there are innate ideas is to inquire if we have in our mind ideas, before receiving any impressions or doing any act.

199. It cannot be maintained that sensible representations are innate. Experience testifies that without the impressions of the organs we cannot have representations corresponding to them; that once these are placed in action in a proper manner, we cannot help experiencing them. This is applicable to all sensations, whether they be actual, existing, or only recollected. They who undertake to maintain that sensible representations exist in our soul previously to all organic impressions, also advance an opinion unsustainable either by facts of experience or by arguments *a priori*.

200. It is to be remarked, that the argument founded upon the impossibility of the body's transmitting impressions to the mind, proves nothing in favor of the opinion we combat. Even were the argument conclusive, the necessity of innate ideas could not thence be inferred, since the physical non-communication of the body and the mind would be saved in the system of occasional causes, and it could at the same time be argued that there are no pre-existing ideas, but that they have been caused in the presence, and on occasion of organic affections.

201. Ideas relative to sensible representations seem to consist, not in forms of the understanding, but in its acts exercised upon these same representations. [16]

To call these ideas innate is to contradict experience, and even to ignore their nature. These acts cannot be performed if the object, which is the sensible representation be wanting; and this does not exist without an impression of the corporeal organs. To call these ideas innate, has then, either no meaning at all, or can mean nothing else than the pre-existence of the intellectual activity, subsequently developed in the presence of sensible intuitions.

202. Neither can those intuitive ideas, not referable to sensibility, such as are those we have when reflecting upon the acts of understanding and will, be innate. What in this case serves as the idea, is the very same act of the understanding or of the will which is presented to our perception in consciousness: to say, then, that these ideas are innate is equivalent to

saying that these acts exist before they exist. Even when the perception does not refer to present acts, but to past acts now recollected, the argument retains the same force: for it can have no recollection of them if they have not previously existed, since our acts cannot exist before we have performed them.

203. Hence it may be inferred that no intuitive idea is innate, since intuition supposes an object presented to the faculty of perception.

204. General determinate ideas are those which refer to an intuition: they cannot, therefore, exist before it: and since, on the other hand, intuition is impossible without an act, it follows that these ideas cannot be innate.

205. Last of all remain general indeterminate ideas, that is to say, those which of themselves alone offer to the mind, nothing either existing or possible. [17] If we observe carefully the nature of these ideas, we shall see that they are nothing else than perceptions of one aspect of an object considered under a general reason. It cannot be doubted, that one of the characteristics of intelligence is the perception of these aspects; and it is no less indubitable, that it does not thence follow, that we must imagine these ideas to a kind of forms pre-existing in our mind, and distinct from the acts by which it exercises its perceptive faculty. We do not see what ground there can be for affirming these ideas to be innate, and to have lain hidden in our mind previously to the development of all activity, just like things stowed away in the corners of a museum, closed however to the curiosity of spectators.

206. Instead of abandoning ourselves to similar suppositions, it would seem that we ought to recognize in the mind an innate activity, subject to the laws imposed upon it by its Creator, the infinite intelligence. Even granting ideas to be distinct from perceptive acts, it is not necessary to admit them as pre-existing. True, that in such a case it would be necessary to recognize in the mind a faculty productive of the representative species, from which, however, we should not escape by identifying ideas with perceptions. These last are acts springing, so to speak, from the very bottom of our soul, and which appear and disappear like the flowers of a plant: and thus we must in every way recognize in ourselves a power which in due circumstances will not fail to produce what before did not exist. Without this it is impossible to form any idea of what activity is.

207. Resuming the doctrine thus far delivered upon innate ideas, we can reduce it to a formula in the following manner:

I. There are in us sensitive faculties which are developed by organic impressions, either as cause or occasion.

II. We perceive nothing by the senses not subject to the laws of organism.

III. Internal sensible representations cannot be formed of other elements than those furnished by sensations.

IV. Whatever is said concerning the pre-existence of sensible representations to organic impressions, besides being said without any reason, is in contradiction with experience.

V. Geometrical ideas, or ideas relating to sensible intuitions, are not innate; since they are the acts of the understanding which operates upon materials provided by the sensibility.

VI. Intuitive ideas of the intellectual order are not innate, because they are nothing else than the acts of the understanding or will, presented to our perception in reflex consciousness.

VII. General determinate ideas are not innate, since they are the representation of intuitions, upon which some act has of necessity been performed.

VIII. There is no ground of affirming that general indeterminate ideas, which seem to be acts of the faculty perceptive of objects under a general reason, are innate.

IX. All that there is of innate in our mind is sensitive and intellectual activity; but both to be put into motion, require objects to affect them.

X. The development of this activity begins with organic affections; and although it goes far beyond the sphere of sensibility, it always remains more or less subject to the conditions imposed by the union of the soul and body.

XI. The intellectual activity has *a priori* conditions totally independent of sensibility, and applicable to all objects, no matter what impressions may have been their cause. The principle of contradiction figures as the first among these conditions.

XII. There is then in our mind something *a priori* and absolute, which cannot be altered, even although all the impressions we receive from objects be totally varied, nor if all the relations we have with them were to undergo a radical change.

BOOK FIFTH
IDEA OF BEING

CHAPTER I
IDEA OF BEING

1. There is in our understanding the idea of being. Independent of sensations, and in an order far superior to them, there exist ideas in our understanding, which extend to, and are a necessary element of all thought. The idea of being, or of *ens*, holds the first rank among these. When the scholastics said that the object of the understanding was being, "objectum intellectus est ens," they enunciated a profound truth, and pointed out one of the most certain and important of all ideological facts.

2. Being, or ens in se, abstracted from all modification and determination, is, considered in its greatest generality, conceived by our understanding. Whatever may be the origin of this idea, or the mode of its formation in our understanding, certain it is that it exists. It is of continual application, and without it it is almost impossible for us to think. The verb *to be*, expressive of this idea, is found in every language: in every discourse, even in the simplest, we meet this expression: the learned and the ignorant, alike, continually employ it in the same sense, and with equal facility.

The only difference, as to the use of this idea, between the rustic and the philosopher, is, that the one does, the other does not, reflect upon it: but the direct perception is the same in both, equally clear in all cases. Such a thing is or is not; was or was not; will be or will not be; there is something or nothing; we had or did not have; we shall have or shall not have, are all applications of the idea of being, applications made alike by all persons, without the least shadow of obscurity; all comprehend perfectly well the sense of these words, and the mind consequently has the idea corresponding to them. The difficulty, if any there be, begins with the reflex act, in the perception, not of being, but of the idea of being. So far as the direct act is concerned, the conception is so perfectly clear as to leave nothing to be desired.

3. Experience teaches this, but it can also be proved by conclusive arguments. All philosophers agree that the principle of contradiction is evident of itself to all men, that it needs no application, to understand the sense of the words sufficing; which could not be true did not all men have the idea of being. The principle is, that "it is impossible for a thing *to be*, and *not to be* at same time." Here, then, is no question of any thing determinate; neither of body nor of mind, of substance nor of accidents, of infinite nor of finite, but of being, of a *thing*, whatever it may be, in its greatest generality; of which it is affirmed that it cannot both be and not be at the same time. Had we no idea of being, the principle would mean nothing: contradiction is inconceivable when we have no idea of the contradicting extremes, and here the extremes are *being* and *not-being*.

4. The same is seen in another principle, closely resembling, if not identical with, that of contradiction: "every thing either is or is not." Here, also, there is question of being in its greatest indeterminateness, considered only as being, as nothing more. Without the idea of *being*, the axiom could have no meaning.

5. The principle of Descartes, "I think, therefore I am," also includes the idea of being: "I am." When he undertakes to explain it, this philosopher relies upon the fact that what is not, cannot act; thus the idea of being enters not only into the principle of Descartes, but is even the foundation upon which he rests it.

6. Whether we make the inward sense the basis of our cognitions, or prefer the evidence by which one idea is contained in another, it is always necessary to make the idea of being a primary element; we must suppose the understanding *to be* before it can think; we must suppose thought *to be* before we can make use of it; we must suppose our sensations and sentiments, the operations and affections of our souls, *to be*, before we can investigate their causes, their origin, and inquire into their nature; we must suppose ourselves *to be*, that *we are*, before we can advance one step in any sense. The idea of being does then exist in our mind, and is an element indispensable to all intellectual acts.

CHAPTER II
SIMPLICITY AND INDETERMINATENESS
OF THE IDEA OF BEING

7. Nothing can be conceived more simple than the idea of being. It cannot be composed of elements. It allows of nothing determinate, since it is in itself absolutely indeterminate. The instant that something determinate is made to enter it, it is in a manner destroyed; it is no longer the idea of *being*, but of *such a being*; an idea applied, but not the idea of the being in all its generality.

8. How shall we make it understood what we would express by the word being, or ens? If we say that it comprises all, even the most unlike and opposite things, there is no reason why it may not be understood what it is. To join to the idea of being any determination, is to introduce into it a heterogeneous element, which in no manner belongs to it, and can only accompany it as a pure aggregation, but can never combine with it, without rendering it what it is not. If the idea of subsistence be combined with that of being, we no longer have the pure idea of being, but that of subsistence.

9. The idea of being is then most simple; it cannot be resolved into elements, and cannot consequently spring from speech, unless as from an exciting cause. If we be asked, for example, what we understand by substance, by modification, cause or effect, we explain it by uniting to the idea of being that of subsistence or inherence, that of productive force, or of a thing produced; but it is impossible for us to explain being, otherwise than by itself. We may make use of the words, something, what is, reality, and the like, but all these are inadequate to explain the thing itself; they are but the efforts we make to excite in the understanding of others the idea we contemplate in our own. If we would give further explanations by showing how the idea corresponding to the word being, is applicable to every thing, and in order to do this enumerate the different classes of being, applying the idea to them all, we only succeed in showing the use of the idea and the applications of which it is susceptible; but we do not decompose it. We

say, indeed, that there is in all something corresponding to it, but we do not decompose this something; we only point it out.

10. From this we infer that the idea of being is not intuitive to us, and that by its very indeterminateness it excludes all that a determinate object can offer to our perception.

CHAPTER III
SUBSTANTIVE AND COPULATIVE BEING

11. For the more thorough understanding of this matter, it will be well to distinguish between the absolute and relative ideas of being; that is between what is expressed by the word being, when it designates reality, simple existence, and when it marks the union of a predicate and its subject. In the two following propositions we see very closely the different meaning of the word *is*; Peter *is*; Peter *is* good. In the former the word *is* designates the reality of Peter, or his existence; in the latter, it expresses the union of the predicate *good* with the subject *Peter*. In the former the verb *to be* is substantive, in the latter it is copulative. The substantive simply expresses the existence; the copulative a determination, a mode of existing. The desk is, signifies the simple existence of the desk; the desk is high, expresses a mode of being, height.

12. Purely substantive being, is nowhere met with, except in the following proposition: being is, or what is is; in all other propositions there is involved, even in the subject itself, some predicate which determines the mode. When we say, the desk is, notwithstanding that the direct predicate of the proposition is the word *is*, there yet enters into the subject *desk* a determination of the being of which we speak, and that is of a being which is a desk. We were, then, right in saying that the verb *to be*, in its purely substantive meaning, is met with in no other proposition than this: being is. This is perfectly identical, absolutely necessary and convertible, that is, the predicate may be observed of all subjects, and the subject of all predicates. Suppose we give the proposition a different form; being is existing; we can still say all being is existing, or the existing is being; that is, all that exists is being.

13. If it be objected that possible being does not exist, we answer that purely possible being is not, strictly speaking, being; but that it does exist, in the same mode in which it is, that is, in the possible order. As we shall, however, treat this question more fully hereafter, we now turn to the propositions in which being is copulative. The desk is, is equivalent to this, the desk is existing. It is true that every real desk is existing, but real is the same as existing; and thus it might, in one sense, be said that the proposition

resembles this other: all being is. But here we detect a difference; it consists in this, that the idea of existence does not necessarily enter into that of desk, for we can conceive of a desk which does not exist, but we cannot conceive of a being as such without a being, that is, of a being which is not being. A very notable difference is every way perceptible between the two propositions; in the former, the subject may be affirmed of all predicates by saying, all that is existing is being; but it is evident that we cannot say all that is existing is desk.

14. The reason of this is that the proposition, being is, is absolutely identical; it is the expression of a pure conception reduced to the form of a proposition; and, consequently, the terms which serve as extremes may be taken indiscriminately the one for the other; being is, whatever is, is being; being is existing; every thing existing is being. But different orders of ideas are combined in all other propositions; and, although the common idea of being is applicable to all, as this idea is essentially indeterminate, it does not thence follow that one of the things to which the general idea corresponds is identical with the other, alike entering into the same general idea. Being belongs to every existing desk; but not, therefore, is every thing a desk.

15. Copulative being may be applied without the substantive; thus when we say that the ellipse is curvilinear, we abstract both the existence and non-existence of any one ellipse; and the proposition would be true although no ellipse at all were to exist. The reason is that the verb *to be*, when copulative, expresses the relation of two ideas.

16. This relation is of identity, but in such a way that more than the union of the two is needed before a predicate can be affirmed of a subject. The head is united to the man, but it cannot, therefore, be said, "man is his head;" the sensibility is united to the reason in the same man, but we cannot say, "sensibility is reason;" whiteness is in union with the wall, but we cannot say "the wall is whiteness."

The affirmation, then, of a predicate expresses the relation of identity, and this is why, when this identity does not exist with respect to the predicate in the abstract, it is expressed in the concrete, in order that something involving identity may enter into it. The wall is whiteness: this proposition is false, because it affirms an identity which does not exist; the wall is white: this proposition is true, because white means something which has whiteness, and the wall is really something which has whiteness; here, then, is the identity which the proposition affirms. [18]

17. The predicate is, then, in every affirmative proposition, identified with the subject. When we perceive, therefore, we affirm the identity. Judgment, then, is the perception of the identity. We do not, however, deny

that in what we call assent there is often something more than the simple perception of identity; but we do not understand how we need any thing more than to see it evidently in order to assent to it. What we call assent, adhesion of the understanding, seems to be a kind of metaphor, as if the understanding would adhere, would yield itself to the truth, if it were presented; but in reality we very much doubt if, with respect to what is evident, there be any thing but perception of the identity.

18. Hence it follows, that if the same ideas were to correspond in the very same manner to the same words, the opposition and diversity of judgments in different understandings would be impossible. When, then, this diversity or opposition does exist, there is always a discrepancy in the ideas.

19. We conceive of things, and reason upon them abstracted from their existence or non-existence; or we even suppose them not to exist, that is, conceive of relations between predicates and subjects without the existence of either predicates or subjects. And as all contingent beings may either be or cease to be, and even the first moment of their being be designated, it follows that science, or the knowledge of the nature and relations of beings, founded upon certain and evident principles, has nothing contingent for its object inasmuch as it exists. There is, then, an infinite world of truths beyond contingent reality.

We conclude, from our reflections upon this, that there must be beyond the contingent world a necessary being in which may be founded that necessary truth which is the object of science. Science cannot have nothing for its object; but contingent beings, if we abstract their existence, are pure nothing. There can be no essence, no properties, no relations in what is pure nothing; something therefore is necessary whereon to base the necessary truth of those natures, properties, and relations which the understanding conceives of in contingent beings themselves. There is, then, a God; and to deny him, is to make science a pure illusion. The unity of human reason furnishes us one proof of this truth; the necessity of human science furnishes a second, and confirms the first. [19]

20. We find a conditional proposition involved in every necessary proposition, wherein substantive being is not affirmed nor denied, but the relative, as in this; all the diameters of a circle are equal. Thus, the one we have just cited is equivalent to this one; if there exists a circle all its diameters are equal. For in reality did no circle exist, there would be no diameters, no equality, or any thing else; nothing can have no properties; wherefore in all that is thus affirmed we must understand the condition of its existence.

21. In general propositions the union conceived of two objects is affirmed; but we must take good care to notice that although we are wont to say that what is affirmed is the union of two ideas; this is not, therefore, perfectly exact. When we assert that all the diameters of a circle are equal, we do not mean that this is so only in ideas, that we conceive it so to be, but that it really is so, beyond our own understanding and in reality, and this abstracting our ideas and even our own existence. Our understanding sees then a relation, a union of the objects; and it affirms that whenever these exist, there will also really exist the union, provided the conditions under which the object is conceived be fulfilled.

CHAPTER IV
BEING, THE OBJECT OF THE UNDERSTANDING, IS NOT THE POSSIBLE, INASMUCH AS POSSIBLE

22. One very important point concerning the idea of being remains to be illustrated, and that is, whether this idea has possible or real being for its object. The scholastics taught that the object of the understanding was being; nor were they altogether without reason in so doing, since one of the things we conceive of with the greatest distinctness, and which is found to be the most fundamental in all our ideas, is the idea of being, containing as it does in a certain manner all other ideas. But as being is distinguished into actual and possible, a difficulty occurs as to which of these categories the idea of being, the chief object of our understanding, is applicable to.

23. The Abbate Rosmini, in his *Nuovo Saggio sull' origine delle idee*, pretends that the form and the light of our understanding, and the origin of all our ideas, consists in the idea, not of real, but of possible being. "The simple idea of being," he says, "is not the perception of any existing thing, but the intuition of some possible thing; it is no more than the idea of the possibility of the thing." [20]

I very much doubt the truth of this; and there seems also to be some confusion of ideas here. He ought to have defined possibility itself for us, before making the idea of it enter into that of being. I will myself give a definition of it, and this may serve greatly to facilitate the understanding of the whole matter.

24. What is possibility? The idea of possibility, abstracted from its classifications, offers us a general idea of the non-repugnance, or non-exclusion, of two things with respect to each other; just as the idea of impossibility presents us such a repugnance or exclusion. A triangle cannot be a circle. A triangle may be equilateral. In the former case we affirm the repugnance of the ideas of the triangle and of the circle: in the latter, the non-repugnance of a triangle having its three sides equal. It may be said that in these cases there is no question of the existence of the triangle or of the

circle; and that the possibility or impossibility is referred to the repugnance of their essences, abstracted from their existence or non-existence, although ideal impossibility draws along with it real impossibility.

25. Since, whenever impossibility is asserted, repugnance also, is asserted, and there can be no repugnance of a thing with itself, it follows that impossibility is only possible when two or more ideas are compared. On the other hand, when there is no repugnance there is possibility; then, no simple idea, of itself alone, can offer to us an impossible object. The object, therefore, of every simple idea is always possible, that is, is not repugnant.

26. Those things only are intrinsically impossible which involve the being and the not-being of the same thing; wherefore they are styled contradictory. When an absurdity of this nature is presented to us, we at once recollect the principle of contradiction, and say, this cannot be, "since it would be and would not be at the same time." Why is a circular triangle impossible? Because it would be and it would not be a triangle at one and the same time.

The idea of not-being does then enter into that of impossibility: without it, there can be no exclusion of being, and consequently, neither contradiction nor impossibility.

27. Possibility may be understood in two ways: I., inasmuch as it expresses only simple non-repugnance; and then what does not exist, is not only possible when it does not involve any contradiction, but also, the existing, the actual; II., inasmuch as it expresses non-repugnance, united to the idea of not being realized; and then it is only applicable to non-existing things. The possible taken in the former sense, is opposed to the impossible; in the latter, it is opposed to the existing; it involves, however, the condition of non-repugnance. In the former case we have possibility simply so called; in the second, pure possibility.

From these remarks we conclude that the idea of possibility adds something to that of being, that is, non-repugnance, non-exclusion; and if there be question of pure possibility, the non-existence of the possible being is likewise added.

28. When the understanding perceives being in itself, it cannot distinguish whether there is or is not repugnance; this is only discoverable by comparison; for the idea of being, in itself simple, does not include comparable terms. The idea of being can encounter no repugnance if it be not applied to some determinate thing, to an essence in which contradictory conditions are imagined, as may be verified by seeking to apply being to a circular triangle.

29. So far is the idea of being in itself from being susceptible of abstraction from the idea of existence, that it is rather the idea itself of existence. When we conceive of being, in all its abstractness, we conceive of nothing else than of existence; these two words denote one and the same idea.

30. We can, in determinate things, conceive of the essence without existence; thus also we can very easily consider all imaginable geometrical figures and examine their properties and relations, abstracted from their existence or non-existence; but the idea of being, as something absolutely indeterminate, if it be abstracted from existence, is also abstracted from itself, is annihilated.

I should be much obliged to any one who would tell me to what the idea of being in general corresponds, abstracted from existence. If, after abstracting all determination, we also abstract being itself, what remains? Some one may answer, there remains a thing which may be. What does *a thing* mean? In case we abstract every thing determinate, *thing* can only signify a being; we should have a thing which may be, and this is equivalent to a being which may be. This is very well: but when we speak of a being which may be, is there only a question of an impure possibility? then we do not abstract existence, and the conditions of the supposition are not kept. Is there question of pure possibility? then existence is denied, and the proposition is equivalent to this: a being which is not, but which involves no repugnance. Let us examine the meaning of this expression: "a being which is not." What does the subject, a being, mean? a thing, or rather, that which is. What does a thing mean? a being: then abstraction is made from every thing determinate. Therefore, either the subject of the proposition means nothing, or the proposition is absurd, since it is equivalent to this, a thing which is, which is not, but which involves no repugnance.

31. The origin of the equivocation we combat consists in applying to the idea itself of being that which belongs only to things that are something determinate, conceivable without existence. Pure being, in all its abstractness, is inconceivable without actual being, it is existence itself.

32. Nor does pure possibility mean any thing except in order to existence. What is possible being if it cannot be realized, cannot exist? The idea of being is therefore independent of the idea of possibility; and the latter is only applicable in relation to the former.

33. The idea, then, of being is the very idea of existence, of realization. If we conceive of pure being, without mixture or modification, and subsisting in itself, we conceive of the infinite, we conceive of God: but if we consider

the idea of being as participated in a contingent manner, by application to finite things, we then conceive of their actuality or realization.

34. When we apply the idea of being to things, we have no intention of applying to them that of possibility, but that of reality. If we say the desk is, we affirm of the subject desk the predicate contained in the idea of being: and still we do not mean to say that the desk is possible, but that it really exists.

35. Nevertheless, the idea of being excludes that of not-being, in such a way that if the idea of being were only of the possible, it would not exclude that of not-being, since the purely possible even includes not-being; possibility, therefore, does not enter into the sole idea of being; and this idea expresses simply existence, reality.

CHAPTER V
A DIFFICULTY SOLVED

36. What means the idea of purely possible being? If we maintain that the object of the idea of being is reality, these two ideas, being, and purely possible, would seem to be contradictory: reality is not purely possible, for were it purely possible, it would not exist, and in the non-existing there is no reality. Let us examine this difficulty, and investigate the origin of the idea of pure possibility.

37. Surrounded as we are by contingent beings, contingent beings ourselves, we are incessantly aware of the destruction of some, and the production of others, that is to say, of the transition from being to not-being, and from not-being to being. Our inward sense attests to us this transition from not-being to being; we have ourselves experienced it; all our recollections are limited to a very brief term, before which the world already existed. Thus, then, reason, experience, and inward sense show us that there are some objects which are, and then disappear, and that others, which before were not, now appear. In those things in which we witness this change, we perceive properties and relations which give occasion to a certain combination of our ideas, and this combination subsists whether the objects to which they refer continue or cease to exist. In this way we form a general idea of things which, although they do not exist, may exist; but this subject *things*, does not express being, but in general finite, determinate objects.

38. Here, then, is the solution of the difficulty. Purely possible being, such as we conceive it to be in the manner explained, involves no contradiction; it does not denote *a reality which is not a reality*, but an object, or a finite, determinate thing, the idea of which we have, although it do not exist, and whose existence involves no contradiction, or repugnance with any of the conditions contained in its idea. The expression, then, purely possible being, if it be explained in this manner, is nothing more than the generalization of these and other similar propositions. A desk which is not is possible. What do we mean by this? Simply that in the idea of desk there is nothing repugnant to its existing; and purely possible being signifies nothing more than that we have many ideas of finite things which may exist without

repugnance. The expression refers to determinate things conceived of by us, but we abstract in this case whether this or that be the essence of which we speak, and comprise all those which offer no repugnance.

39. If it be objected that an infinite, non-existing being would then be a contradictory thing, we admit it without hesitation. If an infinite being do not exist it is an absurdity; and if, when we compare these two ideas, infinity and non-existence, we do not see the repugnance between them with perfect clearness, it is because we do not comprehend the nature of infinity. This is the only reason why the demonstration of the existence of God founded simply on his idea, has been and still is exposed to difficulties. But it is certain that if the infinite being did not exist, it would be impossible. For that is impossible which cannot exist; and did it not already exist it could not exist. This existence could not come from another, since the infinite cannot be a being produced; nor from itself, since it would not exist. We do, it is true, imagine the infinite in its essence, abstracted from its existence; but I repeat that this abstraction is only possible to us because we cannot well comprehend the infinite; could we comprehend it, we should see the repugnance between these terms, infinity and non-existence, with the same clearness as we see that of the triangle and circle.

CHAPTER VI
IN WHAT SENSE THE IDEA OF BEING IS
THE FORM OF THE UNDERSTANDING

40. When it is asserted that the object of the understanding is being, there is room to doubt whether it is meant that the idea of being is the general form of all conceptions, or only that all the understanding conceives is being; or, in other words, whether the quality of object is attributed to being, as being, in such a way that under this form alone objects are conceivable, or only that the quality of being belongs to all that the understanding conceives.

In the first case the proposition might be taken in a reduplicative sense, and would then be equivalent to this: "The understanding conceives nothing save inasmuch as it is being;" in the second it might be taken formally, and be equivalent to this: "whatever the understanding conceives is being."

41. We are of opinion that it cannot be said that the object of the understanding is being only inasmuch as being; in such a way as to make the idea of being the only form of the understanding's conceiving; but that this form is an essential condition to all perception.

42. If we remark that the idea of being, in itself considered, neither includes any determination or variety, nor expresses any thing more than being, in its greatest abstractness, we shall not fail clearly to perceive that this idea of being is not the only form conceived by the understanding; if, therefore, the understanding do not perceive any thing besides this idea in its objects, it cannot know their differences; nor can its perception go beyond that which is common to all, being.

43. If it be said that the differences perceived are modes of being, modifications of that which is represented in the general idea, it is at once agreed that being in itself is not the only form perceived; since both modification and mode of being add something to the idea of being. The rectangular triangle is a kind of triangle: its idea is a modification of the general idea, and no one will pretend that the idea of rectangular adds nothing to that of triangle, or that they are both the same thing. The same is verified in the idea of being and its modifications.

44. We have already seen [21] that indeterminate ideas by themselves alone do not lead to positive cognitions; and certainly no idea better merits the name of indeterminate than that of being. Were our understanding limited to it, perception would be nothing but a vague conception, incapable of any combination.

45. Negation itself, as we shall hereafter see, is known to us, but this it could not be were we to admit that the understanding knows nothing save inasmuch as it is being; in which case the indispensable condition of all cognition, the principle of contradiction, would deceive us.

46. These reasons suffice to place beyond all doubt what we have proposed to show, but as this point is intimately connected with what is most transcendental in logic and metaphysics, we will endeavor to explain it more at large in the following chapter.

CHAPTER VII
ALL SCIENCE IS FOUNDED IN THE
POSTULATE OF EXISTENCE

47. We have said that the idea of being is not the sole form perceived, but that it is a form necessary to all perception. We do not mean by this to say that we cannot perceive without the actually existing; but that existence enters in some degree as a condition of every thing perceived. We will explain ourselves. When we simply perceive an object, and affirm nothing of it, it is always offered to us as a reality. Our idea certainly expresses something, but it has nothing excepting reality. Even the perception of the essential relations of things involves the condition that they exist. Thus, when we say that in the same circle or in equal circles equal arcs are subtended by equal chords, we suppose impliedly this condition, "if a circle exists."

48. Since this manner of explaining the cognition of the essential relations of things may seem far-fetched, we will endeavor to present it under the clearest possible point of view. When we affirm or deny an essential relation of two things, do we affirm or deny it of our own ideas or of the things? Clearly of the things, not of our ideas. If we say, "the ellipse is a curve," we do not say this of our idea, but of the object of our idea. We are well aware that our ideas are not ellipses, that there are none in our head, and that when we reflect, for example, upon the orbit of the earth, that this orbit is not within us. Of what, then, do we speak? Not of the idea, but of its object; not of what is in us, but of what is without us.

49. Nor do we mean that we *see* it thus, but that it *is* thus; when we say the circumference is greater than the diameter, we do not mean that we see it thus, but that it is thus. So far are we from speaking of our idea, that we should assert it to be true although we did not see it, and even although it were not to exist. We speak of our idea only when we doubt of its correspondence with the object; then we do not speak of reality, but of appearance, and in such cases our language is admirably exact, for we do not say, *it is*, but, *it seems to us*.

50. Our affirmations and negations, therefore, refer to their objects. Now, we argue thus: what does not exist is pure nothing, and nothing can

either be affirmed or denied of nothing, since it has no property or relation of any kind, but is a pure negation of every thing; therefore, nothing can be affirmed or denied; there can be no combination, no comparison, no perception, except on condition of existence.

We say *on condition*, because we know the properties and relations of many things which do not exist; but in all that we do know of them, this condition always enters: if they exist.

51. Hence it follows that our science rests always on a postulate; and we purposely use this mathematical expression in order to show that those sciences which are called exact by antonomasy do not disdain this condition which we exact from all science. The greater part of them commence with this postulate: "Let a line be drawn, &c.," "Suppose B to be a right angle, &c.," "Take a quantity A greater than B, &c." This is the way the mathematician, with all his rigor, always supposes the condition of existence.

52. It is necessary to suppose this existence, otherwise nothing could be explained. Common sense teaches us what has escaped some metaphysicians. To prove it, let us see how a mathematician, who never dipped into metaphysics, would talk. We will suppose the interlocutor to set out to demonstrate to us that in a rectangular triangle the square of the hypothenuse is equal to the sum of the squares of the base and perpendicular; and that we, in order to exercise his intelligence, or rather to make him show us, without himself being aware of it, what is passing in his own mind with respect to the perception of its object, put various questions to him, in reality searching, although apparently asked out of ignorance. We will adopt the form of a dialogue for the sake of greater clearness, and will suppose the demonstration to be given from memory, without the aid of figures.

Demonstration. Drop a perpendicular from the right angle to the hypothenuse.

Where?

Why, in the triangle of which we speak, of course.

But, sir, if there be no such triangle——

Why then, what are we talking of?

We are talking of a rectangular triangle, and the case supposed is that there is none.

Is not, but can be. Take paper, a pencil, and ruler, and we will have one right away.

That is to say, you speak of the triangle we may make?

Yes, sir.

Ah, I understand; but then we should have it; now, we have not got it.

All in good time. But if we had drawn it, could we not drop the perpendicular?

Certainly.

That is all I meant to say.

But you were saying drop— —

No doubt we cannot drop a perpendicular in a triangle unless the triangle exists, since then there is neither vertex of a right angle, hypothenuse, nor any thing else; but when I say, drop a perpendicular, I always suppose a triangle; and as it is evident that the triangle may exist, I do not express the supposition, but understand it.

I comprehend this; but then we should drop the perpendicular only in this triangle, but you spoke as if we might drop it in all triangles.

I only took this triangle for an example; we can clearly do with all others what we can do with this one.

With all?

Certainly. Can you not see how, in every rectangular triangle, a perpendicular may be drawn from the right angle to the hypothenuse?

Yes, in your figure; but since what is in my head is not a triangle, for I imagine some with sides a thousand miles long, and there is not in my head room enough—

There is no question of what is in your head, but of triangles themselves—

But these triangles do not exist; therefore, we can say nothing of them.

Yes; but may they not exist?

Who doubts it?

Well then, if they do exist, be they large or small, in one position or another, here or there, is it not true that a perpendicular may be drawn from the vertex of the right angle to the hypothenuse?

Evidently.

I have then only to say that, in every rectangular triangle, this perpendicular may be drawn.

Then you do not speak of those which do not exist? Is it not so?

I speak of all, whether they do or do not exist.

But a perpendicular cannot be drawn in a triangle which does not exist. What does not exist is nothing.

But perhaps that which does not exist may exist; and I see with perfect clearness how every thing said would be verified, *supposing it to exist*. Thus we can and do speak of all existences and non-existences without any exception.

We leave it to the reader to judge if we have not, while thus rudely troubling our good mathematician with our importunate questions, made him reply as would have replied every one not at all acquainted with metaphysics. It is evident that these replies ought to be accepted as reasonable, as satisfactory, and as the only ones in this case that all the mathematicians in the world could give.

This being so, all that we have advanced is found in these replies and explications. All science is founded on the postulate of existence; every argument, to demonstrate even the most essential properties and relations of things, must start with the supposition of their existence.

CHAPTER VIII
THE FOUNDATION OF PURE POSSIBILITY, AND THE CONDITION OF ITS EXISTENCE

53. We have said that the foundation of the pure possibility of things, and of their properties and relations, is founded in the essence of God, wherein is the reason of every thing. [22] And it may at first sight seem that science needs only this foundation, and does not require to rest upon the condition of the existence of things; because, if essences are represented in God, the object of science is found in the Divine essence; and consequently, the argument founded upon the impossibility of asserting any thing of nothing, is not conclusive. Supposing there to be such a representation, science is not occupied with a pure nothing, but with a real thing; and it has consequently in view a positive object, even when it abstracts the reality of the thing considered.

Let us see how we can solve this difficulty.

54. The necessary relations of things, independently of their existence, must have a sufficient reason; and this can only be in necessary being. The condition, therefore, of existence, presupposes the representation of the essence of the contingent being in necessary being; the condition, therefore, "if it exist," cannot be brought in unless it presupposes the foundation of possibility.

55. This remark shows that there are two questions:—1st: What is the foundation of the intrinsic possibility of things? 2d: Supposing possibility, what condition is involved in so much as it is affirmed or denied of the possible object? The foundation of the possibility is God; and the condition is the existence of the objects considered.

Both are requisite to science; if the foundation of intrinsic possibility be wanting, the condition of existence cannot come in; and if, admitting the possibility, we omit the condition, science has no object.

56. We would remark, for the better understanding of this whole subject, that we do not, in affirming or denying the relations of beings represented in God, treat of what these beings are in God, but of what they would be in

themselves were they to exist. In God, all are the same God; for all that is in God, is identical with God. If, then, we consider things only as they are in him, we shall have God, not the things, for object. Certain it is, that in God is the foundation, or the sufficient reason, of geometrical truths: but geometry does not consider them such as they are in God, but such as they are or may be realized. In God, there are neither lines nor dimensions of any kind; he, therefore, is not the object of geometry properly so called. Geometrical truths have in him an objective value or representative value, but not subjective; we should otherwise be obliged to say that God is extensive.

57. Here, then, is seen that what we said above in the place cited, does not conflict with what we have here established; and that to make God the foundation of all possibility, does not exclude the scientific necessity of the condition of existence.

58. We will, in order to place this beyond all doubt, present the question under another aspect, by showing that when God knows finite truths, he sees in them this condition likewise: "If they exist." God knows the truth of this proposition: "Triangles of equal base and altitude are of equal superfices:" this is true as well in the eyes of infinite intelligence, as in ours; were it not thus the proposition would not be true in itself, and we should be in error. This being so, there are in God, who is most simple being, no true figures, although he has the intellectual perception of them. The cognition, then, of God, in what relates to finite things, refers to their possible existence, and consequently involves the condition that they exist.

The cognition of God does not refer to their purely ideal representation, but to their actual or possible reality; when God knows a truth of finite beings, he does not know it from the sole representation of those truths which he has in himself, but from that which they would be were they to exist.

59. Every object may be considered either in the real or in the ideal order. The ideal is their representation in an understanding, which has a value only inasmuch as it refers to possible or actual reality. In this manner alone can the idea have objectiveness, since otherwise it could only be a purely subjective fact, of which, excepting the purely subjective, nothing could be either affirmed or denied. The idea which we have of the triangle aids us, in so far as it has a real or possible object, to know and combine: we refer what we affirm or deny of it to its object: if this disappear, the idea is converted into a purely subjective fact, to which we cannot apply the properties of a triangular figure without an open contradiction.

CHAPTER IX
IDEA OF NEGATION

60. It is said that the understanding does not conceive nothing: this is true in the sense that we do not conceive nothing as something, which would be a contradiction; but it does not therefore follow, that we do not in any mode conceive nothing. Not-being is nothing, and yet we conceive not-being. This perception is necessary to us; without it we could not perceive contradiction; for which reason the principle of contradiction: "It is impossible for a thing to exist and not to exist at the same time:" fundamental as it is in our cognitions, would fail us.

61. It may be said that to conceive nothing, not-being, is not to conceive, but to not-conceive: this, however, is false, for it is not the same thing to conceive that a thing is not, and not to conceive it. The former involves a negative judgment, and may be expressed by a negative proposition; and the latter is the simple absence of the act of perception; the former is objective, the latter subjective. We do not when asleep perceive things; but this non-perception is by no means equivalent to perceiving that they are not. It may be said of a stone that it does not perceive another stone; but not that it perceives the non-being of the other stone.

62. The perception of not-being is a positive act; and it would be a contradiction to say that it is the very perception of being; for it would follow, that whenever we perceive being, we perceive its negation, not-being, and *vice versa*, which is an absurdity.

63. When we perceive not-being, we do, it is true, perceive it in relation to being; and it is equally true, an understanding perceiving absolute not-being, without any idea of being, is altogether inconceivable; but this does not prove the two ideas not to be distinct and contradictory.

64. It is remarkable that the idea of negation, besides entering into the fundamental principles of our understanding: "It is impossible for a thing to be and not to be at the same time:" "Every thing either is or is not:" is also necessary to almost all of our perceptions. We do not conceive distinct beings without conceiving that one *is not* the other, and we cannot form a negative judgment into which negation does not enter. Hence it results that

just as the idea of being is absolute and relative, also is the idea of not-being: thus, we say, "The sun *is;*" "All the diameters of a circle *are* equal;" and we also say, "The phœnix *is not:*" "The diameters of an ellipse *are not* equal."

65. We may ask those who hold that every idea is the image of the object, what sort of an image the idea of not-being would form? This confirms what we have already advanced, that it is a mistake to imagine all ideas as a kind of types, similar to things, and that we cannot oftentimes explain any of those inward phenomena, called ideas, notwithstanding we know and explain their objects by them.

66. It is also said that the object of the understanding is being; but this is inexplicable in the sense that the understanding does not perceive not-being; and can be understood only in the sense that we perceive not-being as coordinated to being, and that not-being of itself alone, cannot be the origin of any cognition.

Remark here an important difference. By the idea of being every thing may be understood; and the more of being there is in the idea, the more do we understand; and if an idea be supposed to represent a being without any limitation, or, which is the same thing, without any negation, we should have a cognition of an infinite being. On the contrary, the perception of not-being teaches us nothing, save inasmuch as it shows us the limitation of determinate beings and their relations; and if we suppose the idea of not-being to be gradually extended, we shall see that in proportion as it approaches its limits, that is, pure not-being, absolute nothing, the understanding loses its object; the points of comparison and the elements of combination fail; all light goes out, and intelligence dies.

67. We know universal, absolute nothing, only as a momentary condition which we imagine, but do not admit. In it we see that it is impossible that something should not exist; for, could any one instant be designated in which nothing existed, nothing could now exist. In this imaginary nothing, we discover no point of departure for the understanding; all combinations become impossible and absurdities; the mind sees itself perishing in the vacuum it has itself created.

68. If the idea of negation be not combined with that of being, it is perfectly sterile; but thus combined, it has a kind of fecundity peculiar to itself. The ideas of distinction, of limitation, and of determination, involve a relative negation, for we do not conceive distinct beings without conceiving that one is not another; nor limited beings, without conceiving that they *are wanting,* that is, that in some sense they *are not;* nor determinate beings, without conceiving something which makes them what they are and not others.

CHAPTER X
IDENTITY; DISTINCTION; UNITY; MULTIPLICITY

69. Let us examine how we may draw from the idea of not-being the explication of the ideas of identity and distinction, unity and multiplicity.

Let us conceive a being, and fix our attention solely on it, and compare it with nothing which is not it, nor permit any idea of not-being to come in; we shall then, with respect to it, have the ideas of identity and unity; or, to speak more exactly, these ideas of identity and unity will be nothing else than ideas of this same being. Ideas of unity and identity are for this reason inexplicable by themselves alone; they are simple, or are confounded with a simple idea in which can be no comparison, and into which if negation enter, it is not noted, nor can be made the object of reflection. Thus, for instance, the idea of not-being enters in some manner into the perception of every limited being; but we can abstract this negation, and consider what the object *is*, not what it *is not*.

70. If we perceive a being, and afterwards another being, the perception that one is not the other gives the idea of distinction, and consequently that also of multiplicity. There is, then, no distinction or number without perception of relative *not-being* combined with *being*; but this perception is all that is requisite to distinction and number.

71. The ideas of identity and unity are simple, those of distinction and number composite; the former involve no negation, the latter imply a negative judgment; "this is not that." It is impossible for A to be presented to us as distinct from B, if we do not perceive that B is not A; and on the other hand, we need only to know that B is not A, in order to enable us to say they are distinct. These expressions, "A is not B," or, "A and B are distinct," are perfectly identical.

72. From this we infer that the primary combination of our intelligence consists in the perception of being and not-being. By it we perceive identity and distinction, unity and number; by it we compare, affirm, or deny; without it we cannot even think. Without the perception of negation, we can have only the perception of being, that is, an intuition fixed upon an identical

object, one and immutable, such as we conceive the Divine Intelligence to be, contemplating the infinity of being in the infinite essence.

73. Does God know negations? Certainly; for when a being ceases to exist, God knows this truth, in which there is a negation. He knows the truth of all negative propositions, whether it expresses substantive or relative being; therefore, he knows negation. But this is no imperfection, since it cannot be an imperfection to know truth; the imperfection is in the objects, which, by the very fact of being finite, include negation, being combined with not-being. Were God not to know negation, it would be because negation is in itself impossible; which would be equivalent to the impossibility of the existence of the finite, and would lead to the absolute and exclusive necessity of one sole infinite being.

CHAPTER XI
ORIGIN OF THE IDEA OF BEING

74. If it be impossible to think without the idea of being, it exists prior to any reflex act, and it cannot have sprung from reflection. The idea of being must therefore be innate. Let us investigate this question.

75. We have shown in the preceding chapter that we cannot think without the idea of being; let whoever doubts this consult his own experience, and make, if he can, a reflex act into which the idea of being will not enter. We have already seen that we cannot exclude it in the conception of first principles, and beyond these it is certain no one will go.

76. Can this idea have come to us from sensation? Sensation in itself offers us only determinate objects, whereas the idea of being is an indeterminate thing: sensation offers us only particular things, whereas the idea of being is the most general it is possible to have: sensation teaches us nothing, tells us nothing, except what it is, a simple affection of our soul, whereas the idea of being is a vast idea, extending to all, and, fecundating our mind in an admirable manner, is the element of all reflection and alone sufficient to found a science: sensation never leaves itself, nor extends to another sensation; the sense of touch has nothing to do with that of hearing; all belong to an instant of time, and only exist during it, whereas the idea of being guides the mind through every class of beings, the corporeal and the incorporeal, the real and the possible, the temporal and the eternal, the finite and the infinite.

If we discover any thing by sensations, if they produce any intellectual fruit, it is because we reflect upon them; but reflection is impossible without the idea of being.

77. Neither does it seem that the idea of being can be formed by abstraction. To abstract is of necessity to reflect; and reflection is impossible without this idea; therefore, it is necessary to abstraction, and consequently cannot have abstraction for its cause.

78. On the other hand, an exceedingly simple explication of the method in which abstraction is made, may be opposed to this argument apparently so conclusive. We see the paper upon which we write; this sensation

involves two things, whiteness and extension. Were we limited to simple sensation, here we should stop, and receive only the impression, extension and whiteness. But having within ourselves a faculty distinct from that of feeling, which makes us capable of reflecting upon the very sensation we experience, we can consider that this sensation has some similarity to others which we recollect to have experienced. We can then consider extension and whiteness in themselves, abstracting the actual affection which they produce in us. Afterwards we can reflect upon the fact that these sensations have something in common with others, inasmuch as they all affect us in a certain manner, and then we have the idea of sensation in general. If, then, we consider that these sensations all have something in common with all that is in us, in so far as they modify us in a certain manner, we shall form an idea of a modification of the *me*, making abstraction, however, of its being a sensation, a thought, or an act of the will; and if, finally, we abstract from these things being in us, their being substances or modifications, and attend only to the fact that they are something, we shall have attained the idea of being. This idea may, therefore, be formed by abstraction. This explication, seductive as it is by reason of its simplicity, is open to grave objections.

79. From the very beginning of this process we make use, without adverting to it, of the idea of being; we therefore deceive ourselves when we imagine that we form it. We cannot reflect upon extension and whiteness without remarking that they exist, that they are *something* similar to other sensations. When we think upon what affects us, we know that *we are*, that that which affects us *is*, and we speak of its being or not being, of its having or not having *something common*; and finally, when we abstract the modifications of our mind as being this or that, and regard them only as *thing*, as *something*, as a *being*, we evidently cannot so consider them if there does not exist in us the idea of *something* in general, that is, of being. Thus being is a predicate which we apply to things; we do, therefore, know this predicate. We only collect in one general and indeterminate idea, particular and determinate things, already existing in our understanding. The successive operations made by means of abstraction are only a decomposition of the object, a classification of it in various general ideas so as to attain to the superior idea of being.

80. It is difficult in view of these reasons, which are all strong, to decide without danger of erring for either of the opinions advanced. Nevertheless, we shall give our own in accordance with the principles we have laid down in different parts of this work. We hold that the idea of being is not innate, in the sense that it pre-exists in our understanding as a type anterior to all sensation and to all intellectual acts; [23] but we see no impropriety in calling it innate, if nothing more be meant than the *innate faculty* of our

understanding to perceive objects under the general reason of being or existence, so often as it reflects upon them. Thus the idea does not flow from sensations; it is recognized as a primary element of pure understanding; but it is not formed by abstraction, which separates it from others, and purifies it, so to speak, itself contributing to this purification. In this sense it may exist before reflection, and yet be the fruit of reflection, according to the various stages in which we consider it. Inasmuch as it is mixed and confused with other ideas, it exists before reflection; but inasmuch as it has been separated and purified, it is the fruit of the same reflection.

81. We must, in order to give a complete solution of the difficulties proposed, give our ideas precision and exactness.

The idea of being is not only general but also indeterminate; it offers to the mind nothing real or even possible, since we do not conceive that a being, which is only being, does or can exist, if no property besides that of being can be affirmed of it. In God is the plenitude of being; he is his own being; with reason does he call himself, I am, who am; but we also affirm of him, with all truth, that he is intelligent, that he is free, and that he possesses other perfections not expressed in the pure and general idea of being.

From this we infer that we ought not to regard the idea of being as a type representing to us something determinate, even something in general.

82. The act by which we perceive being, existence, reality, is necessary to our understanding, but it is confounded with all other intellectual acts, as a condition *sine qua non* of them all, until reflection comes to separate it from them, purifying it, and making it the object of our perception.

Since, when we perceive, we perceive something, it is evident that the reason of being is always involved in all our perceptions; by the simple fact of knowing we know being, that is, we know *a thing*. But as we do not always, when we fix our perception upon an object, distinguish the various reasons into which it may be decomposed, although the idea of being is contained in every object perceived, it is not directly perceived by our understanding until reflection separates it from all else.

83. If we reflect upon an azure object, evidently the idea of color enters into that of azure; but without reflection we shall not distinguish the genus, color, and the difference, azure. These two things are not really distinguished in the object perceived; for it would be ridiculous to pretend that in a particular azure-colored object, color is one thing and azure another. Nevertheless we can, when we reflect upon the object, very easily distinguish between the two ideas of color and azure, and we can discuss one without paying attention to the other. Must we say we have the idea of color in general, prior to the sensible representation? Most certainly not: it is only necessary to recognize an innate force of the mind to generalize what is

presented to it in particular, and to decompose a simple object into various ideas or aspects.

84. Our understanding is endowed with an intellectual force, by virtue of which it can conceive unity under the idea of multiplicity, and multiplicity under the idea of unity. We discover an example of the latter when we unite what is really multiple in a single conception. Our understanding may be compared to a prism which decomposes a ray of light into many colors; hence different conceptions relating to one simple object. When multiplicity is to be reduced to unity, the intellectual force operates in an altogether contrary manner; instead of dispersing, it unites; the variety of colors disappears, and the ray of light is restored in all its purity and simplicity.

85. Our mind, from the fact that it is limited to know many things by conceptions only, and not by intuitions, requires the faculty of composing and decomposing, of seeing a simple thing under distinct aspects, and of joining different things under a common reason.

We must not fail to observe that the power of generalizing and of dividing, given to our understanding, is a great help to it, indicating, however, its weakness in the intellectual order, and continually warning it to proceed with due circumspection, when it has to decide upon the intimate nature of things.

86. According to this doctrine, general, and more particularly indeterminate ideas result from the exercise of reflection upon our own perceptive acts; and there is in the general idea nothing more than is seen in the particular perception, excepting its own generality produced by the elimination of all individuating conditions. This is especially verified in the idea of being, which, as we have seen, enters as a necessary condition into all our perceptions, and is, moreover, requisite to all operations as well of composition as of decomposition.

We cannot conceive, without conceiving *some thing, a being*; and this is substantive being. We cannot affirm or deny without saying, *is,* or *is not*; and this is copulative being. The idea of being is, therefore, less an idea than a condition necessary to enable our understanding to exercise its functions; it is not a type representing nothing determinate; it is rather the very condition of its life, without which it cannot possibly exercise its activity.

87. But we can, by reflection, perceive this condition of all our thoughts; the idea of being, standing, as it does, involved with the others, is then presented purified to our eyes, and we conceive that general reason of *being,* or *thing,* which enters into all our perceptions, but which we had not previously distinguished with sufficient clearness.

CHAPTER XII
DISTINCTION BETWEEN
ESSENCE AND EXISTENCE

88. It has been much disputed in the schools whether existence is distinct from essence. At first sight, this seems an indifferent question; but such it is not, if we attend to the consequences which, in the opinion of respectable authors, flow from it; for they pretend to no less than establishing upon the distinction between essence and existence a characteristic note of the finite, attributing to infinite being alone, the identity of its essence with its existence.

89. That we distinguish between the essence and the existence of things is beyond all doubt; for inasmuch as we know an object realized, we conceive its existence; and inasmuch as we know that this object exists with this or that determination, constituting it in such or such a species, we conceive its essence. The idea of existence represents to us pure reality; the idea of essence offers us the determination of this reality. The schools, however, not satisfied with this, have endeavored to transfer to things that distinction which we discover in our conceptions; but their opinion seems to be subtle rather than solid.

90. The essence of a thing is that which makes it what it is, and distinguishes it from all else; and existence is the act which gives being to essence, or that by which essence exists. It would appear, from these definitions, that there really is no distinction between essence and existence. To render two things distinct, it is requisite that one be not the other; but since essence, abstracted from existence, is nothing, we cannot say that there is a real distinction between them. To what is the essence of a man, if we abstract his existence, reduced? To nothing; and therefore, no relation between them is admissible. We grant that when we abstract the existence of man, we do yet conceive the essence of man; but the question is not whether we distinguish between the idea of man and his existence, but whether there is a real distinction between his own essence and existence.

91. In God are the essences of all things, and in this sense they may be said to be distinguished from finite existence; this does not, however,

if we consider it well, at all affect the present question. When things exist in God, they are not any thing distinct from him; they are represented in the Infinite Intelligence, which is, with all its representations, the infinite essence itself. To compare, therefore, the finite existence of things with their essence, as this is in God, is entirely to change the state of the question, and to seek the relation of things, not with their particular essences, but with the representations of the Divine understanding.

92. It may be objected that, if the existence of finite beings is the same as their essence, it will follow that existence will be essential to these beings; for, since nothing is more essential than essence itself, finite beings would exist of necessity, as all that pertains to essence is necessary. The radii of a circle are all equal, for equality is contained in the essence of the circle; and in like manner, if existence belong to the essence of things, they must exist, and non-existence would be a veritable contradiction.

This difficulty rests upon the ambiguous meaning of the word *essence*, and the want of exactness in joining the ideas of essential and necessary. The relation of essential properties is necessary, for we cannot destroy it without falling into contradiction. The radii of a circle are equal, because equality is involved in the very idea of the circle; consequently, if this be denied, it would be affirmed and denied at one and the same time. There is, however, no contradiction when some properties are not compared with others; but this comparison is not made when there is question of essence and existence, for in this case one thing is not compared with another, but with itself; if the distinction be introduced, it does not refer to two things, but to one and the same thing considered under two aspects, or in two different states, in the ideal order and in the real.

When we consider essence abstracted from existence, the object is the union of the properties which give to beings such or such a nature; we abstract their existence or non-existence, and attend only to what they would be were they to exist. The condition of existence is either expressly or impliedly involved in all that we affirm or deny of properties; but when we consider essence realized or existing, we do not compare property with property but the thing with itself. In this case, non-existence does not imply contradiction; for when existence disappears, the essence also disappears, with all that it included. There would be a contradiction were we to assert that essence implies existence, and to endeavor, while the former remains, to make the latter disappear, which is not verified in this supposition. The equality of the radii of a circle cannot fail, so long as the circle does not fail; and the contradiction would be to make the radii unequal while the circle continues to be a circle; but were the circle to cease to be a circle, there would be no reason why the radii should not be unequal. Essence is the same as existence; so long as there is essence, so long will there be existence; if the essence fail the existence will likewise fail; where, then, is the contradiction? Life is of the essence of man, and yet man dies; we may then say man is destroyed, and therefore there is in this no contradiction. If the essence cease to exist, it also will be destroyed, and existence, which is identified with it, may fail without any contradiction.

93. The scholastics taught that the being whose essence was the same as its existence would be infinite and absolutely immutable, because, since existence is the complement in the line of being or of act, it could receive nothing more. This difficulty also originates in the equivocal sense of words. What is meant by *complement* in the line of being or act? If it mean that nothing can supervene to essence identified with existence, here is a begging of the question, since what was to be proved is asserted. If it mean that existence is the complement in the line of being or act in the sense that, given it, nothing more is wanted to make the things, whose existence it is, really existing, an indubitable truth is advanced, but not one from which what was to be demonstrated can be inferred.

94. It would seem, therefore, that there is no real distinction in things corresponding to the distinction between essence and existence in our conceptions. Essence is not distinguished from existence, but it does not therefore cease to be finite, nor existence to be contingent. In God existence is identified with essence; but in such a manner, that his non-existence implies contradiction, and his essence is infinite.

CHAPTER XIII
KANT'S OPINION OF REALITY AND NEGATION

95. Kant numbers among his categories reality and negation, or existence and non-existence, and, conformably to his principles, defines them thus: "Reality is a pure conception of the understanding; it is what corresponds, in general, to any sensation whatever, consequently that whose conception denotes a being in itself, in time. Negation is that whose conception represents a not-being in time. The opposition of these two things consists in the difference of the same time, as full or void. Since then, time consists solely in the form of the intuition, and consequently in the form of the objects as phenomena, it follows that that which in them corresponds to the sensation, is the transcendental matter of all objects, as things in themselves, essential reality. Every sensation has a degree or intensity, by which it may fill more or less the same time, that is, the inward sense relatively to the representation of an object, until it be reduced to nothing = 0 = negation."

There is in this passage a fundamental error which ruins the whole basis of all intelligence: there is also much confusion in his application of the idea of time.

96. According to Kant, reality alone refers to sensations; therefore the idea of being will be the idea of the phenomena of sensibility in general; this idea will mean nothing, if applied to the non-sensible; the very principle of contradiction will necessarily be limited to the sphere of sensibility; and we neither shall know, or be able to know any thing without the sensible order. Such are the consequences of this doctrine; let us now examine the solidity of the principle from which they flow.

97. Were the idea of reality only the idea of the sensible in general, we could never apply it to non-sensible things, which, however, experience teaches we can do. We speak incessantly of the possibility and even of the existence of non-sensible beings, and we even distinguish the phenomena of our mind into those belonging to sensibility, and those which correspond to the purely intellectual order. The idea of being, therefore, for us, denotes a general conception non-circumscribed by the sensible order.

98. Kant will answer that the applications we make of this idea, extending it beyond the sphere of sensibility, are vain illusions expressed in unmeaning words. To this we reply.

I. There is now no question of ascertaining whether the applications of the idea of being or reality beyond the sensible order be founded or unfounded; there is question only of ascertaining what it is that this idea represents to us, whether the object represented be illusory or not. Kant, when defining reality, regards it as one of his categories, and consequently, as one of the pure conceptions of the understanding. To make his definition good, he ought to employ this conception in its greatest possible extent: but as he has demonstrated that conception, in itself, is not limited to the sphere of sensibility, it must follow that his definition is inadmissible. Had he said that the applications of the conception beyond the sensible order were unfounded, he would indeed have erred, but would not have destroyed conception itself; yet he equivocates not only in the uses of conception, but also in its nature, which he can only ruin, if he limit it to the sphere of sensibility.

II. The principle of contradiction is founded in the idea of being, and extends as well to the non-sensible as to the sensible. It would follow, were we to admit Kant's doctrine, that the principle of contradiction, "It is impossible for a thing to be and not to be at the same time," would be equivalent to this proposition; "It is impossible for a phenomenon of sensibility to appear and not to appear at the same time." Evidently neither philosophy nor common sense ever gave such a meaning to the principle of contradiction. When the impossibility of a thing's being and not being at the same time is affirmed, this is asserted in general, and abstraction is absolutely made of the things pertaining or not pertaining to the sensible order. Were it not thus, we should be obliged to say that non-sensible beings are absolutely impossible, which even Kant does not venture to maintain, or, supposing them to exist, to doubt whether the principle of contradiction is applicable to them. Who sees not the absurdity of such a doubt, and that, if it be admitted for a single instant, all intelligence is destroyed? If we limit the generality of the principle of contradiction, the impossibility is no longer absolute: and supposing it to fail in certain cases, who shall assure us that it does not in all?

III. Kant himself admits the distinction between the phenomena of sensibility and purely intellectual conceptions: with him, therefore, reality comprises something more than the sensible. Purely intellectual conceptions are a reality, are something at least as subjective phenomena of our mind, and yet are not sensible, as Kant himself confesses; he therefore falls into a contradiction, when he limits the idea of reality to the purely sensible.

99. Kant conceives reality and negation only as filling, or leaving void, time, which, in his opinion, is the primitive form of our intuitions, and a kind of back-ground upon which the mind sees all objects, even its own

operations. According to this doctrine, the ideas of time precede those of reality and negation, since only in relation to it are the two latter conceivable. And now we see the singularity of a form, or whatever else it be called, to which the ideas of reality and negation are made to refer when nothing is conceivable without the idea of reality. Kant, scrupulous as he is in the analysis of the elements of our mind, and contemptuous as he is towards all metaphysicians who preceded him, ought to have explained to us the nature of this form in which we see reality, and which, nevertheless, is not contained in the idea of reality. If it is something, it will be a reality; and if it is not something, it will be a pure nothing; and consequently, it cannot be a form which can, by filling and becoming void, present to our mind the ideas of reality or negation. It would be easy to show, by an abundance of reason, the German philosopher's equivocation, when he so inexactly determines the relations between time and the idea of being; but as we propose to explain at length the idea of time, we will pass over here what belongs to another part of this work.

CHAPTER XIV
RECAPITULATION AND CONSEQUENCES
OF THE DOCTRINE CONCERNING
THE IDEA OF BEING

100. We wish now to recapitulate the doctrine brought out in the preceding chapters, so that it may be seen at a glance in all its bearings and connections.

The idea of being is so fruitful in results, that we must sound it under all its aspects, and never lose sight of it in investigating transcendental philosophy.

101. We have the idea of *ens*, or of being in general; reason and our inward sense both attest it.

102. This idea is simple, and cannot be resolved into other elements: it expresses a general reason of things, and its nature is in a certain manner destroyed if it be mingled with particular ideas. It is intuitive, but indeterminate to such a degree that, by itself alone, it affords us no idea of a real or possible being. We not only know that every being is, but that it is *some thing* which is its predicate: even the Infinite Being is not only a being, but is an intelligent and free being, and formally possesses all perfections which imply no imperfection.

103. The idea of being may express either simple existence, in which case it is substantive, or the relation of a predicate with a subject, and then it is copulative. In the proposition, "the sun *is*," being is substantive, that is, expresses existence; in the proposition, "the sun *is luminous*," being is copulative, that is, it denotes the relation of the predicate with a subject.

104. The ideas of identity and distinction originate in the ideas of being and of not-being; and thus the idea of copulative being, which affirms the identity of a predicate with a subject, flows also in a manner from the idea of substantive being.

105. Being, which is the principal object of the understanding, is not the possible inasmuch as possible. We conceive possibility only in order to

actuality. Possibility flows from actuality, not actuality from possibility. We could not conceive pure possibility, that is, possibility without existence, did we not conceive finite beings in whose idea being is not of necessity involved, and of whose appearance and disappearance we are incessantly reminded by experience.

106. The understanding perceives being, and this is a condition indispensable to all its perceptions; but the idea of being is not the only one offered to it, since it knows different modes of being, which, by the very fact that they are *modes*, add something to the general and absolute idea of existence.

107. When we consider the essences of things, and abstract their reality, our cognitions always involve this condition,—if they exist. There can be only a conditional science of the purely possible, insomuch as it is not; that is, provided the object pass from possibility to reality. We must, in order to establish pure possibility so that it may have necessary relations, subject to the condition of existence, have recourse to a necessary being, origin of all truth.

108. The essences of things in the abstract mean nothing, nor can they become the object of affirmation or negation, unless we suppose a necessary being in which is the reason of the relations of things, and of the possibility of their existence.

109. Pure truth, independent of all understanding, of all being created or uncreated, is an illusion, or rather an absurdity. With pure nothing there is no truth. Truth cannot be *atheistic*; without God there is no truth.

110. We not only know being, but also not-being. We have an idea of negation, and it always refers to some being. Absolute nothing cannot be the object of intelligence. The idea of not-being has its own peculiar fecundity; combined with that of being, it gives the principle of contradiction, engenders the ideas of distinction and multiplicity, and makes negative judgments possible.

111. The idea of being does not flow from sensations; neither is it innate, in the sense that it pre-exists in our understanding as a type prior to all perceptions. There is no reason why it may not be called innate, if this mean only a condition *sine qua non* of all our intellectual acts, and consequently of the exercise of our innate faculties. The idea of being is mingled in every intellectual perception, but it is not offered to us with perfect clearness and distinctness until we separate it by reflection from the particular ideas which accompany it.

112. Essence is not distinguished from existence even in finite beings. It is a distinction in conceptions, to which there is no real distinction corresponding.

113. The identity of essence with existence does not involve the necessity of finite things. The arguments by which some pretend to establish this consequence are founded upon an ambiguous meaning of words.

114. Kant's opinion, which limits the idea of reality, and that also of negation, to the purely sensible order, would destroy all intelligence, since it overthrows the very principle of contradiction. This doctrine of the German philosopher is also in opposition with what he himself taught concerning purely intellectual conceptions, distinct from sensible representations. When he refers the ideas of reality and negation to that of time, as the primitive form of the inward sense, he leaves out of the idea of reality what no less pertains to it, and presents the idea of time under a point of view wholly equivocal.

115. As sensible representation is based upon the finite intuition of extension, so the perceptive faculties of the pure understanding receive the idea of being as their foundation. In the same manner that extension is presented to sensibility as limitable, and from limitability results figurability, and consequently all the objects of geometrical science; so also does the idea of not-being, combined with that of being, fecundate in a manner the metaphysical sciences. The parallelism of the two ideas, extension and being, is not of such a nature as to render the former independent of the latter. So far as science is concerned, the idea of extension is sterile, if it be not combined with the general idea of being and not-being. This may be shown in many ways; but it will suffice to recollect that geometry cannot take a single step without the principle of contradiction, into which the ideas of being and of not-being enter. [24]

116. All our cognitions flow from the idea of being and not-being, combined with intuitive ideas. We shall have occasion in the following books to remark this admirable fecundity of an idea, which, although it cannot of itself teach any thing, can yet, when united with others, and modified itself in various ways, so illuminate the intellectual world as to merit to be called the object of understanding.

BOOK SIXTH
UNITY AND NUMBER

CHAPTER I
PRELIMINARY CONSIDERATIONS
ON THE IDEA OF UNITY

1. Before analyzing the idea of number, let us examine its simplest element, unity. Number is a connection of unities. We cannot know what number is, if we do not know what unity is. [25]

2. What is unity? When is a thing one? We all seem to know what unity is, since upon it we found the fabric of all our arithmetic cognitions. We all know when a thing is one, and we never equivocate on the meaning of the word. In this the learned and the unlearned stand on the same footing. The word *one*, in our language, has only one meaning for all who understand it. The same may be said of the word which in other languages expresses the same idea. When we meet the figure 1, which corresponds to this idea, and expresses it in a general manner, abstracting the difference of idioms, all men understand and apply it in the same manner.

3. The idea of unity is the same in all men; it is a common patrimony of the human race. It is not bound to this or that object, nor to this or that act of the mind; it extends to all in the same manner. Even composite and multiple things are called one only, inasmuch as they participate in a general idea. The indivisible point is one. The line composed of many points could not be one were there not a contiguous enchainment of these points, and did they not all unite to form *one* object, which gives us *one* impression, and is submitted to *one* act of our understanding.

4. The idea of unity is not a particular sensation, since it applies to all; neither is it sensation in general, since it pertains to what is not sensation. The sensation of color is one; so, also, the consciousness of the *me* is one, although this is not a sensation. The size of the rectangle which I see is one, and the relation of the equality of its angles is also one, but is not a sensation.

5. The idea of unity is a simple idea, and accompanies our mind from its first steps; we find it everywhere, and understand it well, but cannot explain it as we would, because it is simple, and cannot be decomposed and expressed by various words. We do not mean to say, however, that we must abjure all explanation of it; we only propose to warn the reader of the kind of explanation he may expect, which can be no other than the analysis of the fact, inasmuch as it is an object, and of the phenomenon as presented to our mind.

CHAPTER II
WHAT IS UNITY

6. The scholastics were right in teaching that every being is one, and that whatever is one is being. Unity is a general attribute of every being, but is not distinct from it. However little we reflect, we cannot fail to perceive that unity and being are not distinguished: the unity of unity, by itself, offers us nothing real or even possible. What then would become of unity, if nothing but unity? This idea is involved in that of being; it is an aspect of it, a reason under which being is presented to the understanding.

7. But what is the conception of unity under which beings are presented to us? There is unity in the object when there is no distinction in the conception presenting it; and there is no distinction, when the perception of relative *not-being* is not combined in the object with that of *being*. We have unity whenever we perceive an object simply. Suppose that we perceive the object B. No matter what B is, it will to us be always one, unless we perceive it as composed of C, D, one of which is not the other. If we perceive in the object B, a distinction between C and D, unity disappears.

Evidently when we are aware of this composition we can abstract it and simply consider the result, the whole, B; and then unity appears anew.

8. We see by this that unity may be either real or fictitious. It is real and existing when there is no distinction in the thing either real or apparent; it is fictitious in those composites which of themselves include distinct things that may be offered to the understanding, inasmuch as they are subordinated to one unity of order, abstraction made of the real distinction contained in them.

9. The schoolmen sometimes defined what is *one* to be, "ens indivisum in se, et divisum ab aliis." The former part seems sufficiently exact if by *indivisum* is meant *non-distinctum* and not *non-separatum*; but the second part must be regarded at the best as superfluous. If there existed only one most simple and sole being, it would yet be one, although we could not say that it was divided from others, *divisum ab aliis*; for as there would be *no others* it could not be divided from them. This part of the definition is therefore superfluous.

10. It is no solution of the difficulty to say that this one being is divided from others, real or possible, and that in the supposition of one only being, others are possible although not real. The only being would be *really one*, and the division from others would be only *possible*; since there can be no real distinction between two terms when one of them is only possible. The division from others, *divisis ab aliis*, therefore is not a necessary element of unity, because unity is real, and this element is only possible.

11. However, in confirmation of this doctrine, we may remark, that in common parlance, unity is opposed to distinction, and there is no unity where there is no distinction. If the only being be not conceived as multiple there can be no distinction; and this is so independently of its being compared with the rest. The words, *others*, and *the rest*, suppose single beings; the idea of unity precedes that of distinction; beings are not considered as distinct between themselves until after they are conceived as individually single.

12. It seems, therefore, that a single being ought to be defined as *ens indivisum in se*, or a being which includes no division. Unity, then, will depend upon non-distinction. If non-division denote *non-distinction*, there will be real unity; but if it denote *non-separation* or re-union, we shall only have a fictitious unity. The molecules without extension, of which many suppose matter to be composed, would be really *one*, because there is no distinction in them. Bodies are fictitiously *one* because their composite parts though united are really distinct.

13. A difficulty may be raised by asking whether a being, indivisible in itself, but not divided from others, would be really *one*, for in case it would not be *one*, it might be inferred that we had unjustly censured the definition of the schoolmen, since whatever wants the second property required by the definition would not be one. We reply, then, a being that includes no distinction in itself, and is not distinguished from others, would indeed be one, but in such a case there would be no *others*, since they cannot be when there is no distinction. In such an hypothesis, there would be only one unity, the unity of pantheism, the *great all*, the absolute in which all things would be identified.

14. We have already said that the unity which is confounded with being, is not the unity which originates number. We here in fact encounter two different conceptions of unity, the one marking only want of distinction, and the other expressing the property of engendering number. But we are not thence to infer that the one which is identified with being is distinct from that which engenders number. All beings, one in themselves, but

distinct from each other, no matter what they may be, may be conceived under the idea of number. The number *three* enters into the august mystery of the Trinity, and we say with all truth that in God there are *three* persons.

15. It is not necessary that the unity which engenders number should be real; it suffices if it be fictitious. When we take a foot measure for unity, we employ a fictitious unity, since the foot is composed of parts, but the number which results therefrom is, nevertheless, a true number.

CHAPTER III
UNITY AND SIMPLICITY

16. Real unity and simplicity are identical. What is really one has no distinction in itself; nor is it composed of parts, of which it can be said, this *is not* that. Evidently simplicity requires nothing more; the simple is opposed to the composite, to what is formed of many beings whereof one *is not* the other.

17. We meet this simplicity in none of the objects of our intuitions, excepting the acts of our own mind; so that even when we know, by discursion, that there are substances really one or simple, we do not see them in themselves.

Extension consists essentially of parts; whence it happens that we never encounter real unity or simplicity in the corporeal world as object of our sensibility. But as the composite must be resolved into the simple, as it is hard to proceed *ad infinitum*, we infer that the corporeal universe itself is a union of substances which, whether called points without extension, or any thing else, cannot be decomposed into others; for which reason they are really one, or simple.

18. Hence we conclude that substances may be said to be in a certain manner simple; and that things called composite are unions of substances, which in their turn form a third substance by virtue of a law presiding over them and giving them that unity which we call factitious.

19. We cannot, then, do less than to remark that the transcendental analysis refutes those who deny simplicity to thinking beings, since we have seen that simplicity is prior to composition, which can neither be nor be conceived if it be not presupposed. Simplicity is a necessary law of every being: a composite being ought to be called a union of beings, rather than a being.

20. We have said that simple substances are not objects of our intuition, which has none worthy to be called simple excepting the acts of our mind. The reason of this is, that the principal medium of our intuition is sensibility, which is founded upon representations, themselves based upon extension. There can be no doubt that the acts of our mind, given us by intuition, in the inward sense are perfectly simple; for who can decompose a perception, a judgment, an act of the reason or of the will?

21. The perception of a certain object requires preparatory acts; and the same may be said of judgments and ratiocinations; yet these operations are in themselves exceedingly simple, and cannot be divided into various parts. Simplicity is met with alike in the acts of the will, whether of the pure, intellectual, or sensible will. How shall we divide such acts as these into parts: *I desire, I do not desire, I love, I abhor, I suffer, I rejoice?*

22. We must take care not to confound the multiplicity of the acts with the acts themselves; there may be many acts, but in themselves they are simple. Thoughts, impressions and affections continually succeed one another in our mind; these phenomena are all distinct from each other, as is proved by their existing at different times, some at one time without the others, and by some being incompatible with others, because contradictory; but each individual phenomenon is by itself incapable of decomposition, and admits in itself no distinction into various parts; wherefore, it is simple.

23. True unity, therefore, is only found in simplicity; where there is no true simplicity, there may be factitious, but not real, unity; since even when there is no separation, there may be distinction between the various parts of which the composite is formed.

24. It may be inferred from this that *indistinctum* ought, perhaps, to take the place of *indivisum* in the definition of a one being; because distinction is opposed to unity of identity, and division to union. Absence of division is all that factitious unity requires; but real unity demands that there be no distinction. However closely united two things may be, if one is not the other they are distinct, and cannot, in strict metaphysical language, be called one.

25. The object of these observations is only to fix our ideas, not to modify our language. In common parlance, the idea of unity is used in a less rigorous sense, and, far from opposing this use, we readily accord it a reasonable foundation. There results from the union of two really distinct things, a conjunction, rightly called one so far as it also is subjected to a certain unity; and, were it not permitted to use this word in a sense less rigorous than that exacted by metaphysical analysis, we should be under the necessity of excluding unity from the great mass of objects. Simple substances, we have said, are not offered to us in immediate intuition, and we see compositions rather than their component elements. Could we apply unity only to simple elements, science would be greatly reduced, language would be impoverished, and literature and the fine arts would be despoiled of unity, one of their characteristic perfections.

CHAPTER IV
ORIGIN OF THE TENDENCY OF
OUR MIND TO UNITY

26. Since we encounter multiplicity in all sensible objects, which are those chiefly demanding our attention, how does our mind acquire the idea of unity? In science, in literature, in the arts, and in every thing, we seek unity; and whence this irresistible tendency towards unity, which makes us seek a factitious when we cannot find a real unity, and this, too, notwithstanding the multiplicity presented by all the objects of our perception?

27. Two origins, if we mistake not, may be assigned to this tendency towards unity, the one objective, the other subjective. The former consists in the very character of unity in which the object of the understanding is mainly comprised; the other is the unity found in the intelligent being, and which it experiences in itself. We will explain these ideas more at length.

28. Unity is being; every being is one; and, properly speaking, being is not found without unity. Let us take a composite object: in it we discover two things; the simple component elements of it, and the union of them. The being, properly speaking, does not consist in the union, but in the united elements. The union is a mere relation, not even possible without the elements to be united. On the other hand, these elements in themselves, abstracted from their union, are true beings, existed before, and will exist after their union. What is an organized body? An aggregation of molecules united under a certain law, conformably to a principle presiding over their organization. The parts existed before their organization, and will continue to exist after its destruction. The being, therefore, properly consisted in the elements; and the organization was a relation of them among themselves.

29. Organization requires a principle to rule it, and subject its functions to determinate laws. Thus we see that even relation is subject to unity, to the unity of end and to the unity of a ruling and directing principle.

30. It is inconceivable how the union of distinct things can have any meaning, or lead to any result, if unity do not preside over it. In objects submitted to our experience, things are united in three ways: by juxtaposition

in space; by co-existence in time; and by association in the exercise of their activity. The elements constitutive of extension are united in the first way; all objects belonging to the same time, in the second; and in the third all those which unite their forces and direct them to one and the same end.

31. The union consisting in the continuity of elements in space, has no value in the eyes of science, save inasmuch as there is an intelligent being who perceives the forms resulting from this continuity, by reducing them to unity under ideal types. Four lines of points, so disposed as to form a quadrilateral figure, have no scientific meaning until there comes an intelligence and perceives the form of a quadrilateral figure under the aspect of unity. We do not deny that the quadrilateral figure exists independently of intellectual perception: these lines will certainly exist, and be arranged in the same manner, although we prescind all intelligence; but this disposition in the quadrilateral form is a relation, not a being distinct from the aggregation of the elements disposed; and this relation, of itself alone, is no object of intelligence except inasmuch as presented to it under the unity of the quadrilateral form.

The intelligence in search of a true being, can find none, save in elements; and if it wishes to perceive their relation, it must recur to the unity of form.

32. Co-existence in time, is a relation, which, of itself alone, neither gives any thing to, nor takes any thing from objects. These exist independently of this relation; for they must, of necessity, exist, in order to co-exist. This relation denotes something perceptible to the understanding, only as it is presented to it under unity, which, in this case, is unity of time, as in the former it was unity of space.

33. Neither has the association of activities any meaning, except when it expresses the convergence of forces towards one and the same object. If unity be wanting to the point of their direction, their union will express nothing, and the intelligence will have for its object only scattered and unrelated activities.

34. We have then shown that unity is a law of our understanding, founded upon the very nature of things. Absolute being is never found in the composite, but only in the simple, and relative being is not even conceivable, if it be not submitted to unity.

35. We discover in the very nature of our mind, the second origin of its tendency to unity. It in itself is one, is simple, and therefore disposed to assimilate every thing to itself under this same unity and simplicity. It feels that it is one in the midst of multiplicity, permanent even in succession, and under all the immense variety of sensible phenomena, intellectual and moral, which it unceasingly experiences. The inward sense attests with

irresistible certainty the identity of the *me*. This unity, this identity, is as certain, as evident to the child who begins to feel pleasure or pain, and is sure that he is one and the same that experiences both impressions, as they are to the philosopher who has spent long years in profoundly investigating the idea of the *me* and the unity of consciousness.

The unity and simplicity which we experience in ourselves force us to reduce the composite to the simple, the multiple to the one. The perception of things the most composite refers to a consciousness essentially one: even were we to perceive the whole complicated universe by a single act, this act would be most simple, since otherwise the *me* could not say, *I perceive*.

36. Two reasons, then, exist why our mind in all things seeks unity. Objects are unintelligible, except so far as subjected to a certain perceptible unity, to a form, under which the multiple is made one, and the composite simple. The object of the understanding is being, and being consists in the simple. The composite involves an aggregation of simple elements with the relation called *union*; but unless this be presented under a certain unity, it does not constitute a perceptible object.

Without the indivisible unity of consciousness, no intelligent subject is conceivable. Every intelligent being requires this link to unite the variety of phenomena of which it is the subject. If this unity fail, the phenomena become an informal aggregation, unrelated among themselves: intellectual acts without an intelligent being.

The tendency to unity originates in the perfection of our mind, and is itself a perfection; but it needs to be carefully watched, lest it go astray, and seek real unity there, where only a factitious unity can be found. This exaggeration is the cause of pantheism, the fatal error of our day. Our mind is one, so also is the infinite essence, cause of all finite beings; but the aggregation of these beings is not one, for even when united by many ties, they cease not to be distinct. There is in the world unity of order, of harmony, of origin, and of end; but there is no absolute unity. Number also enters into unity of harmony, but it is incompatible with absolute unity, as reason and experience both show.

CHAPTER V
GENERATION OF THE IDEA OF NUMBER

37. Unity is the first element of number, but does not of itself alone constitute number, which is not unity, but the collection of unities.

38. *Two* is a number. What is our idea of the number *two*? Evidently it is not confounded with its sign, for signs are many and very different, but it is one and always the same.

39. It would seem at first sight that the idea of two is independent of the mode of its generation, and that, being one, it may be formed by addition or subtraction, by adding one to one, or taking one from three: 1 + 1 = 2; 3 - 1 = 2. But if we reflect upon these two expressions, we shall see that the latter is impossible without the former. We should not know that 3 -1 = 2 if we did not previously know that two entered into the composition of three, and how it entered. We could know nothing of this had we not already the idea of two, and this idea is nothing else than the perception of this sum.

40. The idea of two is no sensation, for it extends alike to the sensible and the non-sensible, to the simultaneous and the successive. In itself it is simple, its object is composite.

41. Since the collection of objects is small in two, the imagination can easily figure to itself what the understanding perceives; and the idea seems clearer to us because made sensible by a representation. The idea of addition made, *in facto*, that is, the idea of the sum, enters into that of two, but not of addition *in fieri*. Our idea of this number is perfectly clear, and yet we do not continually think of one plus one.

42. The idea of two refers to the simultaneous as well as to the successive; but our mind does not discover it until after it has the idea of succession. The object of this perception is the relation of united things; the understanding perceives them as such, and then only has it the idea of two.

43. Neither the successive nor simultaneous perception of two objects unaccompanied by relation is the idea of two. Hence the saying: a man and a horse do not make two, but only one and one; and the reason of this is that the man and the horse are represented to the understanding by their

difference, not by their resemblance; and things must be presented to the mind under a common idea in order to give number. Thus, if we abstract their difference, and consider them only as animals, or corporeal beings, or beings simply, or things, they will make two.

44. In objects, then, totally unlike, or not comprehended under some common idea, there can be no number. Abstract number is number by excellence; because it eliminates all that distinguishes the things numbered, and considers them only as beings, consequently as similar, as contained in the general idea of being. Concrete numbers are only numbers so far as they participate in this property. *Two* is applicable to one horse and another horse, but not to a horse and a man, unless we identify them under the idea of animal, and abstract rationality and irrationality. Concrete number requires a common denomination; otherwise it is not number.

45. The idea of distinction, that is, that the one is not the other, enters into the idea of two, so that this idea necessarily involves an affirmation and a negation. The affirmation is of the real, possible, or imaginary existence of the things counted; the negation is of the one with respect to the other. Affirmation without distinction or negation involves identity. The idea of two, as well as that of every other number, includes the ideas of identity and distinction. The identity is of each extreme with itself; the distinction is of the extremes among themselves. Identity in the thing is the thing itself: identity in the idea is the simple perception of the thing. Distinction in the thing is the negation of it with respect to others: distinction in the idea is the perception of negation. We always perceive a thing as identical, and consequently every perception includes the idea of unity. But we do not always, when we perceive a thing, observe its negation with respect to others, and consequently do not always perceive number. The idea of number originates in comparison, when we see an object which *is not* another.

46. The ideas of being, distinction, and similarity enter into that of two. The idea of being, because nothing cannot be counted: that of distinction, or negation of the one being the other, because the identical does not constitute number: that of similarity, because things are only numbered when abstraction is made of their difference. Being is the basis of perception; distinction, of comparison; and similarity, of union. Perception begins with unity, proceeds with distinction, and ends with similarity, which is a kind of unity. The perception of this similarity unites what is distinct; but the union need not always be of the things, but may be in the idea comprising them. There are two poles of the world, but they are not united. The perception of the number two requires something more than the simple perception of objects; they must be susceptible of comparison, and consequently united

in a common idea. This perception, therefore, demands comparison and abstraction, and this is why animals cannot numerate; they can neither compare nor generalize.

47. The analysis of the idea of two is the analysis of all numbers; the difference is not of nature, but of more and less; in the repetition of the same perception.

48. If any one now ask whether number be in the things, or in the mind alone, we reply that it is in things as in its foundation, because both distinction and similarity are in the things; that is, the one is not the other, and both have something in common; but it is the mind that sees all this.

49. After having perceived the distinction and union of two objects, we can also perceive another object, which will be neither the one nor the other of them, and will yet be comprehended in one general idea with them. This is the perception or idea of the number *three*. No matter how many numbers be imagined, nothing will ever be discovered in any of them except a simultaneous perception of objects, distinction of objects, and similarity of objects. If these be determinate, we shall have concrete number; if they be comprised in the general idea of being, of thing, we shall have abstract number.

50. The limits of our mind prevent it from comparing many objects at one time, and from easily recollecting the comparisons it has already made. To assist the memory, and the perception of these relations, we make use of signs. When we pass beyond three or four, our power of simultaneous perception fails, and we divide the object into groups which serve us as new units, and are expressed by signs. Ten is clearly the general group in the decimal system; but before we reach the number ten we have already formed other subalternate groups; since to count ten, we do not say one and one and one, etc., but one and one, two; two and one, three; three and one, four, etc. Each unit added forms a new group, which, in its turn, serves to form another. With two, we form three; with three, four, and so on. This affords an idea of the relation of numbers with their signs; but, as this matter is too important to be here dismissed, we will further develop it in the following chapters.

CHAPTER VI
CONNECTION OF THE IDEAS OF
NUMBER WITH THEIR SIGNS

51. The connection of ideas and impressions, in a sign, is a most wonderful intellectual phenomenon, and at the same time of the greatest help to our mind. Were it not for this connection, we could scarcely reflect at all upon objects somewhat complex, and above all our memory would be exceedingly limited. [26]

52. Condillac made some excellent remarks upon this matter: in his opinion, we cannot, unaided by signs, count more than three or four. If, indeed, we had no sign but that of unity, we could readily count two, saying one and one. Having only two ideas, we could easily satisfy ourselves that we had twice repeated one. But it is not so easy to be certain of the exactness of our repetition when we have to count three, by saying one and one and one; still, this is not difficult. It is more so to count four, and next to impossible to go as far as ten. If we undertake to abstract the signs, we shall find that it is impossible to form an idea of ten by repeating one; and that it will be alike impossible, if we employ no sign, to make sure that we have repeated one exactly ten times.

53. Suppose the sign two, and one half of the difficulty is obviated; thus it will be much easier to say two and one, than one and one and one. In this supposition four will be no more difficult than was two, since, just as we before said, one and one, two; we now say, two and two, four. The attention before divided four times by the repetition of one, is now only divided twice. Six was before a hard number to count, but, in the present supposition, it is as easy as three was before; for, if we repeat two and two and two, we shall have six. The attention before distracted by six signs, is now distracted only by three. Evidently, if we continue to form the numbers three, four, and so on, expressive of distinct collections, we shall gradually facilitate numeration, until we attain the decimal simplicity now in use.

54. It may here be asked if the actual system be the most perfect possible? And if facility depend upon the distribution of collections in signs, can there be any thing more perfect than this distribution? Either there is

question of new signs to denote new collections, or of the combination of signs. There can be no number which we cannot express with our present system, and consequently there is no need of inventing any thing to denote new collections. New signs might perhaps be invented for these collections, and these collections might possibly be distributed in a simpler and more convenient manner. In this case we admit an amelioration to be possible, though very difficult; but none in the former. In a word, the only possible progress would be in expressing better, not in expressing more.

55. The sign connects many ideas which, without it, would be isolated; hence its necessity in many cases, its utility in all cases. With the word hundred, or its numerical representative, 100, we know that we have one repeated a hundred times. Were this help to fail, we could not speak of a hundred, base calculations upon it, or even form it. It is, however, well said that we do not succeed in forming it except by tens, by repeating the calculation ten ten times.

56. Let it not, therefore, be thought that the idea of the number is the idea of the sign; for evidently the same idea of ten corresponds to the word ten, whether written, spoken, or numerically represented by the figures 10, although these three signs are very different. Every language has a word of its own to express ten, and all people have the same idea of it.

57. This last remark creates a difficulty as to what the idea of ten consists in. We cannot say that it is the recollection of the repetition of one ten times; first, because we do not think of this recollection when thinking of ten; and second, because, according to what has already been said, a clear recollection of this repetition is impossible. Neither is it the idea of the sign, for the idea signified existed before the sign was invented, otherwise the invention would have had no object, and would even have been impossible. There can be no sign where there is nothing to signify.

The idea of number includes more difficulties than Condillac ever imagined; who, if he had, after his close analysis of what facilitates numeration, profoundly meditated upon the idea itself, would not so readily have censured St. Augustine, Malebranche, and the whole Platonic school, for having said that numbers perceived by the pure understanding are something superior to those perceived by the senses.

CHAPTER VII
ANALYSIS OF THE IDEA OF NUMBER IN ITSELF AND IN ITS RELATIONS WITH SIGNS

58. In order clearly to conceive the idea of number, and the way it is engendered in our mind, let us study its formation in a deaf and dumb person.

We have no better way of giving such a one an idea of unity than by presenting an object to him. Now, if we would convey to him the idea of two, we show him two fingers, then two oranges, then two books, and in each of these operations make a sign which must be always the same. If we repeat this operation a number of times, the deaf and dumb person will associate the idea of two with that of the sign, and one will suggest the others; and he will endeavor to show us that he has seen two objects of some kind, by uniting the expression of the object with the sign of two. The same will take place with three, or four. When we reach higher numbers, the sign becomes more indispensable; since the less easily the idea of number is represented, the more necessary is the sign to secure it. But what we do to convey an idea of number to the deaf and dumb person, what he himself must do to express the number which he conceives, we must all do if we would obtain the idea.

59. Numeration is a repetition of operations; and the art of facilitating it consists in instituting signs which recall to our memory what we have done. It is an exceedingly complicated labyrinth, and we cannot trust ourselves to its windings with any expectation of finding our way out again, if we do not take care to mark the path we have followed.

It is to the admirable simplicity of the decimal system, united to its inexhaustible variety, that the facility and fecundity of our arithmetic are due. Algebra, going a step beyond, expresses without determining numbers, and presents the results of its operations without effacing its footsteps on the road travelled, is far superior to arithmetic, and has made the human mind take gigantic strides. But how? Solely by aiding the memory. Thus, the very principle that enables the child to say four and one, five, instead of adding unity five times to unity, the dumb man to express five by a hand, a hundred by a grain, enables the algebraist to express the result of his longest operations by a formula easy of retention by the memory. Both attain their object simply by aiding the memory. A grain of wheat denotes to the dumb man the idea of hundred, and this he applies to all similar collections; a few letters combined in a simple manner designate to the mathematician a property of certain quantities, and this he applies to all which are found in the same case.

60. Numeration is only an aggregation of formulas; and the more easy these are of mutual transformation with a slight modification, the more perfect will be the numeration. The better one knows the relations of these formulas and the manner of transforming them, the better will he know how to count. The greater a person's intellectual power of fixing simultaneously the attention upon many formulas, and of composing them, the more perfect arithmetician will he be, because the simultaneous comparison of many, leads to the perception of new relations.

61. What is our idea of hundred? The union of the units composing it, a union which we have made more or less frequently when learning to count. But how do we know that it is the same union? Because we have a formula called a hundred, expressed by a sign 100. This formula is so easily recollected that we have no difficulty in recollecting the idea of hundred and all the properties connected with it. We may be asked if a hundred is more than ninety. Were we under the necessity counting one and one and one, we should be bewildered, and never succeed in distinguishing the greater; but knowing as we do that to reach the formula hundred, we must pass by another formula ninety, and that this was in ascending, we know, once for all, that hundred expresses ninety and something more, that is, a hundred is more than ninety. And if it be further inquired what is the excess, we shall not undertake to ascertain this by adding units, but by the two formulas ninety and ten which compose the formula hundred.

62. By generalization we unite many similar things in one idea. The general idea is a kind of formula. Numeration unites in one sign many things contained in a general idea, but this sign has, at the same time, its own distinctive character. Thus the general idea belongs as a predicate to each of its particular objects; number belongs to no one in particular, but to all joined. We perceive in abstraction a common property, and lay aside all the particular objects which it presents; in numeration, we perceive similarity, but always with distinction. Abstraction is the result of comparison, but not comparison. Numeration implies a permanent comparison, or the recollection of it.

63. The idea of number is not conventional; a hundred is always a hundred with all its properties and relations, and this, too, prior to all convention and even to all human perception. The sign, and the sign only, is conventional. Were there no intellectual creature, and a hundred beings distinct among themselves were to exist, there would really be this number. The number three exists in the august mystery of the Trinity, from all eternity, and of absolute necessity. Number requires only the existence of distinct things; since, however unlike they may be, they always have something in common being, which may be included in a general idea, and consequently they fulfil the two conditions necessary to number.

64. The perception of being and of distinction, that is, of substantive being and of relative not-being, is the perception of number. The science of the relations of every collection, with its measure, which is unity, is the science of numbers.

BOOK SEVENTH
ON TIME

CHAPTER I
IMPORTANCE AND DIFFICULTY
OF THE SUBJECT

1. The explanation of the idea of time is not a matter of mere curiosity, but of the highest importance. To convince ourselves of this we have only to consider that the explanation of the whole edifice of human cognitions is based upon it. The most fundamental and indispensable principle which supports all others, includes the idea of time. A thing cannot be and not be at the same time: "impossibile est idem simul esse et non esse." The impossibility of being and of not-being regards only the *simul, the same time*. Therefore, the idea of time necessarily enters into the very principle of contradiction.

2. The idea of time is involved in all our perceptions; it extends to many more objects than does the idea of space. We estimate not only the movements of bodies by time, but also the operations of the mind. We know that a series of thoughts may be measured by time the same as a series of corporal movements.

3. The idea of succession necessarily enters into that of time, and *vice versa*, the idea of time into that of succession. We may conceive that one thing *succeeds* another; but this would be impossible without succession, without a *before and after*, that is, without time. This reasoning, apparently vicious, shows, perhaps, that we must not explain the ideas of time and succession, the one by the other, since they are identical.

4. Time does not seem to be distinct from things; for who can imagine duration without that which lasts, or a succession without that which succeeds? Is it a substance? Is it a modification inherent in things, or distinct from them? Whatever is something exists; and yet we nowhere meet time existing. Its nature is composed of instants divisible to infinity, essentially

successive, and consequently incapable of simultaneousness. Imagine the minutest instant you can, and it does not exist, for it is composed of others infinitely minute, which cannot exist united. To conceive an existing time, we must conceive it as actual, and in order to do this, we must surprise it in an indivisible instant; but even this is not time; it involves no succession; it is not *duration*, containing *a before and an after*.

5. Nothing is easier than to calculate time, and nothing more difficult than to conceive it in its essence. As to the former the learned and the ignorant are on the same footing; both have equally clear ideas; the latter is excessively difficult even to the most eminent men. The passage in the *Confessiones* of St. Augustine, in which the Holy Doctor endeavors to penetrate this mystery is well known.

CHAPTER II
IS TIME THE MEASURE OF MOVEMENT?

6. Time is said by many philosophers to be the measure of movement. This idea is fruitful, but it needs to be illustrated.

When we measure movement we refer to something fixed. Thus we measure the rapidity with which we have traversed a certain space by noticing the time denoted by a watch. But how do we measure time by a watch? By the space passed over by the hand on the dial. If we reflect carefully, we shall see that this is purely conventional, or rather, that it depends upon an arbitrary condition. For if we suppose the time marked to be an hour, the space passed over by the minute hand, that is, the circumference of the dial, has no relation with the hour except what the artificer gave it by so constructing the watch that the minute hand would make one revolution every hour. If the watchmaker had constructed it differently, as he did the hour hand, the time would be the same, but the space passed over is very different.

7. The time, therefore, indicated by the watch is no measure, save as itself is subject to another measure; consequently it is not the primitive measure. The same can evidently be said of all other watches which must have been regulated one after another, until we come to the first of all watches. There was no other watch to regulate this; it follows, therefore, that no one of the measures furnished by art is the primitive measure.

8. Not finding this measure in the works of man, we must seek it in nature; and here we discover fixed measures. If we regard the course of the sun, and take for unity the time it requires from the time it leaves the meridian until it returns, we shall have the day; this divided into twenty-four parts gives us the hours. Here we have a great watch which will serve to regulate all others.

9. Nevertheless, however lightly we reflect upon this, we cannot help seeing that the solution is not so satisfactory as it seems at first sight.

Solar time and sidereal time do not agree. Thus, if we note the moment when a star is in the meridian conjointly with the sun, we shall the next day see that the star reaches the meridian a little before the sun. Which is right?

Has the star taken just twenty-four hours, or the sun? If time be a fixed thing independently of movement, neither of these measures corresponds exactly to time.

10. This argument, which may be called practical, is corroborated by another purely theoretical. If we take celestial movement for the measure of time, will it be true that whenever the movement, which serves as the rule, shall be verified, that there has passed a fixed and determinate time? If we be answered in the affirmative, we must infer, that even were this movement to be accelerated or retarded, as, for instance, if a solar revolution were to be made with a half, or with twice its ordinary velocity, it would continue to mark the same time, which, however, is absurd. If it be said that the movement is supposed to be uniform, we reply, that this is a begging of the question. Uniformity of movement consists in equal times recurring after equal intervals. Did time, then, in its nature depend upon the movement of the sun, or of any star, as primitive measure, neither uniformity nor variety would have any meaning. If the space of twenty-four hours depended upon a revolution's being made, no matter in what manner whether at a snail's pace, or with the velocity of light, we should never have more or less than twenty-four hours. But if these depend upon another measure, if prior to them, there was a time which measured the velocity of movement, and determined whether it had been accelerated or retarded, then the movement of the stars is not the primitive measure; they are in the same category as our watches, they marked the time passed, but time has not passed because they mark it. Time is the measure of their movement, not their movement the measure of time. Movement is in time, not time in movement.

11. To appeal to the movement of the superior heavens, is evidently no solution of this difficulty, for what has been said of the sun, may also be said of the remotest star in the firmament. Whether we appeal to annual, solar, or sidereal movements, the same difficulty remains. Would sidereal years be the same, if the movement be made with greater or less velocity. If they would, an absurdity would follow; if not, this is not the primitive measure.

12. Moreover, we perceive, when considering movement, that we seem to conceive of greater and less velocity; and thus the idea of time, of necessity, enters into that of velocity, since velocity is the relation of space passed over in a given time. The idea of time is therefore prior to, consequently independent of, *every* particular measure.

13. We measure time by movement, and in order to measure the velocity of movement we need that of time. Here then, perhaps, is a vicious circle; but possibly this only shows that these are correlative ideas, the one explanatory of the other; or, rather, they are different aspects of one and

the same idea. The difficulty of separating them, and the intimate union which unites them on the one hand as much as it divides them on the other, confirms this conjecture. To show this, we ask, what time has passed? Two hours. How do we know this? By our time-piece. But what if it be too fast or too slow? The measure fails. This time is thus to us as a fixed measure, prior to that of the watch by which we undertake to measure it. But what are these two hours, if we abstract the measure of the watch, that also of the stars, and every other measure? Two hours, in the abstract, can be found in no category of real or possible beings; and we cannot, without a measure, give any idea of them, nor form one for ourselves. The idea of hour refers to a determinate movement of known bodies; and this in its turn refers to others; and finally, we come to one in which we can discover no reason why it should be exempted from the general law to which the others are subject. No farther reference being possible, all measure fails; and this failing, time, by the force of analysis, vanishes.

14. Therefore, the referring of time to movement, explains nothing; it only expresses a thing known, and that is, the mutual relation between time and movement, a relation known to the unlearned, and of constant and common use; but the philosophic idea stands intact; the same difficulty remains; what is time?

CHAPTER III
SIMILARITIES AND DIFFERENCES
BETWEEN TIME AND SPACE

15. Time seems to us to be something fixed. An hour is neither more nor less than an hour, no matter how our time-pieces go, or the world itself; just as a cubic foot of space is always a cubic foot, neither more nor less, whether occupied or not occupied by bodies.

16. Time exists independent of all movement, of all succession; if it is something absolute, has a determinate value of its own, is applicable to all that changes without itself changing, the measure of all succession without itself being measured, what is it? That it is something accidental cannot be reconciled with its immutability and universality. Every thing lives in it, but it lives in nothing; every thing dies in it, but death has no power over it. When the substance perishes, the accident perishes; but time continues the same although no substance exist. Before all created beings, we conceive ages and ages, that is, time; and after the destruction, the annihilation of all beings, we still conceive a successive although unending succession, which is time. The idea, then, of time, does not demand that of the universe; it existed before it, and will survive it: but without time the universe is inconceivable.

17. The idea of time seems to be independent of the idea of any being; of all duration in it; every thing may endure in it; but it does not begin or end with what endures in itself; it is applicable to all that endures, but it is not itself an endurable thing. We imagine it to be one in the multiple, uniform in the various, fixed in the movable, eternal in the perishable; and it even seems to contain some features of the attributes of Divinity; but it is, on the other hand, essentially despoiled of every property excepting that of succession in its abstractest signification. It is essentially sterile, has no power of its own, no condition of being or action, and consequently leads to the highest imaginations of what a pure idea really is, an abstraction, which, like space, we have imagined in the presence of things.

18. The points of similarity between time and space are worthy of our attention. Both are infinite, immovable; both are a general measure; both essentially composed of continuous and inseparable parts. Limit them

you cannot, determine any limit you chose, and beyond it you will see an ocean extended. Your powers are impotent; beyond the highest heaven are unbounded abysses of space; before the beginning of things there was a long chain of interminable ages.

In vain would you undertake to move space; you can only move yourself in it, or survey its various points. Its points are all fixed; you may mark out distances and directions with respect to them, but you cannot change them. The result will be analogous if you attempt to move time. The present instant is not the one just past, nor the one next to succeed; they are of necessity distinct, and of necessity exclude each other. Their very nature is to succeed each other. If their place be changed with respect to time, it ceases to be the same. Imagine, if you can, that to-morrow is to-day, that to-day is yesterday. It is impossible for that which was at a certain time not to have then been; but this would not be impossible if time could be moved; for in order that what was yesterday may not be, it is necessary to convert yesterday into to-morrow; but this would be an absurdity. The past, the present, and the future, are essentially distinct things.

A simple space, a space without parts, is no space at all, it is a contradiction; neither is a simple time, a time without parts, a time, but is a contradiction.

A space whose parts are not continuous, is not a space; neither is a time whose parts are not continuous, a time. The parts of space are inseparable; you may distinguish them one from another, count them one after the other, compare them one with another, and consider them one after another, but you cannot separate them. All imaginable bodies may exist in the apartment where we write, one or many, at rest or in motion; but the space which we conceive is one, fixed, and always the same; we can estimate its extent in cubic feet, if we choose, but these feet are fixed and inseparable; we cannot separate one cubic foot from another, even if we would; for even while we annihilate it, it is present to us, and in the same distance that we need in order to conceive separation. We cannot conceive separation, if we do not conceive distance; nor conceive distance, if we do not conceive space. We separate bodies from each other, but not one space from another. Space remains with the same continuity when bodies are separated, and it is by this continuity remaining unalterable that we measure the extent of their separation. The same happens with time; it is a chain which cannot be broken. Can we conceive three successive, immediate instants, A, B, C, and then suppress B? Certainly not; such a suppression would be impossible, or it would be a poor diversion. We destroy B in our caprice, and A and C are continuous; since being only separated by B, when it disappears the extremes meet. But in this case it is no longer A, but B, for B is the instant which precedes C. We have no other distinction than that of priority with respect to C, and continuity with A. When, then, by the imaginary disappearance of B, A is brought into contact with C, it is converted into B. Moreover, A is not only connected with C, but is preceded by others; if, then, by the disappearance of B, it makes a step, so also must the whole infinite chain which precedes it. Each one is then a soldier, or rather no soldiery is possible, for we have taken an instant from the infinite chain, and so rendered it finite. Or, more distinctly; can we conceive yesterday or to-morrow without to-day, a future or a past without the present? Evidently we cannot. Time, then, is essentially composed of inseparable parts.

19. This similarity between time and space naturally leads us to believe that time is an abstract idea just as space is. What we have said of space is applicable to time, only with a few modifications exacted by the very nature of the thing. It can in no case be without utility, in scientific investigations, to approximate and compare these great ideas, which are as immense receptacles wherein our mind deposits its treasures. The actual corporeal universe, and all possible universes, are included in the idea of space; and all finite beings, corporeal or incorporeal, are included in that of time.

20. We may well suspect that these ideas, so intimately united to our perceptions, are formed in a similar manner; for it is probable that they belong to the order of those primitive laws which govern the development of our intellect.

21. The similarity between space and time must not make us ignore the differences which distinguish them.

I. All the parts of space are co-existent; otherwise, that continuity which is essential to them, would be inconceivable. Time is composed of successive parts; to imagine them co-existent, is to destroy the essence of time.

II. Space refers solely to the corporeal world, under only one aspect, that of continuity. Time extends to all that is successive, corporeal or incorporeal.

III. Consequently, the idea of space exists only in the geometrical order, of which it is the basis. The idea of time is mingled with every thing, and more especially with our own acts.

IV. Our soul, when reflecting upon itself, can totally prescind space, and forget all its relations with extended objects; but it cannot prescind time, which it finds necessary even to its own operations.

This last difference is a great help to the understanding in what the idea of time consists; and we venture to recommend it to the attention and memory of the reader.

CHAPTER IV
DEFINITION OF TIME

22. Time is duration; but duration without something which endures, is an absurdity. There can then be no time without something existing. The duration which we conceive, after reducing every thing to nihility, is a vain imagination; it is not an idea, but is rather in contradiction with ideas.

An important consequence flows from this; it is, that time in itself, cannot be defined with absolute elimination of every thing to which it refers. Time, then, has no proper existence; and separated from beings is annihilated.

23. Hence, also, it follows that that infinity which we attribute to time, has no rational foundation. We have no other reason to affirm this infinity than a vague conception, which presents it as such; but we cannot fail to perceive that this conception also exists, even if we suppose all to be reduced to nothing. If, then, there is in this supposition a vain diversion of the imagination, it is not an idea, but a contradiction with ideas; and what has once deceived us, no longer deserves any credit. Those infinite ages of time which we conceive prior to the creation, are not nothing; they are an imaginary time, similar to an imaginary space.

24. Time has no necessary relation with movement, since if nothing were to move, or even no bodies to exist, we should nevertheless conceive time in the succession of operations of our soul. This last is indispensable; we must have some succession of things in order to conceive time. If we suppose nothing to change or to be altered, a being subject to no external or internal change, having one single thought always the same, one single will always the same, having no succession of ideas or acts of any kind whatever, we conceive nothing to which the idea of time is applicable.

Time is a measure; but what is it to measure in a being of this kind? Succession? But there is no succession. Duration? But what is there to measure in a duration always the same, which is only the same being? Duration must have parts given to it before it can be measured; but what parts has it? Those of time? But this would be a begging of the question, since time is applied to it when we are inquiring whether time is applicable to it. When theologians say that the existence of God cannot be measured by time, that there is no succession in eternity, but that all is united in a single point, they utter a profound truth; and Clarke, before ridiculing it, should have studied to understand it.

25. Time commences with mutable things; if they perish, it perishes with them. There is no succession without mutation; and consequently, no time.

26. What, then, is time? The succession of things considered in the abstract.

What is succession? Being and not-being. A thing exists; it ceases to exist; here we have succession. Whenever time can be calculated, there is succession; and whenever succession can be calculated a being and a not-being are considered. The perception of this relation, of this being and not-being, is the idea of time.

27. Time cannot exist without being and not-being; because in this, succession consists; wherever there is succession, there is some mutation; and there is no mutation without something being in another manner, and this other manner is not possible unless the prior manner ceases to be.

Substances, modifications, and appearances have no succession without this being and not-being. What is motion? The succession of the positions of a body with respect to various points; and this succession is verified by occupying some of these positions and destroying others. What is the succession of thoughts or affections of our mind? The not-being of some which were, and the being of others which were not.

28. Time, then, in things, is their succession, their being and not-being. Time in the understanding, is the perception of this mutation, this being and not-being.

CHAPTER V
TIME IS NOTHING ABSOLUTE

29. Is time something absolute? The definition given in the last chapter shows clearly enough that it is not. Time in things is not being only, nor not-being only, but the *relation* of being and not-being. Time in the understanding, is the perception of this relation.

The measure of time is nothing else than the comparison of mutations among themselves. To us, those mutations which seem to be unalterably uniform serve as the primitive measure. For this we have taken the movement of the sun. This movement varies when compared with that of the stars, and ceases to be the primitive measure when referred to this: and it was upon this the scholastics rested when they taught that the movement of the first heavens was the primitive measure of time.

30. But what if the velocity of the sun were augmented, and it should make its revolution in one half of its time? Would the hours continue the same? We distinguish. If this alteration should be verified solely in the solar movement, we should perceive the discordance between this and all other movements; and perceiving this alteration in the sun, we should continue to refer our hours as things fixed to other measures, to our own movements, to our time-pieces, or to other heavenly bodies.

But if we suppose every thing to be changed at one and the same time, and in the same proportion; the movement of all the heavens and of every thing terrestrial to be doubly accelerated, but in such a way as not to increase the rapidity of our thoughts; we should indeed discover an alteration, but we should not know whether to attribute it to the world or to ourselves; we should perceive a discrepancy between our thoughts and these movements, but should not know whether these were accelerated or our thoughts retarded.

If this rapidity be also communicated to us, so that such or such a series of thoughts formerly corresponding to so many minutes is now made in one half the number, we should then witness a perfect correspondence in all things; we could perceive no mutation. An hour, for example, is to us only the perception of the relation of certain mutations: so long as this relation continues the same, there will be no alteration in the hour.

31. To take away from time every idea of absolute, seems an absurdity to the imagination, but not to reason. This case will make this evident. Not the man, the best skilled in perceiving the succession of time, can, if he look at no time-piece, nor refer to any measure for twelve hours, say whether eleven hours and a half or twelve hours have passed. If he live long in this way, he will become totally incapable of estimating time; if locked up in a dark dungeon for several months, he will believe he has spent years there. The idea, therefore, of the measure of time, is nothing absolute; it is essentially relative; it is the perception of the relations between various mutations. So long as these relations remain whole and intact, time will be to us the same.

CHAPTER VI
DIFFICULTIES IN THE
EXPLANATION OF VELOCITY

32. Here arises a serious difficulty: if time be nothing absolute, greater or less velocity is inexplicable. This seems to result even from what we have said, that if the relation of movements be not changed, any augmentation or diminution of velocity is impossible; because, if velocity be in necessary relation to time, and time itself be nothing but the relation of mutations, it is inconceivable how time, and consequently how velocity, can be changed without changing the relation of mutations. Thus it would be impossible for the velocity of the whole mechanism of the universe to be changed, just as it would be absurd to say that the stars and every thing that exists may now experience the same changes of velocity. This would destroy the very idea of velocity; at least if taken as something absolute, wherein different grades may be considered.

33. Let us now examine this difficulty, which indeed deserves to be examined, for it seems to contradict our most common ideas.

First of all, we must premise that velocity is not something absolute, but a relation. Physicists and mathematicians express it by a fraction whose numerator is the space run over and whose denominator is the time consumed. Making V the velocity, S the space, and T the time, we shall have $V = S/T$. This shows the velocity to be essentially a *relation*; for it cannot be otherwise expressed than by the ratio of the space to the time.

34. This mathematic formula expresses the idea we all have of velocity; it expresses in three letters what the unlettered man repeatedly says to himself. The velocity of two horses is ascertained not solely by the space they have passed over, nor solely by the time they have consumed in their career, but by the greater or less space passed over in a given time; or by the longer or shorter time required to pass over a given space.

To deny, then, to velocity an absolute nature, is nothing new; for we all of us make it essentially consist in a relation.

35. In the expression V = S/T two terms enter, space and time. Viewing the former in the real order, abstraction made of that of phenomena, we more easily come to regard it as something fixed; and we comprehend it in a given case without any relation. A foot is at all times a foot; and a yard, a yard. These are quantities existing in reality; and if we refer them to other quantities, it is only to make sure that they are so; not because their reality depends upon the relation. A cubic foot of water is not a cubic foot because the measure so says, but on the contrary, the measure so says because there is a cubit foot. The measure itself is also an absolute quantity; and in general, all extensions are absolute, for otherwise, we should be obliged to seek measure of measure, and so on to infinity. True, to call things large or small depends upon comparison; but this does not change their own quantity. The diameter of the earth, compared with an inch measure, is immense; but it is an almost imperceptible point compared with the distance of the fixed stars; yet this does not prevent the inch measure, the diameter of the earth, and the distance to the fixed stars, from being values in themselves determinate, and independent of each other. [27]

If the denominator in S/T were a quantity of the same kind as space, that is, having determinate values, existing and conceivable by themselves alone, the velocity, although still a relation, might also have determinate values, not indeed, wholly absolute, but only in the supposition that the two terms, S and T, having fixed values, are compared. Thus, if we require a velocity of 4, we have only to take a fixed quantity of space, and another fixed quantity of time, having the relation to each other of 4 to 1; and this is quite easy, when S and T are both absolute quantities. If, in this supposition, an acceleration or delay be required in the whole universe, nothing more would be required than to augment or diminish the time in which each part would have to traverse its respective space. But from the difficulties which we have on the one hand seen presented to the consideration of time as an absolute thing, and from the fact that, on the other hand, no solid proof can be adduced to show such a property to have any foundation, it follows that we know not how to consider velocity as absolute, even in the sense above explained.

36. Hence a consequence not less important than striking, as to the possibility of a universal acceleration or retardation. If we would have an acceleration or retardation of the whole machine of the universe, and should abandon all motion to which we might refer time, should at once change all, not excluding the operations of our own soul, we should have a problem proposed to us that appears insolvable, nothing less than the realization of an impossibility; the relation of many terms would have to be changed without undergoing any change. If velocity be only the relation of space and

time, and time only the relation of spaces traversed, it is the same thing to change them all in the same proportion, and not to change them at all; it is to leave every thing as it is.

37. The singularity of such consequences ought not to be a sufficient excuse for abandoning them. We must not forget that we are examining the common ideas of time and velocity in their most transcendental aspect, and that it is by no means astonishing that our mind finds itself, as it leaves its ordinary walks, in an entirely new atmosphere, wherein it seems to discover contradictions. When we examine the ideas of time and velocity, we unwittingly fall into the error of uniting them in the same explanation. We would prescind them; but this we do only with great difficulty, and we often fall into a vicious circle. Hence it is that when, by a great effort, we succeed in really prescinding, the consequences that follow seem contradictory; but this apparent contradiction arises solely from our not having persevered with due firmness in our prescision; and as, in this case, the understanding starts from two different suppositions, whereas it believes that it starts from one alone, the results seem to it contradictory, which in reality they may not be. The same thing occurs in the examination of the idea of space. [28]

CHAPTER VII
FUNDAMENTAL EXPLANATION
OF SUCCESSION

38. The reasons that destroy the absolute nature of time, inasmuch as it is subject to measure, do not seem fully to obviate another difficulty, arising from the consideration of time in itself. If indeed time be succession, what is this succession? It is evident that things succeed each other; but if there be no *before* or *after*, that is, time existing before succession, since succession consists in some things coming *after* others, what is the meaning of succeeding each other? Thus, time is explained by succession, and succession by time. What is *afterwards* but a part of time that is in relation with a *heretofore*?

39. What we said in the fourth chapter does not seem completely to solve the difficulty; for being and not-being do not form succession, save only inasmuch as one comes *after* the other, that is, inasmuch as it presupposes the time to be explained already to exist. There may be a simultaneous being and not-being of distinct things; and there is in one and the same thing no repugnance between being and not-being, if not referred to the same time. In such a case, therefore, this is always presupposed so to be; since in one and the same thing, being and not-being are inconceivable unless at different instants of time. Hence it follows that being and not-being do not sufficiently explain time.

40. This difficulty is indeed grave; and we must, in order to solve it, elaborate a fundamental explanation of succession. This we shall endeavor to do, and without in any sense supposing the idea of time.

41. There are things which exclude, and things which do not exclude each other. When we have existence of things which exclude each other, we have succession. If in a line a————b————c, a body be at a, it cannot pass to b, without ceasing to be at a. The situation at b excludes that at a; and so also that at c excludes that at b. When we see things exist notwithstanding this reciprocal exclusion, we find succession.

42. Succession is, in reality, the existence of things mentally exclusive of each other. What each involves is the being of that which excludes, and the not-being of that which is excluded.

43. This exclusion prevails in all variations; and therefore, we find succession in every variation. Variation is the mutation of states; the loss of one, and the acquisition of another; therefore, there is exclusion, for being excludes not-being, and not-being, being.

44. When we perceive these distinctions, these exclusions realized, we perceive succession, time. When we compute these exclusions, these distinctions in which distinct and exclusive things are offered to us, such as being and not-being, we compute time.

45. Here arises a difficulty. If succession involves exclusion, and there is no succession without exclusion, it follows that things which do not exclude each other are simultaneous; and from this we infer the absurdity of saying, that the things happening in the time of Adam, which do not exclude those of our own time, are simultaneous. The motion of the plants of Paradise excludes not that of plants in gardens now existing; this motion, then, is simultaneous with that; the motion that was then is the present; and the present motion was then; which is inconceivably absurd.

This difficulty is serious: it seems to be based upon a reason founded in evident truths; but it is not impossible to give a solution of it.

46. Were there to exist one thing which excluded nothing, and was excluded by nothing, it would be simultaneous with every thing. Know you what this thing is? There is but one, God. It is therefore that the theologians say, with great truth, and with a profoundness which has not, perhaps, been at all times understood even by those who have made the remark, that God is present to all times; that to him there is no succession, no *before* or *after*; that to him every thing is present, is *now*.

47. Of God alone is this true; in all else there is some exclusion, being and not-being, and therefore succession. Let us now, for example, examine how the motion of the plants in our gardens is excluded by that of the garden of Eden. How are those of our gardens moved? By existing, and also by being subject to conditions necessary to motion. How do they exist? By a development of the germs they themselves contain. What is this development? A series of motions, of being and of not-being, and consequently of things that exclude each other. There is, then, no simultaneousness between those of the garden of Eden and those of our own gardens; for between the former and the first germ, there was no mediation other than the movement of the first development; whereas, between the movements of those of our gardens and the first germ, many others have intervened. Here we have exclusion, being and not-being. The number of exclusions necessary to existence is very different in the two cases; therefore, there is no simultaneousness. Considering all the developments, and all

the changes of the orb, as a dilated series of terms interlaced by a mutual dependence, as in fact they are by the laws of nature; and calling these terms A, B, C, D, E,—N, the plants of the garden of Eden belong to the term A, and those of ours, to the term N.

48. The non-simultaneousness of motion is proved in the same manner as the non-simultaneousness of existence, for motion is a manner of existing. Moreover, the air which agitates the plants of our gardens has been moved by another, and this other by yet another; and these motions, subject to all the fixed and constant laws of nature, are all interlinked from the very first motion, just as the wheels are interlocked in a system of machinery. But as the curvature of one wheel is not that of the other, so these motions are different, and exclude one another down to the last, which is the air which moves the present plants.

49. This explanation of succession and time, throws much light on the idea of eternity; and shows that eternity, or the simultaneousness of all existence, belongs only to the immutable being. All mutable beings, which necessarily imply a transition from not-being to being, and from being to not-being, involve a succession, if not in their substance, at least in their modifications.

50. This explains how the idea of time is found in almost all our conceptions, and is expressed in all languages. Man continually perceives being and not-being in all around him. He perceives it within him, in the multitude of his thoughts and affections; at one time agreeing, at another disagreeing; sometimes connected, and sometimes separated; but always distinguished from one another, always producing different modifications in the mind: they therefore exclude each other, and cannot co-exist; because the existence of one excludes the existence of the other.

CHAPTER VIII
WHAT IS CO-EXISTENCE?

51. If the succession of time involves exclusion, there must be co-existence where there is no exclusion: therefore, supposing that God has created other worlds, they must necessarily be contemporaneous with the present; for it is evident that they would not be excluded; and as they have not the mutual relation of cause and effect like the phenomena of the present world, we cannot apply to them the explanation which we gave to show that the motion of the plants of Paradise was not contemporaneous with the motion of the plants in our gardens. We must, therefore, hold that it would have been impossible for another world to exist before the present world; and that though God might create as many beings as he pleased, yet, so long as they do not exclude each other, they must be contemporaneous.

52. This difficulty is not easy to solve, unless we have perfectly understood the meaning of the word exclusion. By exclusion is meant, not only the intrinsical repugnance of one being to another, but that, for one reason or another, whether intrinsical or extrinsical, the existence of one implies the negation of the existence of the other. This explanation solves the difficulty.

53. Two worlds, entirely independent of one another, could have been subjected to this exclusion by the will of God. God can create one without creating the other; in this case, we find the existence of the first and the negation of the existence of the other. God can cease to preserve the first, and create the second; we then find the existence of the second and the negation of the first. In both these cases, there is *before* and *after*, a succession in existence. God can create both; we can conceive the existence of both without the negation of the existence of either; this is co-existence.

54. We shall understand the whole question much better, if we examine for a moment the meaning of co-existence. Two beings co-exist, or exist at the same time, when there is no succession of one to the other, when both exist, when there is not the existence of one and the negation of the other. In order to conceive co-existence, we need only conceive the existence of two beings: we form the idea of succession, by combining with the idea of the

existence of one the idea of the negation of the other. The co-existence of two beings is their existence; their succession is the being of one, and the not-being of the other. Being refers only to the present; the past and the future are not being. That only is which is, not that which was, or which will be. There is a profound truth, a sound philosophy, and an admirable ontology in those words of the sacred text: "I am who am. He who is, hath sent me to you."

55. Without being and not-being, there is no succession, there is no time, there is only the present, there is eternity. To a being immutable in itself, and in all its acts, one in its intelligence, one in its will, always its own object, unchangeable, in the plenitude of its being, without any kind of negation, — to such a being there is neither *before* nor *after*; there is only *now*. If you give to it the succession of instants, you apply to it, without any ground, the work of your imagination. Reflect well on the meaning of *before* and *after*, in that which can change in nothing, by nothing, and for nothing, and you will see that succession is in this case a word without any meaning. We attribute to it succession because we judge the object by our perceptions, and our perceptions are successive; they have an alternative of being and not-being, even when applied to an immutable object.

56. Every one may experience this in his own mind. Conceive two beings to exist; add to this thought nothing accessory, neither the negation of being, nor of time, nor of any thing else, — merely conceive the existence of two beings, and see if any thing is wanting to complete your idea of their co-existence. If, on the contrary, you wish to perceive succession, or difference of instants, you must perceive the existence of one, and the negation of the existence of the other. Therefore, the idea of co-existence is simple, and implies only the existence of the beings, but the idea of succession is composed of the combination of being with not-being.

57. I must here call attention to the fruitfulness of the idea of being, which, combined with the idea of not-being, furnishes the idea of time. We have before seen, that the ideas of unity and number were favored in the same manner, and we shall soon have occasion to observe, how, from the ideas of being and not-being, spring others, which, although secondary in respect to these, are the most important of all the ideas which the human mind possesses. I call attention to this, from a desire that the reader may become accustomed to refer all ideas to a few points where they are united, not by a factitious chain imposed by arbitrary methods, but by the internal nature of things themselves. What extension is, in relation to sensible intuitions, the idea of being is, in relation to conceptions. The intuition of extension, and the idea of being, are the two fundamental points in all ideological and ontological science; they are two primitive data possessed by the mind, by

means of which it can solve all problems, either in the sensible order, or in the purely intellectual. Regarded from this point of view, every thing becomes clear, and is arranged in the most logical order, because it is the order of nature.

58. I wish to make one observation on the method which I have followed in this work. I did not think it well to explain separately my opinion of these general connections of all ideas; for then it would have been necessary to treat philosophy in a systematic order, placing at the beginning what ought to be at the end, and trying to establish as a preliminary doctrine, what ought only to be the result of a collection of doctrines. To attain my object, it was necessary to go on analyzing in succession facts and ideas, without reference to system, without doing violence to them, in order to make them conform to a system, but only examining them, in order to ascertain their result. This, undoubtedly, is the best method. We thus obtain the knowledge of truth as a fruit of our labors on facts, and are not obliged to alter objects for the sake of forcing them to bend to the author's opinion. After the application which we have been making of the ideas of being, and not-being, to one of the most abstruse points of metaphysics, it is not out of place to call the reader's attention to this for a moment, so that he may be able to see the connection of doctrines.

CHAPTER IX
PRESENT, PAST, AND FUTURE

59. After explaining the idea of co-existence, we came to the definition of the various relations which time presents. They are principally three: present, past, and future. All others are combinations of these.

60. The present is the only absolute time: by this I mean, that it needs no relation, in order to be conceived. The present is conceived without relation to the past or to the future. Neither the past nor the future can be conceived without relation to the present.

61. The *past* is an essentially relative idea. When we speak of the *past*, we have to take some point to which it refers, and in respect to which we say it is past. This point is the present, either in reality, or in the ideal order; that is to say, that by the understanding, we place ourselves in that point, and make it present to us, and in reference to it, we speak of the past.

To prove that the idea of past is essentially relative, we may observe, that by varying the points of reference, the past may cease to be considered as such, and may be presented as present or future. Speaking of the events of the time of Alexander, they are presented to us as past, because we consider them in relation to the present moment; but if we are speaking of the empire of Sesostris, the epoch of Alexander ceases to be past, and is converted into future. If we were relating events contemporary with the deeds of Alexander, this epoch would cease to be past or future, and would become present.

The past, therefore, is always in reference to a present point, taken in the course of time, and it is only in respect to this, that any thing is said to have been, to be past; without this relation, the idea of past is absurd, and it is impossible to conceive it.

62. What is the relation of past? According to the definition which we have given of time, when we perceive the being of any thing, and then its not-being, and the being of something else, we say the first is past in relation to the second.

63. What would take place, then, if we should perceive the being of something, and then its not-being, without relation to any other being? This hypothesis is absurd; for we must always have this other being, if we perceive being and not-being.

But it may be replied that we may suppose the disappearance of ourselves, and then the objection would be good. Even though we should disappear, there would still remain intelligences capable of perceiving being and not-being. If there were no finite intelligence, there would still be the infinite intelligence.

64. Here arises a new difficulty; for it may be asked whether the thing would be passed with relation to the infinite intelligence. If we admit that it would be, we seem to introduce time with the duration of God, by which we destroy his eternity, which excludes all succession. If we say that to the eyes of the infinite intelligence the thing would not be past, then it would not be past in reality; for things are as God knows them. Then there would be the idea of being and of not-being, and still there would not be the idea of past. This difficulty arises from a confusion of terms.

Let us suppose that God had created only one being, and this being had ceased to exist; and let us see what would be the result of this hypothesis. God knows the existence and the non-existence of the object. This intellectual act is most simple; there can be no succession in it. There is properly no past with respect to God, and applied to the object this idea can only mean its non-existence in relation to its existence which is destroyed. When the ideas are presented in this light it is easy to understand that there is no past in God, but that there is the knowledge of past things.

65. On this hypothesis, how can the time of only one creature be measured? By its changes. But if it has none? On this imaginary supposition there would be no time.

This conclusion is absolutely necessary, although it may at first sight seem strange. We must either abandon our definition of time, or else admit that there is no time where there is no change.

66. Whatever conclusions we form on questions founded on imaginary suppositions, this, at least, is certain—that the idea of past is essentially relative, and that on no supposition can we conceive the past, if we take from it all relation. The expression *has been* implies both being and not-being,—the succession which constitutes time. In this relation the order is such that not-being is perceived after being, and this is why it is called past.

67. The idea of the future is also relative to the present. The future is inconceivable without this relation. The future is that which is to come,— that which is to be with respect to a real or hypothetical *now*; for we may apply to the future what we said of the past, that it is changed by changing the point of its reference. The future for us will be past to those who come after us; that which was future to those past, is present or past to us.

The point of reference of the future is always a present moment; it cannot be referred to the past as its ultimate term; for it is in itself referred equally to the present.

68. Therefore all that we find in the idea of time that is absolute is the present. The present needs no relation. It not only needs none, but it admits none. We can neither refer it to the past nor to the future, because these two times both presuppose the idea of the present, without which they cannot even be conceived.

69. Time is a chain whose links are infinitely divisible. There is no time which we cannot divide into other times. The indivisible instant represents something analogous to the indivisible point; a limit which we approach without ever reaching, an unextended element producing extension. A geometrical point must be moved in order to generate a line; but no motion is conceived as possible unless we presuppose space in which the point moves; or in other words, when we treat of the generation of extension, we commence by presupposing it. A similar thing happens in relation to time. We imagine an indivisible instant, from the fluxion of which results the continuity of duration which we call time. But this fluxion is impossible, unless we suppose a time in which it flows. We wish to examine the generation of time, and we suppose it already existing, prolonged infinitely, as an immense line on which the fluxion of the instant takes place. What are we to infer from these apparent contradictions? Nothing but a strong confirmation of the doctrine which we have established.

Time distinguished from things is nothing. Duration in the abstract, distinguished from that which endures, is a being of reason, —a work which our understanding produces from the materials furnished by reality. All being is present. That which is not present is not-being. The present instant, the *now*, is the reality of the thing; it is not sufficient to constitute time, but it is necessary to time. There can be present without either past or future; but there can be neither past nor future without the present. When besides being there is not-being, and this relation is perceived, time begins. To conceive past and future without the alternation of being and not-being, as a sort of line infinitely produced in two opposite directions, is to take an empty play of the phantasy for a philosophical idea, and to apply to time the illusion of imaginary space.

70. Therefore, if there is only being, there is only absolute, present duration; therefore no past nor future, and, consequently, no time. Time is in its essence a successive, *flowing* quantity; it cannot be seized in its actuality; for it is always divisible, and every division in time constitutes past and future. This is a demonstration that time is a mere relation, and in so far as it is in things, it only expresses being and not-being.

CHAPTER X
APPLICATION OF THE PRECEDING DOCTRINE TO SEVERAL IMPORTANT QUESTIONS

71. This theory will be much better understood by its application to the solution of several questions.

I. How long a time had passed before the creation? None. As there was no succession, there was only the present, the eternity of God. All else that we imagine is a mere illusion, contrary to sound philosophy.

II. Was it possible for another world to have existed when this world's existence began? Undoubtedly it was; this would only require that God had created it, without creating this world; it would only require the being of the one and the not-being of the other. And as there was not-being because there was no creation, it follows that if God had created the one without creating the other, and had ceased to preserve the first when he created the second, there would have been succession and priority of time.

III. Here is another question which is somewhat strange, and at first seems very difficult. Was the existence of a world *prior* to this possible *in any time*? or, in other words, could another world have *ceased* to exist *some time before* the beginning of the existence of this world? This question implies a contradiction. It supposes an interval of time, that is, of succession, without any thing to succeed. If a world had ceased to exist, and no new world should exist, there would be nothing but God; there would then be no succession, there would be only eternity. To ask, therefore, how long a time they were apart, is to suppose that there is time, where there is none. The proper answer is, that the question is absurd.

But we shall be asked, were they distant, or were they not? There is no distance of time where there is no time; this distance is a mere illusion, by which we imagine time, while, by the state of the question, we suppose that there is no time.

Then it may be objected, that the two successive worlds must be necessarily immediate, that is to say, that the first instant of one must be immediately connected with the last instant of the other. I deny it. For immediateness of instants supposes the succession of beings mutually connected in a certain order; the two worlds in question would have no mutual relation; consequently, there would be neither distance nor immediateness between them.

But, it may be replied, there is no medium between being and not-being, and distance being the negation of immediateness, and immediateness the negation of distance, by denying one, we affirm the other; they must, therefore, either be distant or immediate. This reply also supposes something which we deny. It speaks of distance and immediateness, that is, of time, as though it were something positive, distinct from the beings themselves. The principle, that every thing is, or is not, *quodlibet est vel non est*, is applicable only when there is something; but when there is nothing, there is no disjunctive. The time of the two worlds is nothing, as distinguished from them; it is the succession of their respective phenomena; the succession of the two worlds, the one to the other, is nothing distinguished from them; it is the being of the one, and the negation of the other, and the being of the second and the negation of the first. God sees this; an intelligent creature would also see it, if he could survive the annihilation of the first world. To the eyes of God, who sees the reality, succession would be simply the respective existence and non-existence of the two objects. The intelligent creature would say, that the two worlds are immediate, if to the perception of the last instant of the annihilated world, the perception of a new existing world had followed without another intermediate perception; and he would say, that there is distance, if he had experienced various perceptions between the annihilation of the old and the perception of the new creation. The measure of this time would be taken from the changes of perceptions of this creature, and would be longer or shorter, according to the number of these perceptions.

72. The idea of time is essentially relative, as it is the ordered perception of being and not-being. The mere perception of one of the two extremes, would not be sufficient to produce the idea of time in our mind; for this idea necessarily implies comparison. The same is true of the idea of space, which has always a great resemblance to time. We cannot conceive space, or extension of any kind, without juxtaposition; that is to say, without relations of various objects. Multiplicity necessarily enters into the ideas of both space and time. Hence, we may say, that if we conceive a being, absolutely simple, with no multiplicity, either in its essence, or in its acts, but in which all is identified with its essence, there is no room for the ideas of space and time; and, consequently, they are mere fictions of the imagination, when we attribute to them any thing real, beyond the corporeal world, and before the existence of the created.

CHAPTER XI
THE ANALYSIS OF THE IDEA OF TIME CONFIRMS ITS RESEMBLANCE TO THE IDEA OF SPACE

73. Having explained the idea of time, and applied it to the most difficult questions, we may explain this doctrine still farther, by examining what we have already intimated concerning the resemblance between time and space. [29] There is analogy in the difficulties; analogy in the definitions of both ideas; analogy in the illusions which hinder the knowledge of the truth. What we announced before with respect to these two ideas, considering the idea of time as only what it appeared at first sight, we may now assert as the secure result of analytical investigations. I call attention in particular to the following parallel, because it greatly explains the ideas of both.

74. Space is nothing in itself, distinguished from bodies; it is only the extension of bodies: time is nothing in itself, distinguished from things. It is only the succession of things.

75. The idea of space is the idea of extension in general; the idea of time is the idea of succession in general.

76. Where there are no bodies, there is no space: where there are no things which succeed each other, there is no time.

77. An infinite space, before the existence of bodies, or outside of bodies, is an illusion of the imagination: an infinite time before the existence of things, or outside of them, is also an illusion.

78. Space is continuous: so is time.

79. One part of space excludes all others; one part of time also excludes all others.

80. A pure space, in which bodies are situated, is imaginary: a succession, a time, in which things succeed, is also imaginary.

81. That which is entirely simple has no need of space, and can exist without it: that which is immutable has no need of time, and can exist without it.

82. The simple and infinite is present to all points of space, without losing its infinity: the immutable and infinite is present to all instants of time, without altering its eternity.

83. Two things are distant in space, because there are bodies placed between them; this distance is only the extension of the bodies themselves: two beings are distant in time, because there are other beings placed between them; this distance is the existence of the beings which are placed between.

84. Extension needs no other extension, in which to be placed, otherwise we should have a *processus in infinitum*: the succession of things, for the same reason, needs no other succession in which to succeed.

85. Just as we form the idea of continued succession in space by distinguishing different parts of extension, and perceiving that one excludes the others, so we also form the idea of continued succession of time by distinguishing different facts and perceiving that one excludes the others.

86. In order to form determinate ideas of the parts of space, we must take a measure and refer to it: to form an idea of the parts of time we also need a measure. The measure of space is the extension of some body which we know: the measure of time is some series of changes which we know. To measure space we seek for fixed things, as far as possible; for the want of something better, men have recourse to the parts of the body, the hand, the foot, the yard, and the pace, which give an approximate, if not an exact measure. The exact sciences having advanced, they have taken for their measure the forty-millionth part of the meridian of the earth: time is measured by the motion of the celestial bodies, by the diurnal motion, the lunar, solar, and sidereal year.

87. The idea of number is necessary in order to determine space and compare its different parts: the same idea is necessary in the same manner to time. The discrete quantity explains the continuous.

CHAPTER XII
RELATIONS OF THE IDEA OF
TIME TO EXPERIENCE

88. If time is nothing distinct from things, how does it happen that we conceive it in the abstract, independently of things themselves? How does it happen that it presents itself to us as an absolute being, subject to no transformation or motion, while within it every thing is moved and transformed? If it is a subjective fact, why do we apply it to things? If it is objective, why is it mingled with all our perceptions? Because it contains a necessity sufficient to be the object of science.

The idea of time, whatever it may be, seems prior to all perception of transformation, the consciousness of all internal acts included. It is impossible for us to know any of these things, unless time serves as a receptacle in which we may place our own changes and those of others.

89. The idea of time is not the result of observation; for in that case it would be the expression of a contingent fact, and could not be the principle of science. We measure time with the same exactness as we do space, and it is one of the most fundamental ideas of the exact sciences, in so far as they have any application to the objects of nature.

90. It might seem to follow from this that the idea of time is innate in our mind; and that it is prior to all ideas, and even sensations; for both are necessarily involved in successive duration.

91. The necessity of the idea of time seems to prove that time is independent of transitory things; in this case we are obliged to convert it into a purely subjective fact, or else to grant it an objective reality, independent of that which is changeable. By the former we destroy it; by the latter we make it an attribute of the divinity. To deny time is to deny the light of the sun; to raise it to the rank of an attribute of divinity is to admit change in an immutable being. If we make it purely subjective, we deny it; if objective, we make it divine: is there no middle way?

92. I agree that the idea of time is not derived from mere experience; for experience could not furnish an element so solid and so fixed, on which

we may with perfect security rest all the observations of science. Still less can it be maintained, that the idea of time is derived from purely sensible experience, or that it is in itself a sensation.

93. The idea of time is not a sensation; for it is relative, and sensation is an affection of our being, without any reference to or comparison with any thing. When we experience sensations, if we had only the sensitive faculty, we should be limited to pure sensation, without any consideration of before or after, or any relation of any kind. Sensation, being limited to certain objects, cannot, like the idea of time, extend to all objects. By time, we measure not only the external world, but also the internal; not only the affections of the body, but also the most concealed and abstract actions of our mind. Time is, in itself, succession, and, in our mind, it is the perception of this succession; it cannot, therefore, present any object to the mind; even when time refers to objects, and is, as it were, the link between them, it is not itself either these objects themselves, nor the intuition of them. The idea of the time which measures the succession of a sound or of a sight, clearly is not either the sound or the sight, but the perception of their succession, of their connection. If it were the sight alone, or the sound alone, either the sight or the sound would alone be sufficient in order to perceive time, which is absurd; for there is no time without succession, and consequently there can be no time which measures two sensations without these sensations. The idea of time is independent of either of the two; it is superior to them; it is a sort of universal form, independent of this or that matter; so that, if after the sound, instead of the sight, another sound should be perceived by us, the measure of the succession would be the same, and this measure is nothing more than the idea of time. Sensations being mere contingent facts, cannot be the foundation of necessary and universal truths, they cannot serve as the basis of a science. But the idea of time is one of the principal ideas in all the physical sciences, and, like extension, is subjected to a very rigorous calculation; therefore, it is not a sensation, and it is not derived from sensation.

94. Purely experimental cognitions are confined to the sphere of experience; the idea of time extends to the whole real and possible order, it teaches us not only what *is*, but what *may*, and what *must* be; its relations are of absolute necessity, and may be subjected to the strictest calculation; therefore it contains something more than the elements furnished by sensible or insensible experience. It is not otherwise possible to explain the

necessity which it involves, or to pass beyond a collection of contingent facts to arrive at the possession of an element of science.

95. Let us observe, as we pass, that here is found another proof that the system of Condillac is neither true nor subsistent. His system has been found insufficient to explain any fundamental idea, and it does not explain the idea of time, any more than the rest, although it seems as though this idea must have the most intimate relations to the sensible order.

96. If the idea of time is not merely experimental, how explain the priority and necessity of time?

CHAPTER XIII
KANT'S OPINION

97. Kant uses the same theory to explain time that he used to explain space. Time, according to him, is nothing in itself, neither is it any thing in things; it is a subjective condition of intuition, a form of the internal sense, by means of which phenomena are presented to us as successive, just as space was the form by which they are presented as continuous. To speak frankly, it seems to me that this is saying nothing; it affirms a well-known fact, but does not explain it. Who does not know that what we perceive we perceive in succession—that we perceive even our own perceptions in succession? But what is succession? This is what he ought to have explained.

98. Kant says that time is only in us; but I should like to ask him, if succession is only in us. He pretends that we know nothing of the external world, but that we perceive certain appearances, or phenomena; but he does not deny that beyond the appearance there may be a reality. If this reality is possible, changes are possible in it; and change cannot be conceived without succession, nor succession without time.

99. According to Kant, the ideas of space and time are *à priori*, they cannot be empirical, or experimental; for in that case they could not be the basis of science; we could only affirm what we had experienced, and this only with respect to the cases in which we have experienced it. This is true, and I have demonstrated it in the last chapter; but, conceding this priority, it proves nothing in favor of Kant's system. The ideas of space and time, although *à priori*, may nevertheless correspond to something in reality, as follows from the theory by which I have explained them.

100. Time is not any thing which subsists by itself, but it is not equally certain that it does not belong, as an objective determination, to things, and that nothing remains of it, if we abstract it from all the subjective impressions of intuition. I have demonstrated that time does not subsist by itself, and that a duration without any thing which endures, is an absurdity; but it does not follow from this that the order represented by the idea of time is not something real in the objects. Abstracting it from our intuition, there still remains something which verifies the propositions by which we express the properties of time.

101. The German philosopher makes time purely subjective, and relies on the following argument: "If time were a condition belonging to the things themselves, or an order, it could not precede the objects as a condition of them, and be known and perceived *à priori* by synthetical judgments. This last is easily explained if time is nothing but the subjective condition under which all intuitions are possible in us. For then this form of the internal intuition can be represented before the objects, and consequently *à priori*....

"If we abstract our manner of perceiving ourselves internally, and of embracing, by means of this intuition, all external intuitions in the faculty of representation, and consequently take objects just as they may be in themselves, time is nothing....

"I can say that my representations are successive, but this only means that we are conscious of them in a succession,—that is, in a form of the internal sense. Time would not therefore be any thing in itself, nor a determination inherent in things." [30]

102. It is easy to see that the philosopher is struggling between two difficulties. The first is, how to explain the necessity involved in the idea of time, if he makes it proceed from experience. The second is, how, if it is not derived from experience, it can be found really in things, or, at least, how we can know that it is found in them.

Hence, he concludes, that it is not possible to save the necessity involved in the idea of time, unless by making it a purely subjective fact, a form of an intuition, entirely independent of the reality of things.

It seems to me, that by attending to the principles established above, we can give an objective value to time, independently of our intuition, and explain its relations to experience, without destroying the necessity contained in its idea.

CHAPTER XIV
FUNDAMENTAL EXPLANATION OF THE OBJECTIVE POSSIBILITY AND OF THE NECESSITY OF THE IDEA OF TIME

103. Things in themselves, abstracted from our intuition, are susceptible of change. Where there is change, there is succession, and where there is succession, there is a certain order in the things which succeed,—an order which is really in the things themselves, although it does not subsist by itself, separated from them.

Kant might object to this, that perhaps the changes are not in things, but in the phenomena, or the manner in which they are presented to our intuition. But he cannot deny, that whether these changes are in the reality, or not, they are, at least, possible, independently of the phenomena. Therefore, he asserts, without reason, that time in the things is nothing, and that it is only the form of our internal sense. If he admits the possibility of real changes, he must also admit the possibility of a real time; if he denies that it is possible for the things in themselves to be really changed, we would ask him how he came to know this impossibility,—he, who limits all our knowledge to the purely phenomenal order. We cannot know that a thing is impossible in an order, if we know nothing of this order; if Kant maintains that we know nothing of things in themselves, he cannot prove that we know the impossibility of their really changing.

104. It is then demonstrated that time, or a real order in things, is, at least, possible. Therefore, we cannot say that time is a purely subjective condition, to which nothing can correspond in the reality.

105. Admitting the possibility of an objective value of the idea of time, not only in reference to the purely phenomenal order, but also to the transcendental, or rather to things considered in themselves, and abstracted from our intuition; we shall see how the objectiveness of the idea of time and its relations to experience can be shown, without destroying the intrinsic necessity which makes it one of the principal elements of the exact sciences.

106. Time, considered in things, is the order of their being, and their not-being. The idea of time is the perception of this order in its greatest generality and abstracted from the objects which are contained in it. As our understanding evidently can consider a purely possible order of things, the idea of time extends to the possibility as well as the reality. This is why we conceive time before and after the present world, similar to the space which we imagine beyond the limits of the universe. The idea of being, elevated to a purely possible region, in which it is abstracted from all individual phenomena, is freed from the instability to which the objects of our experience are subject: it can then be an absolutely necessary element of science; for it expresses a relation which is not affected by any thing contingent. These observations are a solution of all difficulties.

CHAPTER XV
IMPORTANT COROLLARIES

107. Is the idea of time derived from experience? This question is answered by what we said of the idea of being. It is not a type existing previous to all sensation and to all intellectual act; it is a perception of being and not-being which accompanies all our acts, but is not presented to us separately until reflection eliminates from it all that does not belong to it. This perception is the exercise of an innate activity, which is subjected to the conditions of experience in all that concerns the beginning and the continuation of its acts, but not with respect to its laws which are characteristic of it, and correspond to the pure intellectual order. This activity is unfolded in the presence of causes or occasions which excite it, and its exercise ceases when these conditions are wanting; but while the activity acts, it exercises its functions in accordance with fixed laws which are independent of the objects exciting it.

108. It is therefore clear that the idea of time is not strictly derived from experience, except inasmuch as the mind is excited to develop its activity by experience. Neither is it entirely independent of experience; for without experience we should have no knowledge of change, and consequently the intellect would not perceive the order of being and not-being, in which the essence of time consists.

109. Hence the idea of time is not a form of the sensibility, but of the pure intellectual order; and although it descends to the field of sensible experience, it does so after the manner of other general conceptions.

110. The idea of time is one of the most universal and indeterminate ideas which our mind possesses; for it is the combination of the two most general and most indeterminate ideas, being and not-being. Here is the reason why the idea of time is common to all men, and is presented to us as a form of all our conceptions and of all the objects known.

The ideas of being and not-being, entering as primitive elements into all our perceptions, generate the idea of time. We therefore find this idea in the inmost recesses of our soul as a condition from which we cannot withdraw ourselves, and from which we exempt the Infinite Being himself only by an effort of reflection.

111. The transition from the purely intellectual order to the field of experience takes place in the idea of time, in the same manner as in the other intellectual conceptions. I have, therefore, nothing to add to what I have already said on this point when explaining it elsewhere. [31]

CHAPTER XVI
PURE IDEAL TIME AND EMPYRICAL TIME

112. Time is not only conceived as a general order of change, or as a relation of being and not-being; but also as something fixed, which can be measured with exactness. Thus, before the creation of the world, we conceive not only an abstract order, or time, but a time composed of years, of centuries, or some other terms. But this, if we closely examine it, is only an idea in which we conceive the phenomena of experience under a general view, taking them out of actuality and contemplating them in the sphere of possibility. Neither the years nor the centuries existed when there was nothing by which they could be measured. If we imagine a sort of vague line of duration prolonged to infinity, abstracting it from the measure and the object measured, we become the sport of our imagination, and are entangled in contradictions from which it is difficult to extricate ourselves.

113. The pure and abstract idea of time admits no measure; it is a mere relation of being and not-being. The measure is possible only when the idea of time is combined with the phenomena of experience.

Subject as we are to change, and situated amid beings as changeable as ourselves, we should certainly fall into the greatest confusion of our ideas, if in this ebb and flow of external as well as internal existences which appear to us, we had not the greatest facility in referring them to fixed measures, which are the thread that guides us in this labyrinth of continual variations.

114. Two things are required for this measure: first, a suitable phenomenon, and secondly, the idea of number. The common idea of time which serves for the ordinary purposes of life of these three elements: the pure idea of time, or the relation of being and not-being; secondly, a suitable phenomenon to which we apply this pure idea; and thirdly, the numeration of the changes of this phenomenon. Apply this observation to all the measures of time, and you will find these three elements always sufficient, but always indispensable also.

115. From this we deduce the necessity of time, even considered empirically; for it involves two ideas, the one metaphysical, and the other mathematical, applied to a fact. The metaphysical idea is the relation of being

and not-being; the mathematical idea is number; and the fact is the sensible phenomenon, as, for example, the solar, or human motion. Metaphysics and arithmetic take charge of the absolute certainty; the fact observed answers for the experimental certainty; and as, on the other hand, this phenomenon is supposed to be certain, because, in case it were necessary we could abstract it from the reality, and attend only to the possibility; it follows that time, even considered empirically, may become the object of the exact sciences.

116. This theory does not make time a purely subjective condition, nor grant it a nature independent of things; it reconciles the pure intellectual order with the order of experience; and places man in communication with the real world, without creating a contradiction in his ideas.

CHAPTER XVII
RELATIONS OF THE IDEA OF TIME AND
THE PRINCIPLE OF CONTRADICTION

117. Let us explain the true meaning of the principle of contradiction. "It is impossible for any thing to be and not be at the same time." The connection of the ideas contained in this principle seems at first sight to be explained without any difficulty; so that, to raise questions as to its true sense is to place ourselves in contradiction with one of the fundamental truths on which rests the edifice of our knowledge. For, if there be any doubt as to the true meaning of the principle, it may be understood in several ways, and then there will be another doubt as to whether the generality of men understand it as they ought to, and whether, consequently, it is for them a solid foundation of knowledge.

This difficulty ceases to be one when we reflect that the most evident axioms may be considered in two manners: empirically, or scientifically; or in other words, inasmuch as they are the application, or the object of analytical examination. In the first manner, they are equally certain and equally clear to all men; in the second, they are subject to difficulties. The principle,—things equal to a third are equal to each other,—considered empirically, is absolutely certain and evident to all men: all men, from the wisest to the most ignorant, compare things with a third, when they wish to ascertain their equality or inequality; this is only an application of the principle. If you ask them the reason of this proceeding, although they may not enunciate the axiom in its precise terms, they refer to it in different ways: "These two tables are equal, because I have measured them, and they are each four feet square." Probably the generality of men, not accustomed to reflect on their knowledge, would not express the principle in universal and precise terms; as, "These two tables are equal, because they have a common measure, and things equal to a third are equal to each other." Yet they are just as clearly certain of the principle, and apply it, without any danger of error, in all real and possible cases. This is what I call the empirical knowledge of principles,—a knowledge which is perfect in the direct order, and is defective only in the reflex order. [32]

It is very easy to reconcile the difficulty in the analysis of the principle, with its clearness when applied to ordinary purposes, or to those of science. Thus, in the example given, the analysis of the term *equal* leads to the analysis of the term *quantity*: reflection can discover in this difficulties which, although they do not disturb mankind in the possession of truth, are difficulties notwithstanding. Geometry is undoubtedly a science perfectly evident and certain; but who can deny that the idea of extension presents serious difficulties, when examined before the tribunal of metaphysics? Universal arithmetic is, beyond all doubt, a science; yet the ideas of quantity and number, which are indispensable to it, give rise to the most abstruse questions of metaphysics and ideology. In general, it may be said that there is no branch of our knowledge which is exempt from difficulties, considered in its root; but these difficulties, arising from reflection, do not in any way lessen the certainty of direct knowledge.

Hence it is no objection that the analysis of the principle of contradiction presents difficulties; nor are we therefore to fear for the firmness of the edifice of our knowledge. It would be of no service to us not to attend to these difficulties, if they really existed; a difficulty does not vanish because we shut our eyes so as not to see it. Let us not, therefore, vainly fear to examine the true sense of the principle of contradiction.

118. It seems that this principle either does not exist, or has no meaning, unless we presuppose the idea of time; and, on the other hand, we cannot conceive time, unless we presuppose the principle of contradiction. Do we thus fall into a vicious circle, and this too in the fundamental principle of all our knowledge? This is a difficulty which I shall first develop and present more clearly.

The principle of contradiction presupposes the idea of time, because there would be no contradiction if being and not-being were not referred to the same time. This last condition is altogether indispensable; for, suppressing the simultaneousness, there is no contradiction in a thing both being and not-being. Not only is there no contradiction in this, but it is a thing which we constantly meet with, in every thing around us. We see being and not-being in things which pass from existence to non-existence, or from non-existence to existence.

Although the simultaneousness may not be expressed in the principle of contradiction, it is always understood, so that we should gain nothing by adopting Kant's formula. [33] In whatever terms the principle may be enunciated, it is always true that the same thing cannot both be and not be at the same time, but may very well be at one time and not be at another time.

The idea of time is therefore necessary in order that the contradiction may follow in some cases, and disappear in others. If the time implies simultaneousness, it generates the contradiction; if it implies succession, it destroys the contradiction; because being and not-being are impossible, unless we presuppose a successive duration, among the different parts of which, things that would otherwise be contradictory are distributed.

119. The idea of time also presupposes the principle of contradiction; for, if time, in things, is only being and not-being, and in the intellect, the perception of this being and not-being; we cannot perceive time without having perceived being and not-being; and as these ideas, without succession, involve a contradiction, we must perceive the principle of contradiction when we perceive time. I have said that succession implies the mutual exclusion of the things which succeed; now, the first exclusion is the principle of contradiction: in perceiving time, we perceive succession; therefore we have already perceived the contradiction.

120. These remarks might incline us to believe it necessary to choose between a vicious circle, which is inadmissible in the foundation of all our knowledge, and an explanation of time, independently of being and not-being. If we conceived time as existing by itself, as a sort of line prolonged to infinity; as a form of things, but distinct from them all; as a vague capacity in which successive beings might be placed, just as we situate co-existences in space, — then the idea of time would not be explained by the principle of contradiction, and we could only say that it was completed by it. "When we say that it is impossible for the same thing to be and not be at the same time, but that it is possible for the same thing to be and not be at different times, the contradiction is affirmed or taken away, accordingly as the being and not-being are referred to the same point or to different points in this vague extension, this infinite line, which we call successive duration, and in which we conceive changeable things to be distributed." This explanation is convenient; but it has a defect, that it cannot stand a philosophical examination, as we have seen in the preceding chapters. We must therefore have recourse to another class of considerations.

121. To solve this difficulty, it is necessary to determine precisely the meaning of our ideas. The expression of *vicious circle* is improperly applied to this case. If we understand this, the whole difficulty is solved at once. In explaining things, which are not identical, a circle is a defect, and is called vicious; but when two things are identical at bottom, although they appear distinct, because presented under various aspects, it is impossible to explain one without stumbling, so to speak, on the other, or to approach one without meeting the other. Because they are presented under different aspects we are led to believe them distinct; but examining them analytically, we abstract

the difference of aspect, and penetrate to the reality, and discover the point where they are united, or, rather, where they are absolutely identified.

122. We may draw from these observations a criterion which we may use in a great many cases. When, in explaining two objects, we find ourselves led alternately from the one to the other, without any possibility of avoiding a circle, we may suspect that objects, which appear distinct, are not so in reality, and that the objects presented to the eyes of our understanding are not two objects, but only one object perceived in different ways.

123. This is true in the present instance. In explaining the principle of contradiction we encounter the idea of time, and in defining time we encounter the principle of contradiction, or the ideas of being and not-being. This is a circle, but an inevitable one; and therefore it ceases to be vicious.

124. What is the meaning of the principle of contradiction? Its true meaning is, that being excludes not-being, and not-being excludes being; that the nature of these conceptions is such that the affirmation of one implies the negation of the other, not only in the order of our ideas, but in reality. Let us call A any being whatever: the principle of contradiction means that A excludes not-A, and not-A excludes A. If we think A, the conception of not-A disappears; and if we think not-A, the conception of A disappears. If we affirm A in reality, we deny not-A, and if we affirm not-A in reality, we deny A. This is the true meaning of the principle of contradiction. If we reflect, we shall find that, as far as possible, we have abstracted the idea of time; for we have only considered the mutual exclusion of A and not-A, in reference to a *simul*, an indivisible point of duration, which, involving no succession, does not give us the idea of time. I said, *as far as possible*; because as soon as we think A and not-A, the idea of succession, and consequently of time, arises in our mind.

125. A and not-A imply contradiction; but not so that they absolutely cannot be realized. The exclusion is conditional; that is, it exists as long as the contradictory extremes are simultaneous, or referred to an indivisible *now*; but we discover no intrinsic necessity of existence in the idea of A: consequently, although we know that while A is, not-A cannot be, we can very well conceive that A may cease to be, and not-A may begin to be. There is, in, that case, no contradiction, and we can easily reconcile in our mind the two ideas of A and not-A, by referring them to different instants.

126. Hence the perception of time implies the perception of beings that are not necessary,—of beings which, when they exist, may cease to exist, and when they do not exist, may begin to exist. The difference between necessary and contingent being is, that the existence of the former absolutely

excludes its non-existence, while the existence of the latter excludes its non-existence only conditionally, or on the supposition of simultaneousness.

127. This is why the principle of contradiction requires the condition of time. The objects which we perceive are changeable; there is nothing either in their nature or in their modifications which involves existence. If they are, they may cease to be; and if this change does not constantly occur in their substance, it does in their accidents. Therefore we cannot affirm the absolute, but only the conditional contradiction of their being and not-being; it exists only on the supposition of simultaneousness.

128. If we conceived only necessary being, we could have no idea of time: its existence absolutely excludes its non-existence, and therefore the contradiction would be always absolute, never conditional.

129. A most important consequence results from this analysis. The perception of time with us implies the perception of the non-necessity of things. When we perceive a being which is not necessary, we perceive a being which may cease to be, in which case we have the idea of succession, of real or possible time. Here another reflection arises which is also important: the idea of time is the idea of contingency: the consciousness of time is the consciousness of our weakness.

130. The idea of time is so deep in our mind, that without it we could not form the idea of the *me*. The consciousness of the identity of the *me* supposes a link [34] which it is impossible to find without memory. Memory necessarily involves the relation of *past*, and, consequently, the idea of time.

CHAPTER XVIII
SUMMING UP

Let us collect together the doctrines of the preceding chapters.

131. Time is a question difficult to explain. Whoever denies this difficulty shows that he has meditated but superficially on the matter.

132. Motion is measured by time; but it is not a sufficient definition of time to call it the measure of motion.

133. It is impossible to find a primitive measure of motion; we must, at last, take some measure or another, and although arbitrarily chosen, we must refer motion to it. It should be the most uniform measure possible.

134. The resemblance between the ideas of time and space creates a suspicion that they ought to be explained in a similar manner.

135. There is no duration without something which endures; therefore there is no duration separate from things. If nothing existed, there could be no duration.

136. There is no succession without things which succeed: therefore succession cannot be realized as a form independent of things, although it may be conceived in the abstract by itself.

137. Time implies *before* and *after*, and, consequently, succession. It is succession itself, because in conceiving succession, we conceive time.

138. Succession involves the exclusion of some things by others. This exclusion may either be founded on the essence of things, or be derived from an external cause.

139. Time, therefore, involves exclusion: it is the general idea of the order of changes, or of the mutual relation of being and not-being.

140. If there were no change there would be no time.

141. No time had passed before the existence of the world. There was no other duration than eternity.

142. Eternity is the existence of the infinite being, without any alteration either actual or possible.

143. Time is not any thing absolute and independent of things, but is really in them. It is the order between being and not-being.

144. Co-existence is merely the existence of various beings. To conceive many beings without the idea of the negation of being, is to have the perception of co-existence.

145. Time may be considered under three aspects; the present, the past, and the future. All other relations of time, differently expressed in different idioms, are only combinations of these.

146. The present is the only absolute time: it is conceived without relation to the past or the future; but the past and the future are not conceived without relation to the present.

147. The idea of present accompanies the very idea of being; or rather, it is confounded with the idea of existence; that which has no present existence is not being.

148. The idea of past time is the perception of not-being, or of a being that has been destroyed, in relation to a present being: the idea of future time is the perception of a possible being proceeding from a cause already determined, and in relation to a present being.

149. The idea of time is excited by experience; but it cannot be called a fact of mere observation; for this would be opposed to its intrinsic necessity, by virtue of which it is the object of the exact sciences.

150. Still less can we say, that this idea is confined to the sensible order, since it includes every manner of change in general, whether sensible or supersensible.

151. The idea of time being the perception of the order between being and not-being, this relation, considered in general, belongs to the pure intellectual order. The transition to experience is realized in the same manner as in other general and indeterminate conceptions.

152. It is necessary to make a distinction between pure ideal time and empirical time: pure ideal time is the relation between being and not-being, considered in the greatest generality and the most complete indeterminateness; empirical time is the same relation subjected to a sensible measure.

153. To measure this succession, three things are necessary, and their union forms the idea of empirical time. They are, first, the pure idea of being and not-being, or of change; secondly, the application of this idea to a sensible phenomenon, as, for example, the solar motion; and thirdly, the idea of number applied to the determining of the changes of this phenomenon.

154. We thus conceive why empirical time implies a true necessity, and is the object of science. Of the three elements which compose it, the first is a metaphysical idea, the second, a mathematical idea, and the third, a fact of observation, to which these ideas are applied. If this fact be not real, it must, at least, be possible, in order to save the necessity of the calculation which is based upon it.

155. There is a close relation between the idea of time and the principle of contradiction. Each is explained by the other, yet this is not a vicious circle. The principle of contradiction consists in the mutual exclusion of being and not-being, and the idea of time is the perception of the order between being and not-being. Analysis must therefore lead to a part which is identical in both, to the comparison of the ideas of being and not-being.

156. Without the idea of time, memory would be impossible; consequently also, the unity of consciousness.

CHAPTER XIX
A GLANCE AT THE IDEAS OF
SPACE, NUMBER, AND TIME

157. We may now mark out and determine with perfect exactness the necessary elements which form the object of the natural and exact sciences. This is not only curious, but highly important; for it presents under the simplest aspect, an immense field of knowledge, the limits of which expand, as we advance; so that, it is impossible to assign a limit to progress.

158. Space, number, and time, are the three elements of all the natural and exact sciences. All else contained in them pertains to mere experience, to the order of contingent facts, which involve no necessity, and cannot strictly be the objects of science.

159. Universal arithmetic is founded on the idea of numbers, geometry on that of space, and the idea of time places us in communication with the sensible world, so as to determine the relations of its phenomena. These phenomena are isolated contingent facts, and cannot become the object of science, until subjected to the general ideas of space, number, and time.

160. Hence, there are two parts in every natural science; the theoretic, and the experimental. The former is founded on necessary ideas, the latter on contingent facts; the first without the second, would not come down to the real world; the second without the first, would not rise to the regions of science.

161. The natural sciences merit the name of science, in proportion to the quantity of necessary elements which they contain, and the closeness of the connection by which they unite with them contingent facts. But as no natural science can be conceived, without contingent facts, so there is none entirely free from the contingency which they communicate.

162. These observations reveal a great simplicity in the elements of science, and we may push this simplicity much farther, if we recollect what has been said when analyzing the ideas of number and time.

163. The idea of number arises from the idea of being and not-being: the same is also true of the idea of time; therefore, at bottom, these ideas are but one, though presented under different aspects.

164. Hence, all the natural and exact sciences may be reduced to two elements: the intuition of extension, and the general conception of being. Extension is the basis of all sensible intuitions: externally, it is a necessary condition of the relations which we conceive in the corporeal world; internally, it is a perception, without which the sensibility could not represent external objects. The conception of being, is the basis of all conceptions; developed in different ways, it generates the ideas of number and time; and these, combined with extension, constitute the necessary part of all the natural and exact sciences.

165. The ideas of space, number, and time are common to all men; the proof that they are identical to all is, that, in their application, all are led to the same results, and in speaking of them they all use the same expressions. All men measure space, and its various dimensions; they all count, they all conceive time: why, then, is there so great difficulty in explaining these ideas? why such difference of opinion among philosophers? Here we have a confirmation of what we have said [35] of the strength of direct perception, and the weakness of reflex. When we content ourselves with the direct perception of space, of number, and of time, our ideas are clear, and the understanding feels its strength and energy, it extends the sphere of its knowledge beyond all limits, and raises the edifice of the mathematical and exact sciences. But as soon as it turns upon itself, and, leaving the direct perception, passes to the reflex, endeavoring to perceive its perception, its strength fails, and it falls into a confusion which gives rise to interminable disputes. We scarce perceive that idea, which, a moment ago, we applied to every thing, which penetrated all our cognitions, and circulated, like our life, through all our perceptions; but in its isolation, and its purity, it continually escapes from us; mingled with all things, we see that it is something distinct from them; we separate it from one, and it unites with another; we make an effort to cut it off from all that is not itself, and the mind feels a kind of dizziness come over it, every thing vanishes from before it, and, unable to reach the reality, it is forced to be contented with names, which it pronounces and repeats a thousand times, turning over in them the little reality which they contain.

167. One of the causes of this weakness and of the errors which are its ordinary consequence, is, as I have before said, our mad desire of representing every idea as an internal form, or image, whereas we ought to consider that in many cases there is only a perception, a simple act in the lowest depth of our mind,—an act, which can be represented by nothing,

which resembles nothing, and which cannot be explained in words, because it cannot be decomposed, and it is only present as a simple fact of consciousness. But this fact of consciousness is an active fact; by it we penetrate into things, and see what they have in common, and separate it from what is particular, establishing in our mind, as it were, a central, culminating point, from which we contemplate the internal and the external world, and roam through the boundless regions of possibility.

BOOK EIGHTH
THE INFINITE

CHAPTER I
TRANSITORY VIEW OF THE ACTUAL
STATE OF PHILOSOPHY

1. In the works on transcendental philosophy which have been published of late years, we find the words infinite, absolute, indeterminate, unconditioned, frequently repeated, and made to play a very prominent part in the explanation of the most recondite secrets which can be presented to the consideration of man. The words finite, relative, determinate, conditional, are easily combined with these; and from this combination they pretend that a ray of light will arise to dissipate the darkness of philosophical questions.

2. In spite of the bad use many make of such words, we must confess that the fact indicated is consoling by reason of the great desire there is to use them. This desire marks an effort in the human mind to raise itself from the mire in which the impious school of the last century has sunk it.

3. What was the world in the eyes of the false philosophers who preceded the French revolution? A mass of matter, subject to simple mechanical laws of motion, the whole explanation of which was given in two words, blind necessity. What was the human mind? Nothing but matter. What was thought? A modification of matter. In what did the difference between thinking and non-thinking matter consist? In a little greater or less subtilty, in a more or less happy disposition of atoms. What was morality? An illusion. What were sentiments? A material phenomenon. What was the origin of man? That of matter,—a phenomenon offered by a quantity of molecules, which at one moment happen to be disposed one way, and a moment after in a very different way. If you inquired if there were a destiny beyond the grave, We argue that question! they would answer with a scornful smile. Have you such a word as religion? The scorn increased and changed into contempt. Do you recognize the dignity of the human race? O, yes! we admit

this dignity, and we are of opinion that it is of the same nature as that of the brutes, only it has reached a higher degree of perfection. We do not deny that your form may be more noble and elegant than that of the monkey, nor do we dispute the superiority of your intelligence; but we would have you take good care not to make pretensions to a nobler origin or a loftier destiny. The course of ages may develop and perfect the monkey form, and render it equal with yours; it may develop and perfect his cerebral organs, so that from this very monkey, whose extravagant motions and ridiculous attitudes now amuse, men will be born such as were Plato, Saint Augustine, Leibnitz, or Bossuet.

4. With such a system, it was useless to deal in ideas: they retained only sensations. Whatever could occupy the mind of man, whether the most imbecile or endowed with the loftiest genius, was nothing more than a sensation transformed. The very brutes possessed all the elements of human intelligence; to think was only to feel more perfectly. Such was the last term of their analysis; such the result of their most accurate observation; such the solution their profoundest philosophy gave to the problems of man's understanding. Plato, Aristotle, Saint Augustine, Saint Thomas, Descartes, Malebranche and Leibnitz were nothing but sublime dreamers, whose genius strongly contrasted with their ignorance of the true nature of things. None of them knew any thing about ideology or metaphysics; these sciences were an unknown world until Locke and Condillac came and discovered them.

5. This school, as fatal as frivolous, has involved and stifled mind in matter. The butterfly could not unfold his wings of fair and various colors; he was forced to lay them off and to change into a stupid and filthy worm, entangled in a covering as loathsome and unclean as itself. In this consisted progress. The limit of ideological perfection was to deny ideas; that of metaphysical studies, to deny spirits; that of morals, to deny morality; that of society, to deny authority; that of politics, to establish license; that of religion, to deny God. Thus, human reason, thinking to advance, marched in a retrograde direction; and proposed to raise the edifice of its knowledge, when there was nothing left to demolish: thus they imagined to attain a scientific result by denying every thing, and by finally denying themselves.

6. At present, there is a reaction against so degrading a philosophy. We have only to open the writings of the philosophers of this age to convince ourselves of this consoling truth. We everywhere meet the word idea in contraposition to that of sensation; that of mind to that of matter; that of activity of thought to that of bodily motion; those of cause, order, liberty, of free will, morality, infinity. The ideas which accompany them are sometimes inexact, sometimes extravagant; but at the bottom of all this

we distinguish an anxious desire to rise from the abyss down to which an atheistical and material philosophy had dragged the human mind. Some who have contributed to the reaction do not admit a free and intelligent God, distinct from the universe. What we have said above is therefore true, that pantheism is atheism in disguise; nevertheless, the atheism of the pantheist now-a-days is an atheism which is ashamed to confess itself such, and which sometimes, perhaps, deceives itself, being persuaded that it is not.

7. The atheism of modern philosophers unites itself with the infinite: it does not reject those great ideas which as relics of a primitive tradition were common in the old world, and were afterwards fixed, cleared up and elevated by the superior teaching of Christianity. The philosophy of the last century sat down in the darkness and shadow of death and declared itself alone in possession of light and life. Philosophy now still remains in obscurity, but it is not satisfied with it, and gropes about in the dark, seeking some outlet to the regions of light. Hence those desperate efforts to resolve itself, not into matter, but into the focus of intelligence, into the *me*, that is, the mind: hence the continual use of the words absolute, unconditional, infinite, words which, notwithstanding they ordinarily lead to absurdities, do yet indicate a sublime aspiration.

8. These observations show that we do not confound the philosophy of to-day with that of the past century; that we do not regard the pantheism of to-day as a pure materialism, and that, notwithstanding the atheism of which we accuse the doctrine of certain philosophers, we do not deny that they have, even in the midst of their extravagance, preserved a kind of horror of it, and that, lost as they are in the labyrinth of their speculations, they seek the thread which shall conduct them to the gates of truth.

9. This act of justice we willingly render to modern philosophers, but it will not prevent us from combating their pretension to a merit they do not possess. They style themselves restorers of the spirituality of the soul, and of human liberty; and when they speak of God they almost exact a tribute of gratitude from him for having replaced him upon his throne. Before making such proud pretensions they ought to have considered that they are even yet far from the truth with respect both to God and to man, not only as Christianity has at all times taught it, but also as the most illustrious modern philosophers have professed it. They are ambitious to be called restorers, but their restoration with its licentious frequency is a new revolution, at times as terrible as the evil it attempts to combat.

10. Another consideration ought to have moderated their zeal to be thought inventors, which is that they have said nothing concerning God,

the human mind, thought, ideas, the liberty of freewill, which may not be read in all the works of the philosophers who flourished before, or even in the beginning of, the eighteenth century. Open the text-books of the schools, and you will find many things which they would have us believe to be important discoveries. The great philosophers gloried in knowing what they had before learned when children. The philosophical tradition of sound ideas was not interrupted during the past century. In many parts of Europe schools existed which taught them with scrupulous fidelity. And besides human schools, there was that of the God-Man, the Church of Jesus Christ, which, among its supernatural dogmas, preserved even natural truths, notwithstanding the senseless efforts which have been made to obliterate them.

11. To what, then, are the invention and restoration reduced? Invention there is not, either with respect to God, to the human mind, or to morality, for nothing true has been said of them which had not already been said. Restoration, properly so called, there is not; for what does not perish cannot be restored. The truth exists; and has been known and revered during the whole six thousand years it has refused to bow the knee to Baal. Let not deserters say, when they turn and come back to the truth that they have restored it, but that they have recovered it; not that they give, but that they receive it; not that they enlighten the world, but that they are blind, and that it is the goodness of Providence which opens their eyes to the light.

CHAPTER II
IMPORTANCE AND ANOMALY OF THE QUESTIONS ON THE IDEA OF THE INFINITE

12. The examination of the idea of the infinite is of the highest importance, not only because we meet it in various sciences, the exact sciences among others, but because it is one of the principal characteristics by which we distinguish God from creatures. A finite God would be no God; an infinite creature would not be a creature.

In the scale of finite beings we discover a gradation, by which they are interlinked; the less perfect, as they are perfected, go on approaching the perfect; and there are, preserving the limits of each one's nature, points of comparison by which we may measure their respective distances. Between the finite and the infinite there is no comparison; all measures are inadequate and as nothing. We pass from an imperceptible drop to an immense ocean; from the atom which escapes observation to the abundance of matter diffused through all space; and much as these transitions express, they are as nothing to the transition from the finite to the infinite; these oceans, compared with the infinite truth, become in their turn imperceptible drops, and thus an interminable scale baffles the efforts of the mind in search of something to correspond to its idea. The examination of the idea of the infinite ought to occupy an important place in the study of philosophy, although it served for no other purpose than the contemplation of infinite greatness.

13. The disputes on the idea of the infinite, not only in relation to its nature, but also to its existence, present a strange anomaly. If it exists in our mind it ought to fill it entirely, so that it must be impossible to cease to perceive it. Yet it is well known that philosophers dispute even on the existence of this idea; although it is an infinite treasure, those who possess it doubt its reality—just as the heroes in romance, when they find themselves in a castle richly and splendidly adorned, imagine it the effect of enchantment.

14. The mere dispute as to whether the idea of the infinite be positive or negative, is equivalent to the question of its existence. If it is negative,

it expresses an absence of being; if positive, the plenitude of being. What question can be more vital to an idea than the dispute whether it represents the absence or the plenitude of being?

15. Here again we meet the fact which we have observed in the preceding discussions. Reason, after digging at its own foundations, is threatened with death under the ruins of its loftiest edifices.

CHAPTER III
HAVE WE THE IDEA OF THE INFINITE?

16. If we had no idea of the infinite, the word would have no meaning to us, and when used it would not be understood.

17. Whatever may be the nature and perfection of our idea of the infinite, it is certain that it involves something fixed, and common to all intelligences. We apply the idea to things of very different orders, and it is always understood in the same sense by all men. Even the difficulty we find in attempting to explain it, in itself or in its applications, proceeds from the idea itself; it is a difficulty which we all meet with, because we all conceive in the same manner what is understood by the infinite, taken in general.

18. Infinite and indefinite express very different meanings. The infinite implies the absence of limits; the indefinite implies that these limits retire continually from us; it abstracts their existence, and only says that they cannot be assigned.

19. Whatever exists is finite or infinite; for it either has limits or it has not: in the first case, it is finite; in the second, infinite: there is no medium between yes and no.

20. Hence, properly speaking, there is in reality nothing indefinite; this word only expresses a mode of conceiving things, or rather a vagueness in the conception, or indecision in the judgment. When we do not know the limits of any thing, and, on the other hand, do not dare to affirm its infinity, we call it indefinite. Thus, space is called indefinite by those who see no way of assigning a limit to it, and yet are unwilling to say that it is infinite. Even in ordinary language we call a thing indefinite which has no limits assigned to it; thus, we say "a concession has been made for an indefinite time," although it is limited to some time which has not been determined.

21. The idea of the infinite does not consist in conceiving that another quantity may always be added to a given quantity, or that a perfection may be made more intense; this expresses only the possibility of a series of conceptions by which we endeavor to approach the absolute idea of the infinite. It is easy to see that the absolute idea is something distinct from those conceptions, because we regard it as a type to which the series of connections is referred, but which it can never equal, no matter how greatly prolonged.

22. Let us consider the words in which we naturally express what passes within us when we think of the infinite.

What is an infinite line? A line which has no limits. Is it a million, or a billion miles in length? There is no number to express its length; it will always be greater than the number. But do we not approach the infinite in proportion as we prolong a finite line? Certainly, in so far as *approaching* means only placing quantities which are found in what we approach; but not in so far as it means that this difference can be assigned. There is no comparison between the finite and the infinite; and therefore it is not possible to assign the difference between them. Would an infinite line be formed by the addition of all finite lines? No; for we can conceive the multiplication of each of the terms of the addition, and therefore an increase in the infinite, which would be absurd. Would the infinity of the line consist in our not knowing its limits, or not thinking of them? No; but in its not having them.

23. Thus, we see, that the idea of the infinite, is in the reach of the most common intellects, and expresses only what any person of ordinary understanding would say, even though he had never occupied himself with philosophical studies; that the idea of the infinite is in our understanding, as a constant type, to which all finite representations are unable to arrive. We know the conditions which must be fulfilled, but at the same time, we see the impossibility of fulfilling them. When any one tries to persuade us of the contrary, we reflect on the idea of the infinite, and say: "No; it is a contradiction of infinity; it is not infinite, but finite." We distinguish perfectly well between the absence of the perception of the limit and its non-existence. If any one tries to make us confound these two ideas, we answer, "No; they must not be confounded; there is a great difference between our not perceiving an object and the non-existence of that object, and we are not now examining whether we conceive the limit, but whether it exists." Though the limit retire and hide itself, so to speak, from our eyes, we are not deceived: it exists, or does not exist. If it exists, the condition involved in the conception of infinity is not fulfilled, and the object is not infinite, but finite; if it does not exist, there is true infinity,—the condition is complied with.

24. When the idea of the infinite is considered in general, it can never be confounded with the idea of the finite. There is a line which divides them, and which prevents all error; for it is the principle of contradiction itself; it is the distinction between *yes* and *no*. When we say *finite*, we affirm the limit; when we say *infinite*, we deny it. No ideas can be clearer or more exact.

CHAPTER IV
THE LIMIT

25. The word *infinite* is equivalent to *not finite*, and seems to express a negation. But negations are not always truly such, although the terms imply it; for if that which is denied, be a negation, the denial of it is an affirmation. This is the reason why two negatives are said to be equivalent to an affirmative. If I say, it has not varied, and you deny it, you deny my negation; for it is the same thing to deny that it has not varied, as to affirm that it has varied. In order, therefore, to determine whether the word *infinite* expresses a true negative, we must know what is meant by the word *finite*.

26. The finite is that which has a limit. A limit is the term beyond which there is nothing of the object limited. The limits of a line, are the points beyond which the line does not extend; the limit of a number, is the extreme where the number stops; the limit of human knowledge, is the point to which we may arrive, but which we cannot go beyond. A limit being a negation, to deny a limit, is to deny a negation, and is consequently an affirmation.

27. It is easy to see from these examples, that a limit in the ordinary sense, expresses an idea distinct from what mathematicians define it. They call a limit every expression, whether finite, infinite, or a nullity, which a quantity may continually approach without ever reaching. Thus, the value $0/a$ is the limit of the decrement of a fraction, the numerator of which is variable x/a; because, if we suppose X to be constantly diminishing, the fraction will approach the expression $0/a$, without ever being confounded with it, so long as X does not entirely disappear. If we suppose $(b\ x)/a$ an expression in which X is decreasing, the expression will continually approach $(b\ 0)/a = b/a$, which will be the limit of the fraction. If we suppose the expression a/x, in which X is decreasing, we shall continually approach the expression $a/0 = \infty$, an infinite value which the fraction can never attain, until X becomes 0, which cannot happen, because X is a true quantity. These examples show that mathematicians admit limits which are finite, infinite, or a nullity, and prove that mathematicians employ the word limit in a different sense from its ordinary as well as philosophical meaning.

28. A limit, therefore, expresses a true negation, and the word finite, or limited, necessarily involves a negative idea. That which is not, is not limited; therefore the finite is not an absolute negation. An absolute negation is nothing, and we do not call the finite nothing. Therefore, in the idea of finite are contained being, and a negation of another being. A line one foot in length, involves the positive value of one foot, and the negation of all value of more than a foot. Therefore, the finite, in so far as finite, involves a negation relatively to a being. If we could express this idea in the abstract, using the word finity, as we have the word infinity, we should say that finity in itself expresses only the negation of being relatively to a being.

29. Hence, the word infinite is not negative; for it is the negation of a negation. The infinite is the not-finite; it is that which has no negation of being, consequently that which possesses all being.

30. We have, therefore, an idea of the infinite, and this idea is not a pure negation. But it must not be supposed that we have arrived at the last term of the analysis of the infinite. We are still far from it, and it is even doubtful whether we shall obtain any satisfactory result after long investigations.

CHAPTER V
CONSIDERATIONS ON THE APPLICATION OF THE IDEA OF THE INFINITE TO CONTINUOUS QUANTITIES, AND TO DISCRETE QUANTITIES, IN SO FAR AS THESE LAST ARE EXPRESSED IN SERIES

31. One of the characteristic properties of the idea of the infinite is application to different orders. This gives occasion to some important considerations which greatly assist to make this idea clear in our mind.

32. From the point where I am situated I draw a line in the direction of the north; it is evident that I may prolong this line infinitely. This line is greater than any finite line can be; for the finite line must have a determinate value, and therefore, if placed on the infinite line, will reach only to a certain point. This line, therefore, seems to be strictly infinite in all the force of the word, because there is no medium between the finite and the infinite, and we have shown that it is not finite, since it is greater than any finite line; therefore it must be infinite.

This demonstration seems to leave nothing to be desired; yet there is a conclusive argument against the infinity of this line. The infinite has no limits, and this line has a limit, because, starting from the point from which it is drawn in the direction of the north, it does not extend in the direction of the south.

33. This line is greater than any finite line; but we may find another line greater still. If we suppose it produced in the direction of the south, it will be greater by how much it is produced towards the south; and if it be infinitely produced in this direction, its length will be twice that of the first line.

34. By the infinite prolongation of a line in two opposite directions we seem to obtain an absolutely infinite line; for we cannot conceive a lineal value greater than that of a right line infinitely prolonged in opposite directions. But it is not so: by the side of this right line another may be drawn, either finite or infinite, and the sum of the two will form a lineal

value greater than that of the first line; therefore that line is not infinite, because it is possible to find another still greater. And as, on the other hand, we may draw infinite lines and prolong them infinitely, it follows that none of them can form an infinite lineal value, because it is only a part of the lineal sum resulting from the addition of all the lines.

35. Reflecting on this apparent contradiction in our ideas, we discover that the idea of the infinite is indeterminate, and consequently susceptible of different applications. Thus, in the present instance, it cannot be doubted that the right line, prolonged to infinity, has some infinity, since it is certain that it has no limit in its respective directions.

36. This example would lead us to believe that the idea of the infinite represents nothing absolute to us; because even among those objects which are presented the most clearly to our mind, such as the objects of sensible intuition, we find infinity under one aspect which is contradicted one by another.

37. What we have observed of lineal values is also true of numerical values expressed in series. Mathematics speak of infinite series, but there can be no such series. Let the series be *a, b, c, d, e,* ....: it is called infinite if its terms continue *ad infinitum*. It cannot be denied that the series is infinite under one aspect; for there is no limit which puts an end to it in one sense; but it is evident that the number of its terms will never be infinite, because there are others greater; such, for instance, is the series continued from left to right, if continued from right to left at the same time, in this manner:

.... *e, d, c, b,* | *a, b, c, d, e,* ....

In this case the number of terms is evidently twice as great as in the first series.

Therefore the series which are called infinite are not infinite, and cannot be so, in the strict sense of the term.

38. But what is still more strange is, that the series is not infinite, even though we suppose it continued in opposite directions; for by its side we may imagine another, and the sum of the terms of both will be greater than the terms of either; therefore neither will be infinite. As it is evident that whatever be the series, we can always imagine others, it follows that there can be no infinite series in the sense in which mathematicians use the word series to express a continuation of terms, not excluding the possibility of other continuations besides the supposed infinite continuation.

39. The objections against lineal infinity apply equally to surfaces. If we suppose an infinite plane, it is evident that we can describe an infinity of planes distinct from the first plain and intersecting it in a variety of angles;

the sum of all these surfaces will be greater than any one of them. Therefore the infinite extension of a plain in all directions does not constitute a truly infinite surface.

40. A solid expanding in all directions seems to be infinite; but if we consider that the mathematical idea of a solid does not involve impenetrability, we shall see that inside of the first solid a second may be placed, which, added to the first, will give a value double that of the first alone. Let S be the empty space which we imagine to be infinite; and let W be a world of equal extension placed in it and filling it; it is evident that S + W are greater than S alone. Therefore, although we suppose S to be infinite, $= \infty$, W also $= \infty$; therefore $S + W = \infty + \infty = 2\infty$. And as this value expresses the size, the first is not infinite because it can be doubled. If we take the impenetrability, the operation may proceed *ad infinitum*.

Therefore the first infinite, far from being infinite, seems to be a quantity susceptible of infinite increase.

CHAPTER VI
ORIGIN OF THE VAGUENESS AND APPARENT CONTRADICTIONS IN THE APPLICATION OF THE IDEA OF THE INFINITE

41. The difficulties in the application of the idea of infinity, seem on the one hand, to prove that either this idea does not exist in us, or is very confused; and on the other hand, that we possess it, and in a very perfect degree. Why do we discover that numbers are not infinite, although at first they seem to be? Why do we deny the infinity of certain dimensions, notwithstanding their infinite prolongation in one sense? Because, on examining these objects, we find that they do not correspond to the type of infinity. If this type did not exist in our mind, how could it be possible for us to make use of it? How could we compare beings with it, if we did not know it? Is it possible to know when any thing arrives at a turn, if we have no idea of that turn? It is comparing without a point of comparison; that is, it is exercising a contradictory act.

42. Although these arguments in favor of the existence of the idea of the infinite, if we examine our own mind, we cannot deny that we find there a certain vagueness and confusion which inspire strong doubts as to the reality of this idea. What is presented to our mind, when we think of the infinite? The imagination abandoned to itself, extends space, expands dimensions, multiplies numbers indefinitely, but it offers nothing to the intellect which has the marks of infinity. If we leave the imagination, and regard the understanding only, it gives a type by which to judge of the infinity or not-infinity of the objects presented to it, but if we reflect on the type itself, it loses the clearness it possessed before, and we even ask if the type really exists.

43. Do we, therefore, deny the existence of this idea? are we going to renounce our intention of explaining it? We do neither. I believe that it is necessary to admit the idea, that it is not impossible to explain it, and that we may even point out the reason of its obscurity.

44. Before passing further, I wish to observe, that one of the causes of the difficulties in the explanation of the idea of the infinite, arises from our not distinguishing the intuitive from the abstract cognition. [36] Many difficulties would be avoided by attending to this distinction. When we say that the idea of the infinite is not intuitive, but abstract, we give the key to the solution of the principal objections brought against it.

45. We have no intuitive idea of infinity; that is to say, this idea does not present to our mind an infinite object; we can have this intuition only when we see the essence of God, which will happen in a future life.

46. If we had now the intuition of an infinite object, we should see its perfections as they are, with their true marks; or rather, we should see how all the perfections dispersed among limited beings, are united in one infinite perfection. We could not refer the idea of the infinite to determinate objects, as, for example, to extension, because these objects contradict the idea. It would be impossible for us to modify the idea in different ways, and apply it first in one sense, and then in another very different sense. The idea is one, and simple; it would, therefore, always relate to an object which is also one and simple, not vague and indeterminate, as now, but with the determination of a necessary existence and an infinite perfection. We should have intuition of infinite being, as we have intuition of the facts of our consciousness: our cognition of it would be that of an object eminently incommunicable, as predicate to any order of finite beings; and it would be as manifest a contradiction, to apply the idea of this infinity to any number or extension, as it would be to identify an act of our consciousness with external objects.

47. The indeterminate character in which the idea of the infinite is presented us, and the ease with which we modify it in various ways, and apply it to different objects, in different senses, proves that this idea is not intuitive, but abstract and indeterminate, that it is one of those general conceptions, by the aid of which the mind obtains a certain knowledge not afforded by intuition.

This will explain the origin of the vagueness of our idea of infinity. Indeterminate conceptions, and because they are indeterminate, relate to no particular object, or quality, which may be conceived by itself alone, as something which may be realized; they do not contain those determinations which fix our cognition in an absolute manner. The indeterminate manner in which they present any property of beings, causes a difference in the application, accordingly as the particular properties, which are combined with the general, are different. If we take a right-angle triangle, in which we know the measure of all the sides and angles, the determinateness of the idea avoids the vagueness of the intellect, and prevents the application of this idea to cases different from that which is determinate and fixed. But if we take a right-angle, in general, without determining the value of its sides and angles, its applications may be infinite. The more general and indeterminate the idea of a triangle becomes, the greater is the variety of its applications.

48. Indeterminate ideas, in order to represent any thing, must be applied to some property which is the condition of their actual or possible realization. Until this application is made, they are pure intellectual forms, which represent nothing determinate. I do not mean by this, that these ideas are empty conceptions, which cannot be applied outside of the sensible order, as was maintained by Kant; [37] but only that granting them an universal value, I deny that they have by themselves alone a value representative of any thing that can be realized, beyond the property which they express. The idea of a *pure* triangle can not be realized, for every *real* triangle would contain something more than is in the idea: it would be a right-angled or oblique-angled, etc., all which, the pure idea abstracts. The object will be indeterminate, in proportion to the indeterminateness of the properties contained in the conception; consequently, that which is presented to the understanding will also be more vague, and the applications which may be made of the idea, will be more varied and numerous, as is the case in the ideas of being, not-being, limit, and the like.

CHAPTER VII
FUNDAMENTAL EXPLANATION OF THE
ABSTRACT IDEA OF THE INFINITE

49. Supposing that our idea of the infinite is not intuitive but abstract, let us see how its true nature may be explained.

We have the ideas of being and of its opposite, not-being; these ideas considered in themselves are general, indeterminate, and may be applied to every thing which is subjected to our experience.

We may affirm and deny something of every limited being: we may affirm what it is: we may deny what it is not: the limit is only conceived as such when something is denied of it.

50. The activity of our being is unceasing, but it is limited by the absence or the resistance of objects; the external world is an assemblage of beings presenting a great variety of limitations.

Therefore both internal and external experience give us the idea of the finite, that is, of a being which involves some not-being. The brute has sensible perception, but no understanding: it *is* sensitive, and herein it has being; it *is not* intelligent, and herein it is limited. Man is sensitive and intelligent; the limit of the brute is not the limit of man. Among intelligent beings some understand more than others; therefore the limit of all is not the same.

51. Since we find a limit in both internal and external experience, it is evident that we can form the general idea of limit, that is, of a negation applied to an object.

52. The same experience teaches that what is the limit of some things is not the limit of others, and that the limit applied to one object must be denied of another. When we compare different beings together, we frequently find ourselves *denying certain* limits. As our understanding has the faculty of generalizing, it is evident that we may conceive in general the negation of *certain* limits, and form an indeterminate conception, including the two ideas of *negation* and *limit*.

53. I do not see what objection can be made either to the possibility or to the existence of this conception; but as this fact is necessary for the explanation of the idea of infinity, I shall make some further observations for the purpose of confirming it.

We have an idea of negation in general; this is a primitive fact of our mind: without it no negative judgments would be possible, nor could we even know the principle of contradiction. It is impossible for any thing to be *and not be* at the same time; when we say *not be* we express a negation, we therefore have the conception of negation. This conception is general, because it involves no determination; we speak of not-being without applying it to any particular object, nor even to any determinate species or genus. Therefore the conception of negation is general and absolutely undetermined.

54. We have the idea of limit; for, as we have seen, it is a negation applied to a being. We have also the idea of the negation of limit; for just as we conceive the limit as applied or applicable, we may and do conceive it as not applied or not applicable. At every moment we deny certain limits; this idea generalized becomes the negation in general of limit in general.

55. After these remarks we may establish what is contained in the idea of the infinite. This idea is a general conception involving the conception of being in general, and the negation of limit in general. The union of these two conceptions constitutes the abstract idea of the infinite.

56. The general conception of the negation of limit gives us an idea of infinity in the abstract, but not any infinite thing. Without the intuitive cognition of an infinite object, and with only a very imperfect idea of it, we may speak of infinity without falling into contradiction, and determine the cases in which it may be applied to a being or to an order of beings, whether real or possible. Man has many ideas of this vague kind, which nevertheless answer his necessities. We shall make this palpable by examples.

57. Suppose we take an uneducated person and point out to him a number of learned men, telling him that one of them knows more than all the rest. The uneducated person has no idea of what the man knows who knows the most, nor the man who knows the least; he has no idea of the degrees of science, nor of what science itself is; but he possesses the general ideas of degree, of more and less, and also of knowledge, and this enables him to speak, without contradiction or confusion, of the greater science of the one and the less science of the others, and even to solve with certainty the questions concerning the science of those individuals, in so far as these questions are contained in the general idea that the science of one is greater than that of all the others.

A servant in an establishment where the most beautiful products of art are collected, may speak of them all without contradiction or confusion, although he may be incapable of knowing their merit, and entirely ignorant of the circumstances which constitute the beauty of the objects. It is sufficient for him to have the idea of perfection or beauty in general, and to arrange by certain arbitrary signs the degrees of perfection or beauty of the objects, in order to be able to point them out to visitors, and talk of the greater skill of one artist, the poorer success of another; the greater effect and value of the works of the former, and the inferiority of those of the second, and to make other remarks of a similar nature, which at first might make us suppose him a consummate artist, or, at the least, an amateur of a great intellect and exquisite taste.

58. It would be easy to show by other examples, how fruitful some general ideas are, and how they may undergo innumerable combinations, without presenting any thing determinate to the intellect. This is precisely what happens with the idea of the infinite: in vain we ask what there is within us which corresponds to it: the conception of being in general and of the negation of limit present nothing fixed, except certain abstract conditions to which we continually reduce the objects which come under our intuition, or are presented to us with certain characteristic properties which permit us to form a less vague idea of the negation of limit.

CHAPTER VIII
THE DEFINITION OF INFINITY CONFIRMED
BY APPLICATION TO EXTENSION

59. We have explained the idea of infinity in general, by the indeterminate conceptions of being and the negation of limit. In order to assure ourselves that the explanation is well grounded, and that we have pointed out the essential marks of the conception, let us examine whether their application to determinate objects corresponds to what we have established in general.

If the idea of infinity is what we have defined it to be, we may apply it to all objects of sensible intuition or of the pure understanding, and we shall obtain the results which we ought to obtain, including the anomalies already referred to. [38]

60. The anomalies, or, rather, the contradictions which we seem to find in the applications of the idea of the infinite, when any thing is presented to us as infinite which we afterwards discover not to be so, originate in the application of this idea under different conditions. This variety would not be possible if the idea represented any thing determinate; but as it only contains the negation of limit in general joined to being in general, it follows that we subject this negation to particular conditions in each case, and therefore when we pass to other conditions, the general idea cannot give us the same result.

61. A line drawn from the point where we are situated in the direction of the north, and produced infinitely, gives us an infinite and a not-infinite. This contradiction is only apparent; there is really only the difference of result caused by the condition under which the general idea is applied.

When we consider a line infinitely produced towards the north, we do not apply the idea of the infinite to a lineal value in the abstract, but to a right line starting from a point and produced only in one direction. The result is what it should be. The negation of limit is affirmed under a condition; the infinite which results is subject to that condition. It may be said that there is no medium between the infinite and the not-infinite; but it is easy to solve this difficulty, if we observe that yes and no, to be contradictory, must be referred to the same thing, which is not the case when the conditions of the object are changed.

62. If instead of a line produced in one direction only, we had wished to apply the negation of limit to a right line in general, it is evident that we should have been obliged to produce the line in the two opposite directions: which would have given us another infinite under a new condition.

We have before seen that not even in this case can we have a lineal value strictly infinite; because this right line only forms a part of the sum of lines which we can imagine. Is it then infinite, or is it not? It is both, if we make the proper distinction. It will be infinite, or we shall have the idea of infinity or negation of limit, applied to a right line *alone*; but if instead of one *right line alone*, we take a lineal value, without any condition, the supposed line will not be infinite; the negation of the limit is not applied under that condition; the result must therefore be different.

63. We find the same anomaly, if we take two lines alone. Let us suppose a right line infinitely produced in both directions, and by its side let us describe a curve with continual undulations extending infinitely in a direction parallel to the right line. Both lines will be infinite if we consider only their direction, abstracting their lineal value; but if we regard this value the curve is greater than the straight line; for it is evident if we take a part of the curve corresponding to a part of the straight line, and extend or straighten this part of the curve, it will be greater than the corresponding part of the straight line; as this may be done throughout the whole length of the lines, the lineal value of the curve must be greater than that of the straight line in proportion to the law of its undulations.

64. This may suffice to show how the idea of infinity may be applied under different conditions and produce different results, without any contradiction. What is infinite under one aspect is not so under another aspect; hence we have the *orders of infinities* which figure so largely in mathematics; but I say again that these contradictions are not susceptible of any explanation if we attribute an absolute value to the idea of the infinite, instead of considering it as the abstract representation of the negation of limit.

65. Is it possible to conceive in a right line or curve an absolutely infinite length or lineal value, to which we may apply the negation of limit absolutely? I think not: for whatever be the line under consideration we can always draw others, which, added to the first, will give a value greater than that of the first above. This is a case in which there is a contradiction between the negation of limit and the condition to which it is subjected. You demand a lineal value to which the negation of limit may be applied absolutely; and on the other hand you require that this lineal value should be found in a determinate line, which by the fact of its being determinate,

excludes the absolute negation of limit. The problem supposes contradictory *data*; therefore the result must be a contradiction.

66. What must we suppose in order to conceive an absolutely infinite lineal value? We need only suppose no condition which excludes the absolute negation of limit. We must here distinguish between the pure conception and the sensible intuition in which it is expressed. The conception of infinite lineal value exists from the moment that we unite the two general conceptions of lineal value and negation of limit. But the sensible intuition, which may represent this conception, is not so easy to imagine, even in general. To arrive at it we must imagine a space without any limit; and then considering in general all the lines whether right lines or curves, which may be drawn in it, in all directions, and under all possible conditions, we must take the sum of all these lineal values; and the result will be an absolutely infinite lineal value; for we shall have applied the negation of limit without any restriction.

67. We may obtain in the same way an infinite superficial value; for it is evident that we may apply to it all that we have said of lineal values.

68. In all these cases we apply the negation of limit to extension considered only in some of its dimensions. If we wish to obtain an absolutely infinite extension, we must abstract no dimension; consequently the absolutely infinite of this order, is extension in all its dimensions with the absolute negation of limit. But it is also to be observed that we must presuppose an absolutely infinite value of extension in order to obtain an absolutely infinite value of lines or surfaces; because it is equivalent to presupposing an infinite space in which the lines and surfaces may be drawn in all directions and under all possible conditions.

CHAPTER IX
CONCEPTION OF AN INFINITE NUMBER

69. Can we conceive an infinite number? On one side, it seems not; because we doubt its possibility, and if we possessed this idea we should have no doubt of its existence. On the other side, it seems that we can conceive an infinite number; for we know immediately when a number is not infinite, and we could not know this if we had not the idea of infinite number.

Our observations on infinite series would seem to prove that the idea of infinite number is an illusion; for we find those numbers which we believed infinite, not to be so.

I think this question may be solved on the same principles as those of the last chapter. I see no difficulty in admitting the idea of an infinite number, nor how any contradiction can proceed from it.

70. Number is a collection of units; it is a general idea, because to conceive the number, we do not need to know of what class, or how many the units may be. The idea of number in general abstracts absolutely all such determinations. It is evident that, whatever number we imagine, we can always conceive another still greater, and if we assign a limit to a number, we can always remove it indefinitely, so that the limit of one is not the limit of the other. To the idea of number, we unite the idea of a limit and of the negation of another limit. Therefore, if we unite to the idea of number in general, the idea of the negation of limit in general, we shall obtain the idea of an infinite number.

71. What does this idea represent? It represents nothing determinate: it is an entirely abstract conception, formed of two other abstract conceptions, those of number and the negation of limit. No determinate object corresponds to it; it is a work of our understanding referred to objects in general, without a determination of any sort. We may now solve the difficulties previously intimated.

72. Why is a series of terms presented to us as infinite, which, when we examine it closely, we find wants some of the marks of infinity? Because, in the first instance, we apply the negation of limit under a condition which we take no notice of in the second instance.

Set us the series $a, b, c, d, e, \ldots\ldots$

It is evident that we may continue it infinitely, and conceive the negation of all limit of this continuation: in this sense, the number of terms is infinite; for the idea of the negation of limit is really applied to the series. When we ask if the number of terms is absolutely infinite, we abstract the condition under which we had united the negation of limit. That, therefore, which is infinite in one instance is not so in another. Still there is not any contradiction because the yes and the no refer to different suppositions.

73. Let us take a line and measure it by feet. Producing this line we multiply the number of feet; and we may conceive the negation of all limit of this multiplication. The number of feet will then be infinite. If instead of a foot we take an inch as the unit of measure, we shall have a number twelve times as great. This number would also be infinite, and thus we should have two infinite numbers, one of them greater than the other. Is there any contradiction in this? Certainly not: there is only a different combination of ideas. In the first case, the idea of the negation of limit was subordinated to the condition of the division of the line into feet: whereas, in the second case, we introduce a different condition; the division of the line into inches.

74. But, it may be said, these numbers, considered in themselves, abstracted from their relation to feet or inches, are equal or they are not equal; consequently they are infinite or not infinite. The objection vanishes as soon as we correct the error which supports it. When we abstract all relation to determinate divisions, we consider number in general; on this supposition there are not two cases, but only one; there cannot then be a relation of greater or less. We have only the conception of number in general combined with the idea of the negation of limit in general; therefore the result must be an infinite number in the abstract.

The difficulty consists in a contradiction which escapes our sight at first. We abstract particular conditions in order to know if the numbers are in themselves infinite or not; and at the same time we do not abstract them, because it is only in reference to them that the objection has any meaning, since it supposes the division into various kinds of units. When, therefore, we speak of particular numbers, and at the same time pretend to consider them in themselves, we fall into a contradiction, because we take the numbers both with and without particular conditions at the same time.

75. From all that has been said, we may conclude that the conception of infinite number, abstracted from the nature and relations of the things numbered, involves no contradiction, since it contains only the two ideas of number, as a collection of beings, and of the absolute negation of limit; but we cannot affirm from this alone, that an infinite number can be realized.

Infinite number cannot become actual without an infinite collection of beings; and these beings, when realized, cannot be abstract beings, which contain nothing else but being; they must have characteristic qualities, and must be subject to the conditions imposed by these qualities. As we absolutely abstract these conditions in the general conception, it is not possible to discover, from the conception alone, the contradiction which they may imply. Hence, although there is no contradiction contained in the conception, there may still be in the reality. In the same manner, certain mechanical theories are perfectly conceivable, but they cannot be reduced to practice on account of the opposition of the matter to which they should be applied. Finite beings are the matter on which indeterminate and metaphysical conceptions are to be realized; the possibility of the conceptions does not absolutely prove the possibility of the beings. The reality may draw with it certain determinations involving a contradiction which was latent in the general conception, and is made manifest by the reality.

CHAPTER X
CONCEPTION OF INFINITE EXTENSION

76. Is infinite extension conceivable? This conception includes two ideas: the idea of extension, and the idea of the negation of limit. The idea of extension is a general conception, referring to the intuition which, whatever may be in itself and in its object, represents extension and the union of the three dimensions, the pure form of which is space. It is evident that we can unite, in one conception, the two ideas of extension in general and the negation of limit; and if this is what is called the idea of infinite extension, it is clear that we have this idea. This conception of infinite extension, abstracts all conditions of the reality; we do not know whether there be, in the nature of extended things, any thing which prevents the absolute infinity of their extension; consequently, we are ignorant whether there is or is not any latent contradiction, which the general conception does not reveal to us.

77. It must be remembered that I am speaking of the idea and not of the sensible representation of extension; for although I hold that it is possible for us to have the conception of an infinite extension, I do not think the same with respect to its sensible representation. The latter may be indefinitely expanded, but it cannot become infinite.

Reason demonstrates this impossibility which consciousness makes known to us. Internal sensible representations are only the repetition of the external, or at least are formed from the elements which these latter furnish. Sight and touch are the two senses which produced the representation of extension, and they both imply a limit. Touch only reaches that which is immediate to it, and sight cannot see with a limit which sends the rays of light to it. Internal sensible representations must always retain this limitation; their object may be expanded, or the limit removed to a greater distance, but to destroy this limit would be to destroy themselves. Therefore, the imagination of an infinite extension is impossible to every sensitive being.

78. I have proposed above (§ 40) an objection against the infinity of extension, in so far as we may represent it as a size without limits.

The objection was, that as the idea of impenetrability is not contained in the conception of a solid, we may imagine an infinite series of infinites placed one inside of another. This difficulty is only conclusive when speaking of the conception of a solid which contains something more than the pure idea of extension. The idea of extension necessarily implies that some parts are *outside* of others, and it is not possible to conceive extension otherwise. It is certain that a body may be situated in a part of space; taking from this body its impenetrability, we may put another body in the same place, and so on to infinity; but in that case we conceive something besides pure extension, we unite something, although in a general and indeterminate manner, to the idea of things situated in space; otherwise we should not distinguish the space, representing pure extension, from the solids placed in it, nor should we distinguish these solids from one another, if we did not recognize in them some difference, although general and undetermined.

79. It seems most probable that the pure idea of an infinite extension is contained in the idea of an infinite size, which is nothing more than the idea of space. Whatever else is introduced into the idea is a foreign element, adding to pure extension something which does not belong to it, such is the difference between extended beings, although conceived in an indeterminate manner.

CHAPTER XI
POSSIBILITY OF INFINITE EXTENSION

80. What are we to think as to the possibility of the infinities which we conceive? Let us examine the question.

Is an infinite extension possible? There is no incompatibility between the idea of extension and the negation of limit, at least, according to our way of conceiving them. It is more difficult for us to conceive extension absolutely limited, than to conceive it unlimited: beyond all limit, we imagine space without end.

81. Neither do we discover any impossibility in the existence of an unlimited extension, if we consider the question in relation to the divine omnipotence. Beyond all extension God can create another extension; if we suppose that he has applied his creative power to all the extension possible, he must have created an infinite extension.

82. Here a difficulty arises. If God had created an infinite extension he could not create another extension; his power would be exhausted, and consequently it would not be infinite.

This difficulty proceeds from understanding infinite power in a false sense. When we say that God can do all things, we do not mean that he can do things that are contradictory: omnipotence is not an absurd attribute, as it would be if applied to things that are absurd. An absolutely infinite extension is contradictory in relation to another distinct extension; for, being absolutely infinite, it contains all possible extensions. If we suppose it to exist, no other is possible: to affirm that God could not produce another, is not to limit his omnipotence, but only to say that he cannot do a thing which is absurd.

83. We will make this solution clearer. The intelligence of God is infinite; and he cannot understand more than he now understands; all progress would suppose imperfection, because it would involve a change from a less to a greater intelligence. If, then, we say that God will never understand more than he does now, do we limit his intelligence? Certainly not. He cannot understand more, because he understands all that is real and all

that is possible, and we cannot, without contradiction, conceive that he can understand more than he now does: this is not to limit his intelligence, but to affirm its infinity: it is not susceptible of perfection, because it is infinite. This will enable us to understand the expression *cannot*, as applied to God. What is denied is not a perfection, but an absurdity: wherefore St. Thomas very opportunely observes, that we should much better say that the thing cannot be done, than that God cannot do it.

CHAPTER XII
SOLUTION OF VARIOUS OBJECTIONS AGAINST THE POSSIBILITY OF AN INFINITE EXTENSION

84. The discussions on the possibility of an infinite extension are of a very ancient date. How could it be otherwise? Must not the glorious spectacle of the universe, and the space which we imagine beyond the boundaries of all worlds, naturally have given rise to questions as to the existence or possibility of a limit to this immensity?

Some philosophers think an infinite extension impossible. Let us see on what they found their opinion.

85. Extension is a property of a finite substance, and that which belongs to a finite thing cannot be infinite; therefore it is impossible to conceive infinity of any kind in a finite being. This argument is not conclusive. It is true that an extended substance is finite, in the sense that it does not possess absolute infinity such as is conceived in the Supreme Being; but it does not follow from this that it cannot be infinite under certain aspects. Neither is it correct to say that no finite substance can have an infinite property, because the properties flow from the substance, and the infinite cannot proceed from the finite. In order that this argument may be valid, it is necessary to prove that all the properties of a being emanate from its substance: figures are accidental properties of bodies, and yet many of them have no relation to the substance, and are mere accidents which appear or disappear, not by the internal force of the substance, but by the action of an external cause. We see extension in bodies; but as we know not the essence of corporeal substance, we cannot say how far this property is connected with the substance, whether it is an emanation from it, or only something which has been given to it and may be taken from it without any essential alteration. [39]

Moreover, when we say that the infinite cannot proceed from the finite, we do not deny that an infinite property may proceed from a substance finite in its essence.

When we admit the infinite property, we admit at the same time all that is necessary in the substance in order that this property may have its root in it, so long as we do not deny the character of finite which essentially belongs to every creature. When we deny that creatures are or can be infinite, we speak of essential infinity, of that infinity which implies necessity of being and absolute independence under every aspect; but we do not deny them a relative infinity, such as that of extension.

To undertake to prove that infinite extension is impossible, because every property of a finite substance must be finite, is equivalent to supposing the very thing in dispute; for the precise question is, whether one of these properties, namely, extension, can be infinite. In order to establish the negative proposition, "No property of a finite substance can be infinite," it is necessary to prove this of extension. Hence the argument which we are imposing implies, in some manner, a begging of the question, when they found it on a general proposition which can only be certain when the present question is solved.

86. Infinite extension ought to be the greatest of all extensions, but there is no such extension. From any given extension God can take away a certain quantity; for example, a yard: in that case the infinite extension would become finite, for it would be less than the first; and as the difference between the two extensions is only a yard, it is clear that not even the first could be infinite; for it is impossible that there should be only the difference of one yard between the finite and the infinite.

This difficulty merits a serious consideration: at first sight it seems so conclusive that no possibility of a satisfactory solution is conceivable.

The proposition that the difference between the finite and the infinite cannot be finite, is not wholly correct. We must first of all take notice that the difference between two quantities, whether finite or infinite, cannot be absolutely infinite, in the sense of diminution. Difference is the excess of one quantity over another, and necessity implies a limit; for as the excess only is considered, the quantity exceeded is not contained in the difference. Calling the difference D, the greater quantity A, and the smaller a, I say that D can in no hypothesis be infinite. By the supposition $D = A - a$; therefore $D + a = A$; in order that D may equal A it is necessary to add to it a; therefore D cannot be infinite. If we suppose $A = \infty$, we shall have $D = A - a = \infty - a$, or $D + a = \infty$. Therefore to make D infinite we must add to it a, and we can never have $D = \infty$ unless $a = 0$; but in that case there would be no true difference, since the equation, $D = A - a$, would be converted into $D = A - 0 = A$, and the difference would not be real but imaginary.

It follows from this that no difference between two positive quantities can be absolutely infinite; if it is so in some sense, it is not so in the sense of diminution; and the union of these two ideas of difference and infinity results in a contradiction. [40]

The difference between an infinite quantity and a given finite quantity cannot be another given finite quantity, but it must be infinite in some sense. Let us suppose an infinite line and a given finite line, the difference between them cannot be expressed by a given finite lineal value. For supposing the second line to be a finite and a given line, we may place it upon the infinite line in any of its directions, and from any point in it it will reach a certain point of the infinite line. If we suppose a second given finite line, representing the difference between the other two lines, we ought to place it upon the infinite line at the point where the other terminates; and it is evident that it will terminate at another point determined by its length; therefore it will not measure the whole of the difference between the infinite and the finite lines.

We obtain the same result in algebraic expressions. If A be a given finite value, the difference between A and ∞ cannot be another given finite value. For, expressing the difference by D, we shall have ∞ - D ± A D. Therefore, D + A = ∞; consequently, if both were given finite values, an infinite would result from two given finite values, which is absurd.

Hence, a difference may be in some sense infinite, according to the meaning we attach to the term infinity. If from the point where we are situated, we draw a line towards the north and produce it infinitely, and then produce it, also, infinitely towards the south, the difference between either of these lines and the sum of them both, will be infinite only in a certain sense. This is also verified by algebraic expressions. If we have the infinite value equal 2∞, and compare it with ∞, the result is 2∞ - ∞ = ∞.

In general, from any infinite value we may subtract any finite difference in relation to it, so long as the subtrahend is not a given finite value. Let ∞ be the infinite value,—I say that we can find in it any finite value; for, ∞ being an infinite value, A contains all finite values of the same order; therefore it contains the finite value, A; consequently we may form the equation, ∞ - A = B. Whatever be the value of B, the relation of B to ∞ is A; for by only adding A to B we obtain ∞. The equation, ∞ - A = B, gives B + A = ∞, and also ∞ - B = A; and as A is a given value according to the supposition, and A is the given finite difference between ∞ and B, it follows that we may find a finite difference to every infinite value.

We may infer from this that the possibility of assigning a finite difference to an infinite extension, does not prove any thing against its true infinity. The infinite, and because it is infinite, contains all that belongs to the order in which it is infinite. We may take any sure value, and considering it as a difference, and we shall obtain a finite difference. But far from proving the absence of infinity, this confirms its existence; for it shows that all the finite is contained in the infinite.

In this case, the subtrahend would be infinite under a certain aspect; but not in the order of diminution, because it wants the quantity which is taken from it.

87. There is another argument against the absolute infinity of extension, which seems to have more weight than any of those which precede, and I cannot see why it has never occurred to those who argue against this possibility. It is this,—we suppose an infinite extension to exist. God can annihilate it, and then create another equally infinite. The sum of both is greater than either alone; therefore neither of them alone is infinite. This annihilation we may suppose as often as we wish; hence we may have a series of infinite extensions. The terms of this series cannot exist at the same time, since one actual infinite extension excludes all others. Therefore, as the sum of the extensions is greater than any number of particular extensions, the absolute infinite extension must be found, not in the particular extensions, but in the sum, and hence an actual infinite extension is intrinsically impossible.

To solve this difficulty we must distinguish between extension and the thing extended: the whole question turns on the intrinsic possibility of the infinity of extension, considered in itself, abstracting absolutely the subject in which it is found. The difficulty places before our sight a series of successive infinite extensions; but in reality this succession is in the beings which are extended, and the number of which goes on increasing; but not in the extension itself. The pure idea of infinite extension in the one case, is not increased by the new extensions which are produced; the extension appears, disappears, reappears, and again disappears, but is not increased. The succession shows the intrinsic possibility of its appearance and its disappearance, its essential contingency, because it is not repugnant for it to cease to exist when it exists, or to pass again from non-existence to existence. If we examine our ideas, we shall find that we cannot increase the infinite extension which we conceive, by any imaginable supposition; and that whatever we may do, is reduced to a succession of productions and annihilations. The idea of infinite extension seems to be a primitive part of our mind; the infinity which we imagine in space, is only the attempt which our mind makes to express its idea in reality. Created with sensible intuition, we have received the power of expanding this intuition on an infinite scale,—to do this we require the idea of an infinite extension.

CHAPTER XIII
EXISTENCE OF INFINITE EXTENSION

88. The question of the possibility of an infinite extension is very different from that of its existence. The first we answer in the affirmative, the second in the negative.

Descartes maintained that the extension of the world is indefinite; but this is a term which, although it has a very rational meaning when it refers to the compass of our understanding, has no meaning when applied to things. There is no objection to saying that the extension of the world is indefinite, if it only means that we cannot assign its limits; but in the reality, the limits exist or do not exist, indifferently of our power of assigning them; there is no medium between yes and no; therefore there is no medium between the existence and the non-existence of these limits. If they exist, the extension of the world is finite; if they do not exist, it is infinite;—in either case, the word indefinite expresses nothing.

The argument of Descartes proves nothing, or it proves the true infinity of the world. For, if we must remove its limits indefinitely because we always conceive indefinitely an extension beyond every other extension, as, on the other hand, we know that this series of conceptions has no limit, we may at once transfer the unlimitedness to the object which corresponds to those conceptions, and affirm that the extension of the world is absolutely infinite. Unfortunately, the argument of Descartes is without any basis; for it consists in a transition from the ideal, or, rather, imaginary order, to the real order, which is contrary to good logic. [41]

89. Leibnitz maintained, that although God could have made the material universe finite in its extension, it is more in conformity with his wisdom not to have done so. "Thus I do not say," he writes, [42] "as is here imputed to me, that God cannot give limits to the extension of matter; but the appearance is that he does not wish it, but preferred to give it more." The opinion of Leibnitz is founded on his system of optimism, which is open to a multitude of objections, but it is not the place here to examine them.

90. To speak frankly my own opinion, I say that this is a question which cannot be solved on purely philosophic principles; for, as the ideas

contain no intrinsic necessity, either for or against the existence of an infinite extension, we must look for its solution to what experience teaches us. All the time occupied in attempting to solve this question is lost. What we can assert is, that the extension of the world exceeds all appreciation; and as the science of astronomy advances, greater depths are discovered in the ocean of space. Where is the shore? or is there any? Reason cannot answer such questions. What do we, poor insects, know, whose life is but a momentary dwelling on this little ball of dust, which we call the globe of the earth?

CHAPTER XIV
POSSIBILITY OF AN ACTUAL
INFINITE NUMBER

91. Is an infinite number possible? Does the union of the idea of number with the idea of the absolute negation of limit, involve any contradiction which prevents the realization of the conception?

Whatever number we may conceive, we can always conceive one still greater: this seems to show that no existing number can be absolutely infinite. If we suppose this number to be realized, an intelligence may know it, and may multiply it by two, three, or any other number; therefore the number may be increased, and consequently it is not infinite.

This difficulty is far from being conclusive, if we examine it carefully. The intellectual act of which it speaks, would be impossible on the supposition of the existence of an infinite number. If the intelligence should not know the infinity of the number, it might make the multiplication, but it would fall into a contradiction through its ignorance; for the number being absolutely infinite, could not be increased; its multiplication would be an absurdity, and the intelligence making it, would combine two ideas which would still be repugnant, although not known to be so by the intelligence. If the absolute infinity of the existing number were known to the intelligence, the idea of multiplication could never be associated with it; for the intelligence would know that all possible products already exist.

92. An absolutely infinite number cannot be expressed in the algebraic or geometrical values; the attempt so to express it limits it in a certain sense, and therefore destroys its absolute infinity. If the expression ∞, represented an absolutely infinite number, it would not be susceptible of any combination which would increase it: to suppose that it may be multiplied by other numbers, finite or infinite, is to take its infinity in another than an absolute sense.

The fraction a/0 does not express an infinite value in all the strictness of the word; for it is evident that whatever be the value of a/0 it will always be less than 2a/0 or, in general, less than na/0 n representing a value greater than unity.

93. Neither can an infinite number be represented in geometrical values.

Let us take a line one foot long. It is evident that if we produce this line infinitely in opposite directions, the number of feet will be in some sense infinite, since the foot is supposed to be repeated infinite times: the expression of the number of the feet will be the expression of an infinite value. Now, I say that this number is not infinite, because there are other numbers still greater. In each foot there are twelve inches; therefore, the number of inches contained in the line will be twelve times as great as the number of feet; consequently the number of feet is not infinite. Neither is the number of inches infinite; for they in their turn may be divided into lines, the lines into points; and it is evident that the number of the smaller quantities will be proportionally greater than the number of the greater quantities. There will be twelve times as many inches as feet, twelve times as many lines as inches, and twelve times as many points as lines; and this progression can never end, because the value of a line is infinitely divisible.

94. Pushing to infinity the divisibility of an infinite line, we seem to have an infinite number in the elements which constitute it; but a slight reflection will dissipate this illusion. For it is evident that we can draw other infinite lines by the side of the supposed infinite line; and since according to the supposition, each of them may be infinitely divided, it follows that the sum of the elements of all the lines will give a greater number than the sum of the elements of any one of them.

95. If we wish to find an infinite number of parts in values of extension, we must suppose a solid infinite in all its dimensions, with all its parts infinitely divided. But not even then should we have an absolutely infinite number, although we should have the greatest which can be represented in values of extension.

Conceding that an infinite extension existed which is infinitely divisible, the number of its parts would not be absolutely infinite; for we can conceive other beings besides extended beings, and considering both under the general idea of being, we might unite them in a number which would be greater than that of extended beings alone.

96. No imaginable species of beings infinitely multiplied, can give an absolutely infinite number. The reason is the same as that given in the last paragraph: the existence of beings of one species does not render the existence of beings of another species impossible. Therefore, besides the supposed infinity of the number of beings of a determinate species, there are other numbers which, united with this, produce a number greater than the pretended infinity.

97. The existence of an absolutely infinite number requires: first, the existence of infinite species of beings; and secondly, the existence of infinite individuals of each species. Let us see if these conditions can be realized.

98. There seems to be no doubt of the intrinsic possibility of infinite species. The scale of beings is between two extremes, nothing and infinite perfection: the space between these extremes is infinite; and beings may be distributed on it in an infinite gradation.

99. Admitting the intrinsic possibility of an infinite gradation in the scale of beings, the question occurs, whether their possibility is only ideal, or also real, that is, may be realized. God is infinitely powerful; if the infinite gradation is intrinsically possible, God can produce it; for whatever is intrinsically possible falls within the reach of divine omnipotence. On the other hand, supposing, as we must, the liberty of God, there is no doubt but God is free to create all that he can create. If then there is nothing repugnant in an infinity of the species of beings distributed in an infinite gradation, these beings may exist if God will it. Therefore denying all limit to the number of species and of individuals of each species, it seems that the infinite number would exist, since it is impossible to imagine any increase or limitation in the collection of all beings.

On this supposition the most perfect created beings possible would exist, and no more perfect being in the sphere of creatures could be conceived. All that can be imagined would already exist, from nothing to infinite perfection.

100. Still it must be observed that the collection of created beings, whatever be their perfection, are necessarily subject to the condition of dependence on another being; a condition from which the infinite being above is essentially exempt. This condition involves limitation; therefore, all created beings must be finite.

101. Does the character of finite, which is met with in all created beings, involve a determinate limit beyond which they cannot pass? If this limit exists, is not the number of possible species also limited? And if these species are not infinite, is not an infinite number an illusion?

Although the intrinsic possibility of the infinite scale of beings seems beyond a doubt, we must beware of solving too quickly the present question. With respect to indeterminate conceptions, we see no possible limit; but would this still be so, if we had an intuitive knowledge of the species? Are we sure that in the particular qualities of beings, combined with limitation and dependence, which are essential to them, we should not discover a term beyond which they cannot go, by reason of the constitution of their nature? How impotent philosophy is to solve such questions!

102. Whatever may be concluded as to this infinity of species and their respective perfection, I do not believe that an actually infinite number can exist. Among these species must be counted intelligences which exercise their acts in succession. This is evidently so; for in this number are included human minds which think and wish in a *successive* manner. The acts of these intelligences may be numbered: this we know from consciousness. Therefore there would never be an infinite number, because these acts, being successive, can never be all at the same time.

103. It may be answered that in this case we might suppose that spirits, including our own, have only one act of intelligence and will. To this I reply, that besides contradicting the nature of created beings, which, because they are finite, must be subject to change, it is also open to another objection, inasmuch as it eliminates at once many species of beings, and thus, instead of preserving the infinity, renders it impossible. Who can deny the possibility of that which exists? If, as our experience informs us, there now exist beings of successive activity, why would not these beings be possible on the supposition that the divine omnipotence had exerted all its infinite creative power?

104. This difficulty, which is founded on the nature of finite intelligences, seems to render the existence of an infinite number impossible, and it becomes still stronger if we examine the question under a more general aspect.

The existence of an absolutely infinite number excludes the existence of any other number. That which is numbered is not substance alone, but its modifications also. This has already been demonstrated with regard to intelligences, and is true in general of all finite beings. Every finite being is changeable, and its changes may be counted. The modifications produced by the changes cannot all exist at once, for some of them exclude others. Therefore, an actual infinite number is never possible.

105. Let us apply these considerations to the sensible world. Motion is a modification to which bodies are subject. This modification is essentially successive. A motion, the parts of which co-exist, is absurd. The co-existence of different states, which result from different motions, is also absurd: things that are contradictory cannot exist at the same time, and many of these situations are contradictory, because one of them necessarily involves the negation of others. If a line falling on another line revolve around a point, it will successively describe different angles. When it forms an angle of 45 degrees, it will not form an angle of 30 degrees, nor of 40, nor 70, nor 80; these angles mutually exclude one another. A portion of matter will form different figures, according to the arrangement which is given to the

parts of which it is composed. When these parts form a globe, they will not form a cube; these two solids cannot exist at the same time, formed of the same portion of matter.

106. This variety of motion and form can be numbered. At every step we measure motion, applying to it the idea of number; at every instant we count the forms of a portion of matter, as for example, a piece of wax, to which different forms have been given successively: whatever be the number of the beings which we suppose to exist, every one of them will be susceptible of transformations which may be counted. Therefore, in the very nature of things, there is an intrinsic impossibility of the existence of an actual infinite number.

107. I believe that these arguments fully demonstrate the impossibility of an actual infinite number; and if I do not dare to say that I am sure of having given a complete demonstration, it is because the nature of the question presents so many and so great difficulties, it so bewilders and confounds the weak understanding of man, that there is always reason to fear that even those arguments, which seem the clearest and most conclusive, may conceal some fault which vitiates their force, and makes an illusion appear an incontestible truth. Still I cannot but observe that to combat this demonstration, it seems, to me that it would be necessary to deny our primary ideas, the exclusion of being and not-being, and the necessity of succession, of time, to the realization of contradictory things.

108. Perhaps it may be objected to me that contradictory modifications are not a part of the infinite number, which only relates to the possible: but this does not destroy my demonstration; it rather confirms it. For as the absolute infinite number implies the absolute negation of all limit, when, in treating of the realization of this conception, I meet with things that are contradictory, I say that the realization of the conception is contradictory, because the general and indeterminate conception is more extended than all possible number.

109. The origin of their greater conception is, that the indeterminate conception abstracts all conditions, that of time included; but the reality does not and cannot abstract these conditions. Hence arises the conflict between the conception and its realization, and this explains why the conception is not contradictory, although its realization is impossible.

Let us suppose a number realized containing all the species and individuals possible, we may reflect on the conception of the infinite number, and say that the true infinity of the number requires the absolute negation of all limit; but thinking of the collection of things which exists, we can find it a limit, for concerning this collection of units in general, we may add to it another number expressing the new modifications which may be produced. At the instant A, the number of units may be expressed by M. At the instant B, there will be a new collection of units which may be expressed by N. The sum of M + N will be greater than either M or N alone. Therefore, neither M nor N will be absolutely infinite. The indeterminate conception abstracts instants and relates to the sum above; hence it includes things which cannot co-exist.

CHAPTER XV
IDEA OF ABSOLUTELY INFINITE BEING

110. We are entering on a difficult question. Serious difficulties are found in the idea of the infinite in general; the idea of absolutely infinite being is not less difficult. We have seen that there are different orders of infinities, each one of which is a conception formed by the association of the two ideas of a particular being and the negation of limit. But it is easy to see that none of the infinities hitherto examined can be called infinite in the strict sense of the term: they are all limited under many aspects,— none of them is an infinitely perfect being. The idea of this being is not fully possessed by us while in this life; still it may be analyzed and explained with more clearness than it is by most authors. The great difficulties, which we meet with in this attempt, show the necessity of deep meditation, and the transcendency of the errors which originate in a wrong understanding of the word infinite when applied to God.

111. What is an absolutely infinite being? It might seem that we had said all that is necessary in defining the absolutely infinite being to be that which has no negation of being: but this is a common notion which leaves much to be desired. It is an indisputable truth that the infinite being has no negation of being; but it is a truth so far beyond our reach that it presents to our weak understanding only a gloomy confusion, as soon as we attempt to determine exactly its true sense.

112. If the absolutely infinite being has no negation of being, it seems that nothing can be denied, but that everything may be affirmed of it, for it must be all; in this case pantheism results from the idea of infinity. If a true negative proposition can be established in relation to the infinite being, there is in it a negation of being, or of the predicate which is denied in the proposition.

It cannot be said that when negative propositions are applied to God, only a negation is denied, for in reality positive things are denied of God. When I say that God is not extended, I deny of him a reality which is extension. When I say God is not the universe, I deny of him the reality of the universe. Therefore negative propositions, as applied to God, deny not only negations, but also realities.

It does not seem to solve the difficulty to say that the realities denied involve imperfection, and are, consequently, repugnant to God. This is very true, but we are treating at present of the explanation of the idea of the absolutely infinite, and the difficulty militates against the supposition that the idea of the absolutely infinite is to be explained by the absolute absence of negation of being. If these realities are any thing, when denied of God some being is denied; and since the proposition cannot be true if there is not in God the negation of the being denied, it follows that it is incorrect to say that the absolutely infinite being is that which has no negation of being.

113. It also seems that a being of this nature could have no properties; for some positive properties exclude others: thus, intelligence and extension, freedom of will and necessity with respect to the same thing are positive properties which mutually exclude one another. Therefore the infinite being cannot have all properties, unless we make it a collection of absurdities, after the fashion of pantheists.

114. The infinite being must have all being which involves no imperfection. This is very true, but there still remain serious difficulties to be solved. What is perfection? What is imperfection? These are questions which it is not easy to answer, and yet we cannot advance a step until we have determined their meaning.

115. The idea of perfection implies being: nothing cannot be perfect, a perfect not-being is a manifest contradiction.

116. Not all being is absolute perfection; for there are modes of being which involve imperfection: what is perfection for one being is imperfection for another.

117. In finite beings perfection is relative; a very perfect barn would be a very imperfect church; a painting may be an ornament in a gallery which would be a profanation if placed in the sanctuary. Perfection seems to consist in a property being conducive to its end. This idea is not applicable to the infinite being which can have no other end than itself. Therefore, perfection in the absolutely infinite being cannot be relative, but must be absolute.

118. If perfection is being, it seems that the perfection of the infinite being must consist in certain properties which are found formally in it, and therefore exclude all imperfection. An absolutely indeterminate being, that is, a being without any property, is impossible. What conception can we form of a *thing* without intelligence, without will, and without liberty? The propositions in which these properties are affirmed of God, are true; therefore these properties really exist in the subject of which they are affirmed.

119. An infinitely perfect being must have all perfection; but in what sense are we to understand *all*? Does it mean all possible perfections? But what perfections are possible? Those which are not repugnant. To what is the repugnance to be referred? It must be either a mutual repugnance, or a repugnance to a third: if the first, it is necessary to presuppose one of the two extremes, in order that the other may be repugnant to it; in that case, which is to be preferred? If the second, what is the third to which they are repugnant? On what is it founded?

If by all perfection is meant all that we can conceive, the same difficulty remains. For if we speak of the conception of a finite being, the conception is not infinite; if of the conception of an infinite being, it is a begging of the question, because in explaining the perfections of the infinite being we appeal to its conception.

These difficulties can only be solved by determining more precisely the meaning of these ideas.

120. A thing may be denied of another in two manners: by referring the negation to a property, or to an individual. When I say a surface is not a triangle, I may refer the predicate either to the species of triangle in general, or to an individual triangle. In the first instance, I deny that the figure is triangular; in the second, I deny that the figure is another given triangle. When I say God is not extended, I deny a property; when I say God is not the world, I deny an individual.

It is evident that in order to attribute absolute infinity to any being, it is necessary that no being should be denied of it, either with respect to properties or to individuals, and that the predicate should be affirmed without destroying the principle of contradiction. This exception is absolutely indispensable, unless we wish to make the infinite being the greatest of all absurdities, a jumble of contradictions.

I believe that this will explain to a great extent the idea of absolute infinity, not considered in the abstract, but applied to a really existent being.

CHAPTER XVI
ALL THE REALITY CONTAINED IN INDETERMINATE CONCEPTIONS IS AFFIRMED OF GOD

121. We have seen that our cognitions are of two classes: some are general and indeterminate, others intuitive. All the objects which we know, whether indeterminately or intuitively, may be affirmed of God, provided they involve no contradiction.

122. General and indeterminate conceptions are the ideas of being and not-being, substance and accidents, simple and composite, cause and effect. All that is real in these conceptions is affirmed of God.

123. Being or that which really exists, is affirmed of God. That which is not has no property.

124. Substance, or being subsistent in itself, is also affirmed of God.

I do not enter into the discussion of the question greatly disputed in the schools, whether the ideas of being and substance are applied in the same sense, or, as logicians say, *univoce*, to God and creatures. It is sufficient for my purpose that the idea of being is applied to the infinite being, as opposed to the idea of not-being, and the idea of substance as opposed to accidents, or rather, as implying a thing which contains all that is necessary in order to subsist by itself without inhering in any other.

125. The idea of accident cannot be applied to the infinite being; but this is not to deny it any thing positive, but rather to affirm a perfection; for we say that it has no need of being inherent in another. This is a perfection; it is being: to deny the quality of accident is to remove a negation. To say that a being is a substance is to deny that it is an accident: these two ideas are contradictory and cannot be attributed to the same subject at the same time.

126. Simplicity is affirmed of God. This attribute denies nothing; to be convinced of this we need only recollect what simplicity is. The simple is one; the composite is a union of beings. If the parts are real, as they must be if there is a true composition, the resultant is a collection of beings

subordinated to a certain law of unity. When, therefore, we say that God is simple, we say that God is not a collection of beings, but one being. This involves no negation: but on the contrary it is the affirmation of an existence not divided into various beings.

127. The idea of cause, that is, of activity which produces in another the transition from not-being to being, or from one mode of being to another, is also affirmed of God. This involves no negation, but is an affirmation of being; for a cause is not only being, but a being which so abounds in perfection as to communicate it to others.

128. The idea of effect cannot be applied to God; but this is an affirmation, not a negation. Every effect is a thing produced, which has, consequently, passed from not-being to being: to deny the quality of effect is to remove the negation of being, and affirm the fulness of being.

129. What has been said of the ideas of cause and effect, may be extended to the ideas of necessary and contingent. The negative proposition, God is not contingent, is an affirmation; for contingency is the possibility of not-being. To deny this possibility is to affirm the necessity of being, which is the fulness of perfection.

CHAPTER XVII
ALL THAT IS NOT CONTRADICTORY IN INTUITIVE IDEAS IS AFFIRMED OF GOD

130. We have seen that all that is positive in general and indeterminate conceptions is affirmed of God. Let us see if the same is true of intuitive ideas. These ideas, in all that touches our understanding, may be reduced to these four; passive sensibility, active sensibility, intelligence, and will.

131. Passive sensibility, or the form under which the objects of the external world are presented to our senses, cannot be attributed to the infinite being. This negative proposition, the infinite being is not passively sensible, is strictly true.

Does this proposition deny any thing positive of God? Let us examine it.

The form of passive sensibility is extension, which necessarily implies multiplicity. The extended is necessarily a collection of parts: to deny extension of God is to affirm his simplicity; to deny that he is a collection of beings, and to affirm the indivisible unity of his nature.

132. Besides extension, there is in the passive sensibility of objects only the relation of causes which produce in us the effects called sensations. This causality can and must be affirmed of God: for it is certain that the infinite cause is capable of producing in us all sensations without the intervention of any medium.

133. The negative proposition: the infinite being is not material, means nothing more than the other; the infinite being is not passively sensible. We do not know the intrinsic nature of matter: all we know is, that it is presented in intuition to our sensibility under the form of extension, as an essentially multiplex object. When we deny that God is material or corporeal, we deny that he is passively sensible, or that he is multiple under the form of extension.

134. The other properties of matter, such as mobility, impenetrability, and divisibility, relate to extension, or to a particular impression caused on

our senses. The difficulties that may be raised on these points are solved by the preceding paragraphs.

Inertness, or indifference to rest or motion, is a purely negative property. It is the incapacity of all action, the absence of an internal principle productive of change, the purely passive disposition to receive all that is communicated to it.

135. It therefore remains demonstrated that to deny to God passive sensibility, or corporeal nature, is to affirm his undivided nature, his productive activity, and the impossibility of his suffering any kind of change.

136. Active sensibility, or the faculty of perceiving, presents two characteristics which must be defined. There are in sensation two things: the affection caused in the sensitive being by the sensible object, and the internal representation of the sensible being. The first is purely passive, and supposes the possibility of being affected by an object, and, consequently, of being subject to change. This cannot be attributed to the infinite being: to deny it is to affirm immutability, or the necessity of remaining always in the same state. The second is a sort of inferior order of cognition, by which the sensitive being perceives the sensible object. The representation of all objects must necessarily be found in the infinite being, consequently all that is intuitively perceptive in the sensitive faculty must be contained in the perception of the infinite being; that is to say, all that sensibility presents to us of external objects, all that it transfers to our intuition of external existence, must be contained in the representation which the infinite intelligence has within itself. Man cannot know under what form objects are presented to the intuition of the infinite being; but it is certain that all the *truth* contained in sensitive representation is presented to this intuition.

137. Intelligence, or the perception of objects without the forms of sensibility, implies the perception of beings and of their relations, which is something positive. In us it is often accompanied by the negative circumstance, of the absence of determinate objects to which the general conception may be referred. The infinite being sees in a single intuition all that exists and all that can exist, and contains all that is positive in intelligence, without what is negative, which is an imperfection.

138. It is evident that will must be affirmed of God; for we cannot deny the infinite being that internal, spontaneous activity which is called *to will*, and the nature of which involves no imperfection.

139. The will of God, although one and most simple, is distinguished into free and necessary, according to the objects to which it is referred. This gives rise to various negative propositions, which it is well to examine.

We say: God cannot will moral evil; this proposition, apparently negative, is, logically considered, affirmative. God cannot will moral evil, because his will is invariably fixed on good, on that sublime type of all holiness which he contemplates in his infinite essence. The impotence of moral evil is in God an infinite perfection of his infinite holiness.

140. The divine will may be referred to external objects, which, being finite, can be combined in different manners, and the existence or non-existence of these combinations depends on the end proposed by the agent which produces or modifies them. The will of God exerted on these objects is free; and to say that he has no necessity of doing this or that is to deny nothing, but to affirm a perfection, namely, the faculty of willing or not willing, or willing in different manners, objects which, on account of their finite nature, cannot bind the infinite will.

141. Hence all the reality contained in general ideas, whether indeterminate or intuitive, that is not contradictory, is affirmed of the absolutely infinite being. As to individual realities, it is evident that those which are finite cannot be affirmed of the infinite being without contradiction. The proposition: the infinite being is the corporeal universe, is equivalent to this: the infinite being is an essentially finite being. The same contradiction will be met with in every proposition where the subject is the infinite being, and the predicate an individual reality distinct from the infinite being. This remark will suffice for the present: they will be more clearly understood when we come to treat of the multitude of substances, in refuting the error of pantheists.

CHAPTER XVIII
INTELLIGENCE AND THE
ABSOLUTELY INFINITE BEING

142. The infinite being is not a vague object presented in the general idea of being, but is possessed of true properties which, without ceasing to be real, are identified with its infinite essence. A being which is not something, of which some property cannot be affirmed, is a dead being, which we conceive only under the general idea of thing, and is presented to us as something which cannot be realized. Such is not the conception which mankind form of the infinite being; the idea of activity has always been associated with the idea of God: this is not a general, but a fixed and determinate activity; internally, it is the activity of intelligence; externally, the activity which produces beings.

143. The idea of activity in general does not exclude all imperfection: activity to do evil is an imperfect activity: the activity by which some sensible beings act on others, is subject to the conditions of motion and extension, and is, consequently, not exempt from imperfection. Pure, internal activity, considered in itself, involves no imperfection; this is intellectual activity. It is an inoffensive activity, and of itself does no harm; it is an immaculate faculty, and of itself is never stained.

144. To know good, is good; to know evil, is also good; to wish good is good; to wish evil is evil; here is a difference between the understanding and the will; the will may be defiled by its object, the understanding never. The moralist considers, examines, and analyzes the greatest iniquities, and studies the details of the most degrading corruption; the politician knows the passions, the miseries, and the crimes of society; the lawyer witnesses injustice under all its aspects; the naturalist and the physician contemplate the most filthy and loathsome objects; and in all this no stain attaches to the intelligence. God himself knows all the evil there is or can be in the physical or in the moral order, and yet his intelligence remains immaculate.

145. Created beings abuse liberty as such; for it is essentially a principle of action, and may be directed to evil; but the intelligence, as regards itself

alone, cannot be abused. It is essentially an immanent or intransitive act in which are represented real or possible objects; the abuse does not commence until the free will combines the acts of the intelligence and directs them to a bad action; there is no evil knowledge until the act of the will is introduced into the combinations of the understanding. A collection of stratagems to commit the most horrible crimes, may be the innocent object of intellectual contemplation.

146. A wonderful thing is intelligence. With it there is relation, order, rule, science, art; without intelligence there is nothing. Conceive, if you can, the world without the pre-existence of intelligence; all is chaos; imagine the order which now exists, destroy intelligence, and the universe is a beautiful picture placed before the extinguished sight of a corpse.

147. We conceive beings as more perfect accordingly as they are higher in the order of intelligence. Leaving the sphere of the insensible and entering the order of sensitive representation, a new world commences. The first degree is the animal in which sensations are limited to a small number of objects, and the summit is intelligence. Morality flows from intelligence, or, rather, is one of its laws, it is the prescription of conformity to an infinitely perfect type. Morality is explained with intelligence; without intelligence it is an absurdity. The intelligence has its laws, its duties, but they proceed from itself, as the sun enlightens itself by its own light. Liberty is explained with intelligence; without it, liberty is an absurdity. Without intelligence causality is presented to us as a farce operating without an object or a direction, without a sufficient reason, and is consequently the greatest of absurdities. When some theologians said that the constitutive attribute of the essence of God is intelligence, they expressed an idea which contains a wonderfully profound philosophical meaning.

148. By the intellectual act being does not go out of itself: intelligence is an immanent act which may be extended to infinity, and exercised with infinite intensity without the intelligent leaving itself. The more profound its understanding is, the more profound is its concentration on the abyss of its consciousness. Intelligence is essentially active: it is activity. See what happens in man: he thinks, and his will awakes and acts: he thinks, and his body moves: he thinks, and his strength is multiplied, all his faculties are subject to his thought. Let us imagine an intelligence infinite in extension and in intensity, an intelligence in which there is no alternation of action and rest, of energy and abatement, an infinite intelligence which knows itself infinitely, and knows infinite, real, or possible objects with an infinitely perfect knowledge; an intelligence, the source of all light without any darkness, the origin of all truth without any mixture of error; we

may then form some idea of the absolutely infinite being. By this infinite intelligence I conceive an infinitely perfect will; I conceive creation, a pure act of will calling into existence, from nothing, the types which pre-existed in the infinite intelligence; I conceive infinite holiness, and all the perfections identified in that ocean of light. Without intelligence I conceive nothing: the absolute being, which is in the origin of all things, seems the old chaos, and I try in vain to induce some order into it. The ideas of being, of substance, and of necessity are knocked about in the greatest confusion in my understanding; the infinite is not a focus of light for me, but an abyss of darkness: I know not whether I am immerged in an infinite reality, or lost in the imaginary space of a vague and empty conception.

CHAPTER XIX
SUMMING UP

149. The examination of the idea of the infinite is of the greatest importance, because it is inseparably united with the idea of God.

150. We have the idea of the infinite; but the disputes concerning its nature, and even its existence, denote its obscurity.

151. The finite is that which has limits.

152. The infinite is not the same as the indefinite. The infinite is that which has no limits—the *not-finite*; the indefinite is that to which no limits are assigned—the *not-defined*.

153. The difference between the infinite and the finite is founded on the principle of contradiction: the finite affirms limits; the infinite denies them: there is no medium between yes and no.

154. Limit is the negation of a being, or of something real, applied to a being: the limit of a line is the point which terminates it; the limit of a force is the point beyond which it does not extend.

155. The idea of the infinite, denying limit, denies a negation; therefore it is an affirmative idea: the idea of the finite is negative, because it affirms a negation.

156. The idea of the infinite is applied to many orders of beings, and presents strange anomalies, which seem contradictions. A line produced to infinity in only one direction appears infinite, since it is greater than all finite lines; and it is not infinite, because it has a limit in the point where it starts. The same thing is verified in surfaces and solids. To explain these anomalies we must attend to the following observations.

157. The idea of the infinite is not intuitive. We have no intuition of an object either absolutely or relatively infinite.

158. The idea of the infinite is an indeterminate conception formed by the union of the two indeterminate ideas of being in general, and the negation of limit in general.

159. The indeterminate conception of the infinite gives us no knowledge of any thing infinite.

160. The anomalies and apparent contradictions, which we find in the application of the idea of the infinite, vanish when we reflect that the difference of the results depends on the different conditions under which we apply the idea of the infinite. Things which would be infinite under one condition cease to be so when considered under other conditions: the apparent contradiction is caused by one not remarking the change of conditions.

161. We have the conception of infinite number, for we can unite in our mind the two indeterminate conceptions of number and the negation of limit.

162. We have the conception of infinite extension, for we can unite the two indeterminate ideas of extension and the negation of limit.

163. The possibility or non-contradiction of conceptions in the purely ideal order does not prove their possibility in the real order. When the conceptions are realized, their reality is not in an abstract extension or an abstract number, but in individual extended beings, or individual numbers: the determinateness implied by the reality may involve contradiction to the true infinity, although it be impossible for us to discover any contradiction in the indeterminate conception, which abstracts the conditions of their realization.

164. Although we have the conception of infinite extension, it is impossible for us to imagine it.

165. No extrinsic or intrinsic repugnance can be discovered in the existence of infinite extension.

166. We cannot know by purely philosophical means whether the extension of the universe is infinite or finite.

167. Although an absolutely infinite number may be indeterminately conceived, it is not susceptible of any arithmetical or geometrical expression: no series of what mathematicians call infinite expresses an absolutely infinite number.

168. The intrinsic impossibility of an *actual* infinite number may be demonstrated from the intrinsic repugnance of the *co-existence* of certain things which may be *numbered*.

169. The idea of the absolutely infinite real being cannot be indeterminate: it necessarily involves positive and formal perfections.

170. All that does not imply a contradiction must be affirmed of the infinite being. That which is absurd is not a perfection.

171. Analyzing indeterminate and intuitive ideas, we find that all the reality contained in them is affirmed of God.

172. The absolutely infinite being must be intelligent.

173. Intelligence is a perfection which does not imply contradiction.

174. Will and liberty must also be found in the absolutely infinite being.

175. The indeterminate idea of the infinite is favored by the combination of the ideas of being and not-being.

176. The idea of an absolutely infinite being consists in the idea of a union of all being that involves no contradiction.

177. The indeterminate idea of a real infinite being, or of God, is formed from the idea of an absolutely infinite being, combined with the intuitive ideas of intelligence, will, liberty, causality, and all others that can be conceived without imperfection, in any infinite degree.

BOOK NINTH
ON SUBSTANCE

CHAPTER I
NAME AND GENERAL IDEA OF SUBSTANCE

1. What is substance? Have we a clear and distinct idea of it? The disputes of philosophers concerning the idea of substance and the continual applications which we make of it, prove two things: first, that the idea of substance exists; and secondly, that its clearness and distinctness are not all that could be desired. A mere name, containing no idea, could not so strongly draw the attention of all philosophers, nor be used so generally, even in ordinary language; a clear and distinct idea could not give occasion to so much dispute.

2. The importance of this idea may be seen in the results to which philosophers are led, according to the way in which they explain it. The entire system of Spinosa is founded on wrong definition of substance.

3. In the present question as in many others, it does not seem to be the shortest way to begin with a definition, unless the thing defined is only a name: to define a thing is to explain it, and we cannot explain it if we are ignorant of what it is, and we are ignorant, or are supposed to be ignorant of this, when we enter on investigations in order to ascertain what it is. If philosophers, at the beginning of their treatises, would not say, substance is this, but only, this is what I understand by substance, they would escape a number of difficulties.

4. After defining the name of substance, and making a clear and distinct idea correspond to it, it is still necessary to show how far the idea represents objects really existing, or, whether it belongs to the class of ideas expressing only the relation of different ideas, without our having any means of ascertaining whether this relation is found in the positive world or not; that is to say, whether the idea of substance is only the work of our understanding, a mere result of the combination of certain ideas, or

is furnished us by experience itself. I shall try not to fall into any of these faults; I know not, however, whether I can escape them. For this purpose, I shall first analyze the word, with respect to its etymological sense, and then examine the various meanings which have been given to it. The analysis of words is very useful for the analysis of ideas: words often contain a great deal of truth, which we lose by not attending to their common meaning.

5. The word substance, *substantia*, implies something which is under, *substat*, which is the subject on which other things are placed; just as its correlative, accident or modification, expresses something which happens to the subject, *accidit*; something which modifies it, which is in it, as a mode of being, *modus*.

6. By substance we seem to understand something constant in the midst of variation, something which, although it is in various ways successively, according to the variety of modifications which affect it, remains constant and identical under different transformations. When we say that the substance has received any new modification, although we understand by this that the substance is, in a new mode, we do not mean that it is different in itself, that it has lost its internal primitive being, and taken a new being; but we only consider this change as external, and as leaving untouched a certain base, which is what we call substance.

If it were not so, if we did not conceive something constant and identical under modifications, we could not distinguish substance from its modifications. The modification passes from not-being to being, and from being to not-being; now it is, and now it resigns its post to another and very different modification. But the substance is the same under different modifications; it does not pass from not-being to being with the succession of its modifications. From the moment that we attribute to substance the instability which belongs to its modifications, it ceases to be distinguishable from them.

Ordinary language confirms this truth. When there is a variation of modifications we say that the substance changes, that is, we conceive something which existed before the change, and exists after it. We say that a modification has entirely disappeared; we do not say this of the substance, but only that it is, or is presented to us, in a different manner. We therefore conceive something which remains constant and identical under different modifications: the subject in which these changes occur, this something which does not disappear with the disappearance of the modifications, which is not changed internally with these changes, we call substance, *substantia, substratum*.

CHAPTER II
APPLICATION OF THE IDEA OF SUBSTANCE TO CORPOREAL OBJECTS

7. Let us apply the ideas contained in that of substance to a corporeal object: this will help explain these ideas, and perhaps suggest others.

The paper on which I am writing is susceptible of various modifications: I may write on it a thousand different things, in various characters, and in different colors; I may fold it in various ways, and give it an infinite variety of positions in relation to the objects around it, and I may move it in all imaginable directions. Under this infinity of changes there is something constant, something which does not change. There are many new things, but there is one which is not new, which is always the same. There is one which suffers these changes, but retains something which does not change. If I make the paper blue and then red, that which is now red is the same that was blue, and before that white, and to this which is constant all those changes are referred. If a white paper is shown me, and then another paper that is blue, and then one that is red, it is clear that it is not the same as though I gave all these transformations to the same paper. The impression which the color produces in me remains the same; in what, then, does the difference consist? The difference is, that in the one case there is something permanent, which has passed through successive changes; in the other case this *something* is not the same, but is another and different thing. In the one case there are different modifications; in the other there are different substances.

8. Let us go deeper into the matter. If we only received the successive impressions without any means of referring them to the same object, to connect them in a common point, we should find no difference between the two cases of which we have been speaking. If a piece of white paper be placed before us, and, after turning our eyes aside for a moment, we find a blue paper in the same place, with the same dimensions, and after again turning our eyes aside we find a red paper: it is clear that it would be impossible for us to distinguish, by the mere succession of the visual impressions, whether the same paper has been differently colored in

succession, or different papers have been substituted for the first. But if we keep our eyes on the place where the paper is, we see whether the paper is colored or changed. In the first case, the appearance of the new color will continue with the same sensation of the paper, unmoved, the transformation is made without our losing sight of it, and the paper receives the continued succession of its motions and positions under the hand of the one who colors it. We are then sure that the paper is the same, because there has been a continuity of sensation, or rather a connection of the different colors with a third, resulting from the situation of the paper and its motions, and from all that by which we know what is common to the first and the second. But if there is no new coloring of the paper, but a substitution of a differently colored paper, we see that the first paper is taken away; the whole order of the sensation is interrupted, and new sensations are presented. These last have no connection with the first; there is, consequently, for us a different *thing*.

9. This shows how the idea of substance with respect to bodies is generated in us, or, to speak more properly, how we apply the idea of substance to bodies. When we discover a link which unites the different sensations in one point, we call that in which they are united, substance. And as we meet in nature with many of these points which are independent of one another, we naturally say there are many corporeal substances.

10. When we perceive an impression we never call it a substance, if we refer it to an object, or consider it as objective: for the object is not, of itself alone, capable of connecting various sensations. We receive the sensations of red, and not only ordinary people, but even philosophers, when not philosophizing, make the color objective, and consider the red, not as a simple sensation, but as an external quality. No one would call this quality by itself a substance; for it is not capable, of itself alone, of connecting other impressions or qualities. If there is a change of color the red disappears, and the new impression is connected in the order of time with the sensation of the red, but does not reside in it. If there is a change of form, although the red continues, we do not conceive this color as the necessary link between the two forms, because we know that the continuance of the red is indifferent to the variety of form, which may be changed with or without the continuance of this color.

As in general we have experienced that no sensation is necessarily connected with another, and that among sensations connected at a common point, some disappear without the rest disappearing, we infer that none of them is a necessary link; and therefore, although we make them objective, we do not give them the character of a substance, of any thing remaining identical through changes, of which it is, as it were, the recipient.

11. There is a property in bodies which is necessary to all sensations, or at least, to the two principal sensations of sight and touch. This property is extension, which, whether considered subjectively or objectively, we regard as a recipient of all sensations. We neither see nor imagine the white or black; we neither touch nor imagine the hard or the soft, the warm or the cold, without the extension in which the whiteness or blackness, the hardness or softness, the warmth or the cold reside. Thus extension might perhaps merit the honor of substance, if it were not subject to another condition, which deprives it of this title.

Although when we conceive extension in general, in the abstract, considering it as a mere continuity, we absolutely abstract it from all form; when we have need of an applied extension as the recipient of sensations, it is impossible to find it without a determinate form and figure. We do not see a color simply, but we see it in a circular, triangular, or other extension. These forms are confounded with extension itself as its applications; and do not serve as a link for other sensations. Sometimes, it is true, the same figure receives different colors, different positions, different degrees of heat or cold, etc., but the contrary also sometimes occurs, and with the same color, and the same degree of heat or cold, with the same continuance of the other sensations, the object changes its form; just as a red circle may become a green circle, a red object may become circular, and afterwards triangular. In the first case, the circular figure is the link connecting the sensations of the colors; in the second, the color is the link connecting the figures.

12. Having deprived extension of the honor of substance, as well as all other sensations, in so far as objective; we may observe that all these variations in the objects are successive, and the sensations are connected with each other. Thus the same circle may take different colors; and the same color different figures; the colors may be again changed, and the first reproduced, the figure remaining the same; or the first figure may be reproduced, the colors remaining the same. We conclude that under this variety there is something constant, that under this multiplicity there is something which is one; that under this succession of being and not-being there is something permanent; and this which is constant, one, and permanent, the recipient of these changes, the point outside of us which connects them, and enables us to conceive them connected,—this is what we call substance.

CHAPTER III
DEFINITION OF CORPOREAL SUBSTANCE

13. What is the permanent subject of transformations in the sensible order? Is it a pure illusion? Is it a reality? What reality can it be? Does it not seem rather an abstraction? A thing which is no color, but lends itself all colors; which is none of the qualities which we experience, but the subject and cause of them all; which is no form, but accommodates itself to all forms; which is not pure extension, because this is an abstraction, and it is something which serves as the ground of other things; a corporeal object which, in itself, can affect none of the senses; what is it? Is it what the Aristotelians call an occult quality, a mysterious, and fantastic being, a mere illusion? Let us examine it by the light of experience.

14. Let us take a piece of wax and without letting it go out of our hands paint it different colors successively, subject it to different degrees of temperature, softening it by warming, and then cooling it; let us give it different forms, of a globe, a cylinder, a parallelopipedon, a table, a vase, or a statue; do all these changes take place in the same thing? Yes. Is this thing not a color, or a figure, or a degree of temperature? No; because all these qualities were and ceased to be whilst the thing remained the same. How do I know that the thing remained the same? Because there was a continuity of sensation in the eye fixed upon the object; in the touch which, although it felt the modifications of warm and cold, hard and soft, experienced also an uninterrupted sensation of an object, which remained constantly in the hand, and the weight of which was continuously felt. Therefore there is something there which is not the modifications, but is that which is modified, something common to them all, which receives and connects them, outside of me and within me.

15. Examining one conception of this permanent something, we find that, after abstracting its qualities, we have:

I. The idea of being. We say the thing, the something, the subject, etc., we therefore speak of a being, of a quality. Without the reality there is nothing; and nothing cannot be the subject of modifications, or the link connecting impressions.

II. The idea of being, which we here find, is not pure, it is not being alone. The qualities exist, are beings; and still we do not confound them with the subject.

III. That which accompanies the idea of being is the idea of permanence amidst succession, and the relation of this permanence as the point of connection, the immovable centre in the midst of succession.

16. If, therefore, we wished to define substance, we could only say that it is *a permanent being in which occur the changes which are presented to us in the sensible phenomena.* Our knowledge is all reduced to this; all that we can add beside, is only hypothesis or conjecture. In vain you ask me, what is this being? Give me the intuition of the essence of corporeal things, and I will tell you; but while I know them only by their effects, that is, the impressions which they produce in me, I cannot answer you. I know that it is something; I know its relation to its forms; I know that the forms are in the subject, and are not the subject; but here is the limit of my knowledge. The object corresponding to the idea composed of a permanent being and its relation to various forms is what I call corporeal substance.

17. Since the substance changes its accidents, remaining the same itself, it follows that its existence is independent of the accidents. Abstracting, for the present, whether it can or cannot exist without any, I only affirm that none in particular is necessary to it. Here we must take note of the difference between substance in itself, and in the medium by which it is manifested to us, and placed in active or passive communication with us. The accidents are this medium; they are the transitory forms it puts on. How can we know the existence of bodies, except by sensations? The object of sensation is not substance in its inner nature, but only its qualities as affecting us.

CHAPTER IV
RELATION OF CORPOREAL
SUBSTANCE TO ITS ACCIDENTS

18. In the idea of corporeal substance the idea of permanence is perfectly included, the idea of unity only imperfectly. The unity which we conceive in every corporeal substance is a factitious unity; since that which is constant is not one but an aggregate of many, as is proved by the divisibility of matter; out of every corporeal substance we may make many which will have the same right as the first to be called substances. A piece of wood is a substance; but we may slit it into several pieces which will be equally substances. These pieces, joined together, formed what are called *one* substance; but it is clear that this unity was very imperfect, and was rather a union than a unity, and that if we consider it as *one*, it was in relation to the unity of effect which it produced in us, by the connection which it gave to our sensations and to the phenomena which resulted from it.

19. Hence, every corporeal substance involves multiplicity, or combination of the elements which compose it. Experience informs us that this combination is not permanent; there is, consequently, no corporeal substance which does not imply at least one modification, namely, the arrangement of its parts. Abstracting the changes which this modification may undergo, it can never be confounded with the substance: although the bodies might be presented constantly to our senses with the same arrangement of the parts, the permanent *being* would be in the parts, not in their arrangement. The latter is something external which is added to the thing existing; there can be no union and combination without parts which are united and combined.

20. A difference which we observe between the substance and its modifications is, that the substance is independent of the modifications, but the modifications are not independent of the substance. The substance, while remaining the same, changes its accidents, but an accident cannot change its substance and remain the same. The same block may receive different figures successively; but a figure, numerically the same, cannot pass from one block to another. Two blocks may have a similar or a different

figure, whether cubic, spherical, or pyramidal, and one may take the figure of the other; but in that case, the figures are not identical, but similar, they are specifically but not numerically the same.

21. If I am asked how I know that there is only similarity and not numerical identity in the figures which bodies take successively, that there is no *permanence* in the figures which change their subject, and consequently that the same figure cannot pass from one substance to another, in the same manner that the same substance passes from one figure to another; I shall not find it difficult to prove what I assert.

There is no one who does not see what an extravagant thing it would be for a cubic figure to leave a body and pass to another. What is this figure separated from the body? How is it preserved during the transition? Why is it not exactly the same in both, but presented with slight modifications? Has it undergone a modification in its passage from one body to another? Then there would be a modification of a modification, and the figure in itself abstracted from all body, would be a kind of substance of a secondary order, permanent under modifications. These are but absurd dreams in which that is applied to the concrete which belongs to the idea only in the abstract. This transition of the forms would suppose their separate existence, and thus we might have all kinds of abstract figures, cubes, spheres, circles, triangles, etc., subsisting in themselves without application to any thing figured.

22. A still stricter demonstration of this truth is possible. If we suppose a figure, numerically the same, to pass from one body to another; the block A, which loses the cubic form, transmits it to the body B. Now, this individual form cannot be in both at the same time. Suppose that after the cubic form has left the block A, we turn it back before it has touched the body B, evidently it will not be the same in both: therefore the body B has not acquired the same, but only a similar form. It is also evident that in order to give the cubic form, we need not take it from another; therefore, the form of one is not *individually* that of the other; otherwise we should have to say that it is and is not, that it is preserved and ceases to exist at the same time.

23. The term *transmission* or *communication* of motion, which is so much used in physical science, expresses something real so long as limited to the phenomenon which is under calculation; but it would be an absurdity, if it meant that the *same* motion which was in one body has *passed* to another. The sum of the quantities of motion is the same in elastic bodies after impact as before it; the velocity being divided between them, and the one gaining what the other loses. This is proved by calculation, and confirmed by experience. But it is evident that one body does not impart the *same* individual velocity which it contained to the other body; for not only can

the velocity not be separated from the body and pass from one subject to another; but it cannot even be conceived except as a relation, the idea of which includes the ideas of a body moved, of space, and of time. It is true that Q representing the quantity of the motion before impact, the value of Q remains the same after impact; but this only expresses the phenomenon in relation to its effects, as subject to calculation; not that the velocity in the second member of the equation is composed of the parts of the first. Let A and B represent two bodies, the individual masses of which are expressed by these two letters; and V, v their respective velocities before impact. The quantity of motion will be Q = A × V B × v. After impact there will be a new velocity which we may call w, and the quantity of motion will be Q = A × w B × u. Mathematically speaking, the value of Q will be the same; but this only means that if the results of the motion be expressed in lines or numbers, we shall have the same after impact as before it; it does not and cannot mean that in the velocity u, considered as united to the subject, there is a portion of velocity which has been detached from V to be joined to v.

24. Hence, we do not conceive the accidents of bodies as possible without a subject in which they are inherent; and that substances are not inherent in another being, but are conceived and really exist without this inherence. A figure cannot exist without a thing figured, but the thing figured may still exist, through all other things are destroyed. The analysis of the nature of substance shows that its existence supposes the existence of another being which produced it; but relation between them is that of cause and effect, not of inherence, or that of the subject and its modification.

25. These last observations explain another mark of corporeal substances. In the third chapter of this book we found the three characteristics of being, the relation of the permanent to the variable, and the subject of the variations; we now find a fourth, which is a negation, non-inherence in another. This negative characteristic is included in the positive one, *permanent subject of variations*; for it is clear that in conceiving a subject *permanent amid variations* we do not include inherence, but rather deny it, at least implicitly. Non-inherence supposes something positive, something on which is founded the denial of the necessity of being inherent. What is this something? We know not. We know that it exists, but its explanation is beyond our reach. It is probably inexplicable without the intuition of the essence of things;—an intuition which we have not.

CHAPTER V
CONSIDERATIONS ON CORPOREAL
SUBSTANCE IN ITSELF

26. The idea of substance, such as we have thus far explained it, implies a relation to accidents in general. The idea we are now examining is not that of an indeterminate substance, but of corporeal substance; and it must be confessed that it is difficult to conceive a particular corporeal substance without any accident. If I take from the paper, on which I am writing, its figure, extension, and all that relates to my senses, what is there left for me to conceive something particular and determinate, something which is not the idea of being in general, but of this being in particular? It is clear that, in order that the object may not disappear altogether, and losing its individuality be confounded in the universal idea, I must reserve something by which I can say *this*: that is to say, that which is here, or which has affected me in this or that manner, or has been the subject of such or such modifications. I consider at least its position with respect to other bodies, or its causality in relation to the effects which it has produced in me, or its nature as the subject of determinate accidents. Just as the idea of finite substance in general involves relation to certain accidents in general, the idea of a particular substance involves relation to particular accidents.

27. We find this relation in our mode of conceiving corporeal substance; we cannot assert that it is involved in the nature of the substance. This nature is unknown to us, and when we attempt to examine it, we pass to another question, that of the essence of bodies.

28. Neither can we say how far the identity of the corporeal substance continues under its different transformations. The partisans of corpuscular philosophy consider all transformations as mere local motions, and all the variations which we see in bodies as mere results of the different position of the corpuscles among themselves. Leibnitz resolved matter into an infinity of monads, differing from the atoms of Epicurus, but conducing to the substantial invariability of bodies, which are only a collection of indivisible substances, which he calls monads. The Aristotelians believed that, of the changes of bodies, some were accidental, as figure, motion, density,

warmth, cold, etc.; others substantial, as the change of wood to ashes. But in all the variety of systems, all admit something permanent, the subject of the changes. The Atomists and Leibnitz evidently admitted the identity of the subject. As to the Aristotelians, although the change which introduced a substantial form different from the first substantially transformed the being, so that after the change of the substantial form it could not be said that one was substantially the other, they still thought there was a common subject in these substantial transformations, and this was what they called the first matter, *materia prima*. All systems of philosophy admit this clear and evident truth, that in the midst of the transformations of the corporeal world, there is something permanent.

29. This corporeal substance being a reality, must not only exist, but it must be something determinate. This substantial determination of the body, which makes it this particular thing, and distinguishes it in its internal nature, in its essence, from all other bodies of other species, the Aristotelians called the substantial form. The subject of this form, or actuality, which was common to all bodies, they called the *materia prima*, which was a pure potentiality, a sort of medium between pure nothing and actual being.

30. Ever since there have been schools of philosophy, these points have been disputed; and it is probable they always will be; but it is to very little purpose. We know the existence of the corporeal world, we know its relations to ourselves, we know its properties and its laws, so far as they are subject to our observation; but its intrinsic nature is beyond the reach of our senses, or our instruments. Increased acuteness of observation and improvement in the power and delicacy of instruments, discovers new mysteries, and man finds the barriers which he believed the *ne plus ultra*, removed from him as he advances. Will he ever be able to pass them? Will he ever make the entire circuit of this scientific world? Is the knowledge of the intrinsic nature of the subject of this infinity of phenomena which astonish us, reserved to the future? It is hard to believe it. The telescope, becoming more perfect, extends the limits of the universe, and seems to behold the infinitely great; the perfection of the microscope, advancing in the opposite direction, regards the infinitely little. Where are the limits? It is probable that man is not permitted to reach them while in this world. The mind of man in its fruitful activity, struggles alternately after the two extremes, but just as he flatters himself he is reaching the last limit, he feels that something stronger than himself withholds him from attaining the object of his noble desires; it is the chain that binds him to the mortal body, and obstructs the flight of his pure spirit.

CHAPTER VI
SUBSTANTIALITY OF THE HUMAN ME

31. We have not found perfect unity in corporeal substances: all that are subject to our senses may be resolved into a number of others equally substances in their turn; a body is rather an aggregate of substances, than one substance. We do not find the unity in the bodies; we attribute it to them either inasmuch as they form a common link of our sensations, or inasmuch as we consider the different substances subordinated to one being and governing substance. Thus the parts of an animated body constitute a sort of unity, inasmuch as they are subordinate to the principle which animates them.

32. We do not conclude from this that true unity does not exist in bodies; if we could know their essence, we should doubtless discover it, whether in the monads, as maintained by Leibnitz, or in something else more or less resembling them. Although this knowledge of their essence is denied us, reason leads us to this unity. The composite is formed of parts; if these parts are in turn formed of others, we must at last come to something which has no parts; here we find the indivisible, or rather, the true unity. This reasoning is equally valid, even though we suppose matter to be infinitely divisible. Infinite divisibility would suppose an infinity of parts into which any body may be divided: these parts would therefore exist; these infinitesimal elements would be real: the unity would be in them.

33. Independently of the external world, we find the idea of substance in ourselves; consciousness reveals its real application and perfect unity. Consciousness makes known to us that we think, desire, feel, and experience an infinity of affections, some of which are subject to our will and are the product of the internal activity of our soul; others are independent of us, they come without our will, and often against it, and it is not always in our power to reproduce them even if we wish it.

This ebb and flow of ideas, volitions, and sentiments, have a point in which they are connected, a subject which receives them, remembers them, combines them, and seeks or avoids them; this being, of which we are internally conscious, philosophers have called the *me*. It is one and identical under all transformations; this unity, this identity, is an indisputable fact which consciousness reveals to us. Who could make us doubt that the *me* which thinks at the present moment is not the same which thought yesterday, which thought years ago? Notwithstanding the variety of thoughts and desires, the changes of opinion and will, who could deprive us of the firm and deep conviction which we have that we are the same who experience them all, that there is something here within us which is the subject of them all?

34. If there were not something in us permanent in the midst of this variety, the consciousness of the *me* would be impossible. Memory and combination would also be impossible; for there would be within us only a succession of unconnected phenomena. Thinking is impossible without something which thinks and remains identical under the variety of the forms of thought. There is, therefore, within us a simple subject which connects all the changes which occur in it: there is a substance. In it there is unity: the unity which we only find in corporeal substances after an infinite series of decompositions, is presented to us in the spiritual substance, at the first instant, as a simple internal fact, without which, all the phenomena which we perceive within us are absurd, and all experience of the external world impossible.

Without the unity of the *me* there can be no sensation, and without sensation no experience of the beings around us.

CHAPTER VII
RELATION OF THE PROPOSITION, I THINK, TO THE SUBSTANTIALITY OF THE ME

35. The proposition, *I think*, can have no sense unless we admit that the soul is a substance. Philosophy loses its resting-point, and all that experience within us is a series of unconnected phenomena, incapable of being observed, or subjected to any rule.

36. My present thought is not individually my thought of yesterday, as my thought of to-morrow will not be my thought of to-day. These thoughts, considered in themselves and abstracted from a subject in which they are found, have no connection with one another: perhaps their objects are without any relation to each other, or even contradictory; perhaps the thought of to-day is the denial of the thought of yesterday.

37. The same is true of all thoughts, all acts of the will, of all sentiments, imaginary representations, and sensations, and, in general, of all that I experience within myself. Turning my attention to all internal affections, whatever they may be, I see in them only a series of phenomena, a sort of current of existences passing away and disappearing, some never to return, others to reappear at a different time, *expressly* presenting this difference. The reappearance is not individual, but similar: the affection which is repeated is not the same, but another resembling it. When the affection returns, I am conscious of its presence at the time, and conscious of its presence at a previous time; this double consciousness constitutes recollection, makes me distinguish between the two affections, and necessarily implies the judgment that one is not the other. There would be no recollection, if the affection *recalling* were identified with the affection *recalled*. A thing *presents* itself, but does not *recall* itself.

38. Therefore every thing passes away within us never to return, the disappearance is real, the reappearance but apparent; that which ceases to be can never return to be again; there may be a similar thing, but not the same; that which was, is passed, and time does not retrace its steps.

39. Therefore, the series of internal phenomena, considered in themselves and abstracted from the subject in which they reside, are necessarily unconnected, and there is no way of subordinating the terms of the series to any law, or connecting link.

40. Still this law exists in all our intellectual acts; reason, without laws which govern it, would be the greatest of absurdities; this link is found in all our affections. That they pass from us with their distinction and difference and resemblance is a fact of our mind, to which we are subjected, as to a primitive and inevitable condition of our existence.

41. The proposition, *I think*, in the sense in which the word *think* includes all internal affections, does not relate to isolated phenomena alone, but it necessarily implies a point, which we call the *me*, in which these phenomena are connected. If this point does not exist, if it is not one and identical, the thought of to-day can have no connection with the thought of yesterday: they are two distinct things, at different times, and perhaps contradictory: when I say to-day, *I think*, and mean that the *I* is the same as in the proposition, *I thought yesterday*, my language would be absurd; if they are mere phenomena, two thoughts without any connecting link, the *me* is nothing, I cannot say, *I thought, I think*; but I must say *there was* thought, *there is* thought. If, then, you ask me, *where? in whom?* I must reply, that there is no *where*, no *who*; I must deny the supposition, and confine myself to repeating, *there was* thought, *there is* thought.

42. To say *me*, it is necessary to suppose a permanent reality; a reality, because that which is not real is nothing; permanent, because that which passes away disappears, ceases to be, and cannot serve as the point to unite other things.

CHAPTER VIII
REMARKS ON THE SOUL'S
INTUITION OF ITSELF

43. The permanent reality of the *me*, considered in itself and abstracted from the things which pass within it, is a fact which we perceive in our intuition, and which we express in all our words. If this presence, this internal experience, be what is called the intuition of the soul, then we have intuition of our soul. This intuition is reproduced in every particular intuition, and in all internal affections in general; for, although they are isolated phenomena, they imply the intuition of the *me*, because they imply the consciousness of themselves.

44. The variety of isolated phenomena instead of proving any thing against the unity of the intuition of the *me*, on the contrary, evidently confirms it. If we conceived only one fixed and identical thought, there would be less necessity of uniting with it the idea of a subject in which it resides; but when there is a multitude of different phenomena, which cannot co-exist without contradiction, we must refer them to something constant, or else the internal world is converted into an absolute chaos.

45. The soul has, therefore, an intuition of itself; that is to say, it is conscious of its unity in multiplicity, of its identity in diversity, of its permanence in succession, of its constant duration in the appearance and disappearance of phenomena. Either we must admit this, or we must renounce the legitimacy of all testimony of consciousness, and embrace the most complete skepticism that ever existed, extending it both to the internal and to the external world.

46. We find within us the realization of the indeterminate conceptions of *being, unity, permanence,* and *subject of modifications*; this realization is revealed by consciousness, and is confirmed by the logical analysis of the series of phenomena in their relation to a point of connection.

47. All that is included in the idea of finite substance is contained in these four terms: *being, one, permanent,* and the *subject of modifications*. All this is in our soul, and we perceive by experience that we are internally affected by it. If this perception is called intuition, we have intuition of the substantiality of our soul.

48. The thinking being not only perceives itself but it knows itself as a real object, to which, by means of reflection, it applies the ideas of being, unity, permanence, and the subject of modifications. Therefore the soul may be the true predicate of propositions resting on logic and consciousness.

49. Have we any other intuition of the soul, besides that which has just been explained? To this I answer, that we have not while in this life, and at the same time I ask whether any other than that of consciousness is possible. Accustomed as we are to sensible intuitions which imply extension in space, we ask what the soul is in itself, and we do not seem to be satisfied without seeing its image. Leaving the order of sensibility and rising to the purely intellectual sphere, who knows whether we can say that there is no other intuition of the soul than that which we now have; whether the soul in itself, in the unity and simplicity of its entity, is the force which we perceive; whether this force is the subject of the modifications, the substance, without its being necessary to imagine another support in which this force might reside? Why may not this force be subsistent? Why must we imagine another *substratum* to support it? If it were so, if we must apply to the substance of the soul what the great Leibnitz thought applicable to all substances, making the idea of substance to consist in the idea of force; why may we not say that the pressure of the internal sense, the consciousness of itself, is all the intuition of itself which the soul can have?

50. You may ask me, what is the soul separated from the body? What will it perceive and know of itself, when it exists *alone*? As though it did not now perceive and know *alone*, or as though the organs, which it uses, could perceive or think. Does it, perchance, know how it uses them, or even know otherwise than by experience that it uses them at all? Is it not alone in the depths of its activity with its thoughts and the acts of its will, its sentiments, its joy and its sadness, its pleasures and its pains? Say, then, that perhaps we do not form sufficiently clear ideas of the *mode* of consciousness which we shall have of ourselves after this life; say that perhaps other intuitions of our self are possible; but do not imagine the soul as inconceivable alone. Leave me thought, will, sentiment, all that is internally present to my consciousness, to find myself; I ask no more. Give me communication with other beings, which affect me or are affected by me, which transmit to me thoughts and wills, which cause me pleasure or pain; I need nothing more in order to have a world which I can very well conceive. I am ignorant of the quality of the things, not of their possibility: the soul changes its state, not its nature.

CHAPTER IX
KANT'S OPINION OF THE ARGUMENTS
PROVING THE SUBSTANTIALITY OF THE SOUL

51. The psychological arguments in favor of the substantiality of the soul are mere paralogisms, in Kant's opinion; although they prove an ideal substance, they can never lead to a real substance. Besides the arguments with which this philosopher attacks the psychological proof of the substantiality of the soul, he had also a personal argument, which, considering the weakness of the human heart, was very powerful. He had either to place the substantiality of the soul in doubt, or else consent to the ruin of his whole system. "It would be," he says, "a great and even the only stumbling-block in our whole *critique*, if there were a possibility of demonstrating *a priori* that all thinking beings are in themselves simple substances, and (which is a consequence of the principle of this demonstration) are inseparably accompanied by personality and the consciousness of their existence distinct from all matter. For, in this case, if we had taken a single step out of the world of the senses, we should have entered into the field of the *noumena*, and no one would dispute our right to extend farther into it, to build in it, and, according to each one's good luck, to take possession of it." [43]

52. In Kant's conception, the first paralogism of pure psychology in favor of the substantiality of the soul is the following:—"Every thing, the representation of which is the *absolute substance* of our judgments, and which cannot serve as a determination of any thing else, is a substance. The *me*, as thinking being, is the absolute substance of all possible judgments, and this representation of itself cannot be the predicate of any thing else; therefore the *me*, as thinking being, is a substance."

These are the terms in which he presents the psychological reasoning which he proposes to attack, in the first edition of his *Critic of Pure Reason;* in the second edition, wishing to be more clear, or, perhaps, more obscure, he expresses the same argument in these words:—"That which cannot be thought otherwise than as subject, does not exist otherwise than as subject, and is therefore substance. Now a thinking being, regarded merely as such, cannot be thought otherwise than as subject. Therefore it exists only as such, that is, as substance." We must confess that if psychology could find no clearer expounders than Kant, and should have to use in its demonstrations the forms which this philosopher employs in these passages, it would have but a small number of proselytes, for the simple reason that very few could understand its language. I am sure that but few readers would be convinced by the syllogisms proving the substantiality of the soul, such as Kant presents them; in this way there is a great advantage in the position of the philosopher; for he has to prove that an argument, the force of which has not been felt, has no force. But let us suppose the philosopher to descend from the Olympus of incomprehensible abstractions, and deign to use the humble language of mortals, presenting the psychological argument under a more simple form, who knows but what the conviction which it would produce would be somewhat more difficult to destroy? Let us see.

53. A substance is a being remaining identical with itself, a permanent reality in which different modifications occur. But there is within me this reality which, remaining identical, has a variety of thoughts, acts of the will, sentiments, and sensations, as is revealed by consciousness. Therefore that which is within me is a substance.

I defy all the philosophers in the world to point out a false, or even a doubtful proposition in this syllogism, or to show a fault in the consequence, without placing themselves in open contradiction with the testimony of consciousness on the one hand, and with all the laws of human reason on the other.

54. Kant pretends that the argument in favor of the substantiality of the soul is not conclusive, because the pure categories, and consequently that of substance also, have absolutely no objective value, except in so far as applied to the diversity of an intuition subject to them: that is to say, the conception of substance is a purely logical function, without any objective value or meaning except as referred to sensible things, and as soon as we leave the sphere of sensibility, it can lead to no result. It is evident that the substantiality of the soul cannot be the object of sensible intuition; consequently, to apply to the soul the idea of substance is to extend the conception beyond what its nature allows. It must be confessed that Kant's reasoning is conclusive, if we admit his principles; and here we have a proof of the necessity of combating certain theories, which, because they are in the realm of abstractions, seem innocent, but in reality are most dangerous, on account of the results to which they lead. Such is the system of Kant as denying the objective value of the pure categories, and this is why I have combated it, [44] demonstrating: I. That indeterminate conceptions, and the general principles founded on them, have an objective value beyond the field of sensible experience, in respect to beings which are in nowise subject

to our intuition; II. That it is not true that we have only sensible intuition, for we have intuitive knowledge of a pure intellectual order, above the sphere of sensibility. This doctrine overthrows the whole of Kant's argument, for it destroys its foundation.

55. The German philosopher seems to have perceived the weak point in his reasoning, and therefore he tries to give the psychological argument in such terms as to show a transition from the ideal order to the real, keeping out of sight the point which unites things so distant. His language is purely ideological: "Every thing, the *representation* of which is the absolute substance of our judgments, and which cannot serve as a *determination* of any thing else, is a substance." Observe that he defines substance by the *representation* and the incapacity of serving as a *determination* of any thing else; that is, by purely ideological or dialectic attributes. The form which he employs in the second edition suffers from the same defect. "That which cannot be *thought* otherwise than as *subject*, does not exist otherwise than as subject, and is, therefore, substance." Why does he not tell us that the substance here spoken of is a permanent being, in which the modifications are realized, but which remains identical with itself? Why does he speak only of *representation*, of *thought*, of the *determination* or predicate? Because it helped his purpose to present the argument as a sophism in which there is a transition from one order to another entirely different order; because it was for his interest to give an obscure form, so that he could make the following observations:—"In the major, a being is spoken of which can be thought under any view in general, and consequently, also, as it is given in the intuition. But, in the minor, the same being is spoken of in so far as it is regarded as subject, in relation only to thought and the unity of consciousness, but not at the same time in relation to the intuition by which the unity is given to the thought as its object. Consequently the conclusion follows only by a fallacy, *per sophisma figuræ dictionis*." And in a note he says: "Thought is taken in the two premises in an entirely different sense; in the major, as belonging to an object in general, and such, consequently, as it may be given in the intuition; but in the minor only as it is in relation to the consciousness of self, where it is not thought in any object, but is merely represented in relation to itself, as subject, as the form of the thought. In the first case, a thing is spoken of which can only be thought as subject; but, in the second, thought is spoken of, not things, since abstraction is made of all objects; and in the thought the *me* always serves as subject of the consciousness; hence the conclusion which follows is not, that I cannot exist otherwise than as subject, but only, that I cannot make use of myself in the thought of my existence, otherwise than as subject of the judgment, which is an identical proposition, revealing absolutely nothing concerning the

manner of my existence. [45] It makes one indignant to see a man attempt, by such a confusion of ideas and of words, to rob the human mind of its existence; for it amounts to the same thing, to deny that it is a substance. It makes one indignant to see a philosopher pretend, by such an absurd confusion, to attack one of the clearest, most evident, and most irresistible arguments which can be presented to human reason. I thought yesterday, I think to-day: in all the variety of my situations, I find myself the same and not another; this reality, which remains identical in the midst of diversity, I call my soul; therefore my soul is a permanent reality, the subject of modifications; therefore it is a substance. Can any thing be clearer?"

56. Psychology does, it is true, make use of the general idea of substance in proving the substantiality of the soul: but it appeals to a fact of experience, to the testimony of consciousness, in order to apply this idea to the present case. What does Kant mean when he pretends to have demonstrated that the conception of a thing which can exist of itself as subject, but not as mere attribute, does not involve any objective reality? When he speaks of *subject*, does he mean a real subject, the subject of modifications? Then the soul is a subject; but we do not say that it is a subject *only*; we conceive its reality under this aspect without, therefore, denying that it has other characters: on the contrary, we expressly acknowledge that it is an active principle, which implies something more that the mere subject of modifications, for this last is a passive, rather than an active, quality. If by subject Kant understands the logical subject, we deny that this is exclusively the character of the soul in such a way that it cannot logically be the attribute or predicate of a proposition.

57. "The conception of a thing," says Kant, "which can exist as its own subject, but not as a mere predicate, draws with it no objective reality; that is, one cannot know whether any object corresponds to it, since one cannot conceive the possibility of such a manner of existing, consequently there is absolutely no cognition. In order that it may indicate under the denomination of substance, an object which may be given, in order that it may be a cognition, a constant intuition must be placed at the foundation, as the indispensable condition of the objective reality of a conception, namely, that by which alone the object is given. But we have nothing constant in the internal intuition, for the *me* is only the consciousness of my thought; if, therefore, we confine ourselves to the thought alone, the necessary condition of the application of the conception of substance, that is, of a subject subsisting in itself as thinking being." [46]

No argument could be more common-place and sophistical. Kant does not admit the substantiality of the soul, because we cannot take the substance itself and present it in sensible intuition; but then he ought not to speak of *pure intellectual conceptions* of *logical functions*, or of *ideas*; for all these are things which are out of the order of sensibility, and therefore cannot be given us in the sensible intuition. Yet they really exist as internal phenomena, as subjective facts, of which Kant is continually talking, and to which he devotes the greater part of his *Critic of Pure Reason*. Will it, perchance, be said that the pure idea of relation means nothing, because we cannot present an abstract relation in sensible intuition? Will it be said that the principles from which proceed the phenomena of attraction, affinity, electricity, magnetism, galvanism, light, and all that charms or astonishes us in nature,—will it be said that they do not exist, that they are not permanent things, but empty words, because we cannot represent them in sensible intuition? Such a manner of arguing is unworthy of a philosopher. It might be excusable in an uneducated person, accustomed only to the phenomena of sensibility, who had never descended to the depths of the soul in the sphere of pure intelligence,—such a person might be pardoned if, when we speak of a *spirit*, a *cause*, or a *substance*, he should ask, *what is it?* and require us to show the insensible under a sensible form: but one who pretends to excel all philosophers, ancient or modern, one who from the inaccessible height of his wisdom looks down with such sovereign contempt on all the arguments which were before regarded as conclusive, ought to produce some other title of his superiority than merely saying: one cannot conceive the possibility of such a manner of existing: we have no internal intuition of this permanent thing which you speak of; the *me* is only the consciousness of my thought. What then! is any thing more necessary in order to prove what we propose, than this consciousness. Is not this consciousness *one* amid the variety of our thoughts? Is there not a point connecting yesterday's, to-day's, and to-morrow's thought? Different and contradictory as they are, do they not all belong to the same thing, to this *thing* which we call the *me*, and which authorizes us to say: *I* who think to-day, am the same who thought yesterday, and who will think to-morrow? Can any reasoning be clearer or more convincing than affirming the real permanence which we perceive in the internal testimony of our consciousness? I do not see my substance, you may say, I have no intuition of it; I only perceive my consciousness. What more do you want? This consciousness which you experience, which is one amid multiplicity, identical amid distinction, constant amid variety, and permanent in the midst of the succession of the phenomena which appear and disappear; this consciousness, which is no one of your individual thoughts, which endures while they pass away, not to return; this consciousness presents to you the substantiality of your soul, it presents it in a certain manner in intuition, not in the intuition of *sensations*, but in the intuition of the *internal sense*, as a thing affecting you deeply, and the presence of which you cannot doubt, as you do not doubt the pleasure or pain in the act by which you experience it.

58. In attacking the psychological for the substantiality of the soul, Kant supposes that those who make use of it, attempt to prove the substantiality of the soul by starting from the pure and simple category of substance. This mistake might have occasioned the form in which Kant presents this argument; but we have seen that, whether intentionally or not, this form is arranged in the best manner for affording weak points for the attacks of the philosopher. Open any treatise on psychology and you will find that although the general idea of substance is employed, it is only made use of after it has been legitimated by a fact of experience; it is not inferred from the pure category of substance that the soul is a substance; but only after we have established the idea of substance as a general type, we scrutinize the depth of consciousness to see if there is any thing there to which this type may apply. This is what has been done in the preceding paragraphs, and if Kant had wished to be more exact in his account of the opinions of his adversaries, he would not have said that the first argument of rational psychology only gives a light, which is pretended to be true, when it presents the constant logical subject of the thought, as the cognition of the real subject of the inherence. "Far from its being possible," he says, "to infer these properties from the pure and simple category of a substance, on the contrary, the permanence of a given object cannot be taken as a principle, except by starting from experience, when we wish to apply to it the empirically general conception of a substance." The philosopher is right: the properties of the pure and simple category of a substance cannot take us out of the ideal order, unless we rest on a fact of experience; but he forgets a part of the psychological argument when he adds that in the present case we have not placed at the foundation any experience, and that we have only drawn our conclusions from the conception of the relation of every thought to the *me* as the common subject with which this thought is connected. The experience exists in this very consciousness of the relation of all thoughts to the *me*; in this point with which they are all connected; the relation to the *me* is not possible if the *me* is not something; thoughts cannot be connected in the *me* if the *me* is a pure nothing. "Referring the thought to the *me*," Kant goes on to say, "we cannot establish this permanence by a certain observation; because, although the *me* is found at the bottom of every thought, besides that there is no intuition to distinguish it from every other perceptible object, it is connected with this representation." It is true that we do not perceive the permanent *me* in the same manner that we do the objects of the other intuitions; but we perceive it by the internal sense, by that presence, of which we cannot doubt, and which, as Kant himself confesses, makes us refer all thoughts to the *me* as to a common subject which connects them.

59. "It may be observed," he says, "that this representation (that of the *me*) is constantly reproduced in every thought; but not that it is a fixed and permanent intuition in which variable thoughts succeed each other." There is an evident contradiction in this passage. The representation of the *me* is constantly reproduced in every thought: but the *me* either means nothing, or it means something identical with itself; for if the *me* which thinks to-day is not the *me* which thought yesterday, the word *me* means something very different from what all the world understands by it; therefore, if the representation of the *me* returns in every thought, the *me* is the same in every thought; therefore the *me* is fixed and permanent, and consequently the *me* is a substance in which all variable thoughts succeed.

60. I cannot see any answer to this argument, founded on Kant's own words when establishing a phenomenon, the existence of which he was unable to place in doubt, namely, the presence of the *me* in every thought. This is not the place to examine the philosophical questions on the uninterruptedness of consciousness, or whether there is any time in which the soul does not think, and is not conscious of itself. Many philosophers believe there is such an interruption; and they rest their opinion on our experience when asleep, and our not recollecting what happens to us in that state; but Leibnitz thinks that thought is never entirely extinguished, that there is never an absolute pause of consciousness, that our thought is a light which sheds but little lustre at times, but which never goes entirely out. Whichever of these opinions be the true one, the permanence of the substance of the soul is beyond a doubt; and it is worthy of remark that the interruption of thought and of consciousness, far from favoring those who oppose the permanence of the soul, confounds them in a most conclusive manner. For if it is impossible to conceive, without supposing something permanent, how different phenomena, continued in an uninterrupted series, are connected in consciousness; it is still more inconceivable how they can be connected, if we suppose this series to be interrupted, and a certain space of time to intervene between the existence of the connected phenomena.

61. Let A, B, C, D be thoughts which are continued without any interval of time between them, and Q the consciousness through which they pass; if this Q is not something, it is impossible to conceive how the terms of the series can be connected, and, how, notwithstanding their difference and diversity, there is found at the bottom of them all something constant and identical, which we call the *me*, and by virtue of which we can say: I, who think D, am the same who thought C, and B, and A.

But if the consciousness is interrupted, if some hours have passed between C and D, during which there was no thought, no consciousness, it is still more inconceivable how at the bottom of the thought *me* there is found the same *me* which was in the thought C; it is still more inconceivable, because in thinking D we may say: I, who think D, am the same who thought C, and who have been for a certain time deprived of thought. Without something permanent, something which lasts during the succession, how explain this connection? Are we, perchance, speaking of unknown facts? Is not this our daily experience on awaking? If this is not conclusive, let us deny consciousness, let us deny reason; but let us not waste time in talking philosophy.

CHAPTER X
KANT'S OPINION OF THE ARGUMENT WHICH HE CALLS PARALOGISM OF PERSONALITY

62. Kant attacks the argument founded on the testimony of consciousness in a particular manner in the examination of what he calls *the Paralogism of Personality*. He gives the argument in this form; "Whatever has the consciousness of its numerical identity at different times is, by this fact alone, a person; this is verified of the soul; therefore soul is a person." Kant uses the word *person* in a very incorrect sense: it not only means an intelligent substance, but one that is the complete principle of its actions, independently of all connection with any other substance, or a union with a *supposition*. At any rate, the German philosopher understands here by person an intelligent substance; and in this sense he proposes to combat the argument proving the personality of the soul.

63. "If I wish," he says, "to know by experience the numerical identity of any external object, I apply my attention to that which is constant in the phenomenon, to which all the rest is referred, as a determination to its subject; and I observe the identity of the subject at the time in which the determination changes. I am an object of the internal sense, and time is only the form of this sense; I therefore refer all my successive determinations, and each one of them in particular, to that which is numerically identical, in all time, that is, in the form of the internal intuition of myself. Hence the personality of the soul ought only to be deduced or concluded as a proposition perfectly identical with consciousness in time; consequently, this proposition is valid *a priori*, because it does not really announce any thing else than that in all the time in which I am conscious of myself, I am conscious of this time as a thing, which is a part of my unity. This is the same as to say: All this time is in me as individual unity, or rather, I am in all this time with numerical identity."

It would have been desirable if Kant had shown why the internal sense of the numerical identity may be expressed by the proposition; all this time is in me as an individual unity, or in this other; in all the time in which I am conscious of myself, I am conscious of this time as a thing, which is a part of my unity. It is true that the numerical unity is perceived in the diversity of time; but it is not true that we are conscious of time as a thing which is a part of us. He is treating of the consciousness of self, as it is found in the greatest part of mankind, who, far from considering time as a thing which is a part of themselves, regard it as a sort of vague extension or succession in which they and all that is variable exist.

It is well known that philosophers themselves dispute on the true nature of time; and that it is the form of the internal sense is an opinion of Kant's, which is not accepted by many others, and which, as I have shown, [47] he explains badly and proves still worse, although he pretends to have raised his theory to the height of an incontestible doctrine. Whether time is an internal or an external form, whether, even, it is an illusion or a reality, we perceive our numerical identity in its succession; therefore when the German philosopher bases himself on his theory of time, in order to attack the solidity of the argument of consciousness, he rests on a supposition which we are not required to admit, and what is more, he explains this sentiment of identity in terms which no one ever used before him. If he wishes to make time enter into the sentiment of numerical identity, he might say: I find myself in all this time in a numerical identity, or: all this time has passed over me as over an individual unit; but not that we are conscious of time as a thing which is a part of ourselves. If we look to consciousness, we should rather be inclined to believe that time is a sort of successive extension, in which we live, and by which our existence is measured.

64. "The identity of the person," continues Kant, "must inevitably be found in my consciousness; but if I regard myself from the point of view of another (as the object of his external intuition) this other observer conceives me only in time; for, in the apperception, time is not strictly represented except within me; therefore he will not conclude my objective permanence from the *me*, which he admits, and which accompanies all representations in all time in my consciousness, and in a perfect identity. The time in which the observer places me not being the same which is found in my own sensibility, but that which accompanies his intuition, it follows that the identity which is necessarily joined to my consciousness, is not joined to his, that is, to the external intuition of my subject." It is difficult to understand precisely what Kant means in this passage, and it seems very doubtful whether he understood it himself; however, let us see what can be deduced from it against the permanence of the soul.

The German philosopher admits that the identity of the person is inevitably found in our consciousness; that is, the *me* finds itself numerically identical in the diversity of time. It is also true that a strange observer conceives the *me* only in time, that is, if one man reflects on the soul of another man, he conceives it only in time. But this does not show why Kant says that the observer would not infer from this the objective permanence of the soul observed. What would happen would be this. If the man who reflects on the soul of another man believes that same passes in the soul of this man which he perceives within himself, he will infer that the other soul is permanent, for the same reason that he affirms the permanence of his own soul. It is true that as he cannot enter into the consciousness of the other, he can only know it by external marks; but if he is convinced that these marks are sufficient to denote a series of phenomena of consciousness similar to those which he experiences in himself, he will infer that the soul which he observes is as permanent as his own. What does Kant mean then, when he says that the identity which is necessarily connected with *my* consciousness, is not connected with that of the observer? Who ever doubted this truth? Who ever supposed that the perception of the identity in relation to one's own consciousness is not very different from that which relates to another's? Our own identity is revealed to us by immediate consciousness; the identity of another is shown to us by a series of external phenomena which lead us by reasoning and analogy to the conviction that outside of us there are beings similar to ourselves.

65. "The identity of the consciousness of myself at different times," Kant goes on to say, "is only a formal condition of my thoughts and their connection; but it does not prove the numerical identity of my subject, in which, notwithstanding the logical identity of the *me*, such a change may take place, as to render it impossible to preserve the identity of this *me*, which does not prevent our always attributing to it the identical *me*, which *me* may still preserve in another state, and even in the metamorphosis of the subject, the thought of the previous subject, and transmit to it all that comes afterwards." This is precisely what Kant ought to have explained; because the phenomenon of the sentiment of identity in the midst of continual variety, is what irresistibly inclines us to believe that the *me* is something permanent. It is not true that we have only the topical identity of the *me*, for we are not speaking of the subject of a proposition, but of a real subject, experienced, perceived in the depth of our consciousness.

Kant imagines that he can explain this sentiment of identity with great simplicity. I will try to express his strange opinion in an intelligible manner. Let A, B, C, D, E, ... be instants of time, and let $a, b, c, d, e,$ ... be thoughts or any other internal phenomena, corresponding to them. At the instant A, the thought a exists. At the instant B, the thought b succeeds. At the instant B, the soul which existed at the instant A, no longer exists. The soul at the instant B, is something entirely new; it is not a but b. The same is true of all the rest. But how, you will say, is it possible for the soul at all these instants to believe itself the same? It is very simple: the subject *a* transmits the thought to the subject *b*; *b* transmits its own and *a*'s to *c*. Nothing remains identical; but the consciousness of the identity always lasts. Does not such an hypothesis seem truly wonderful and philosophical? What could be imagined clearer and more satisfactory?

The reader may perhaps think that I am jesting, and that I present Kant's opinion under a ridiculous aspect for the sake of combating it more easily; but it is just the reverse; the exposition which I have just made of Kant's philosophy is more serious than his own. These are his words: "One elastic ball striking another in a right line, communicates to the latter its whole motion, and consequently its whole state (considering only their positions in space). Admit now, by analogy with these bodies, certain substances, of which one transmits representations to another, with the consciousness which accompanies them; we may then conceive a whole series of such representations, in which the first communicates its state, and the consciousness of its state to the second; the second communicates its state, together with that of the preceding substance, to the third; the third, in like manner, communicates the states of both of the preceding substances together with its own, and the consciousness which accompanies them to the fourth. The last of the series will then have the consciousness of all the states of the substances which preceded it, as of its own; because these states, and the consciousness of these states have been transmitted to it. Still it will not have been the same person in all these states."

Kant, in trying to refute the psychological argument founded on consciousness, overthrows and destroys the character of consciousness: a transmitted consciousness is not a true consciousness; it is only the cognition of a previous thought.

These substances, existing successively and transmitting their consciousness from one to another, would be something distinct from the act of consciousness, or they would not. If distinct, we must admit a subject of the consciousness, which in itself, and as subject, does not come under the sensible intuition; and consequently we may argue *ad hominem*, and retort Kant's objection against himself. If these transitory substances are only the act of the consciousness, when the act ceases, nothing remains of the substances, and therefore, there is nothing transmissible.

Transmission supposes something which may be transmitted; if, then, the act of consciousness is transmitted, it must be something permanent in itself, in the midst of the succession of the substances; and this is a very strange conclusion to which the German philosopher is brought by his theory of transmission. All psychologists had said that the substance of the soul is permanent, and its phenomena transitory; now, on the contrary, we find that the transitory is the substance, and that which is permanent is the phenomenon, or the act of consciousness which is transmitted.

66. Perhaps it may be answered that by transmission is not meant the communication of any thing constant, but merely the succession of phenomena united by any tie among themselves. Thus, supposing the instants A, B, C, D, the acts of consciousness, a, b, c, d, corresponding to them, will not be strictly identical in number, but successive, and connected. But this reply, which avoids the necessity of admitting the permanence of the act of consciousness, explains nothing, and makes it incomprehensible, how, at the instant D, for example, there can be consciousness of the acts c, b, a, which there is an irresistible inclination to believe have at bottom something numerically identical. When d exists there is no longer any thing of c left; there is no substance remaining, because, by the supposition there either is no such substance, or it is something transitory; there is no act of consciousness remaining, because a is numerically distinct from c, and besides, we have seen that the permanence of the phenomena cannot be admitted. Therefore it is absolutely impossible to explain or to comprehend how there can be in the act a the representation of c.

67. To say that the phenomena are united by any tie whatever is to elude the difficulty by a foolish play upon words. What is the meaning, in this case, of uniting, of a tie? They are metaphors which if they mean any thing must express the permanence of some *thing* amid the variety of the phenomena; the tie, the bond, must extend to the various things which it connects and unites: therefore it must be *common* to them all; and this something, whatever it be, which remains constant in variety, we call substance.

68. The mere succession of the phenomena or acts of consciousness is not sufficient to transmit the belief of the numerical identity; if it were, all men would be conscious of the previous acts of others. Let a, b, be two successive acts of consciousness: if, in order that the act b, which is numerically distinct from a, may represent the numerical identity of consciousness, it is sufficient that b should succeed a; since this succession is met with in the acts of consciousness of different men, it must follow that all men have consciousness of all the acts of the others. *Risum tematis?* And yet this conclusion is absolutely necessary: it cannot be avoided by saying that there is a form of the internal sense, and that the succession takes place in each man in his respective internal sense, and that therefore the succession of the internal phenomena of one is in a different time, in a different form from what it is in another. The words, *respective* internal sense, internal form of *each* man, have a meaning, if we admit something permanent in our interior; but if there is nothing but successive phenomena,

the word *respective* is absurd, because there can be no respective internal sense if there is nothing to which it can refer. Suppose the man M, and the man N be merely a succession of phenomena, and in *each* one there is only a mere succession: there is the same reason why the phenomena of N should be connected with each other as with those of M. Therefore, if there is a community of consciousness in the phenomena of M, without any other sufficient reason than the mere succession, this community should be found in all the phenomena, because they all have the same sufficient reason.

69. It must be observed that in all this argument, I abstract the nature of the substance of the soul, and only purpose to demonstrate that we must admit something constant in the midst of the variety of the phenomena, and common to them all. Call it a tie, a form, an act of consciousness, or what you will, it is either something real or it is not. If it is not something real, whoever expresses it, employs a word without any meaning: if it is something real, the substantiality of the soul is acknowledged, because a permanent reality is admitted in the midst of the variety of the phenomena. We, who admit this substantiality, do not pretend that the soul can be given in sensible intuition, nor that we can express in an exact definition its internal properties abstracted from the phenomena which we experience in it. What we say is, that we know its real existence, its permanence, and its numerical identity in the midst of the succession and diversity of the phenomena. Therefore from the moment that it is admitted that there is within us something real, permanent, and numerically identical in the midst of diversity, the substantiality of the soul, which we defend, is admitted. Disputes may arise on the distinctive character of its nature; whether it is or is not a force, as Leibnitz maintained, whether its essence consists in thought, as was the opinion of Descartes: but these questions are foreign to the matter now in hand. Is there something real and permanent amid the variety of internal phenomena? If there is not, the consciousness of numerical identity is absurd; if there is, then the substantiality of the soul is demonstrated.

70. "The opinion of some ancient philosophers," says Kant, "that all is transitory and nothing constant in the world, although it cannot be maintained if we admit substances, still it cannot be refuted by the unity of consciousness; because we cannot even judge by consciousness, whether, as something, we are or are not permanent; for we attribute to our identical *me* only that of which we have consciousness, and thus we must necessarily judge that we are precisely the same in all the durations of which we are conscious." Kant expressly acknowledges that the judgment that we are the same is necessary, that is, that the identity of the *me* is for us a necessary fact of consciousness. It would be difficult to imagine a confession more injurious

and more conclusive against the arguments of the German philosopher. If we are forced to judge ourselves identical, if consciousness tell us so, can we deny or doubt this identity without destroying the fundamental fact of all psychological investigations, and consequently falling into the most complete skepticism? If the testimony of consciousness is not valid, if the judgment to which it *necessarily* forces us is not certain, what shall we catch hold of in order that we may not be precipitated into the most absolute skepticism? where shall we look for a solid foundation for the edifice of our knowledge?

71. "But," Kant continues, "from the point of view of another, we cannot hold this judgment valid, because, finding in the soul no other constant phenomenon than the representation of the *me* which accompanies and unites all the other phenomena, we can never decide that this *me* (a simple thought) is not as fleeting as the other thoughts, which are respectively connected by it." Do not, then, admit that the representation of the *me*, although essentially representing an identity, is valid; say that, although transitory it *necessarily* brings us to the illusion of permanence; but draw also all the consequences of this doctrine, and maintain that human reason avails nothing, absolutely nothing; say that recollection is a pure illusion, that although we are necessarily induced to believe that the thought which we now have is the recollection of another previous thought, that all this is pure illusion; that we are not sure that there is the relation of recollection, and that we only know that at present we have the consciousness of a thought which *seems* to us connected with another previous thought; say too that reasoning has no validity, for all conviction of ideas is impossible without memory; and that, although an internal representation necessarily produces an assent, we must distrust the judgment which necessity demands: say too that all that we think, all that we perceive, all that we will, all that we experience within us, cannot enable us to know any thing, that we are condemned to a complete impotence of acquiring any certainty of any thing; and that the language of every philosopher should be the following: "This now seems so; I am conscious of it; I know nothing further; I experience a necessity of believing it, but perhaps this belief is a pure illusion; I know nothing of the external world; I know nothing either of the internal world; all knowledge is denied me; I myself am only a succession of phenomena which pass away and disappear; an irresistible necessity impels me to believe that these phenomena have a common tie, but this tie is nothing; because when a phenomenon disappears nothing is before it; if I acknowledge any reality, no matter what, I fall into the substantiality of the soul, which I have resolved not to admit; all is illusion, all is nothing, because, as I am not even certain of the facts of consciousness, I am not certain even of the illusion." Who can encounter such consequences?

CHAPTER XI
SIMPLICITY OF THE SOUL

72. I have confined myself in the preceding chapters to proving the substantiality of the soul; to do which it was only necessary to demonstrate by the testimony of consciousness that there is within us a permanent reality, the subject of the modifications which we experience. I shall now demonstrate that this substance is simple.

To proceed methodically, let us fix the meaning of the word *simple*. When many beings are united and form a collection, the result is called a composite being; so that there is a true composition wherever beings substantially distinct are united; the band which unites them may be of different species, which produces the diversity of compositions. Simplicity is opposed to composition; the idea of simplicity essentially excludes the idea of composition; as this last includes a *number* of distinct things which are united to form a whole, the idea of simplicity essentially excludes the idea of number of things united to form a whole. Therefore the simple is strictly one, and there is simplicity in a substance when it is not a collection of substances.

When, therefore, we say the substance of the soul is simple, we mean that it is not a collection of substances, but one substance.

73. The idea of simplicity thus determined with exactness, let us see if it belongs to our soul. As the soul is not given us in intuition after the manner of sensible things, and we only know it by the presence of the internal sense, and by the phenomena which we experience in the depths of our consciousness, we must examine these two sources to see if we can find simplicity in them.

It is an indisputable fact that in all our acts, in all our internal affections, we perceive the identity of the *me*. [48] There is no identity between things that are distinct: consequently the internal sense at once rejects the multiplicity of the soul. It may be said that this identity does not exist between distinct substances, but that a composite substance is identical with itself, and perhaps the identity revealed by consciousness is only the identity of a composite with itself: but this reply is destroyed by merely examining the testimony of consciousness. That which we perceive as various and multiple is not the *me*, but that which takes place in the *me*: we think, we will, we perceive different things; but consciousness attests that what thinks them, wills them, and perceives them, is one and the same, the *me*. Therefore, the testimony of consciousness alone proves the simplicity of the soul; for it is impossible to explain otherwise how we perceive within us the permanent unity amid the multitude of internal phenomena.

74. Abstracting the testimony of the internal sense, and looking only at the nature of the internal phenomena, it may be demonstrated that the subject of them is a simple substance. If it were not so, the thinking substance would be composed of various substances; let us see what would follow from this supposition. Let the component substances be three, for example, A, B, C; I say that this collection cannot think. To demonstrate it with the most complete evidence, let us take this judgment: metal is a body, and let us see if it is possible for the collection of A, B, C, to form this judgment. Let us suppose the representation of the subject, *metal*, to be in the substance A; the idea of the predicate, *body*, to be in B; and the general idea of the relation of the predicate to the subject, or the copula, *is*, to be in C; can a judgment be the result? By no means. A will perceive the metal, B the body, and C the general idea of the copula, *is*. Each of these substances will have consciousness of its own; but as it is not conscious of what is in the other two, it can form no judgment, for this essentially consists in the relation of the predicate to the subject.

75. If you say that each of the substances contains the representations of the three things, we shall have three judgments, and there will not be one thinking being, but three. Besides, either of the three substances A, B, C, is composed of others, or it is not. If it is not, is simple, and we have a simple and perceptive substance, why then suppose three when one is enough? If it is composed of others, the difficulty is increased; for supposing A to be formed of two substances, which we may call *m, n*; the representation of metal which was in A will be distributed between *m* and *n*, in which case, far from obtaining a judgment, we should not even have a subject; for it would not be possible to form the representation of metal, supposing it to be divided between *m* and *n*.

If it is not possible to form a judgment, or even the idea of one term, it is evident that all reasoning and thought would be impossible; for reasoning implies a connection of judgments from which it deduces the conclusion contained in the premises.

76. Acts of the will are also impossible in a composite substance; there is no will where there is no cognition, and this latter is, as we have just seen,

inseparable from simplicity. But we may extend the demonstration still further. An act of the will implies an inclination, tendency, or whatever it may be called, towards an object known. Let us suppose the two substances A and B to compose a substance which has a will; and let us suppose all that is necessary for the act of willing to be divided between them in such manner that the knowledge of the object willed is in it, and the inclination or tendency in B; I say such an act or will is absurd. To feel the force of this truth let us suppose that the act of the will is to be formed of the cognition of one man, and the inclination of another towards the object known by the first; the pure cognition of one is not the act of the will, and the inclination of the other towards an object is impossible unless he has the cognition of the object towards which he is inclined, because this is equivalent to supposing a relation without any term to which it relates. These contradictions must be admitted by every one who denies the simplicity of the substances which will; for either the inclination and the cognition must be divided between the parts of the substances, or all concentrated in one part, and then the others are unnecessary.

Moreover, the substances composing the substance which will are either simple or composite; if simple, then there are simple substances which know and will; if composite, each act of the will would be an aggregate of the action of the parts, and what would an act of the will be which should consist in an aggregate?

77. The union which we conceive in distinct substances is either juxtaposition in space, simultaneousness in time, or the concourse of forces producing a common effect: juxtaposition in space or simultaneousness of time does not help us to explain thought, the act of the will, nor any internal phenomena; and neither does the concourse of forces producing a common effect solve the problem. On this supposition we should have to conceive internal phenomena as the products of an elaboration to which various substances have occurred. Let us for a moment admit this absurdity; we advance nothing by it, for we then ask, where does the phenomenon reside? If in all the substances jointly it must be in itself composite, and its consciousness would also be composite; none of the component substances could say *I* with respect to this phenomenon; there would, therefore, be a multiplicity of consciousnesses. Either these consciousnesses would be united in a point in order to form a common consciousness, or they would not. If they are united, their point of union must be a simple substance, or we relapse into the multiplicity of consciousnesses: if they are not united, the different internal consciousnesses of each man will be like the consciousnesses of different men; each substance will think its own, without knowing what the other thinks.

78. Finally, this divisibility of substance and of consciousness will extend to infinity, or it will not; if the former, instead of one thinking being, there will be an infinite number of thinking beings within each one of us; if the latter, we must come to simple substances with thought and consciousness, which is precisely what our adversaries are opposed to. Infinite divisibility does not save them from simplicity; the division separates the parts, but it supposes them distinct; therefore, infinite division must suppose an infinite number of simple beings which make the division possible.

CHAPTER XII
KANT'S OPINION OF THE ARGUMENT PROVING THE SIMPLICITY OF THE SOUL

79. Kant calls the argument, by which we have just proved the simplicity of the soul, the second paralogism of psychology. He gives it in these terms: "Every thing, the action of which can never be conceived as the concurrence of many agents, is simple: the soul or thinking substance is of this nature; therefore the soul is simple." The German philosopher admits that this argument is not a mere sophism, invented by some dogmatist for the purpose of giving his assertions a slight appearance of truth; and he confesses that it seems to defy the most attentive examination and the most profound reflection. Still he flatters himself that he can expose its fallacy, showing that this principal support of rational psychology is a false foundation, and that, consequently, the whole edifice of this science is built in the air.

80. Kant observes that the *nervus probandi* of the argument is in the fact that many representations cannot form a thought, except inasmuch as they are contained in the absolute unity of the thinking subject; "but no one," he says, "can prove this proposition *by conceptions*. Where could he begin? The proposition: 'A thought can only be the effect of the absolute unity of the thinking subject,' cannot be analyzed; the unity of thought (and even thought results from many representations) is collective; and as to simple conceptions, their unity may just as well be referred to the collective unity of substances which contribute to produce the thought (just as the motion of a body is the motion of all its parts) as to the absolute unity of the subject. The necessity of the supposition of a simple substance cannot consequently be known by the rule of identity in a composite thought. No one who understands the reason of the possibility of synthetic judgments *a priori*, as we have explained them above, will dare to affirm that this proposition can be known synthetically, and perfectly *a priori*, or by pure conceptions." This reasoning is pure sophistry, and will vanish in the light of evidence.

81. In the first place, it is not correct to say that all thoughts result from many representations; in the perception of a simple idea, as of being, for

example, there are not many representations; therefore Kant's argument fails at the first step; for if there be even one thought which requires simplicity, it has already been demonstrated that, if the soul is simple in one instance it cannot cease to be so in another.

82. Let us now examine how the diversity of representations enter into those thoughts which admit of this diversity. When these representations form what is called a thought, they are united, as it were, in a point which requires the unity of the perception and of the subject perceiving. In the thought called judgment various representations are combined, that of the subject and that of the object; but these different representations do not constitute the thought called judgment, except inasmuch as they are presented as connected with the relation which authorizes us to affirm or deny the predicate of the subject; therefore at the bottom of the diversity there is unity, that is to say, the relation; therefore the thought by which this relation is perceived is one, and the action of perceiving is essentially one, notwithstanding the variety of the representations.

83. There is no order in our thoughts except as we compare them with each other: all our intellectual acts are reduced to the perception and comparison of ideas; in perception there is simplicity, as there must also be in comparisons, since there can be no comparison of that which is varied, except by reducing the varied to that which is one, that is, to the relation which is perceived in the comparison. Therefore in every thought there is unity; thought can never be conceived as the concurrence of many agents; therefore the proposition, which Kant considered indemonstrable, is demonstrated, — that many representations cannot form a thought except in so far as they are contained in the absolute unity of a thinking subject.

84. Let us present the same demonstration under a stricter form. Suppose A, B, C, to be the three agents concurring in the formation of the thought; each part will yield its contingent; let us suppose a to correspond to the first, b to the second, and c to the third, the result will be the union composed of a, b, and c; this will be the thought; it will therefore be triple and can never constitute a point of comparison; therefore, we must either reject this hypothesis, or deny thought. Kant's sophism proceeds from his attending solely to the diversity of the representations, and abstracting the unity which is always met with in the perception of this diversity; hence it is nothing strange that he does not find unity in the conception of thought. He presents this conception incompletely, or rather, falsely; he presents thought as a collection of representations, and not as a most simple point in which representations unite, in order to be perceived in the relation which they have among themselves. The diversity of the representations does not form a collection after the manner of sensible objects; the thought, in which

the relation of two different triangles is known, cannot be expressed by the sum of the figures of the two triangles; it is something different from them; something which is in the midst of them; which unites them by comparing them, and which joins their diversity in the unity of their relation.

85. The example brought by Kant manifests the rudeness of his idea of the character of the union of the representations in the formation of a whole thought. The unity of the thought is, he says, collective, and may be referred to the collective unity of many substances, just as the motion of a body is the motion composed of all the parts of the body. Here we see clearly wherein Kant's equivocation consists; he takes the collection of the representations for the thought which relates to them, and therefore it is no wonder that he cannot see the unity implied in the diversity, on the supposition that this diversity has to be thought.

To carry conviction to the farthest point, let us take this example of motion, and suppose a cube to be moved. Let us call its eight verticles A, B, C, D, E, F, G, H; they all move, and the collection of their motions, with those of the points which are between them, forms the whole motion. What is there common in the result of this concurrence of agents? Nothing, except juxtaposition in space, and the relation which they preserve by the equal velocity of the motion. But the motion of the vertex H is not the motion of the vertex A, as is evident if we consider that the vertex A may be cut off from the cube, and remain at rest without discontinuing or altering the motion of the vertex H; therefore, the two motions are things absolutely distinct. It is evident that the same holds true with respect to the other points; therefore the unity of the composite motion is purely factitious; what there is, in reality, is a multiplicity of substances, and of motions, without any other than a purely extrinsical connection, the relation of positions in space.

Let us change the vertices into representations, and see what will be the result. Do they exist without any other connection than their co-existence? Then they do not form a thought, but only a collection of phenomena which may be considered as a *union* of things, but not a thought; in that case the sum of all the representations will be similar to the sum of the motions; but it will produce no result in relation to the object which we are now examining. If we give these representations a point of union, that is, the relation under which they are perceived, we shall have a thought; but what has this act, which is *one* and most simple, in common with, the totality of a number of points in motion?

86. If Kant had wished to present a more seductive example, he ought to have made use of a theory in mechanics, the application of which to the present case presents, if not more difficulty, at least a more deceitful appearance; I mean the resultant of a system of forces and their point of application.

When several forces act upon a line, a plane, or a solid, they produce an effect equal to that one force alone, which is called the resultant: this force has a determinate direction and a point of application, as though it were simple or had not emanated from others; why cannot this be applied to thought? Why may not a thing, although it is simple, be the product of the concurrence of various agents? This example is more specious, because it presents the result of the composition concentrated in a point, but if we examine it well, we shall find that it proves nothing against us.

The disparity is this: thought is a simple act in itself, whilst the resultant of the forces is so only in its relation to the effect experienced, which is all that comes under our calculation. If two forces are applied at the two extremities of an inflexible right line the effect will be the same as though we applied one force equal to the sum of them both at one point of the line, at a distance from either extremity inversely proportioned to the value of the first forces. But the unity of this effect depends on the cohesion of the parts, which, not permitting isolated motions, must make the force act on a single point; but the component forces do not cease to be distinct and separate, so that at the moment the cohesion should cease, the respective parts would each feel the action of the force corresponding to it, and move in the direction and with the velocity which the force impresses on them. If, while the cohesion lasts, it were possible to give each of the component forces the consciousness of its action, there would be two consciousnesses really distinct, which could never form one common consciousness, and could only be united in the production of an effect. If the point of their application should have the consciousness of the action which it experiences, it might have a consciousness similar to that of the action of one force, equal to the sum of the components, if it did not know the manner in which their action is transmitted to it; but from the moment that it becomes conscious of their respective action, it would know that the result is owing to the impossibility of each of them producing its effect in an isolated manner. If, therefore, we compare the thinking subject to this point of application of the forces, we must attribute to this subject the consciousness of the origin of the representations which concur in the production of the whole effect.

Perhaps it may be said that by the very analysis of the example, we have prepared the way for the triumph of the adversaries of the simplicity of the soul; because after arbitrary suppositions we have at last come to a simple effect inherent in a simple thing, and produced by the concurrence of various agents; but if we look closer to it, we shall find that this pretended triumph was never farther from being realized than it is in the last result to which we are led by the analysis of the forces. For, in order to arrive at a simple result produced by the concurrence of various forces, we also require a simple point in which this result is concentrated. Then, and precisely because we have arrived at this simplicity, we can abstract the component forces, and consider the result as a simple effect, produced by a simple force, and inherent in a simple subject, which is the indivisible point, to which we consider the force as applied. Therefore, continuing the comparison, we ought to say that, whatever may be the number of the agents concurring in the production of the thought, this thought must reside in a simple subject, and in that case the simplicity of the soul is admitted. It is true that we should then suppose a certain number of agents acting on the soul in order to produce the thought; but the thought once produced, the soul alone would be the thinking subject, just as the indivisible point is the only one which unites the action of the component forces.

Thus all that our adversaries would have gained would be the burden of the ridiculous invention of the concurrence of agents, and be forced notwithstanding, to admit a simple thinking substance, which is all that we proposed to demonstrate.

87. Kant pretends that it is impossible to deduce from experience the necessary unity of the thinking subject, as the condition of the possibility of all thought, because experience reveals no necessity, and the conception of absolute unity belongs to an order different from that which we are here considering. It is certain that experience alone does not reveal any necessity; for it is limited to particular, contingent facts, and does not reach the universal reason of objects; but this is not true of experience regarded objectively, or in relation to the cognition of the general reasons of things; for although this cognition, considered subjectively as an individual act, is a contingent fact, still inasmuch as it exists it represents a true necessity in certain objects; unless we wish to renounce the certainty of all the sciences, mathematics included.

It is clear that in speaking of thought and the thinking subject, we cannot forget experience, since it is impossible to abstract the basis of all psychological investigations,—I think,—a proposition which expresses a fact of consciousness, an act of internal experience; but with this experience is combined the idea of unity in general, or the exclusion of distinction and multiplicity from the act of thought and from the thinking subject. Thus the demonstration of the simplicity of the soul follows in the same path as all demonstrations which are confined to the purely ideal order, and which consequently are formed of one premise which contains a necessary truth, and another which establishes a fact of experience. In the present instance, the necessary premise is the very definition of unity and simplicity; the other expresses the fact experienced, that is, the nature of the thought, as it is revealed in consciousness.

88. Hence the demonstration of the simplicity of thinking beings is not limited to the human mind, but extends to all the subjects in which the fact of consciousness exists. When Kant says we cannot extend this demonstration, because we then go out of the field of experience, we reply with this argument: our demonstration is founded on the idea of unity and the fact of consciousness; the idea of unity is general, and consequently is valid in all cases; the fact of consciousness is a thing which is found in every thinking being, since thought is inconceivable without a subject, which may say, *I think*; therefore, we proceed legitimately in extending the demonstration of simplicity, unless you mean to give to the word *think* a very different meaning from that which we all give to it, in which case we go out of the arena of philosophy and enter on a discussion of words.

89. We must have received the idea of a thinking being from internal experience: we may expand or restrict this idea, increasing or decreasing its perfection; but at bottom it remains always the same, and we cannot conceive thought in another being without attributing to it something similar to what we experience in ourselves. In this respect Kant is therefore right when he says that if we wish to represent to ourselves a thinking being we must put ourselves in the place of the object. According to him, we require for thought the absolute unity of the subject, only because without this unity it would be impossible to say, *I think*; since, although the totality of the thought may be distributed among the various subjects, the subjective *me* cannot be divided or separated, and every thought supposes this *me*. The proposition, I think, is the foundation on which psychology raises the edifice of its knowledge: Kant admits this, but I cannot understand why, admitting that this proposition is the form of the apperception which is joined with and precedes all experience, he still says that it is not experimental; as though the thought were not just as subject to a real experience as its form; whereas if we closely examine it, we should rather say that the form is experienced than the thought itself, on the supposition that the latter is distinct whilst the form is identical in every instance; for the form in itself is only the consciousness of the unity identical in the midst of diversity.

90. In conceiving this absolute unity in the *me*, we do not, as Kant pretends, conceive a topical unity, but a real unity, if we suppose it to remain really the same through the variety of thought. When we enunciate this unity in the proposition, I think, we do not speak of a form in the abstract, common to all perceptions, but of something positive which is within us, and the reality of which is indispensable to the possibility of thought.

91. The German philosopher further says: "This subjective condition of all knowledge cannot with propriety be converted into a condition of the possibility of a knowledge of the objects; that is, into a conception of

thinking being in general, since we cannot represent this being to ourselves without putting ourselves in its place by the formula of our consciousness." I do not believe that the psychologists who have pretended that they could demonstrate the simplicity of the soul, ever flattered themselves with arriving at a perfect idea of thinking beings, or denied that we obtain the type of this idea from our own experience; what they have pretended is, that reason leads them to infer that there is absolute unity of the subject wherever there is a thinking being; whether its thought may belong to a higher or lower order than our own.

92. When Kant observes that the subject in which the thought inheres is only indicated in a transcendental way, without its properties being discovered, and that, therefore, we do not know the simplicity of the subject itself, he declares a fact which is in some sense admissible, but he deduces from it a false consequence. It is true that we only know the substance of the soul by the presence of the internal sense, and by its relation to its acts; and consequently that the soul in itself abstracted from all the phenomena which we experience, is not given in immediate intuitions, and that when we arrive at this point we are reduced to the idea of a simple being, but this indeterminateness, and vagueness, in the knowledge of the substance of the soul, does not prevent our knowing its simplicity, if this simplicity is revealed by the internal sense, and also by the nature of the phenomena by which we know the thinking subject.

93. Some persons may believe that the indeterminateness of the knowledge of the substance of the soul is a fact recently discovered by the German philosopher; but it is easy to show that it had been observed long before, and is laid down in a very special and interesting manner in the writings of St. Thomas. This eminent metaphysician proposes the question whether the intellectual soul knows itself by its essence, *utrum anima intellectiva seipsam cognoscat per suam essentiam*, and after the various remarks on intelligence, and the intelligibility of objects, he solves it in these remarkable words: "Our understanding does not know itself by its essence, but by its act; and this in two ways: in one way, in particular; inasmuch as Sortes or Plato perceives that he has an intellectual soul, because he perceives that he understands: in the second way, in general; inasmuch as we consider the nature of the human mind in the act of the understanding. But it is true that we derive the judgment and efficacy of the knowledge by which we know the nature of the soul, by the light of the divine truth of which our intellect participates, and in which are contained the reasons of all things, as was said above. Hence, Augustine says, in the ninth book on the Trinity: We have intuition of the inviolable truth by which we perfectly determine, as far as possible, not what the mind of each man is, but what it

should be according to the eternal reasons. But there is a difference between these two cognitions, for, to have the first, we only need the presence of the mind, which is the principle of the act by which the mind perceives itself, and, therefore, we say that it knows itself by its presence; but for the second, the presence of the mind is not sufficient, but a careful and subtle investigation is necessary. Hence many are ignorant of the nature of the soul, and many also have erred on the nature of the soul; wherefore in the tenth book on the Trinity, Augustine, speaking of this investigation, says: The soul should not try to see itself as something absent, but endeavor to distinguish itself as something present; that is, to know its difference from other things, which is to know its quiddity and nature." [49]

94. It is to be observed that St. Thomas admits two cognitions of the soul by itself;—that of its presence, as we perceive it in perceiving our thought, *percipit se habere animam intellectivam ex hoc quod percipit se intelligere*; and another which we deduce from the analysis of the intellectual act reasoning from general considerations, and reflecting on the light which the eternal reasons shed upon this fact of experience. This is how St. Thomas explains the knowledge of presence or consciousness contained in the proposition, *I think*; and the general knowledge which we deduce from the same intellectual act in its relations to the unity of the subject exercising it. That this last contains something abstract and indeterminate no one denies; and when Kant calls attention to it, he tells us nothing which the holy Doctor had not already told us when he expressly affirmed that the soul knows itself not in its essence, but in its acts. These few laconic words express all the truth which is contained in Kant's diffuse explanation of the limitation of our cognition to the acts of consciousness, and the absence of the intuitive knowledge of the substance of the soul, the transcendental subject of the thought.

CHAPTER XIII
IN WHAT MANNER THE IDEA OF
SUBSTANCE MAY BE APPLIED TO GOD

95. In the idea of substance as formed from the beings around us and from the testimony of our consciousness we find the relation to changes which occur in it as their subject or recipient. But we have before remarked that besides this relation there is a negation of inherence in another as the modifications are inherent in the substance; this negation implies a perfection which exempts it from the necessity of inherence to which the changeable and transitory beings which we call accidents or modifications are subject. As we are ignorant of the intrinsic essence of substances, we do not know what this perfection is; yet we cannot doubt that it exists in the very nature of the subject, and is independent of the modifications which transform it. If then the essence of the substance must consist in any thing, it must be in this perfection of which we have a knowledge, but not an intuitive cognition. When therefore substance is defined in relation to accidents, *quod substat accidentibus*, it is rather defined by the manner in which it is presented to us than by what it is in itself.

96. Hence, of the two definitions usually received in the schools: *Ens per se subsistens*, a being subsisting by itself, and, *id quod substat accidentibus*, the subject of accidents; the first is the more correct, because it comes nearer the expression of what it is in itself. Although we know finite substances only inasmuch as revealed by accidents, and even our own mind knows itself only in its acts, reason tells us that in order to be known things must exist, and in order that our mind may find in them something permanent, it is necessary that this something should be in them. Our knowledge does not produce its objects; in order to be known they must exist.

97. These reflections manifest the possibility of the existence of a substance not subject to accidents or change of any kind; and that this substance not only does not lose the character of substance by being immutable, but possesses it in a much more perfect degree. The perfection of substance is not in its changes but in what is permanent in it, not in having a succession of modifications inherent in it, but in existing in such

a manner as not to need to inhere in another. The substance which should possess this permanence, this perfection enabling it to exist by itself, and at the same time should have no modification, should experience no change, would be infinitely superior to all other substances. This substance is God.

98. Now it is easy to answer the question whether when applied to God the idea of substance is understood in the same sense as when applied to creatures; or, to speak in the terms of the schools, whether it is taken univocally or analogously.

99. In the idea of every substance is contained the idea of being; what does not exist cannot be a substance. Inasmuch as we conceive being as a reality, as opposed to nothingness, the idea of being belongs both to God and to creatures: God is, that is to say, God is a real thing, not nothing. But if from this general idea, such as we conceive it in opposition to nothingness, we pass to its realization in objects, to the manner of its application, so to speak, we find all the difference that there is between the contingent and the necessary, the finite and the infinite. Although we do not intuitively see the infinite being, nor the essence of finite beings, still we have evident knowledge that the word *being* applied to the infinite means something very different from what it does when applied to the finite.

100. In the idea of substance is also contained the idea of something permanent; this permanence belongs also to God: the infinite being is essentially permanent.

101. In the substances around us we find this permanence combined with the succession of the modifications which affect them; these changes are impossible in God. The relation to modifications is a characteristic quality of finite substances.

102. Substances are not inherent in others as modifications are inherent in them; this non-inherence also belongs to the divine substance.

103. Substances must contain something which exempts them from the necessity of inherence and raises them above the things which so rapidly succeed each other, and in their existence always need another to sustain them; this perfection is found in the divine substance which is being essentially, the fountain of perfection.

104. It follows from this analysis that all the perfection contained in the idea of substance may be applied to the infinite being; and that all that is contained in this idea which cannot be applied to this being is what implies negation or imperfection.

CHAPTER XIV
AN IMPORTANT REMARK, AND SUMMARY

105. When we say, that a substance is a being subsisting by itself, we do not mean that it is a being which has absolutely no need of another for its existence. To confound these two things would produce a frightful confusion of ideas, and is itself produced by a not less frightful confusion of the relation of cause and effect with the relation of substance and accidents.

106. The relation of cause and effect consists in the cause giving the effect its being; the relation of substance and accident consists in the substance serving as subject to the accident. So great is the difference between these two relations that not only does reason show them to be distinct, but at every moment experience presents them as separate. Our soul is the subject of many accidents in the production of which it has no part, but on the contrary opposed to their production as far as it is able. Such are all painful sensations, all disagreeable impressions, all troublesome thoughts which present themselves in spite of us, and when we wish to think of something else. In these cases the soul is the subject, and not the cause: it has the relation of substance to things of which it is not the cause, and with respect to which it is entirely passive. If I am not greatly mistaken, this example is conclusive, and marks the line which divides causality from substance, effect from accident.

107. To be subsistent by itself expresses an exclusion; if this exclusion is referred to causality, to be subsistent by itself is to be not caused; if referred to inherence, it means to be not inherent in another as accidents are in their substance. When substance is defined a being subsistent in itself, it is understood in the second sense, not in the first, and this distinction is sufficient to overthrow the whole system of Spinoza, and all the pantheists, whatever be the aspect under which they present their error.

108. In order to enter on the question of pantheism free from all confusion, let us sum up in a few words all that reason and experience teach concerning substance.

I. Within us there is a being, one, simple, identical, permanent, the subject of the phenomena which we experience.

II. Outside of us there are objects which preserve something constant through the variety of this phenomena.

III. In the idea of substance are contained the ideas of permanence and non-inherence in another as a modification.

IV. The relation of a subject to its modifications, is found in all finite substances.

V. Relation to modifications is not inseparable from the ideas of being, permanence, and non-inherence in another.

VI. An immutable substance implies no contradiction.

VII. To subsist by itself is not the same as to be independent of all other beings. The relation of cause and effect ought not to be confounded with the relation of substance and accident.

VIII. *Non-inherence* in another is characteristic of substance; but this negative idea must be founded on something positive; on the *force* to subsist by itself without the necessity of adhering to another.

CHAPTER XV
PANTHEISM EXAMINED IN
THE ORDER OF IDEAS

109. The idea of substance and all its applications, as well to the external as to the internal world, are far from leading us to infer the existence of a *single* substance; on the contrary, reason according with experience forces us to acknowledge a *multitude* of substances. Why should we admit only one substance? This is one of the most important questions of philosophy, and from the most ancient times has given occasion to the most serious errors; it consequently deserves a careful investigation.

110. Those who admit only one substance must found their opinion either on the idea of substance or on experience; our mind can have no other recourse than to its primitive ideas, or the teachings of experience. Let us begin with the *a priori* method or that which is founded on the idea.

111. What do you understand by substance? we ask. If by substance you understand a being subsisting by itself, and by this subsistence you mean that it has no need of another, and never had any need of another in order to exist, then you are speaking of a being that is *not caused*, of a necessary being which has in itself the sufficient and necessary reason of its existence. If you say this being is only one, or that there is no other of its kind, we agree with you, only we tell you that you take the name of substance in an improper sense. But at bottom the difference would be only in the name; and in order to come to a mutual understanding it is only necessary for us to know that by substance you understand an absolutely necessary, and consequently absolutely independent being. But if you assert that this being is the only one in the sense that there is nothing, and can be nothing beside it, then your assertion is gratuitous and we ask for joint proof.

Why should the necessary being exclude the possibility of other beings? Is it not more reasonable to conclude that it contains the reason of their possibility and existence? The being which has in itself the necessity of existing, must possess activity, and the external term of this activity is production. Why may not other beings be the result of this production? Inasmuch as produced they would be distinct from the being producing them.

112. Without going beyond our ideas we find contingency and multiplicity. Experience reveals a continual succession of forms within us; these appearances are something; they cannot be a pure nothing, for they must be something, though only appearances. In them we behold a continual transition from not-being to being, and from being to not-being; therefore there is a production of something which is not necessary, since it is, and ceases to be; therefore there is something besides the being which is supposed the only one. This argument is founded on the purely internal phenomena, and, therefore, is valid even against the idealists, against those who take from the external world all reality, and reduce it to mere appearances, to simple phenomena of our mind. These appearances exist at least as appearances; they are then something, they are contingent, they are not therefore necessary being. Therefore besides this being there is something which is not it; therefore the system which asserts the existence of only one being is not sustainable.

The idea of a being absolutely independent by reason of its absolute necessity does not exclude the existence of contingent beings; it only shows that the necessary being is the only necessary being, not that it is the only being.

113. Neither does it follow from the idea of necessary being that there cannot be contingent beings, *caused*, and yet subsisting by themselves in the sense that they are not inherent as modifications in others. Not to be caused and not to be inherent are two very distinct things; the first implies the second, but the second does not imply the first. Every being not caused must be free from inherence, because if it is not caused it is necessary, and contains in itself all that is necessary in order not to inhere in another. If necessary, it must be absolutely independent of all others, which it would not be if it needed them as a modification needs a substance. But not every thing which is not inherent is necessarily not caused, for its cause may have made it such that it does not need to be inherent as a modification in another. It would then depend on another as an effect on its cause, but not as an accident on its substance; there would be between them the relation of causality, but not that of substance; things which we have shown in the last chapter to be very distinct.

114. Never will the pantheists be able to prove that because a thing is not a modification it must be not caused; and this is precisely what they must prove in order to carry their system through in triumph. Once prove that whatever subsists in itself is not caused, and you will have proved whatever subsists in itself to be necessary. And as the necessary being must be only one, you will have proved that there is only one substance.

115. The secret of pantheism is the confounding of non-inherence with absolute independence; and the means of overthrowing its arguments is always to distinguish these two things. All that is not caused is substance, but not all that is substance is uncaused. All that is not caused is necessary and therefore not inherent, but not every substance is necessary. Finite substance is not inherent in another being, but it is caused by another being. It cannot exist without this other being, it is true; but this dependence is not the dependence of a modification on its substance, but that of an effect on its cause.

The cause gives being to the effect; the substance sustains the accident: the cause is not modified by the effect; the substance is modified by the accident. These ideas are clear and distinct; by them pantheism is destroyed in all its transformations, and forced, as old Proteus was by Menelaus, to resume its primitive form. Atheism is its nature, and should be its name. Many of the erroneous systems which disturb the ideal world are founded on an equivocation; to oppose them with success, we must fix ourselves on the point which clears up their equivocation, and not go out of it. The equivocation will assume different forms, but we must not suffer ourselves to be deceived or confounded by it; we must always return to the same distinction and make that the battle-ground. The passage of the immortal poet in the place just alluded to, might be taken as a fable giving an excellent method of defeating sophisms: "Collect all your strength and courage," says the goddess Idothea to Menelaus, "and, throwing yourself upon him, hold him tightly despite all his efforts; for he will metamorphose himself in a thousand ways in order to escape from you: he will take the semblance of all the most savage animals. He will also change himself into water; he will become fire: but let none of these frightful forms terrify you, or force you to let him go; on the contrary, hold him and strain him the more tightly. But as soon as he returns to *the first form* in which, he was, ... then use no more violence, but let him go. [50] " So it is with pantheism, it will speak of matter, of mind, of the reality of phenomenal, of the *me*, of the *not-me*, of subsistence and non-subsistence, of the necessary and the contingent; but do not allow it to go beyond the fundamental ideas, lead it to them; it will at last return to its first form, and when it has returned to this, then let it go, showing it to the world as it is, saying: "See it in its horrible deformity; it has always been what it is now; notwithstanding all its transformations, it is nothing but atheism."

CHAPTER XVI
PANTHEISM EXAMINED IN THE
ORDER OF EXTERNAL FACTS

116. If pantheism is unsustainable in the region of ideas, it is not less so in the field of experience. The latter, far from leading us to the exclusive unity of substance, shows us on all sides multiplicity.

117. There is unity where there is no division, when in the thing that is one no others can be distinguished, when it admits no negative judgment. Nothing of all this is observed in the external world; but a constant experience presents directly the contrary.

118. In the external world division is visible, palpable; there is no other unity than that of order, of direction to an end; besides this, all is multiplicity. The only medium by which we are placed in communication with the external world are the senses, and they encounter multiplicity on every side—sensations distinct in number, diverse in species, graduated in a thousand different ways, distributed into infinite groups, which, although they are connected in this or that point, may be divided and are divided in a thousand others.

119. Multiplicity is as truly revealed by the testimony of the senses as the very existence of objects. If we deny the competency of their testimony in the first, we must deny it also in the second. They not only tell us that such a body exists, but that it is not another body. We know nothing with more certainty than that an external object corresponds to a sensation, that the objects of two distinct sensations are distinct.

To say that the senses are not good judges in this matter, because they are limited to mere sensation, and consequently cannot judge of the objects of the sensation, is to appeal to idealism, for by the same reason we may assert that the senses, limited to mere sensation, cannot give us certainty of the existence of their respective objects.

120. To establish unity outside of ourselves is to annihilate the corporeal world. The idea of extension contradicts unity. In that which is extended some parts are not the others. This is evident, and whoever attempts

to doubt it attacks the basis of the certainty of geometry. If the world is something real, it is extended; if it is not extended, we cannot be certain that it is any thing real. We have the same certainty of its extension as of its existence. Its very existence is manifested by the extension presented to our senses. If, then, this extension does not exist, sensations are a mere internal phenomenon, a pure illusion, in so far as we attribute to them a correspondence to the exterior.

121. This argument seems to me one of the most conclusive than can be brought against Spinosa, who, together with the oneness of the substance admits extension, as one of its attributes. The extended is essentially multiplex; it always involves the distinction between its parts; we can always say of it: "The part A is not the part B." Pantheism cannot escape this argument except by taking refuge in pure idealism; and in this respect Fichte and Hegel are more logical than most persons give them credit for being. In order to maintain the exclusive oneness of substance, it is necessary to convert the external world into mere phenomena, whose only reality consists in their being thus presented to us. This is to absorb the world in the *me*, and concentrate the reality in the idea; but this absorption, this concentration, notwithstanding its obscurity, is a necessary and logical consequence of the principle established. There is absurdity, but there is at least the consequence of the absurdity.

122. Those who call Spinosa the disciple of Descartes, have not observed that there is a necessary contradiction between the two systems. The argument founded on extension, which I have just presented, although conclusive under every hypothesis, is still more so against those who admit with Descartes, that the essence of bodies consists in extension. In that case, the various parts of extension are essentially distinct, since each part constitutes an essence. The essential and substantial multiplicity of bodies would be in proportion to the multiplicity of extension.

123. If you maintain that extension is not the essence of bodies, but an attribute or modification of bodies, whether a determination founded on their essence or an accidental determination, and pretend that this modification or attribute may belong to the only substance, we ask you whether this substance in itself abstracted from extension is simple or composite. If composite, it implies multiplicity, and Spinosa coincides with the common opinion of a corporeal world, composed of many parts, one of which will have no more right than another to be the true substance. For then there would not be a single substance, but one composed of many; and the corporeal universe cannot be called a substance except in the sense in which it is commonly called one, that is, not taking the oneness in a strict sense, but inasmuch as all its parts are connected together, and disposed in a certain

order to conspire to the same end. If the substance, the subject of extension is simple, the result will be a simple substance determined or modified by extension, a simple extended substance, which is a contradiction. A thing cannot be conceived as a modification of another unless it is modified by it; this is what the words express. A modification modifies, giving to the thing modified the form of the modification, applying itself to the thing modified. Extension cannot modify except by making the thing modified extended; and to be extended, and to have extension, are absolutely identical expressions. Therefore it is repugnant for a simple substance to have extension for one of its modifications; therefore Spinosa's system is absurd.

CHAPTER XVII
PANTHEISM EXAMINED IN THE ORDER OF INTERNAL FACTS

124. The multiplicity of substances is no less attested by the consciousness of ourselves, or of the internal world. Our first reflex act reveals within us something which is one, indivisible, and remaining always the same through all the transformations of our being. This unity of the *me* is indispensable to the connection of all the phenomena in a point; without it all memory, all combination, and all consciousness are impossible; our own being disappears, and there remains only a series of unconnected phenomena. But this unity, which we must take as an internal fact which consciousness places beyond all doubt, and the conviction of which it is impossible for us to withstand,—this unity produces the knowledge of multiplicity. There is something which affects us and which is not ourselves. Our will, our activity, is impotent to resist other activities which act upon us; there is, then, something which is not ourselves, which is independent of us. There is something which is not a modification of ourselves, because very often it does not affect us, does not modify us. This something is a reality, for nothing cannot affect any thing. It is not inherent in us; it is, then, in itself, or in something which is not ourselves. There is, therefore, a substance which is not our substance; and the *me* and the *not-me* which have made so much noise in German philosophy, far from leading to the unity of the substance, lead to multiplicity; and destroy pantheism entrenched behind idealism.

125. At the very first we meet at least with duality, the *me* and the *not-me*; but carrying our observations a little farther, we find a striking multiplicity.

Our mind is not alone: the consciousness of what we daily experience proves our communication with other minds, which, like our own, have the consciousness of themselves—a sphere of activity of their own, and, like our own mind, are subjected to other activities without their will, and sometimes even against it. The *me* and the *not-me* existing for our consciousness, exists also for theirs; what in us alone was duality becomes a wonderful multiplicity by means of the repetition of the same fact which we have experienced in ourselves.

126. To attribute this variety of consciousnesses to the same being, to take them as modifications of the same substance, as revelations of itself to its own eyes, is a gratuitous assertion; and not only gratuitous but absurd.

With full confidence I can defy the greatest philosopher of the world to assign any reason, I do not say satisfactory, but even a specious reason, proving that two individual consciousnesses belong to a common consciousness, or are consciousnesses of the same being.

127. In the first place, this doctrine is in contradiction to common sense, and is rejected with irresistible force by the internal sense of every man. The sentiment of our existence is always accompanied by the sentiment of our distinction from other beings like us. We are not only certain that we exist, but that we are distinct from others; and if in any thing the sentiment of this distinction is profoundly marked, it is in what regards the phenomena of our consciousness. Never at any time, in any country or phase of society, could men be persuaded that the consciousness of all their acts and impressions belonged to one and the same being in which individual consciousnesses were united. It is a bad philosophy which begins by struggling against humanity, and placing itself in open contradiction to an irresistible sentiment of nature.

128. The very idea of consciousness excludes this monstrous absurdity, which attempts to transform individual consciousnesses into modifications of one universal consciousness. Consciousness, that is, the internal sentiment of what a being experiences, is essentially individual, it is, so to speak, incommunicable to every other. To others we communicate the knowledge of our consciousness, but not our consciousness itself. It is an intuition or a sentiment which is completed in the innermost recesses of our being, in that which is most our own. What, then, would that consciousness be which does not belong to us as individuals, which is not our own which is nothing of what we believe it to be, but only a property of an unknown being, — a being of which we have no knowledge, and of which we are only a phenomenon, a passing modification? Where would be the unity of consciousness in the midst of such diversity, opposition, and mutual exclusion? This being, modified by so many consciousnesses, would have no consciousness of its own, for it could give itself no account of what it experiences.

CHAPTER XVIII
FICHTE'S PANTHEISTIC SYSTEM

129. I am going to fulfil a promise made in the beginning of this work, [51] to explain and refute the system of Fichte. We have seen the cabalistic forms employed by the German philosopher to obtain a simple result, which amounted to neither more nor less than Descartes' principle, "I think, therefore, I am." The reader could never imagine that any one should attempt to found pantheism on this fact of consciousness, and that the human mind, because it finds itself, should have the arrogance to maintain that nothing exists beside itself, that whatever there is, proceeds from itself, and what is still more extraordinary, that it is itself produced by itself. In order to believe that such things have been written we have to see them, and therefore in explaining Fichte's system, I shall copy his own words.

Thus, although he may suffer a little from the foreign garb, and the reader may be fatigued with deciphering enigmas, he will have an idea of the matter and of the form of the system, which he could not have, if we should take from the philosopher his extravagant originality, which, however, relates to the form, rather than to the substance.

130. "This act, namely X = I am, is founded on no higher principle." [52]

This is true to a certain extent, inasmuch as it affirms that in the series of the facts of consciousness, we come to our own existence as the last limit, and can go no farther. The reflex act, by which we perceive our existence, is expressed by the proposition, *I am*, or, *I exist*; but this proposition by itself alone, tells us nothing as to the nature of the *me*, and is very far from proving our absolute independence. On the contrary, from the moment that we begin to reflect, internal facts are presented to us which incline us to believe that our being is dependent on another; and in proportion as we continue to reflect, we acquire a deep conviction of this truth, arising from a rigorous demonstration.

In no way can we affirm that the act, *I am*, does not depend on any higher principle, if we mean by that, that the act does not spring from any *principle of action*, and that by itself alone, it produces existence. Besides plainly contradicting common sense, this assertion is without any proof, and is also opposed to the most fundamental notions of sound philosophy.

131. Fichte thinks differently, and without knowing why, he deduces from the above propositions these consequences: "Therefore it (the act, X = *I am*) is *supposed absolutely*, and *founded on itself*, as the principle *of a certain* (and, as will be seen by the whole *Doctrine of Science, of every*) act of the human mind, consequently, also of its pure character,—the pure character of activity in itself, abstracted from its particular empirical conditions." It is no great discovery that the character of *act* is *activity*; but this character is not *pure*, since in us no act is pure activity, but it is always a particular exercise of activity.

"Consequently," he continues, "the supposition of the *me* by itself is its pure activity. The *me supposes itself*, and it *is*, in virtue of this mere supposition by itself; and on the other hand, the *me is* and it *supposes* its being, by virtue of its mere being. It is at the same time the acting, and the product of the act; the active, and that which is brought about by the activity; act and fact are one and precisely the same thing; and, therefore, *I am* is the expression of an act, and also of the only one possible, as must be seen from the whole *Doctrine of Science.*"

He that can, may understand what is the meaning of a being which is at the same time producing and produced, principle and term of the same action, cause and effect of the same thing. He that can, may understand the meaning of existing in virtue of a mere action, and exercising this action in virtue of existence. If these be not contradictions, I know not what is. In God, who is infinite being, essence, existence, and action are identical; but we cannot say that the action *produces* his being, that he *supposes* himself by his action; we say that he exists necessarily, and that it is therefore impossible that he should have been produced, that he should have passed from not-being to being.

132. There occurs to me here a rational explanation of Fichte's language, an explanation which even if admissible would not excuse the philosopher for expressing very simple things in contradictory terms. However, it is this. The soul is an activity; its essence consists in thought, by which it is manifested to its own eyes, and finds itself in the act of consciousness. In this sense we may say that the soul supposes itself, that is, knows itself, takes itself as subject of a proposition to which it applies the predicate of existence. The soul is the principle of its act of consciousness; and thus it is productive; it is also presented in the act of consciousness as object, hence it may also be said, though inexactly, that in the ideal order it is produced; in this way it is the principle and the term of the action, but under different respects. This explanation, whether more or less founded, is at least reasonable and even intelligible, and the basis on which it rests, that the essence of the soul consists in thought, has the name of Descartes in its favor. Thus although we

do not defend the words of Fichte, we might at least defend his ideas. But unfortunately, the philosopher has taken good care to prevent even this; his words could not have been more opposed to it.

"We now consider once more," he says, "the proposition: *me is me.*

"The *me* is supposed absolutely. If it is admitted that the *me* which in the above proposition stands in the place of the formal subject is the *me supposed absolutely*; and that in the place of the predicate means the *existing me*; it is expressed in the judgment which is absolutely valid, that both are completely one, or supposed absolutely; that the *me* is, *because* it has supposed itself."

Every judgment implies identity of the predicate and the subject; but in the proposition: *me is me*, the identity is not only implied but explicitly asserted; for which reason, the proposition belongs to the class of what are termed identical propositions, because its predicate explains nothing concerning the idea of the subject, but only repeats it. Whence then does Fichte deduce that the *me* exists because it has supposed itself? So far we have only the *me* saying: *me is me*; it affirms itself and thus *supposes* itself as subject and predicate of a proposition: but it is clearer than day-light that to *suppose by affirming* is altogether different from *supposing by producing*: on the contrary, common sense and reason alike teach that the existence of the thing affirmed is necessary to the legitimacy of the affirmation. To confound these two ideas, to consider it the same thing to *affirm* as to *suppose by producing*, is an inconceivable absurdity. [53]

133. Explaining this in a note, Fichte adds what follows: "It is also certainly so according to the logical form of every proposition. In the proposition A = A, the first A is that which is supposed in the *me* either absolutely as the *me* itself, or on any other ground as every determined *not-me*. In this case the *me* represents the absolute subject, and hence the first A is called the subject. The second A denotes what the *me*, which takes itself as the object of reflection, finds as *supposed* in itself because it has first supposed it in itself. The judging *me* predicates something, not properly of A, but of itself, namely, that it finds an A in itself; and hence the second A is called the predicate. So in the proposition: A = B, A denotes that which is supposed now; B that which is found already supposed. *It* represents the transition of the *me* from the act of supposing to the reflection on that which is supposed."

What does Fichte mean by this comparison of ideas and of language? Does he mean that in this proposition the *me* is subject and predicate according to the different aspects under which it is considered? Does he mean that the *me*, in so far as it occupies the place of subject, expresses simply existence, and that as predicate it is presented as an object of reflection? What does he mean by the word *suppose*? If he means by it to produce, how is it possible for a thing which is not to produce itself? If he means by it the manifestation of itself, so that the object manifested may serve as the logical term of a proposition, why does he tell us that the *me* exists because it supposes itself? But let us follow the German philosopher in his wandering deductions.

134. "The *me* in the first acceptation and that in the second must be absolutely the same. We can therefore invert the above proposition and say: the *me* supposes itself, absolutely *because* it is. It *supposes* itself by its mere being, and *is* by its mere supposition."

Without defining the sense of the word *suppose*, without saying any thing more than what all the world knows; that the *me* is the *me*; he infers that the *me* exists because it supposes itself, and supposes itself because it exists: he identifies existence with supposition without even noticing that at least some preliminary remarks were necessary before placing himself in direct opposition with common sense and the doctrines of all philosophers, including Descartes, who make existence necessary for action, and regard it as a contradiction for a thing to be active without existing. Leibnitz thought that there was nothing and could be nothing without a sufficient reason; but thanks to the author of the *Doctrine of Science*, we may henceforth people the world at pleasure with finite or infinite beings, and if asked whence they came, we may answer that they have been supposed; if we are further asked why they have been supposed, we may answer; because they exist; and if still again asked why they exist, we may say, because they have been supposed; thus we may pass from supposition to existence, and from existence to supposition, without any danger of refutation.

135. Although this philosophy is any thing but clear, it seems to have satisfied its author, who goes on with admirable gravity to say: "Thus, then, it is *perfectly clear* in what sense we here use the word *me*, and we are led to a determinate explanation of the *me* as absolute subject. *Every thing whose being (existence) consists solely in its supposing itself as being*, is the *me*, as absolute subject. So far as it *supposes* itself, it *is*; and so far as it *is*, it *supposes* itself; and the *me* is therefore absolute and necessary for the *me*. That which is not for itself is no *me*." Ideal pantheism could not be established more explicitly, and at the same time more gratuitously; one is astonished to find one's self seriously occupied with such extravagances. They have made a noise, because they have not been known; they ought therefore to be presented to the reader as they are, even at the risk of fatiguing him.

136. Fichte tries to make his ideas clearer, but we may be always sure that each explanation will add to their obscurity. Let us permit him to continue:

"Explanation! One often hears the question asked, *what* was I before I came to the consciousness of myself? The natural answer to this is: *I* was nothing at all; for I was not the *me*. The *me* is only in so far as it is conscious of itself. The possibility of this question is founded on a confusion of the *me* as *subject*, and the *me* as *object* of the reflection of the absolute subject, and is entirely inadmissible. The *me* represents itself, takes itself so far under the form of the representation, and is now for the first time *something*, an object; consciousness receives under this form a substratum which *is*, and although without actual consciousness, is here thought corporeally. Such a case is considered, and it is asked: what was then the *me*; that is, what is the substratum of consciousness? But even then we think the *absolute subject* as that which has intuition of this substratum, *together with it*, although we do not take note of it; we also, without taking note of it, at the same time think that which we pretended to abstract, and thus fall into a contradiction. We can think absolutely nothing without at the same time thinking the *me* as conscious of of itself; we can never abstract our own consciousness: hence all questions of this kind are unanswerable; for they would be, if well understood, unaskable."

That the *me* did not exist as the object of its reflection before it had consciousness of itself, is an evident truth; before thinking itself, it does not think itself; who ever doubted it? But the difficulty is, whether the *me* is any thing, independently of its own reflections or its objectiveness in relation to itself; that is, whether there is in the *me* any thing more than the being thought by itself. The question is not contradictory, but it is one which naturally presents itself to reason and to common sense; for reason as well as common sense resist the taking as identical, that which exists, and that which is known; that which knows itself, and that which produces itself. We are not now examining whether we have or have not a clear idea of the *substratum* of consciousness; but it is curious to hear the German philosopher remark that when we do not conceive the *me* as the object of reflection, we conceive it under a bodily form. This is to confound imagination with ideas, things, as I have elsewhere [54] shown, which are very different.

137. It follows from Fichte's doctrine that the existence of the *me* consists in its supposing itself by means of consciousness; and that if consciousness should not exist, the *me* would not exist. In this case to be and to be known are the same thing. Although I might ask Fichte for his proofs of so extravagant an assertion, I shall confine myself to insisting on the difficulty which he proposes, and which he only eludes by a confusion of ideas. What would the *me* be, if it were not conscious of itself? If to exist is to have consciousness, when there is no consciousness there is no existence. Fichte answers that the *me* without consciousness is not the *me*, in which case, it does not exist;

but that the question rests on an impossible supposition, the abstraction of consciousness. "We can think absolutely nothing," he says, "without at the same time thinking the *me* as conscious of itself; we can never abstract our own consciousness." I say again; these words do not solve the difficulty; they only elude it. I pass over his assertion that consciousness is the same as existence: but it is certain that we conceive an instant in which the *me* is not conscious of itself. Has this conception never been realized? Has there, or has there not, been an instant in which the *me* was not conscious of itself? If we admit this instant, we must admit that at this instant the *me* did not exist; therefore it never could have existed, unless Fichte will concede that the *me* depends on a superior being, and thus admit the doctrine of creation. If we do not admit this instant, the *me* has always existed, and with the consciousness of itself; therefore the *me* is an eternal and immutable intelligence; it is God. There is no way for Fichte to escape this dilemma. There is no room here for the distinction between the *me* as subject and the *me* as object: we are speaking of the *me* as having consciousness of itself,—that consciousness in which Fichte makes its existence consist,—and we ask whether this *me* has always existed or not; if the first, the *me* is God; if the second, you must either acknowledge creation, or hold that a being which does not exist can give itself existence.

138. Fichte does not retreat from the first consequence, and although he does not call *me* God, he gives it all the attributes of divinity. "If the *me*," he says, "is only in so far as it supposes itself, it is only *for* the supposing, and supposes only for being. *The me is for the me*,—but if it supposes itself absolutely as it is, it supposes itself necessary, and is necessary, for the *me*. *I am only for myself; but I am necessary for myself*—(in saying *for myself* I always suppose my being.)

"*To suppose itself*, and *to be*, are, speaking of the *me*, entirely the same. The proposition: I am, because I have supposed myself, can, therefore, be also expressed in this manner: *I am absolutely, because I am.*

"Moreover, the *me* which supposes itself, and the *me* which is, are entirely identical; they are one and the same thing. The *me* is for that *which* it supposes itself; and it supposes itself as *that* which it is. Therefore, *I am absolutely, what I am.*

"The immediate expression of the act which we have now developed would be the following formula: *I am absolutely, that is, I am absolutely, because I am; and am absolutely, what I am; both for the me.*

"But if the enunciation of this act is intended to be placed at the head of a doctrine of science, it should be expressed somewhat in the following manner: *The me originally supposes its own being absolutely.*" [55]

There is only one fact which is clear in all this extravagance of expression; and that is, the pantheism openly professed by Fichte; the deification of the *me*, and, consequently, the absorption of all reality in the *me*. The *me* ceases to be a limited spirit; it is an infinite reality. Fichte does not deny it: "The me determines itself, the absolute totality of reality is ascribed to the *me*. The *me* can determine itself only as reality, for it is supposed absolutely as reality, and no negation whatever is supposed in it. [56]

"But reality is supposed in the *me*. Therefore the *me* must be supposed as the *absolute totality* of reality, (therefore as a quantity, which contains all quantities, and which may be a measure for them all;) and this, too, originally and absolutely, if the synthesis, which we have just explained problematically, be possible, and the contradiction is to be solved in a satisfactory manner. Therefore:

"The *me* supposes absolutely, without any foundation, and under no possible condition, the *absolute totality of reality*, as a quantity, than which, by virtue of this supposition, none greater is possible; and this absolute maximum of reality it supposes *in itself*. All that is supposed in the *me* is reality: and all reality that is, is supposed in the *me*....

... "The conception of reality is similar to the conception of activity. All reality is supposed in the *me*, is the same as: All activity is supposed in the *me*, and reversely; all in the *me* is reality, is the same as: The *me* is *only* active; it is the *me* only in so far as it is active; and in so far as it is not active, it is the *not-me*." [57]

"Only in the understanding is there reality; it is the faculty of the *actual*; *in* it the ideal first becomes real." [58]

"The *me* is only that which it supposes itself; it is infinite; that is, it supposes itself infinite....

"Without the infinity of the *me*,—without a productive faculty whose tendency is unlimited and illimitable,—it is impossible to explain the possibility of representation."

139. Let us give a glance at these ravings. Psychology starts from a fundamental fact—the testimony of consciousness. The human mind cannot think without finding itself; the starting-point of its psychological investigations is the proposition, I think; in this is found the identity of which Fichte speaks—the *me* is the *me*. All thought, from the first moment that it exists, perceives itself subject to a law; the perception of every thing involves the perception, either explicit or implicit, of the identity of the thing perceived. In this sense, the most simple formula in which we can express the first law of our perception is: A is A; but this formula is as sterile

as it is simple; and it is impossible to conceive how any one could pretend to raise upon it a system of philosophy. This formula, supposing it to be enunciated, involves the existence of the *me* which enunciates it. It cannot be said that A is A, if there is not a being in which the relation of identity is supposed. If the proposition A = A is true, it is necessary to suppose an A, or a being in which it exists. A purely ideal truth, without any foundation in a real truth, is an absurdity, as we have elsewhere proved and explained at great length. [59]

140. But the existence of an ideal truth, *in so far as it is represented in us*, that is to say, in so far as it is a fact of our consciousness, is not necessary, but hypothetical, it exists when it exists; but when it exists it may not exist, or when it does not exist it may exist. Necessity cannot be inferred from existence: the testimony of consciousness assures us of the fact; but in this consciousness we find no proof that the fact is necessary, that it has not depended on a higher agent; quite the contrary, the sentiment of our weakness, the shortness of the time to which the recollections of our consciousness extend, the natural and periodical interruptions of them which we experience during sleep, every thing shows that the fact of consciousness is not necessary, and that the being which experiences it has but a little while ago commenced its existence, and might lose it again as soon as the infinite being should cease to preserve it. The *me* which we perceive within us knows itself, affirms itself; the word *supposes* itself has no reasonable meaning, unless it mean that the *me* affirms its existence; but this knowing itself is not producing itself; whoever asserts such an absurdity is under obligation to prove it.

141. In truth it requires all the gravity of Fichte to pretend to connect such a collection of extravagant absurdities into science. It was reserved for modern times to see a man seriously occupied with a system whose existence will, with difficulty, be believed by those who read the history of the aberrations of the human mind. The system of Fichte is already judged by all thinking men, and there is no surer means to make it forgotten than to expose it to the eyes of the judicious reader.

142. Having established the necessary and absolute existence of the *me*, Fichte proposes to demonstrate that from the *me* proceeds the *not-me*, that is to say; all that is not the *me*. "But the *not-me* can only be supposed in so far as a *me*, to which it is opposed, is supposed in the *me* (in the identical consciousness).

"But the *not-me* must be supposed in the identical consciousness.

"Therefore the *me* must also be supposed in it in so far as the *not-me* is supposed in it."

... "If *me* = *me*, all is supposed which is supposed in the *me*.... "The *me* and the *not-me* are both products of original acts of the *me*, and the consciousness itself is a product of the first original act of the *me*, of the supposition of the *me* by itself." [60]

This, then, is how according to Fichte, the *not-me*, that is to say; this which we call the external world, and all that is not the *me*, is born of the *me*; the distinction of one thing from another is a pure illusion, a play of relations by which the *me* conceives itself as *not-me* in so far as it limits itself; but the *me* and the *not-me* are absolutely identical. "The *me* and the *not-me* inasmuch as they are supposed identical and opposed by the conception of mutual limitation, are something in the *me* (accidents) as divisible substances, supposed by the *me*, the absolute and illimitable subject, to which nothing is identical and nothing opposed. There all judgments, the logical subject of which is the limitable or determinable *me*, or something which defines the *me*, must be limited or defined by something higher; but all judgments, the logical subject of which is the absolutely illimitable *me*, cannot be determined by any thing higher, because the absolute *me* is not determined by any thing they are founded on, and defined absolutely by themselves." This is the last result of Fichte's system, the *me* converted into an absolute being, which is determined by nothing above itself, into an unlimited and illimitable subject, an infinite being, into God. Every thing emanates from this absolute subject. "In so far as the *me* supposes itself as infinite, its activity (that of supposing itself) is spent on the *me* itself, and on nothing else than the *me*. Its whole activity is spent on the *me*, and this activity is the ground and the compass of all being. The *me* is therefore *infinite in so far as its activity returns to itself*, and consequently so far also is its activity infinite as its product, the *me*, is infinite. (Infinite product, infinite activity; infinite activity, infinite product; this is a circle, but not a vicious one, for it is one from which reason escapes, for it expresses that which is absolutely certain by itself, and for its own sake. Product, activity, and active are here one and the same thing, and we separate them only in order to express ourselves.) The *pure activity* of the *me* alone, and *the pure me alone* are infinite. But pure activity is that which has no object, but returns to itself."

"In so far as the *me* supposes limits, and, according to what we have said, supposes itself in these limits, its activity is not spent immediately on itself, but on a *not-me* which is to be opposed to it." [61]

How shall we sum up this doctrine? In the words of Fichte: "In so far as the *me* is absolute, it is *infinite* and *unlimited*. It supposes all that is; and that which is not supposed, is not (*for* it; and *out of* it there is nothing). But all that it supposes, it supposes as *me*; and it supposes the *me* as all that it supposes. Hence in this respect the *me* contains in itself all, that is, an infinite, unlimited reality.

"In so far as the *me* opposes to itself a *not-me*, it necessarily supposes *limits*, and supposes itself in these limits. It divides the totality of the being supposed in general between the *me* and the *not-me*; so far supposes itself necessarily as *finite*." [62]

143. Thus Fichte in a few words destroys the reality of the external world, converting it into a modification or development of the activity of the *me*. Is it necessary to stop any longer to refute such an absurd doctrine, one, too, founded on no proof? I believe not: especially since I have established on solid principles the demonstration of the existence of an external world, and have explained the origin and character of the facts of consciousness, without having recourse to such extravagant absurdities. [63]

CHAPTER XIX
RELATIONS OF FICHTE'S SYSTEM
TO THE DOCTRINES OF KANT

144. I have already shown [64] how Kant's system leads to Fichte's. When a dangerous principle is established, there is never wanting an author bold enough to deduce its consequences, whatever they may be. The author of the *Doctrine of Science*, led astray by the doctrines of Kant, establishes the most extravagant pantheism that was ever invented. In concluding his work, he says that he leaves the reader at the point where Kant takes him; he ought rather to have said that he takes the reader at the point where Kant leaves him. The author of the *Critic of Pure Reason*, by converting space into a purely subjective fact, destroys the reality of extension, and opens the door to those who wish to deduce all nature from the *me*; and by making time a simple form of the internal sense, he causes the succession of phenomena in time to be considered as mere modifications of the *me* to the form of which they relate.

145. But it is far from being necessary for us to hunt after deductions; the philosopher himself, in the midst of his obscurity and enigmatical language, does not cease to lay down in the most precise manner this monstrous doctrine. Let us hear how he speaks in his transcendental Logic, where he proposes to explain the relation of the understanding to objects in general, and the possibility of knowing them *a priori*. "The order and regularity in phenomena, that which we call nature, *is consequently our own work*; we should not find it there if we had not placed it there by the nature of our mind; for this natural unity must be a necessary unity, that is to say, a certain unity *a priori* of the connection of the phenomena. But how could we produce a synthetic unity *a priori*, if there were not in the primitive sources of our mind subjective reasons of this unity *a priori*, and if these subjective conditions were not at the same time *objectively valid*, since they are the grounds of the possibility of knowing in general an object in experience?" [65] Who does not see in these words the germ of Fichte's system, which deduces from the *me* the *not-me*, that is to say, the world, and gives to nature no other validity than that which it has received from the *me*?

146. But Kant is still more explicit, where he is explaining the nature and attributes of the understanding. He says: "We have before defined the understanding in different ways; we have called it a spontaneity of knowledge, (in opposition to the receptivity of sensibility,) a faculty of thought, or rather, a faculty of conceptions or judgments; these definitions, rightly explained, are but one. We may now characterize it as a *faculty of rules*. This character is more fruitful, and comes nearer to the essence of the thing: sensibility gives us forms (of intuition) and the understanding rules. The latter is always applied to the observation of phenomena in order to find in them some rule. The rules, if objective, (if, consequently, necessarily united to the knowledge of the object,) are called laws. Although we know many laws by experience, still these laws are only particular determinations of other higher laws, the highest of which (to which all the others are subjected) *proceed* a priori *from the understanding itself*, and are not taken from experience, but, on the contrary, they give to the phenomena their validity, and therefore make experience possible. The understanding, then, is not simply a faculty of making rules for itself, and comparing phenomena; *it is also the legislation for nature; that is to say, that without the understanding there would be no nature*, or synthetic unity of the multiplicity of phenomena according to certain rules. For the phenomena, as such, cannot exist out of us; on the contrary, they only exist in our sensibility; but this, as the object of the knowledge in an experience, with all that it can contain, is only possible in the unity of the apperception. The unity of the apperception is the transcendental foundation of the necessary legitimacy of all the phenomena in an experience; this unity of the apperception in relation to the multiplicity of the representations (in order to determine the multiplicity by starting from only one) is the rule, and the faculty of these rules is the understanding. All phenomena, then, as possible experiences, are *a priori* in the understanding, and from it they derive their formal possibility, in the same manner that they are pure intuitions in the sensibility, and are only possible by it in relation to the form."

In the *deduction of the pure conceptions of the understanding*, Kant not only pretends that the objects of our knowledge are not things in themselves, but that it is impossible that they should be, because we could not then have conceptions *a priori*. He adds, that the representation of all these phenomena, consequently all objects which we know, are all in the *me*, and are determinations of *my identical me*, which expresses the necessity of a universal unity of these determinations in only one and the same apperception.

147. From these passages it clearly follows that Fichte's system, or the ideal pantheism which reduces every thing to modifications of the *me*, accords with the principles established in the *Critic of Pure Reason*, and is even expressly laid down, although it does not form its principal object in that work. For the sake of impartiality I cannot do less than refer the reader

to the seventeenth chapter of the third book, where I have intimated that the German philosopher attempts to explain his expressions so as to escape idealism, which he professes to refute. But this he seems to me to do only by an inconsequence.

148. However, my opinion of the connection of modern pantheism with the *Critik der reinen Vernunft* is confirmed even by the Germans. "From these depths," says Rosenkranz, speaking of this work, "the results of the transcendental æsthetics and logic receive a new importance in the great problems of theology, cosmology, morals, and psychology, which was not even suspected by the dull sense of the greater part of its admirers. They know nothing of the chain which unites Fichte's *Doctrine of Science*, Schelling's *System of Transcendental Idealism*, Hegel's *Phenomenology and Logic*, and Herbart's *Metaphysics*, with Kant's *Critic*....

"I may say that the English and French in particular will understand nothing of the development of German philosophy since Kant, until they have penetrated the *Critic of Pure Reason*, for *we Germans always look to that*.... Just as we use the houses, the palaces, the churches, but most of all the towers which rise over every thing to guide us in a large city; so also in contemporary philosophy, amid the labyrinth of its quarrels it is impossible to take a single step with security unless we keep our sight fixed on Kant's *Critic*. Fichte, Schelling, Hegel, and Herbart made this work the great centre of their operations for attack or defence." [66]

149. I do not mean by this that the German philosophers since Kant have added nothing to the *Critic of Pure Reason*: I have already observed (in the seventh chapter of the first book) that the cause of the greater obscurity which is found in Fichte's words, proceeds from his having gone farther than Kant in his abstraction of all objectiveness both external and internal, placing himself in I know not what pure primitive act, from which he pretends to deduce every thing; in which he differs from the author of the *Critic of Pure Reason*, whose labors did not so absolutely annihilate the objectiveness of the internal world, and therefore his observations are less incomprehensible, and even present here and there some few luminous points: I only wished to show the baneful importance of Kant's works, to place those incautious persons on their guard, who, judging from what they have heard, are inclined to regard him as the great restorer of spiritualism and sound philosophy, when, in reality, he is the founder of the most pernicious schools which the history of the human mind has known, and would be one of the most dangerous writers that ever existed, were it not that the obscurity of his ideas, increased by the obscurity of their expression, renders him intolerable to the immense majority of readers, even of those versed in philosophical studies.

CHAPTER XX
CONTRADICTION OF PANTHEISM TO THE PRIMARY FACTS OF THE HUMAN MIND

150. I do not know how any philosopher who has meditated on the human mind can incline to pantheism. The deeper we go into the *me* from which it is pretended to deduce such an absurd system, the more we discover the contradiction in which pantheism appears in respect to the primary ideas and facts of our mind. My development of this observation will be brief, for it turns on questions largely examined in their respective places.

151. We have seen (Bk. VI., Ch. V.) that the idea of number is found in every understanding, and experience teaches that we employ it explicitly or implicitly in almost all our words. We scarcely speak without using the plural, and this can have no meaning without the supposition of the idea of number. Pantheism reduces all existence to an absolute unity; multiplicity either has no real existence, or is limited to phenomena, which, in the judgment of some followers of this system, contain no reality of any sort, and, in the opinion of all pantheists, can contain no substantial reality. According to them, therefore, the idea of number either has no correspondence in the reality, or it relates only to modes of being, to the various modifications of the same being, and therefore does not extend to the beings themselves, for in this system there is only one being. If this be so, how is it that the idea of number exists in our understanding? how is it that we conceive not only many modes of being, but many beings? In the system of the pantheists not only is there no multiplicity of beings, but it is impossible that there should be; why, then, has our understanding this radical vice which necessarily leads it to conceive the multiplicity of *things*, if this multiplicity is absurd? why is this ideal defect confirmed by experience which also necessarily leads us to believe that there are many distinct *things*?

152. In the system of the pantheists our understanding is only a modification, a manifestation of the only substance; but it is impossible to explain this disagreement between the phenomenon and the reality, this necessary error into which the phenomenon of the substance leads us in

respect to the substance itself. If we are a mere manifestation of the unity, why do we find the idea of multiplicity as a primitive fact within us? Why this continual contradiction between the being and its appearances? If we are all one same unit, whence do we obtain the idea of number? If the phenomena of experience are only evolutions, so to speak, of this one unit, why do we feel ourselves irresistibly inclined to suppose multiplicity in the phenomena, and to multiply the *things* in which they succeed?

153. The idea of distinction opposed to that of unity is also fundamental in our mind; [67] yet pantheism gives it no correspondence in the reality. If there is only being, if all is identical, there is nothing distinct, and the idea of distinction is a pure chimera. In this system distinction not only does not exist, but it is impossible; consequently the idea of distinction is absurd; therefore one of the primary facts of our mind is a contradiction.

154. Negative judgments form a considerable part of the wealth of our understanding; [68] pantheism destroys them. In this system the proposition: A is not B, can never be true; for, if all is identical, one thing cannot be denied of another, there would be no distinct things, there would be no *one* or *another*; all would be one; the negative judgment must be limited to the following: in reality A is the same as B, there is only the appearance of distinction; B is A existing or *presented* differently.

155. The idea of relation is also absurd in the pantheistic system; there is no *relation* without a term of *reference*, and there is no reference without distinction. According to the pantheists the subject referred and the term of the reference are absolutely identical; there are, consequently, no true, but only apparent, relations; thus we find another of the primary facts of our understanding radically absurd, because it is in contradiction with the reality, and even with the possibility.

156. The support of all our knowledge, the principle of contradiction, it is impossible for the same thing to be and not to be at the same time, is without meaning, and can have no real or possible application, if the doctrine of pantheism be admitted. When we say that it is impossible for the same thing to be and not be at the same time, we understand that there is the possibility of not-being; in our mind the idea of being excludes that of not-being only with respect to the same thing and at the same time. If there is only one being, and all other being is impossible, it follows that the idea of not-being is absolutely contradictory, and all the propositions in which it is expressed are absurd. There is in this case only one being which is every thing, to this being negation of being can never be applied; this negation, then, is absolutely absurd, and another idea of our mind is absolutely contradictory.

157. The idea of contingency is also contradictory if pantheism be admitted; all that can be is, and all that does not exist is impossible; therefore when we distinguish contingency from necessity we contradict both the reality and the possibility. Hence there is another primary illusion of our mind which presents to us as possible, and even existent, that which in itself is absurd.

158. Neither can the ideas of finite and infinite co-exist in the system. One of them must be contradictory; if the only being is infinite, there is and can be nothing finite; therefore the opposition between the finite and the infinite is a chimera of our mind, to which there is nothing in reality corresponding. There is only one thing; it must be finite or infinite; in either case, one of these terms must disappear, one of these ideas is contradictory, since it is in opposition to an absolute necessity.

159. The system of absolute unity destroys the idea of order. In this idea is contained the arrangement of distinct things, distributed in a convenient manner to conspire to an end. If there is no distinction there is no order, and the distinction is impossible if there is absolute unity. The idea of order is still one of the fundamental ideas of our mind; literary and artistic unity, and in general that of all sensible beauty, is the unity of order: substitute for this absolute unity, and you destroy all beauty of the imagination; art becomes absorbed by chaos.

160. It is useless to add that pantheism destroys liberty of will; this liberty of which we are so clearly and vividly conscious, and which accompanies us through every moment of our existence. In this monstrous system absolute unity is inseparable from absolute necessity; the existent and the possible are confounded; nothing which is can cease to be; nothing which is not can be. The action must spring from the only substance by a spontaneous development; understanding by spontaneity the absence of an external cause; but this action cannot but exist, it will be an irradiation, as it were, of the only substance, just as light radiates from luminous bodies. Without liberty of will merit is absurd; a being that acts by absolute necessity can have no merit or demerit. Then laws are to no purpose, rewards and punishments useless; the history of individuals as of all mankind is only a history of the phases of the only substance, which goes on eternally developing itself in subjection to absolutely necessary conditions which have no other foundation than the substance itself.

161. Pantheism not only destroys freedom of will, but it renders unintelligible all affections which relate to *another*. If there is only one being, what mean the sentiments of love, respect, gratitude, and in general, all those which suppose a person distinct from the *me* which experiences them? No

matter how distinct we suppose the term of these affections, they can never have any; and although they seem to proceed from different principles, they spring from only one. The man who loves one man and hates another is the *me* loving and hating itself; appearances denote diversity and opposition, but at bottom there is unity, identity. Who can accept such absurdities?

162. Thus pantheism, after destroying the intellectual man, annihilates the moral man; after declaring the fundamental ideas of our mind contradictory, it attacks the most precious fact of our consciousness,— the freedom of will; it destroys the sentiments of the heart, denying our individuality, it precipitates us all into the deep abyss of the only substance, the absolute being, confounding and identifying us with it, till we lose within it our own existence, as the molecules of a grain of dust are lost in the immensity of space.

CHAPTER XXI
RAPID GLANCES AT THE PRINCIPAL
ARGUMENTS OF PANTHEISTS

163. The principal arguments on which pantheism rests are founded on the unity of science, the universality of the idea of being, the absoluteness and exclusiveness of the idea of substance, and the absoluteness and exclusiveness of the conception of the infinite.

164. Science must be one, say the pantheists, and it cannot be completely so, unless there is unity of being. Science must be certain, and there cannot be absolute certainty, unless there is identity of the being which knows with the thing known.

The solution of these difficulties consists in denying the gratuitous propositions on which they are founded.

It is not true that human science must be one, nor that unity of being is necessary for the unity of science. They must prove both these assertions; to triumph in a discussion it is not enough to assert. Far from either of them being sufficiently proved, they are both contradicted by reason and by experience. It is unnecessary to repeat here, what I have explained at full length when treating of the possibility and existence of transcendental science as well in the absolute intellectual order as in the human. For this I refer the reader to the fourth, fifth, sixth, and seventh chapters of the first book.

The second proposition which exacts the identity of the subject knowing with the object known, has also been sufficiently refuted. I have elsewhere shown that the system of universal identity does not help to explain the problem of representation, and I have proved by incontestible arguments, that besides the representation of identity, there are the representations of causality and ideality. [69] I have also demonstrated the objective value of ideas, in so far as distinguished from objects, founding my proof on the unity of consciousness. [70]

The doctrines of Kant which convert the external world into a purely subjective fact, and thus give rise to Fichte's transcendental idealism, are refuted in the second book, where I have demonstrated the objectiveness of sensations, — in the third book, where I have proved the reality of extension, and in the seventh book, where I have proved that time is not a pure form of the internal sense.

165. The argument founded on the idea of the universality of being, that is, the impossibility of more than one being, because the idea of being is absolute and embraces every thing, is a sophism in which there is a transition from the ideal order to the real, by which an indeterminate and abstract idea is converted into an absolute being. To form a perfect conception of this idea and its relations to the reality, see what has been said in the fifth book, when treating of the idea of being.

166. Spinosa, Fichte, Cousin, Krause, and all who have taught pantheism under one form or another, start with a wrong definition of substance. It is impossible to overrate the necessity of acquiring clear and distinct ideas of this definition, for there is no doubt but that here is the origin of the error of the pantheists, and the secret to put a stop to their progress. When one examines profoundly the principles of systems which have made so much noise in the philosophical world, one is surprised at contemplating their insubsistency in its nakedness. The doctrines summed up in Chapter XIV. should be kept always in sight.

167. In the importance and transcendency of the definition, the notion of the infinite may compete with that of substance. It is incredible to what extent this word has been abused without any care to explain its different senses, or its origin, or the legitimacy of its applications.

All the arguments which the pantheists pretend to found on the idea of the infinite vanish like smoke when we clearly understand the character, the origin, and the application of this idea. [71]

168. I will conclude with one remark. I am profoundly convinced that the most baneful systems in philosophy arise in great part from confusion of ideas, and the superficiality with which the most fundamental points of ontology, ideology, and psychology are examined. My ruling idea in the present work is to prevent this evil; this is why I have so greatly extended the part of *fundamental philosophy*, abstracting, as far as possible, all secondary questions. These last are easily answered, after we have once acquired a clear and exact knowledge of the fundamental ideas of human science. (4)

BOOK TENTH
NECESSITY AND CAUSALITY

CHAPTER I
NECESSITY

1. Beings are divided into two c∞∞lasses: necessary and contingent; necessary being is that which cannot but be; contingent is that which may be and cease to be. In these definitions every thing is said; but their laconism does not permit all that is expressed in them to be easily understood. Necessity and contingency may refer to different aspects and give rise to very diverse considerations. This makes a careful analysis of the ideas expressed by them necessary.

2. What is meant by necessity? In general that is called necessary which cannot but be; but the expression *cannot,* may be taken in different senses: in a moral sense, as when we say: I cannot but fulfil this duty; in a physical, as in this proposition; a paralytic cannot move himself; and in a metaphysical sense, as: A triangle cannot be a quadrilateral. In the first example, the obstacle is founded on a law; in the second, it arises from nature; in the third, it follows from the essence of the things. In all these suppositions, necessity implies the impossibility of the contrary, and this impossibility results from the necessity.

3. Hence it follows that the ideas necessity and impossibility are correlative, and that is metaphysically necessary whose opposite is metaphysically impossible. Impossibility consists in the exclusion of one thing by another; thus, "a circular triangle is impossible," means the same as "the nature of a triangle excludes the nature of a circle." In all impossibility, therefore, there is a term denied; as in all necessity there is a term affirmed; the metaphysically necessary is that whose opposite is contradictory; the existence of the absurd is impossible, the non-existence of the necessary is absurd. It is contradictory for a triangle to have four sides; and it is absurd for a triangle not to have three angles.

4. In the purely ideal order we see many necessities without any relation to existence; such are all geometrical truths. Even in the real order we conceive many hypothetical necessities in contingent beings: such are those which are obtained by applying absolute principles to any hypothesis furnished by experience. The principle of contradiction serves in an infinity of cases to found a certain necessity even in contingent beings. There is no absolute necessity of the existence of extended beings; but on the supposition that they exist, it is necessary for them to have the properties proceeding from extension.

5. In no finite being can there be an absolute necessity; the only necessity which it can have is hypothetical. The relation of its essential attributes is necessary; but, as its essence does not exist necessarily, whatever is necessary in it is so only hypothetically, that is, on the supposition that it exists.

6. We must then distinguish two necessities: one absolute, the other hypothetical. The latter relates to the essences of things, abstracting their existence, although implying it as a condition, and supposing another necessary as the ground of its possibility; [72] the former relates to the existence of the thing. The absolutely necessary is that whose existence is absolutely necessary.

7. The essence of the necessary being must contain existence; its idea must involve the idea of existence, not only logical and conceptual, but also realized.

8. We can conceive the existence of the necessary being distinct from its essence, but the reason of this is in the imperfection of the idea, which with us is not intuitive, but discursive; and consequently, we can distinguish between the logical order and the real order.

Here we find the defect of Descartes' argument by which he pretends to demonstrate the existence of God from the fact that the predicate, existence, is included in the idea of a necessary and infinite being. The idea of necessary being involves existence, but not real existence, only logical and conceptual; since after we have the idea of the necessary being, it still remains to be proved that there is an object which corresponds to this idea; the predicate belongs to the subject according to the manner in which the subject is taken, and as this is only in the purely ideal order, the predicate is also purely ideal.

9. The reality of the necessary idea cannot be demonstrated from its idea alone; but it may be demonstrated with complete evidence by introducing into the argument other elements which experience furnishes us.

Something exists; at least ourselves; at least this perception which we have in this act; at least the appearance of this act. I leave aside for the present all the questions disputed between the dogmatists and the skeptics; I only suppose a *datum* which no one can deny me, though he carry skepticism to the utmost exaggeration. When I say that something exists, I only mean to affirm that not every thing is a pure nothing.

If something exists, something has always existed, or there is no moment in which it could be said with truth: there is nothing. If such a moment of universal nothingness had ever been, nothing would now exist, there never could have been any thing. Let us imagine a universal and absolute nothingness; I then ask: Is it possible that any thing should come from nothing? Evidently not; therefore on the supposition of universal nothingness reality is absurd.

10. Therefore something has always existed, with a cause, without a condition on which it depends; therefore there is a necessary being. Its existence is supposed always, without relation to any hypothesis; therefore its *not-being* is always excluded under all conditions; therefore there exists an absolutely necessary *being*, that is, a being whose *not-being* implies a contradiction.

11. Summing up the doctrine which precedes, we may say:

I. That we have the idea of a necessary being.

II. That we deduce its existence from its idea alone.

III. That in order to demonstrate the existence of a necessary being, it is sufficient to know that something exists.

IV. We know by experience that something exists; for experience presents to us, if nothing else, the existence of our own thought.

CHAPTER II
THE UNCONDITIONED

12. The words, conditioned and unconditioned, are greatly used in modern philosophy; as the ideas which these terms express have a great analogy to those explained in the last chapter, I will briefly consider them here.

13. The conditioned is that which depends on a condition; that is to say, that which is supposed if another thing, which is called the condition, is supposed. If the sun is above the horizon, there is light; here the light is the conditioned, the sun the condition. The unconditioned is that which supposes no condition, as its name expresses.

14. The universe is an assemblage of conditioned beings; this is manifested by both internal and external experience: does any thing unconditioned exist? Yes.

15. Representing the universe by a series A, B, C, D, E, F, ... etc., the condition of F is in E; the condition of E in D; that of D in C; that of C in B, and so on successively. If there is nothing unconditioned this retrogression will extend to infinity, and we shall have an infinite series of conditioned terms.

To arrive at any term, for example, B, it will have been necessary to pass through the infinite conditions which precede it: the infinite series will have been exhausted: this is contradictory. And as what is said of B may be said of A, or of any other of the preceding or succeeding terms, it follows that they are all impossible: therefore the series is absurd.

16. In the supposed series all is conditioned, there is nothing unconditioned; and still the existence of its successive totality is necessary. Therefore the series in itself is unconditioned; therefore a collection of conditioned terms is unconditioned, although it is supposed impossible to assign any thing, out of the series, which is unconditioned. Who would admit such an absurdity?

17. Let us give a more precise formula to the argument. Taking any three terms in the series; A ... F ... N, we may form the following propositions.

If A exists, F and N will exist.

If N exists, F and A have existed.

If F exists, A has existed and N will exist.

Objections.—I. Whence arises the connection of the conditions with one another?

II. Why should any one of them be supposed?

18. By admitting a necessary, unconditioned being which contains the condition of whatever exists, every thing is explained. To the first objection it may be answered, that the connection of the *conditioned* conditions depends on the *unconditioned* condition. To the second, it may be said that the primitive condition has no need of any other condition, supposing it to be a necessary being. To ask *why* it should be supposed, is to fall into a contradiction; since it is unconditioned it has no *why*, the reason of its existence is in itself.

19. But if we admit nothing necessary, nothing unconditioned, neither the terms nor their connection can be explained. Infinite terms would exist, necessarily connected, with any internal or external sufficient reason. There would be no more reason for the existence of the universe than for its non-existence; being and nonentity would be indifferent to it; and it cannot be conceived why existence should have prevailed. For nothing it is evident that nothing is required; why then is there not an absolute and eternal nothing?

20. The more we examine the necessity of the connection of the conditions, one with another, the stronger this difficulty becomes; for if it be said that one condition cannot exist without another; with still more reason we ask why a first condition is not necessary for the collection of the conditions, or the entire series.

21. Therefore the conditioned supposes the unconditioned; the first given, we can conclude the second. The conditioned is given us in the external and in the internal world. Therefore there exists an unconditioned being, whose existence has no reason in any thing outside of itself.

CHAPTER III
IMMUTABILITY OF NECESSARY
AND UNCONDITIONED BEING

22. The absolutely necessary and unconditioned is immutable. For its existence *is*, or, to speak in modern language, is *supposed* absolutely, by intrinsic necessity, without any condition; and with this existence its *state* is also supposed. We abstract for the present the nature of this state, whether it be of this or that perfection, this or that degree, or even finite or infinite. Its existence being supposed unconditionally, its state is supposed unconditionally also; therefore as its *non-existence* is contradictory, (Ch. I.) its *no-state* is also contradictory. Change is only a transition from one state to another state which implies the *no-state* of the first; therefore change in the necessary is contradictory.

23. In order to present this in a clearer and more precise manner, we will call E the necessary and unconditioned being. As E is supposed absolutely by intrinsic necessity, without any condition, the *not-E* must be contradictory. E is not abstract but real being, consequently it must have certain perfections, as intelligence, will, activity, or any other whatever; and it must have these perfections in a certain degree, abstracting for the present, whether it be greater or less, finite or infinite. With the absolute existence of E a state of perfection, which we shall call N, is also supposed. What has determined the state N? By the supposition, it can have been determined by nothing; since the state is unconditioned. Therefore, if the state N is absolutely and necessarily, the *not-N* is contradictory. Therefore the change by which E would pass from N to *not-N* is contradictory.

24. But let us for a moment suppose a change in the necessary being, and suppose it to have proceeded from this being itself. As the reason of the change must be necessary and eternal, we should have to admit an infinite series of evolutions, and should again fall into the impossibility of reconciling the infinity of the series with the existence of any one of its terms. [73]

25. Thus it is demonstrated that the necessary and unconditioned being can suffer no change which would cause it to lose its primitive state.

The necessary being can lose nothing; it cannot pass from N to *not-N*; but who knows but what it is possible that without losing N, or passing to *not-N*, it might acquire something which could be united to N in one way or another. In other words; N being given, *not-N* is contradictory, but would N P be contradictory, P expressing a perfection, or degree of perfection? This would be impossible; because P which is added must emanate from N; therefore all that is in P was already in N; therefore there has been no change, and to suppose it is contradictory.

26. It may be replied that P was in N virtually, and that the new state only adds a new form. But does this form, as such, involve something *new* in reality? Either it does or it does not: if it does not, there is no change; if it does, it was either contained in N or not contained in it; if contained in it, there is no change; if not contained in it, whence does it come?

27. To elude this demonstration, some have imagined various necessary beings acting on each other, and mutually producing changes in each other,—by this means they attempt to explain whence the *new* states come. But these are not only fictions, and evidently groundless cavils in contradiction with the principles of ontology, but they may be destroyed by one conclusive argument.

Let A, B, C, D, be the necessary and unconditioned beings; each is supposed absolutely, and with primitive states, which we shall respectively call *a, b, c, d*. Then, taking them in their primitive state, the collection of the existences will be united with a collection of necessary and unconditioned states, which we may represent in this formula: A*a*, B*b*, C*c*, D*d*, (1.) This expression represents a primitive, necessary, and unconditioned state: now I ask: whence come the changes? All is unconditioned; how then is the conditioned, the mutable introduced?

28. The force of the argument is not weakened by supposing the primitive and mutual action of A, B, C, D, to be implied in the primitive states *a, b, c, d*. For the mutual actions, being primitive and absolute, would produce primitively and absolutely a result in their respective terms. This result would be primitively necessary, and would be contained in the formula. (1) Therefore the formula would suffer no variation by the new supposition; and consequently there would have been no change of any kind.

29. By imagining that the mutual action does not suppose a primitive state, but a successive series of states, we fall into the infinite series, and consequently into the impossibility of arriving at any term of it, without supposing the infinity to be exhausted, (Ch. II.).

30. Again, the essences of the necessary and unconditioned beings A, B, C, D, being distinct, what reason is there for supposing them to be in

relations of activity? What is the ground of this relation if they are all four necessary, unconditioned, and therefore independent of each other?

31. But let us leave such absurdities, and go on with our analysis of the idea of a necessary and unconditioned being. Immutability excludes perfectibility, so that it is necessary either to suppose the summit of perfection primitively in the necessary being, or to admit that it can never attain this perfection. Perfectibility is one of the characteristics of the contingent, which improves its mode of being by a series of transformations; the absolutely necessary is what it is, and can be nothing else.

32. The contingent must emanate from the necessary, the conditioned from the unconditioned; therefore all perfections, of whatever order, must be found in the necessary and unconditioned being; therefore all the perfections of existing reality must be in it, at least, *virtually*, and those which imply no imperfection must be contained in it *formally*. [74]

33. The possibility of the non-existent must have a foundation; [75] possible perfections must exist in a real being, if their idea is possible; therefore the infinite scale of perfections, which we conceive in the order of pure possibility, besides those which exist, must be realized in the necessary and unconditioned being.

CHAPTER IV
IDEAS OF CAUSE AND EFFECT

34. We have the idea of cause; the continual use which we are always making of it shows this. Philosophers do not alone possess it; it is the inheritance of mankind. But what do we understand by cause? All that makes any thing pass from not-being to being, as the effect is all that which passes from not-being to being. I am not now considering whether that which passes from not-being to being is substance or accident, nor the manner in which the cause influences this transition. Hence the definition includes every class of cause, and every species of causality.

35. The idea of cause contains:

I. The idea of being.

II. The relation to that which passes from not-being to being, as of a condition to the conditioned.

The idea of effect contains:

I. The idea of being.

II. The idea of the transition from not-being to being.

III. The relation to the cause, as of the conditioned to the condition.

36. Axiom I.—Nothing cannot be a cause; or in other terms: every cause is a being, or exists.

37. I say that this is an axiom, because it cannot be demonstrated, since the predicate existence, is evidently contained in the idea of cause. That which is a cause, is; if it is not, it is not a cause. To affirm the cause and deny that it is, is to affirm and deny at the same time. Therefore this proposition is an axiom. To be convinced of its truth, we need only to attend to the ideas of cause and effect, and we see the idea of being evidently contained in the idea of cause. The explanation which I give must not be regarded as a demonstration, but as an illustration, for the purpose of better comparing the two ideas. Whoever compares them as he ought will want no demonstration, he will see it intuitively, and this is what constitutes the character of an axiom.

38. Axiom II.—There is no effect without a cause.

39. To understand the sense of this axiom it must be observed, that here the word *effect* only means that which passes from not-being to being, whether it be caused or not; for, if by effect was meant a thing caused, the axiom would be an identical and useless proposition. Substituting for effect its meaning, it would be, "There is nothing caused without being caused," — which is very true, but of no use. The sense then is this: whatever passes from not-being to being, requires something distinct from itself, which produces this transition.

40. I say that this proposition is an axiom, and to be convinced of it, we need only fix our attention upon the ideas contained in it. Let us consider a thing that is, and transfer it to the time when it was not. Let us abstract all that which is not it, let us suppose no other being which may have produced it or taken part in its production; I assert that we see evidently that the transition to being, will never be made. Not only is it impossible for us to make the object emanate from the pure idea of its not-being, but we also see that it can never emanate from it. There is no being, no action, no production of any kind; there is pure nothing; whence will the being emanate? The truth, of the proposition is then intuitively presented to us: we not only do not see the possibility of the apparition of being in the pure idea of not-being by itself, but we see in this idea the impossibility of this apparition. They are ideas which exclude each other; not-being is possible only by the exclusion of being, and *vice versa*.

41. When we conceive a productive action, we either refer it to the thing which from not-being must pass to being, or to something distinct from this. In the first case, we fall into contradiction; because we suppose an action and do not suppose it, since there is no action in pure nothing. Let us suppose that the thing is cause before being; we then find ourselves in contradiction with Axiom I, (§ 36). In the second case, we already conceive the cause, since cause is only that which produces the transition from not-being to being.

42. The common expression, "ex nihilo nihil fit," is a truth, if understood in the sense of Axiom II.

CHAPTER V
ORIGIN OF THE NOTION OF CAUSALITY

43. Are there in the world any cause and effect? This is equivalent to asking whether there is any change in the world. All change involves a transition from not-being to being. The least change is inconceivable without this transition. Whatever is changed is, after changing, in *another* way than it was before the change; therefore it has this mode of being which it had not before. This mode did not exist *before*, it exists *now*; it has passed, therefore, from not-being to being.

44. Even if we were not in relation with the external world, and our mind was confined to internal facts alone, to the consciousness of the *me* and its modifications, we should know that there is transition from not-being to being, by the testimony of the successive appearance of new perceptions and affections. Within ourselves we experience the ebb and flow of modifications which pass from not-being to being, and from being to not-being.

45. It is clear, from what has been said, that the ideas of cause and effect suppose a real or possible order of contingent beings. If there were only necessary and immutable beings, there could be no causes and effects.

46. I said (Chap. IV.) that the idea of cause contains the idea of being and the idea of relation to the not-being which has passed or passes to being. The idea of cause is not a simple idea; it is composed of these two. The idea of being alone is not sufficient to constitute it; for we may conceive being without conceiving cause. What the idea of cause adds to the idea of being is something distinct from the idea of being, and not contained in it; it may be called causality, power, productive force, activity, or any such term; they all express the relation of one being to realize in another the transition from not-being to being.

47. In the idea of causality is likewise included another simple idea, which, though accompanying the idea of being, must not be confounded with it. If any one should call it a modification of the idea of being, I should have no objection.

48. Whence does the idea of causality arise? The mere intuition of the idea of being does not seem sufficient to produce it. The idea of being

is simple, it expresses nothing but being; we can, therefore, find in it no relation to the transition from not-being to being.

49. Does it, perchance, spring from experience? Here we must distinguish between the idea of causality, and the knowledge of the existence of the cause. Experience reveals the succession of beings, that is, their transition from not-being to being, and *vice versa*. We have already remarked that in the intuition of not-being with relation to being we see the impossibility of a transition, without the mediation of some being which executes it; therefore the certainty of the existence of the cause arises from experience, combined with the intuition of the ideas of being and not-being.

50. If this experience did not exist, we should not know that causality is possible; because in the idea of being, as we possess it, we do not see the idea of force: we might perhaps conceive the force, but we could not know whether any thing in reality corresponds to it. We should thus have the *notion* of the force, but not the *notice* of its existence, nor even the certainty of its possibility.

51. But if we examine it well, this want of experience is an impossible supposition; because a limited intelligent being, as uniting intelligence with limitation, feels the succession of its perceptions, and, consequently, experiences within itself the transition from a not-being to being. And as, on the other hand, it perceives its power of combining ideas, it perceives within itself the existence of causality, of a power which produces its reflections.

52. The exercise of our will, whether with respect to internal or external acts, likewise gives us the knowledge of the dependence of some things upon others; and the impressions which we receive without our will, or against it, confirm us in this conviction. Without this experience we should see the succession of the phenomena, but should not know their relations of causality; for it is clear that the inclination to assign as the cause of a phenomenon that which preceded it, supposes the idea of cause and the knowledge of the dependence of the phenomena in the relation of causes and effects.

53. Some philosophers say that man has no idea of the creation, from which, without intending it, they come to the conclusion that we have not the idea of any cause. By creation is meant the transition of a substance from not-being to being, by virtue of the productive action of another substance. I hold that this is only the idea of causality in its highest degree, that is, as applied to the production of a substance; but since therefore we have the idea of cause, the idea of creation is not a new and inconceivable idea, but a perfection of an idea which is common to all mankind. We have seen that the idea of cause contains the idea of producing a transition from not-

being to being; this power is an attribute of every active being, but with this difference, that finite causes have only the power to produce modifications, whilst the infinite cause has also the power to produce substances.

54. Here we find the same thing as in other branches of our philosophical cognitions: the idea of the essence pertains to reason, the knowledge of its existence depends on experience. The first is independent of the second, and we may reason on the essence by means of the condition of existence, that is, by means of a postulate. [76] We always have this postulate, if in nothing else, at least in the phenomena of our consciousness.

CHAPTER VI
FORMULA AND DEMONSTRATION OF
THE PRINCIPLE OF CAUSALITY

55. The principle of causality, or the proposition: all that commences must have a cause; has been somewhat disputed latterly; hence it is necessary for us to place it beyond the reach of attack. I believe it possible to do this, by presenting the doctrine of the preceding chapters under a clear point of view, which shall drive away all doubt and clear up all difficulty. I beg the reader's attention for a few moments to the argument which I am going to propose.

56. Let us take any being, A. In order that the principle of causality may be applied to it it is necessary that it should have begun to be, and that it should not have existed before; for, if we do not suppose this beginning, A must have existed always.

We can then assign a duration in which A was not, and in which there was not-A. Therefore in the order of duration there has been a little series of two terms:

not-A ... A.

To begin is to pass from the first term, not-A to A. The principle of causality says: the transition from the first term to the second is not possible without the intervention of a third term, B, which must be something real.

57. What does the term not-A represent by itself alone? the pure negation of A, the mere nonentity of A. In the conception of not-A, instead of A, we find its contradictory term; so that, instead of the second being contained in the former, they mutually exclude each other, and make the proposition: it is impossible for not-A and A to exist at the same time, absolutely true. Thus it is impossible for A ever to emanate from the conception not-A, and consequently without a real term to produce the transition it is impossible to pass from not-A to A, even in the purely ideal order.

58. Observe, however, that I do not pretend to say that, conceiving not-A so as to deny A as known, it would be impossible to conceive A; for it is evident that whoever conceives not-A, must have just conceived A, and

he might conceive it entirely alone, by simply destroying the negation; but I say that on the supposition that there is an absolute conception of not-A, conformed to the absolute objective not-A, A could never emanate from this conception; and if we reflect on it we shall see that there could not even be this conception, since the thought of pure negation is no thought, no conception. There would then be an absolute absence of conception; and in the purely ideal order, we should find ourselves in the first term of the series, in a pure negation, in not-A, without any means of passing to the second term, A.

59. Those, then, who deny the principle of causality, conceive the transition from not-A to A without any reason, or any intermediary: those who deny creation, admit what is a thousand times more incomprehensible than creation. Whence do they infer the possibility of this transition? Not from experience; because experience presents only succession, and therefore not absolute appearance in the manner which they suppose: not from reason; because reason cannot make a positive conception emanate from a pure negation.

60. How is the transition from not-A to A effected? Those who admit the principle of causality, say it is effected by the action of B, which they call the cause. If it is a substance which is produced, they suppose the intervention of an infinite power. But those who deny the principle of causality can only answer that the transition from not-A to A is made absolutely. They imagine the instant M, in which A did not exist; and then the instant N, in which A exists. But why? They allege no reason: without their knowing how, A has arisen from nothing, without the action of any thing. This is a manifest contradiction.

61. The principle of causality is founded on the pure ideas of being and not-being. Suppose only not-being, and we see evidently that being cannot begin. The principle then is purely ontological: those who, in order to establish, or oppose it, appeal *only* to reasons of experience, put the question badly; they take it from its true field; they confound the *notice* of causality with the *notion* or idea of causality.

Those philosophers who keep within the sensible order, cannot give a solid foundation to this principle; for this reason, they who admit no other ideas than sensations, have all fallen into errors or doubts on this point; and all sensists would have fallen into the same doubt if they had only been logical enough to draw the last consequences of their doctrine.

CHAPTER VII
THE PRINCIPLE OF PRECEDENCY

62. The transition from not-being to being implies succession: to conceive that something begins, we must conceive that something did not exist. The series

not-A, A,

has no sense if either term is wanting; and these terms, inasmuch as they are contradictory, cannot exist at the same time.

63. Let us imagine absolute nothingness. The first term, not-A, stands alone. All existence is denied: nothing can be affirmed without contradicting the supposition. Then there is no time; for time being only the succession of things, or of being and not-being, [77] cannot exist when there is nothing which can succeed. If we suppose any thing to begin, we establish the series not-A, A; in which case we imagine two different instants M and N, to which the terms of the series respectively correspond in this manner:

not-A .. A.
M .... N.

It may be said with truth: M is not N. What is the meaning of this proposition? Since time and duration in general is not distinct from the things that endure [78] , N can only represent the existence of A, in relation to not-A; M in the same manner can represent only not-A, in relation to A. Hence the conception of A, in so far as it begins, contains the relation to not-A, without which it could not be conceived as *begun*.

64. What we have explained is conceivable on the supposition at least of one intelligence; because this intelligence would refer not-A and A to their proper duration, successively, if this duration were successive like ours; in some other way, if this duration were not successive. But if there is absolutely nothing, the series, not-A ... A, is inconceivable, since the relation of A, in so far as it begins, has no real or conceived term of comparison, unless we imagine a pure time, entirely empty, in which we suppose the terms of the series to be placed.

65. Thus it seems that by the mere fact of thinking A, in so far as begun, we think also a preceding existence, because there is no beginning unless not-A preceded A; and this precedence means nothing unless there is an existence to which it relates, either as to a successive series, or as to an immutable duration.

66. If A must be preceded by an existence B, then nothing can begin independently of a preceding existence, or unless something already exists; or the simple conception of succession implies the necessity of something *always* existing, in order that something may begin.

67. As duration is nothing distinct from things, the two terms of the series, B, A, of which one precedes the other, cannot be placed in an absolute duration distinct from the things themselves, as in two distinct instants, independently of the things. The relation, then, which exists between B and A is not a relation of one instant to another, since the instants in themselves are nothing, but of one thing to another. Therefore A, inasmuch as it begins, has a necessary relation to B. Therefore B is the necessary condition of the existence of A. Therefore it is demonstrated that every being which begins, depends on an existent being.

68. This demonstration, though differently developed, is found in the works of Baron Pascual Galuppi, Professor of Philosophy in the University of Naples; [79] and although it is impossible to deny that it is very profound, still it does not leave the understanding wholly satisfied. These are the words of the Italian philosopher:

"Is the proposition: there is no effect without a cause, an identical proposition? I have demonstrated its identity in this manner: whatever has a beginning of existence must have been preceded either by an empty time or by a being; because otherwise the thing of which we are speaking would be the first existence, and the first letter of the alphabet of beings, and it could not be said that it begins to be, for the notion of *beginning of existence* implies a priority in relation to the being which begins. These two notions, *existence begun*, and *existence preceded by another*, are then identical; but is it possible for an existence to be preceded by an empty time? I have proved that an empty duration is a chimera, a product of the imagination, without any reality. The development of this proof, which I shall not give in this place, may be found in my *Essays on the Critique of Knowledge*. I have there established that time is nothing else than the *number of productions*. Aristotle said that time was the *number of motion*. Therefore an *existence begun is an existence preceded by another existence*. This proposition is identical; but how can an existence be preceded by another? Is that which precedes, perchance, found in an instant of time prior to that in which that which is preceded is found? Then we fall again into the doctrine of a time distinct from existent things. Thus we must admit that the existence which precedes is such as to make the existence preceded *existence begun.* It is not begun because it is preceded; the *priority* of the existence which precedes, is a priority of *nature,* an objective priority, which makes the beginning of the existence which is preceded; it is therefore the *efficient cause* of this existence. Thus the great principle of causality stands invincibly demonstrated,—it is an identical proposition."

69. I say again that this demonstration does not leave one wholly satisfied; not because it is not conclusive in itself, but because it needs greater development. The nerve of the proof is in the impossibility of conceiving a *beginning,* without conceiving something pre-existent; or to conceive precedency, without the relation of that which begins to that which pre-exists. It is not easy to conceive how from this may be inferred the intrinsic dependence of the things; and founding the argument upon so difficult an idea as that of time, greatly increases the doubt.

70. Let us suppose the world to exist, and something to begin now. Precedence is then conceived without dependence. This, in fact, happens continually; since beings are continually beginning which are preceded by others on which they do not depend. It may be said that they do not depend on all those which precede them, but still they depend on one of them. This is precisely what is to be proved. In order to prove that the principle of causality is demonstrated by the mere idea of the order of duration, it is necessary to prove that the relation of precedence is a relation of dependence. That which begins supposes something: certainly; but it remains to be proved that it depends on this thing as on something producing it, and not only as on a condition which makes the conception of beginning possible for us. Until it is proved that the *action* of a being is indispensable for the transition from not-being to being, the principle of causality does not seem to be proved, but only that of precedency; and as the order of things in duration, as priority and posteriority, can represent no other dependence than that of pure succession, it would follow that if we should confine ourselves to precedency, we should not prove that every thing that begins must depend on another, but that every thing that begins must succeed another; this last is not the principle of causality, but of succession.

71. We will make these ideas clearer. The difficulty raised against the former demonstration will be better understood, if we observe that those who reject the principle of causality, do not conceive it impossible for *any* thing to begin at *any* moment without any cause. Let us represent the successive beings of the universe by the series ... A, B, C, D, E, ... and the times in which they exist, by the series ... *a, b, c, d, e....* According to the

demonstration which we are examining, no term could have begun, unless another had preceded it; wherefore, D *begun* means the same as D *preceded*. Therefore D has a necessary relation to C, because the instants *d* and *c* are nothing in themselves, as distinguished from D and C.

Any one who does not admit the principle of causality will say that D may begin without any dependence on C; and that in order that the conception of beginning may be possible, it is only necessary that there should *always* have been something existing, although the terms *preceding* and those *preceded* have no relation to each other. Thus as the order of beings is represented by the series ... A, B, C, D, E, ... another series ... M, N, P, Q, R, ... may be imagined, to both of which the series ... *a, b, c, d, e,* ... corresponds. Then D may begin without any *necessary* dependence on C, for it is sufficient that P pre-exists at the instant *c*, in order to make the conception of beginning possible for us; in which case, D will have no *necessary* relation, either to C or to P; since the precedence of either is sufficient. And as it is evident that what we have said of C and P may be said of any other terms of these or other series, it follows that the demonstration only leads us to the necessity of conceiving something *pre-existent*; and this only in order to make the conception of a beginning possible. If to this we add the peculiar difficulty proceeding from the nature of the ideas of time and of all duration, I think we must conclude that the demonstration is not so satisfactory as might be desired. Those who have not examined the idea of time very profoundly will scarcely understand the meaning of the proof; the others will see the contradiction involved in an absolute beginning demonstrated, and therefore the necessity of something having been *always* existing; but not the intrinsic dependence implied in the relation of an effect to a cause. These difficulties render a more rigorous and profound examination necessary.

72. The principle of precedency leads us to an important result. Our understanding conceives absolutely an external existence; since it is impossible for it to conceive an absolute beginning without a preceding being.

73. The conception of absolute nothing is impossible. I. Because this conception would be entirely void, or rather, the absence of all conception. We conceive negation relatively to an existence, [80] but not absolutely. II. Because a conception is not possible without consciousness, and consciousness implies the idea of a being, of something, and this is contradictory of absolute nothing.

74. Unable to conceive absolute nothing, we always conceive something existing; and since, as we have demonstrated, we cannot conceive an absolute beginning, it follows that we cannot think without our thought implying an eternal existence.

How luminous a truth! What reflections it inspires! Let us continue to meditate on it.

75. Hence the necessity of thinking the necessary and eternal is a primitive fact of our mind, and the confusion which we feel in thinking on duration in the abstract, and the inclination to imagine time before the world existed, arise from the necessity of conceiving the eternal,—a necessity, from which our mind cannot emancipate itself so long as it thinks.

76. The basis of the principle of contradiction, the idea of being, is found in our conceptions in an absolute manner; its opposite, the conception of not-being is found only in relation to the contingent, and is a sort of condition implied by contingency.

77. Every thing contingent includes some not-being, so far as contingent it can *not be*, and therefore its not-being is at least in the order of possibility. But these transitions from not-being to being are not even conceivable without presupposing something existing, necessary, and eternal.

78. Thus in our ideas we find being as absolute, and not-being only as relative; and we can conceive being which has proceeded from not-being, or has begun, only in relation to an absolute being.

79. This relation considered objectively does not seem at first sight to be the relation of causality, but only of succession; but it presents a subjective fact which brings us to the knowledge of the objective truth. Our conceptions of not-being and being are connected in such sort that we cannot conceive the transition from not-being to being without conceiving a pre-existent being: here we find a reflex of objective causality which is revealed to us in subjective facts. Duration, as distinct from things, is a pure imagination; the relation of durations is therefore a relation of beings. True, in this relation of durations we discover only succession, and not intrinsic dependence; but this dependence, though not known intuitively, is represented in the very connection in which we conceive beings in duration. It is certain that we can imagine different series; but that of time is a pure imagination in so far as we conceive it distinct from others. If the series of times disappears, there remains only the series of things: the relation between the terms will be the relation between the things; and what is called the dependence of *succession* will be the dependence of *reality*. The real relation of that which passes from not-being to being, with that which is absolutely, is a dependence of causality.

80. Let us imagine any series of realities. A, B, C, D, E, ... M, N, P, Q, R....

The series of times *a, b, c, d, e,* in so far as distinct from the others, means nothing. In this case it may be eliminated, and all the relations of some of the terms on others will be relations of things, not of time.

Now, it has been demonstrated that a term, D, for example, cannot be conceived as passing from not-being to being, or as beginning, without a relation, and it has been shown that this relation is a real relation of D to any of the terms. It has been objected that D, in order to begin, requires only a term which would make the conception of priority, and consequently, of beginning, possible, which term might be sought in another distinct series; but this is really only to change a name; for, if the term which is necessary for the beginning is found in another series, the cause is found in it also, for in it is found that which is necessary for the effect.

81. All the terms begun presuppose another, either one or more, for we here abstract their unity; therefore we must come at last to one or more terms not begun. Those which have begun could not have begun without the existence of those which have not begun; therefore the existence of these is necessary for the existence of those. Therefore the existence of these last contains the reasons of the beginning of the existence of the others; therefore they contain true causality.

82. The difficulties opposed to this demonstration arise from inadvertently violating the supposition by attributing to duration an existence distinct from the beings. In order to perceive the whole force of the proof, it is necessary to eliminate entirely the imaginary conception of pure duration: and then it will be seen that the dependence represented as the relation of duration is the dependence of the beings themselves,—a dependence which represents nothing else than the relation expressed by the principle of causality.

83. After completely eliminating the conception of pure duration as a thing distinct from the beings, there remains only the transition from not-being to being as all that is expressed by the word, beginning. In this case we find that the principle of precedency is the same as the principle of causality; and as we have had to abstract entirely duration in itself in order to solve the difficulties, we find that if the principle of causality is to be placed beyond all doubt, and to be regarded as an axiom, it can only rest on the contradiction between not-being and being, or the impossibility of conceiving a being which suddenly makes its appearance, without any thing more than a pure not-being preceding it.

84. Thus, after examining the question on every side, we come to what we established in the preceding chapters: a not-being cannot arrive at being without the intervention of a being: the series not-A, A, is impossible without the intervention of a being, B. We find it so even in our ideas, and to contradict this truth is to deny our reason.

I believe, then, that the principle of causality is completely explained only in the manner in which we have treated it in the preceding chapters. To begin supposes a not-being of that which begins; and it is impossible and contradictory to deduce being from the conception of not-being. The principle is true subjectively, because it is founded on our ideas; but it is also true objectively, because in these cases objectiveness is necessarily joined with subjectiveness. [81] The being which suddenly appears, without a cause, without a reason, without any thing, is an absurd representation which our intellect rejects as instantly and as strongly as it accepts the principle of contradiction.

As time is the relation of not-being to being — the order of the variable — it is a contradiction to conceive succession without any thing which pre-exists; and thus the principle of precedency confirms the principle of causality; or rather, it shows that the two are one, though presented under different aspects: the principle of precedency relates to duration, that of causality to being; but both of them express an application of the fundamental principle: it is impossible for the same thing to be and not be at the same time.

CHAPTER VIII
CAUSALITY IN ITSELF.—INSUFFICIENCY
AND ERROR OF SOME EXPLANATIONS

85. Causality implies relation: if in exercise, it implies actual relation; considered not in exercise, but *in potentia*, it implies a possible relation. Nothing causes itself; causality always relates to another. There is no cause where there is no effect; and there is no effect where there is no transition from not-being to being. If this transition takes place in a substance which was not, but begins to be, it is called creation; and is said to be passive, relatively to the effect, and active, in relation to the cause. If the transition is of accidents only, the effect is a *new* modification; we do not then say that there is a new being, but that the being is *in another manner*.

86. From this it may be inferred that causality is not the same as activity: all causality is activity, but not all activity is causality. God is active in himself; but he is cause only in relation to the external. His intelligence and his will are certainly infinite activity, considered in themselves, and abstracted from creation, as we conceive God from all eternity before the beginning of the world; yet, inasmuch as they are purely immanent, they are causality, for they produce nothing new in God. His intelligence is a pure act, infinitely perfect, and can never suffer any change; the same must be said of his will: therefore the divine intelligence and will with respect to God himself are not acts of causality. Even as referred to external objects, they are a producing cause in reality, only by subjection to the free will of the Creator; for otherwise we should have to admit that God created the world necessarily.

Activity in creatures, even in immanent operations, is always causality; for they cannot exercise their activity without producing new modifications. Acts of understanding and will are the exercise of an immanent activity, and yet they modify us in different ways. When we think or will we are in *a different manner* from that in which we are when we do not think or will; and when we pass from thinking or willing one thing to think or will another, this transition cannot take place without our experiencing *new modes* of being.

87. In what does the relation of efficient causality consist? What is the meaning of the dependence of the effect in relation to the cause? This is a difficult and a profound question; one of the most difficult and most profound which can be presented to science. The majority of men and even of philosophers imagine that they can solve it, by using words which, rightly analyzed, explain nothing.

88. To cause, it is said, is to give being. What means to give? To give is here synonymous with to produce. What means to produce? With this the explanations are at an end, unless one should wish to fall into a vicious circle, saying that to produce is to cause or give being.

A cause, it is also said, is that from which a thing results. What is understood by resulting? To emanate. What is to emanate? To emanate is to proceed, to flow from another. Always the same thing: metaphorical expressions which at bottom have all the same meaning.

It is said that a cause is that which *gives, produces, makes, communicates, generates,* etc., and that an effect is that which *receives, proceeds, emanates, results, flows, comes, springs,* etc.

89. Causality implies succession, but is not identified with it. We can clearly conceive that B is after A, without A being the cause of B.

Internal and external experience present continual examples of succession distinct from causality. A man goes out into the field, another follows him: between the going out of both there is succession, but there may be no causality. The two phenomena, whether considered objectively in themselves, or subjectively, as known by us, are connected by the relation of succession, but not by that of causality. There is as great a difference in philosophy as in ordinary language between *post* and *propter, after* and *because* of. The same is true in purely internal phenomena. I think of a question of philosophy, and then pass to a literary question: the two thoughts are successive, but one is not the cause of the other.

90. The relation of causality is not the connection of the ideas of things. The representations of A and B may be strongly connected in our mind without our even thinking of the relation of causality. We have seen in a place a scene which made a profound impression on us; ever afterwards the remembrance of the place recalls the scene, and the recollection of the scene reminds us of the place; here we find two internal representations strongly connected, without our therefore attributing to the objects the relation of causality. We know that two persons arrive at the same place and without the coming of the one influencing the coming of the other. The idea of the coming of the one will be associated in the mind with the idea of the coming

of the other. There will then be a connection of representations, although we deny to the objects the relation of causality.

91. Although the connection of the ideas in our understanding may, in consequence of a constant experience, be such that one is always preceded by the other, as the conditioned is by the condition, this is not enough for true causality. An observer may have remarked the correspondence of the ebb and flow of the tide with the motion of the moon; but whether for reasons of philosophy, or because it has never occurred to him that the motion of the moon could influence the motion of the sea, he considers these phenomena entirely independent of one another, although he may try hard to explain so strange a coincidence. In the mind of this observer the two phenomena will be always joined, in such a way that the phenomenon of the moon will always be that of the ebb and flow, without its being possible to invert the order and make the ebb and flow precede the motion of the moon. Here then is a necessary priority in an idea, and yet true causality is not attributed to the object.

92. There is a fact in the history of philosophy which proves with the greatest evidence the truth of what I have just said. This fact is the system of occasional causes maintained by eminent philosophers. If a body, they say, strike another body at rest, it will communicate to it its motion; but this communication does not imply a true causality, but that the motion of the impinging body is a mere occasion of the motion of the body impinged. Here then a thing is conceived as a necessary condition of the existence of another, and yet it is denied that there is between them the relation of causality. In thinking of the two phenomena we cannot invert the order, and conceive the motion of the body impinged as the condition of the motion of the impinging body, yet we can deny the relation of causality between the condition and the conditioned. Therefore the idea of causality represents something besides the necessary order of things among themselves.

93. This brings us to a new phasis of the question. Is the relation of causality faithfully represented in the conditional proposition: if A exists, B will exist? The connection expressed by this proposition is not the relation of causality. If the fruit-tree N flourishes in a certain country, M will flourish. A constant experience proves it. The conditional proposition in this case does not express the relation of causality of the flourishing of N with respect to the flourishing of M; yet the proposition is true. One phenomenon may be the sign of the immediate approach of another, without being its cause.

94. Conditional propositions, in which the existence of one object is affirmed as the condition of the existence of another, express a connection; but this may not be a connection of the objects with each other, but with a

third. If a gentleman's servant goes to a place, and then another servant of the same gentleman goes to the same place, the cause of the going of the second may not be the going of the first, but simply that their master wished them to go one after the other. The crops in one field indicate the state of the crops of another field, and this indication may be expressed by a conditional proposition. Why so? Is it on account of the causality of the crops in one field in relation to those in another? Certainly not; but because the circumstances of the climate and the soil produce a sufficiently fixed order between them to verify the conditional proposition, without the intervention of the idea of the causality of one in relation to the other.

95. There are many cases in which the relation between the condition is necessary, and yet the condition neither is, nor can be, the cause of the conditioned. We are here treating of efficient cause, of that which gives being to the thing, and it would often be absurd to attribute this kind of causality to conditions which on the other side are necessarily connected with the conditioned. Take away the pillar on which a body rests, and the body will fall; the connection of the condition with the conditioned, or of the taking away the pillar with the fall of the body is necessary; the proposition in which this connection is expressed is true and necessary in the natural order; and still it cannot be said that the removal of the pillar is the *efficient* cause of the fall of the body.

96. Even a purely occasional connection is all that is necessary for the truth of the conditional proposition; and no one ever confounds the occasion with the cause. In the present example, the body cannot fall unless the pillar is removed; and it must necessarily fall if it is removed; but the cause of the fall is not in the removal of the pillar, but in the weight of the body, as is evident if we suppose the specific gravity of the body to be equal to that of the fluid in which it is submerged, since in that case, the removal of the pillar is not followed by the fall of the body.

97. Causality cannot express a necessary relation of the condition to the conditioned, unless we deny all free causes. Supposing the idea of causality to be correctly expressed in this proposition: if A exists, B will exist; by substituting God and the world for A and B, it will become: if God exists the world will exist; which would lead us into the error of the necessity of the creation. By substituting man and determinate actions for A and B, we shall have the proposition: if man exists, his determinate actions will exist, which implies necessity, and destroys free will.

98. Here arises the question: would the relation of causality be correctly expressed by a conditional proposition, taken in an inverse sense, or with the effect, as the condition and the cause as the conditioned, (not conditioned in

the order of existence, but only as a thing necessarily supposed,) that is, if, instead of saying: if A exists, B will exist, we say: if B exists, A exists? In this case, the proposition may be applied even to the dependence of creatures on God, and in general of all free actions on their causes; for we can say with truth: if the world exists, God exists; if there is a free action, there is a free agent.

99. Although at first sight this seems to explain the relation of causality, this new formula cannot be regarded as correct. For, though it is true in general, that if there is an effect there is a cause, it is also certain that oftentimes one thing supposes another, not as its cause, but as a mere occasion, as a condition *sine qua non*; which is far from being true causality. Supposing the body supported by the pillar to be so placed that it cannot fall unless the pillar is removed, we might form the conditional proposition: if the body has fallen, the pillar has been taken away; the proposition is true, although the removal of the pillar is not the efficient cause of the fall of the body.

100. God could have so created the world that creatures would have no true action of causality upon one another, and yet have so arranged them that the phenomena would correspond with each other in the same manner as they now do. This is the opinion of defenders of the doctrine of occasional causes, and to this is reduced the *pre-established harmony* of Leibnitz, according to which all the monads constituting the universe are like so many clocks, which, though independent of one another, agree with admirable exactness. On this hypothesis we might form infinite conditional propositions expressing the correspondence of the phenomena without the idea of causality entering into any of them.

101. From what has been said we must infer that this idea is something distinct from the necessary connection, and that it is not correctly expressed in all its purity by the relation contained in the conditional propositions, whether the cause be taken as the condition or as the conditioned. The dependence of the effect on its cause is something more than the simple connection. To say that whatever is necessarily connected, even successively and in a fixed order, is connected by the relation of causality, is to confound the ideas of common language as well as those of philosophy.

CHAPTER IX
NECESSARY AND SUFFICIENT CONDITIONS
OF TRUE ABSOLUTE CAUSALITY

102. We have just seen that the necessary connection of two objects is not enough to establish the character of causality; what circumstances are then necessary?

103. If we conceive an object, B, which begins, and suppose that the object A was *necessary* to its existence, and that *of itself alone* it was sufficient for the existence of B, we find in the relation of A to B the true character of the relation of a cause to its effect. For the complete character of *absolute* cause, two conditions are indispensable: I. The necessity of the existence of A for the existence of B. II. That the existence of A be sufficient for the existence of B, without any thing more being requisite.

These conditions may be expressed in the following propositions or formulas:

If B exists, A exists.

The existence of A alone is sufficient for the existence of B.

When the relation between two objects is such that both these propositions are true at the same time, there is a relation of absolute causality.

104. From this explanation it is evident that the character of cause must be denied to all mere occasions, since the second proposition cannot be applied to them. When two facts are occasionally connected, it may be said that if the one exists the other must exist, and the first proposition is verified in this case; but it cannot be said that the existence of the one is sufficient for the existence of the other; and therefore the second proposition fails of its application. If two men have agreed that the one shall fire a pistol when the other gives a signal with his hand, it may be said that if the signal is given the pistol will be fired, but not that the signal alone contains what is sufficient for the firing of the pistol. For, supposing the man with the pistol to be asleep, the signal may be repeated a number of times without the firing of the pistol.

105. The character of cause must also be denied to every condition which is only the removal of an obstacle (*removens prohibens*). To such the first proposition is applicable, but not the second. In the case of a body resting on a pillar so that it cannot fall unless the pillar be removed, we may say: if the body has fallen, the pillar has been taken away; but not that the removal of the pillar is sufficient for the fall of the body; because if the body were of a less specific gravity than the fluid in which it is submerged, or united to another body which would prevent its falling, it would not fall. It is evident that the removal of the obstacle is not sufficient for the fall, but that something more is required, as the force of gravity, or an impulse.

106. All phenomena connected in succession of time necessarily and in a fixed order, must be denied the relation of cause and effect, unless the application of these ideas is made legitimate by something else; because, although the constant order authorizes us to say that if A happens, B will happen, and then C, and then D, and so on successively, it cannot be said that in the existence of A is contained that which is sufficient for the existence of B, nor in the existence of B what is sufficient for the existence of C, since we suppose an indispensable condition outside of the series.

107. The first proposition: if B exists, A exists; is true of every cause whether necessary or free. The second proposition is likewise applicable to both these classes of causes. It is necessary to observe with care that the proposition does not say that if A exists, B will exist; but that the existence of A is all that is requisite in order that B *may* exist. If, supposing A, B is necessarily supposed also, the cause is necessary; but if, supposing A, only that which is sufficient for the existence of B is supposed, the cause remains free; because the existence of B is not affirmed, but only the possibility of its existence.

108. Let us apply this doctrine to the first cause. If the world exists, God exists: this proposition is absolutely true. If God exists, the world exists; this proposition is false, because, God existing, the world might not have existed. If God exists, the world may exist; that is, in the existence of God is contained that which is sufficient for the possibility of the existence of the world: this proposition is true; because in the infinite being is contained the possibility of finite beings, and in him is found sufficient power to give them existence, if he thus freely wills it.

CHAPTER X
SECONDARY CAUSALITY

109. In determining in the last chapter the conditions of true causality, I spoke only of *absolute* causality; the reason of this, which I shall now explain, turns on the difference between the first cause and second causes.

110. We have seen that the pure idea of absolute causality is the perception of three conditions: the necessity of one thing for the existence of another; the sufficiency of the first alone for the existence of the second; and lastly (when the cause is free) the act of the will necessary for the production of the effect. These three conditions are fulfilled absolutely in the first cause, since nothing can exist unless God exists; and for the existence of any object the existence of God, with the free will of creating the object, is sufficient. It is evident that causality cannot be applied in the same sense to second causes; of none of them can it be said that its existence is absolutely necessary for the existence of the effect, since God could have produced it either by means of another secondary agent, or immediately by himself; neither is its existence alone sufficient for the existence of the effect, since whatever exists presupposes and requires the existence of the first cause.

111. Thus, then, the idea of causality applied to God has a very different meaning from that which it has when applied to second causes: it is necessary to bear this in mind, and not to raise questions concerning second causes before the meaning of the word *cause* is strictly defined. It is certain that the relation of an effect to its cause is a relation of dependence; but we have seen that the words dependence, connection, condition, etc., are susceptible of different meanings; if they are not clearly and strictly determined it is impossible to give any solution to these questions.

112. What then is meant by secondary causality? After the observations which we have made, it is not difficult to say. In the order of created beings A will be the cause of B when the following conditions are fulfilled.

I. That the existence of A is necessary (according to the order established) for the existence of B; which may be expressed by this formula: if B exists, A exists or has existed.

II. That in the order established B and A form a series which goes back to the first cause, without the concurrence of the terms of any other series being requisite.

This last condition will not, perhaps, be understood, unless explained by some examples.

113. The motion of my pen is the effect of the motion of my hand; here I have the true relation of secondary causality, for I pass through a series of conditions, which do not require the conditions of any other series: the motion of the pen depends on the motion of my hand; that of my hand depends on the animal spirits (or whatever cause physiologists may please to assign); that of the animal spirits depends on the command of my will; and my will depends on God, who created it, and preserves it. I here find a series of second causes to which I give the true character of causality, in so far as it can exist in a secondary order; and the efficient cause, the principal among secondary causes is my will; because in the secondary order of it is the first term of the series. The motion of the pen of my secretary depends on my will, not however as its true efficient cause, but as its occasion; because in the secretary is found the same series as in the former example: the first term of this series is his will, which I cannot absolutely determine, since being free, it determines itself. There is true efficient causality in the will of the secretary; because there ends the series whose first term is at my disposal only in an improper sense, that is to say, so long as the secretary pleases.

114. The body, A, in motion strikes upon the body, B at rest: the motion of the body A is the cause of the motion of the body B, and the causality will be found in all the terms of the series, that is, in all the motions whose successive communication has been necessary in order that the motion might reach the body B. Let us suppose that in the series of these communications obstacles have been removed which impeded the communication of the motion; the removal of the obstacles is an indispensable condition on the supposition that they existed, but it is not a true cause, since it is a term foreign to the series of the communications, and might not have existed, without the motion therefore ceasing to exist. For, supposing there had been no obstacles, they would not have been removed, and yet the motion would have been communicated. But it is not the same with respect to the terms which form the series of the communications; for if we represent them by A. B. C. D. E. F. . . . . the motion of A cannot reach F if one of the

intermediate bodies serving as the vehicle of the communication be taken away.

115. From this theory it follows that the idea of secondary causality represents a concatenation of various objects forming a series, which terminates in the first cause, whether by a necessary order, as in the phenomena of corporeal nature, or by the medium of a first term in the secondary order with a determination of its own, as is the case in things which depend on free will.

CHAPTER XI
FUNDAMENTAL EXPLANATION OF THE ORIGIN OF THE OBSCURITY OF IDEAS IN WHAT RELATES TO CAUSALITY

116. It may be asked, of what nature is this connection of the terms of the series; *how* one communicates with another; *what* it is which is communicated; by virtue *of what quality* they are placed in relation. All these questions arise from a confusion of ideas which has been the occasion of interminable disputes. In order to avoid them we must remember the difference between intuitive and discursive knowledge, and between determinate and indeterminate, intuitive and not-intuitive ideas, as explained in its proper place. [82]

117. I there said [83] that the pure intellect may exercise its functions by indeterminate ideas, or those representing general relations which are not applied to any real or possible object, until a determination furnished by experience is added to them. [84] The idea of cause is indeterminate; [85] and, consequently, taken in general, it cannot be presented to us without the relation of being and not-being, or of beings united among themselves by a certain necessity, but in an absolute indeterminate manner. [86] Therefore the idea of cause is not enough to determine the character of this activity and its means of communication; this idea by itself can tell us nothing of the particular; it can only teach us certain truths *a priori*; the application of these truths to beings rests on experience.

118. I said [87] that our intuition is confined to passive sensibility, active sensibility, intelligence, and will; whatever lies outside of this sphere we can know only by indeterminate conceptions, and, consequently, it is impossible for us to expose to the intuition of another that which we feel to be wanting to our own. We may develop this doctrine farther by applying it to the philosophical questions on causality.

119. There have been great disputes as to whether bodies exercise a true action on each other; and those who hold the negative are always asking, *how* one body can cause any thing in another? *what* that is which is

transmitted, and what is the *character* of its active quality? Various replies have been made; but I greatly doubt if it is possible to make any which is satisfactory, without considering the doctrine which I have just explained, — what answer, then, can be made? It is this: we know nothing intuitively of bodies except passive sensibility, which, in the last result, is only extension with its various modifications. [88] Now these modifications are reduced to figure and motion; whatever would make us depart from these two intuitions, requiring an explanation with characteristic determinations, would ask for that which is beyond the power of man. The limits of our intuition on this point are confined to extension and motion, and their relations to our sensibility; we must, therefore, be contented with observing the phenomena of bodies, and subjecting them to calculation within the circle of this intuition: all beyond this is impossible. We know that the body A moves with a certain velocity, which we measure by the relation of space to time; when it arrives at the place where it meets B, B moves in a corresponding direction and with a corresponding velocity. Here there is a succession of phenomena in time and space; the phenomena are subject to constant laws, which are known by experience. Our intuitive cognitions go no farther; when we attempt to go beyond this we find the general relations of being and not-being, of being *before* and being *after*, of condition and conditioned, which present nothing determinate by which we can explain the true character of secondary causality.

120. Philosophy, when treating of bodies, is limited to what is strictly called physics; when it attempts to rise to the region of metaphysics bodies disappear, in so far as they are phenomena subject to sensible observation, and there remains only the general and indeterminate ideas of them.

121. As regards the sensitive faculty, we are in some sort passive, inasmuch as we receive the impressions which we call sensations. Whatever activity we possess in sensation does not depend on our free will, supposing that we are subject to the conditions of sensibility. If you put your hand in the fire it is impossible for you not to experience the sensation of heat. In what regards the causality which we have as to the reproduction of past sensations or the production of new sensible sensations, it is vain to ask us the *manner* in which we exercise this activity: its exercise is a part of consciousness; all we know about it is that it exists in such or such a manner in our consciousness.

122. The same may be said of the elaboration of ideas. None of the philosophers can explain the *manner* of this immanent production; ideological investigations go no farther than the characterizing and classifying these phenomena and showing the order of their succession; they can tell us nothing concerning the manner in which they are produced.

123. The exercise of the will presents to our intuition, or if you please, to our consciousness, another series of phenomena, of the manner of the production of which we know nothing. Consciousness testifies that the free principle which exercises this activity is within us: this is all that we know about it. These phenomena are found at times connected with motions of our bodies, which a constant experience presents as depending on our will, but how things so different are connected, we know not: philosophy will never know.

CHAPTER XII
CAUSALITY OF PURE FORCE OF THE WILL

124. In what does creation consist? How can God produce things from nothing? Such a thing is incomprehensible. This is the language of many who do not reflect that the same incomprehensibility is found in the exercise of secondary causality, both in the corporeal and in the incorporeal world. If we knew God in the intuitive manner in which, according to the Catholic dogma, the blessed see him in the mansion of glory, we might know intuitively the manner of the creation. As it is, we say that in so far as we can form any idea of the action of the Creator, he produces all things from nothing by the force of his will; which besides according with the teachings of religion, is in harmony with what we experience in ourselves. God wills, and the universe springs up out of nothing: how can this be understood? To him who asks this, I say: man wills, and his arm rises; he wills, and his whole body is in motion. How can this be understood? Here is a small, weak, and incomplete, but true image of the Creator: an intelligent being which wills, and a fact which appears. Where is the connection? If you cannot explain it to us in so far as concerns finite beings, how can you ask us to explain it with respect to the infinite being? The incomprehensibility of the conception of the motion of the body with the force of the will does not authorize us to deny the connection; therefore the incomprehensibility of the connection of a being which appears for the first time with the force of the infinite will cannot authorize us to deny the truth of the creation: on the contrary, the finding a similar thing in ourselves greatly strengthens the ontological arguments which demonstrate its necessity. In the dogmas of the Christian religion, besides what they reveal that is supernatural, we find at every step philosophical truths as profound as they are important.

125. The causality which relates to purely possible effects can only be understood by placing it in an intelligence. The cause which does not produce an effect, but which may produce it, involves a relation of the existent to the non-existent; the cause exists, the effect does not exist; the cause does not produce it, but may produce it; what is the relation of that which exists to that which does not exist? is not a relation without a term to which it relates, a contradiction? It is certainly, if abstracted from the

intelligence: the intelligence alone can relate to that which does not exist; for it can *think the non-existent*. A body can have no relation to a body which does not exist; but an intelligence may have a relation to that which does not exist, even knowing that it does not exist; we may ourselves wander at pleasure through the regions of pure possibility.

126. The will also participates of this character of the intellect. Desire relates to an enjoyment which is not, but which may be; we will and will not, we love and hate things that are often purely ideal, and whose identity we know perfectly well, still this does not prevent our willing them. Thus we desire things to happen which are not, and we may even desire things which we know to be impossible. We may wish to recover that which we know is lost forever; we may wish for the presence of a friend whom we know to be at so great a distance as to render his coming impossible; we may wish that time would stop or hurry on in conformity to our wants or our caprices.

127. Thus we find both the intellect and the will in relation to that which does not exist;—a relation which is not even conceivable in a being destitute of intellect. This leads to an important result. The absolute beginning of any thing is not possible unless we conceive causality as having its root in the intellect. That which begins passes from not-being to being, and how is it possible that a being has produced in *another* a transition from not-being to being, if the relation to the *other* before it existed was intrinsically impossible? An intelligent being may think another although the other does not exist; but for an unintelligent being if the other does not exist in *reality* it does not exist at all; consequently no relation to it is possible, any such relation that may be imagined is contradictory, and therefore it is absurd to suppose that which is not to begin to be.

128. This reasoning proves that in the origin of things there is an intelligent being, the cause of every thing, and that without this intelligence nothing could have begun. If something has begun, something must have existed from all eternity; and that which began was *known* by that which existed. Not admitting intelligence, beginning is absurd. Imagine in the origin of things a being without intelligence, its relations can only be to that which exists; it can have no relation to the non-existent; how then is it possible for the non-existent to begin to exist, through the action of the existent? In order that the non-existent may begin to be, some reason is necessary; for otherwise the beginning of one thing or of another, and even its beginning or not-beginning would be indifferent. Unless we suppose a being which knows that which does not exist, and may establish, so to speak, a communication with nothing, the being which does not exist can never exist.

CHAPTER XIII
ACTIVITY

129. To understand more clearly the idea of causality, it will be useful to reflect on the ideas of activity and action, as also on those of inertness, or inactivity, and inaction.

130. An absolutely inactive being is a being without intelligence, without will, without sensibility, without any kind of consciousness, containing in itself nothing which can change its own state or that of any thing else.

Thus absolute inactivity or inertness requires the following conditions: I. The absolute denial of all principle, of intelligence, of will, of sensibility, and in general of every thing which is accompanied by consciousness. II. The absolute denial of all principle of change in itself. III. The absolute denial of all principle of change in others. The union of these three conditions forms the idea of absolute inactivity or inertness: the state of such a being is that of absolute inaction.

131. A being of this nature, regarded in general, presents only the idea of an existing thing: we may also consider it as a substance, supposing it not to inhere as a modification in another, or rather, supposing it as a substratum capable of receiving modifications by the action of other beings upon it.

The only means by which we can characterize to a certain extent this general idea, so that it may be presented to our intuition, is to add to it the idea of extension, by which we make in some manner the idea of inert matter.

132. After the ideas of inertness and inaction are explained, their opposites, the ideas of activity and action, are clearly understood.

When we conceive a being which has the reason of its changes within itself, we conceive an active being.

When we conceive a being which has within itself the reason of the changes of other beings, we conceive an active being.

When we conceive a being which knows, wills, perceives, or has consciousness in any way, we conceive an active being.

Hence activity may represent three things to us: the origin of its own changes; the origin of the changes of others; and consciousness.

133. The first kind of activity can belong only to changeable beings; the second also to immutable beings, which are causes; the third is an activity which belongs to mutable or immutable beings, abstracting absolutely the idea of causality.

134. The general relation of principle of its own or another's changes, is an indeterminate idea; consequently the only activity of which we can have an intuitive idea is that of intelligence, of will, and in general of whatever relates to the phenomena which require the perception called consciousness.

135. We must consider consciousness as an activity, and include in this order the idea of intelligence and will abstracted from all relation to their own or another's changes, unless we mean to say that God was from all eternity an inactive being, because he had no other action than the immanent acts of knowing and willing.

136. Therefore not all activity is transient, but there is a true immanent activity, of which we have an intuitive knowledge in the phenomena of our consciousness.

137. The activity which we can conceive in bodies is reduced to a principle of their own changes or those of some other being; it is therefore something of which we can have no intuitive knowledge. In fact, we are in relation with bodies only by means of the senses, which present but two orders of facts with respect to corporeal nature; subjective facts, or the impressions which we experience and call sensations, and which we believe to emanate from the action of bodies upon our organs; and objective facts, that is, extension motion, and the different modifications which the senses discover in extended things which move. Neither the first class of facts nor the second give us an intuitive idea of the activity of corporeal beings.

Subjective facts or sensations are immanent, that is, are in us, not in the things; and inasmuch as subjective tell us nothing of what is outside of us, but only what is within us. Even supposing sensations to be a true effect of the activity of bodies, this activity is not presented in the effect. When our hand is warmed by the fire we have the intuitive perception of the sensation of heat, inasmuch as it is in us; if we suppose that this sensation is really an effect of the activity of the fire, we know the relation of our sensation to this activity considered in general, and indeterminately as the origin of our sensation; but we do not know the activity intuitively in itself, because as such it is not represented in our sensation.

Neither do objective facts, that is, extension, motion, and whatever we conceive which is not in our sensation, but in the object itself, give us any intuitive idea of the activity of corporeal things. The modifications of extension, or figures, motion with all its accidents, and in general all that presents the corporeal world to our senses, are the changes themselves and their relations, but not the principle of these relations or of these changes. The body A, which is in motion, strikes upon the body B at rest; B after the impact begins to move: without considering whether the impact of A is the cause of the motion of B, that which we are certain of is, that we have no intuition of the activity producing the motion. What do the senses tell us of the body A? They only tell us that it has moved with a certain velocity towards the point M where the body B was situated. What do they tell us of the body B? Only that it began to move the instant the body A reached the point M: so far we have only the relations of space and time between the two extended objects A and B. Where is the intuition of the activity of A, and of its action on B? We see absolutely nothing of it. By reasoning, by analogy, by considerations of order, of agreement, and such like, we may prove with more or less evidence that in the body A there is an activity which causes the motion of the body B; but this gives us only an indeterminate idea, not an intuition of activity.

138. These considerations are conclusive as applied to all the phenomena of corporeal nature. Take any one you please, select that one which leads us most strongly to imagine a true activity; analyze it well, and you will find our intuition limited to relations of extension in space and in time.

That all bodies are heavy is a fact of experience; do we know intuitively the principle from which the phenomena of weight proceed? By no means. Let us examine it in the subjective order and in the objective. What does weight as perceived by us present to us? Only that affection which we call heaviness, that is, the pressure on the members of the body. What does it present objectively? Only the direction of bodies towards a centre with a certain velocity depending on circumstances. We find in all this only a purely internal fact, which is the unpleasant sensation of weight or heaviness, or the pure relations of extended objects in space and time.

139. The fire burns objects and reduces them to ashes; nothing could be better suited to give us the idea of activity. Still we cannot say that we know it intuitively. In the subjective order we have the painful sensation of burning, which thus far is a purely internal fact; in the objective order we have the disorganization of the bodies burnt, which presents to the senses only a change in the size, figure, color, and other qualities relative to our senses—all this may be the effect of the activity, but it is not the activity itself.

140. The light reflected from an object strikes our eyes, painting on the retina the object which reflects it. Have we in this case an intuition of the activity of light. Not at all. In the subjective order we find the sensation called *seeing*; in the objective order, we find the size, figure, and other qualities of the object in space. If we consider the light itself, we find a fluid whose rays have this or that direction in subjection to determinate laws, but we have no intuitive knowledge of its activity; and in order to persuade ourselves that the activity exists, we reason from principles which are not within the sphere of our intuition.

141. The four intuitions of passive sensibility, active sensibility, intelligence, and will, may be reduced to two: [89] extension and consciousness; including in extension all its modifications, and in consciousness all the internal phenomena of a sensitive or intellectual being; in so far as they have the common ground of consciousness. We therefore know intuitively two modes of being: consciousness and extension; consciousness is within us, it is a subjective fact; extension is external, its existence is revealed by sensations, particularly those of sight and touch.

142. The classification of these two intuitions is important beyond measure for the distinction of the active from the inert. In consciousness we find a type of true activity; in extension, as such, we have a type of true inertness. In thinking of consciousness, we think of something active without adding any other idea; when we think of extension, it presents to us the image of a thing susceptible of various modifications, the principle of none of which is contained in extension; in order to think of a corporeal activity we have to go out of the pure idea of extension, and consider a principle of change in general, which is not the object of the intuition of the extended.

143. Thus the only activity which we know intuitively is that of consciousness; for we have only indeterminate ideas of corporeal activity. The words action, reaction, force, resistance, impulse, express only indeterminate relations, and represent something fixed and determinate, only in their effects. Mechanists express forces by lines or numbers, that is, by results subject to calculation. Even Newton, in establishing his system of universal attraction, declares his ignorance of the immediate cause of the phenomenon, and confines himself to assigning the laws to which the motions of bodies are subjected.

144. Activity in changeable beings represents a principle of their own and others' changes, a sort of superabundance of being which constantly develops itself, and, in proportion as it is developed, perfects itself. We find an example of this development in our own mind. The child at its birth

receives in a confused manner the impressions of all that surrounds it. By the repetition of these impressions its activity is developed; that which was obscure becomes clear, the confusion is put into order, that which was feeble becomes strong, thought arises, comparison begins, reflection is unfolded, and the being which was torpid and almost inert becomes perhaps a genius which astonishes the world. Materials have come to it from without, but of what use would they have been without that living fire of activity which transformed them and deduced from them new and valuable products? The same phenomena of nature are presented to the eyes of brute animals as to Kepler or Newton; but what for the first is only a sensible impression is for the latter a starting-point of sublime and wonderful theories.

145. The active being possesses virtually the perfections which it is to acquire; it may be compared to the acorn which contains the mighty oak, whose development depends on circumstances of soil and climate. On the other hand, the inactive being can give itself nothing; it has a state, and it preserves it till some other changes it; and it remains in this new state until another action from without takes it away and communicates another.

146. Activity is a principle of its own or another's changes; this activity may operate in two ways: with intelligence and without it. When the being is intelligent its inclination to that which is known is called will. The will is inclined to the object necessarily or not necessarily: in the first case, it is a necessary spontaneity; in the second, it is a free spontaneity. Liberty, then, does not consist solely in the absence of coaction; it requires the absence of all, even spontaneous, necessity; the will must be able to will or not will the object; if this condition is wanting there is no freewill.

147. It is worthy of remark that our intuition of the external relates only to the inactive, to extension; and that internal intuition relates principally to activity, to consciousness. By the first we know a substratum of changes, since all change seems to take place in extension; by the second we know no subject intuitively, but only the changes themselves. We prove the unity of their subject by reasoning, but we do not see it intuitively. [90] Extension, as such, is presented to us as simply passive: consciousness, as such, is always active; for, even in those cases in which it is most passive, as in sensations, in so far as there is consciousness, it implies activity; for by it the subject gives itself an account, explicitly or implicitly, of the affection experienced.

CHAPTER XIV
POSSIBILITY OF THE ACTIVITY OF BODIES

148. Having marked the limits of our intuitive knowledge with respect to causality and activity, it is easy to answer the objections against secondary causality, which arise from confounding intuitive and indeterminate ideas; but we have still to examine whether there are true second causes, that is, whether there really is in finite beings a principle of their own and others' changes. Some philosophers, among others the illustrious Malebranche, have denied the efficacy of second causes, thus reducing them to mere occasions. The author of the *Investigation de la Vérité* goes so far as to maintain that secondary causality not only does not exist, but is impossible.

149. The universe contains two classes of beings,—immaterial beings, and corporeal beings: each presents difficulties which it will be well to examine separately. Let us begin with matter. It is said that matter is incapable of all activity, that its essence is indifferent to every thing, susceptible of any sort of modification. I cannot discover on what this general proposition is founded, nor do I see how it is possible to prove it either by reason or by experience.

150. In order to maintain that matter is completely inactive, or incapable of any activity, it would be necessary to know its essence; but this we do not know. By what right do we deny the possibility of an attribute when we are ignorant of the nature of the object to which it should belong, when we do not know even one of its properties to which this attribute is repugnant? It is true that we deny to matter the possibility of thought, and even of sensation; but we can do so only because we know enough of matter, to establish this impossibility. In matter, whatever may be its intrinsic essence, there are parts, consequently there is multiplicity; and the facts of consciousness necessarily require a being which is one and simple. [91]

It is not the same with respect to activity; for activity, when it does not present the intuitive idea of consciousness, gives us only the indeterminate conception of a principle of changes in itself or in other beings. This does not contradict the idea of multiplicity. Suppose bodies in motion to have a true activity which really produces motion in others, there is no contradiction in this activity being distributed among the different parts of the other body, which at the moment of impact produce their respective effects, causing motion in the parts of the other body with which they come in contact.

151. Consequently, examining the question *a priori*, or considering the idea of body, we can find no reason for denying the possibility of its being active. It is true that the extension of bodies, inasmuch as extension, is presented to us as something without life, indifferent to all figures and to all motions, and that we do not discover in it any principle of activity; [92] but this can prove nothing, unless we suppose that the essence of bodies consists in extension, and that extension contains nothing more than is presented to our senses, that it includes nothing on which its activity can be founded. The first is an opinion, but one without any foundation; the second can never be demonstrated, because it escapes all observation, and cannot be the object of investigations *a priori*.

152. How can it be proved that the essence of bodies consists in extension? [93] What we may say is, that we experience it, and that all corporeal nature is presented to us under the form of extended. If we assert any thing more than this we do so without any foundation, we substitute for the reality a play of our fancy. The essence of any thing is that which constitutes it what it is, that which serves as the internal ground or root of the properties: who can say that we know this ground, this root, in corporeal objects? Our senses, it is true, perceive nothing not extended: we cannot conceive to what bodies would be reduced if deprived of extension; but from this we can only infer that extension is a form under which bodies are presented to our senses; that this form is a necessary condition of the affection of our sensibility; but not that the form is the essence of the thing, not that there is in the object nothing more intimate in which the form itself has its root.

153. If the essence of bodies consisted in extension, such as it appears to our senses, extension being equal there would be equality of essence; the essences of bodies might be measured like their dimensions; two globes of equal diameters, would be two essentially equal bodies. Experience, and even common sense are opposed to this. It may be said, that pure dimension, in so far as subject to measure, is not enough to form equality of essence; but that the equality of nature of the extension of both bodies is also requisite; but what, I ask, is the meaning of the *nature* of extension? If the word nature here means any thing, it must mean something distinct from extension, in so far as subject to our sensibility; in which case I infer that just as in order to diversify the essences of bodies something is imagined which is not contained in extension in so far as subject to sensible intuition, something

may in the same manner be supposed which is capable of activity, and which offers to our understanding an accessory idea giving life, so to speak, to the dead matter which we find in extension, considered as the simple object of purely geometrical ideas.

154. Experience cannot demonstrate the impossibility of the activity of bodies. Absolute inactivity cannot affect us, and therefore cannot be known by experience. We can only experience action, or the exercise of activity; inaction, or the state of an absolutely inactive thing, cannot be the object of experience without a contradiction.

CHAPTER XV
CONJECTURES AS TO THE EXISTENCE
OF CORPOREAL ACTIVITY

155. Experience, far from authorizing us to infer the absolute inertness of bodies, on the contrary inclines us to believe that they are endowed with activity. Although the senses do not give us intuition of any corporeal activity, they present a continuous series of changes in a fixed order in the phenomena of the corporeal world; and if the true activity of some on others can be inferred from the coincidence of their relations in space and time, from the constant succession in which we see some follow others, and the invariable experience that the existence of some suffices for the existence of others; then we must admit true activity in bodies. Whatever this argument may be worth at the tribunal of metaphysics, it has always been sufficiently powerful to convince the majority of mankind, and hence it is that the denial of the activity of bodies is contrary to common sense.

156. If we consider our relations to the corporeal world, we are equally led to believe that there is true activity in bodies. Whatever may be our ignorance of the manner in which sensations are produced within us, it is certain that we experience them in the presence of bodies which are connected with us in space and time, and in a fixed and constant order, which authorizes us to prognosticate with safety what will follow in our senses if such or such bodies are placed in relation with our organs. The idea of activity presents to us the idea of a principle of changes in other beings; bodies are continually producing real or apparent changes in us. The exercise of the sensitive faculties implies a communication with corporeal beings; in this communication the sensitive being receives from bodies a multitude of impressions causing continual changes.

157. It is said that experience shows bodies to be indifferent to rest or motion, and some works on physics at the very beginning lay it down as a thing beyond all doubt, that a body placed at rest would remain in the same state for all eternity, and if put in motion it would move for all eternity in a right line, and always with the same velocity which it at first received. I do not know how they could have learned this from experience; and I maintain that not only they could not know it, but experience seems to prove directly the contrary.

158. Where was there ever a body that was indifferent to rest or motion? In all terrestrial bodies we find a tendency to motion, if no other, at least that of gravitation towards the centre of the earth. Celestial bodies, so far as our observation extends, are all in motion; calculation agrees with experience in showing them to be subject to universal attraction: where, then, is the indifference to rest or motion, revealed by experience? We should rather say that experience reveals a general inclination of bodies to be in motion.

159. It would be objected that this inclination does not flow from any activity in the bodies, but that it is a simple effect of a law imposed by the Creator. Let it be so: but at least do not tell us that experience presents bodies as indifferent to motion or rest; explain motion, if you will, without activity, maintain that there is no activity, despite the appearances of experience; but do not tell us that these appearances show the absence of activity.

160. If I place a body on my table, it remains at rest, I find it there the next day, and if I return after many years I still find it there. But this body is not indifferent to motion or rest; here it is at rest, but it is continually exercising its activity, as is evident from its pressure on the table which supports it. This exercise is incessant, it is experienced at every moment; try to raise it and it offers resistance, take away the table and it falls, place your hand under it and it will press upon your hand, and it changes the form of soft bodies on which it rests.

161. To say that the attraction of the centre of the earth acts upon the body, proves nothing against corporeal activity but rather confirms it; for this centre is another body, and thus you take activity from one body to give it to another. Moreover, all observations show that attraction is mutual, and therefore attractive activity is a property of all bodies.

162. The corporeal world, far from appearing to us as an inert mass, presents the appearance of an activity developing its colossal forces. The mass of bodies which move in space is colossal; the orbit which they describe is colossal; their velocity is colossal; the influence, at least apparent, which they exercise upon each other, is colossal; the distance at which they communicate is colossal. Where is the want of activity revealed by experience? Rays of light inundate space, producing in sensitive beings the wonderful phenomena of sight: rays of heat extend in all directions, and motion and life spring up on all sides; where is the want of activity revealed by experience? Do not the vegetation which covers our globe, the phenomena of life which we experience within us, and in the animals around us, require a continual motion of matter, an ebb and flow, so to speak, of action and reaction of bodies on each other, in reality or in appearance? Do not the phenomena of electricity, of magnetism, of galvanism, appear to be

principles of great activity, the origin of motion wherever they exist, rather than objects indifferent to motion or rest? The ideas of activity, of force, of impulse, are not alone suggested to us by our internal activity, but also by the experience of the corporeal world, which displays before our eyes, and in obedience to constant laws, a continual variety of magnificent scenes, whose origin seems to indicate a fund of activity surpassing all calculations.

163. With how little reason then do you appeal to experience to combat the existence of causality in bodies, and how much more in accordance with experience are those philosophers who give a true activity to bodies, is apparent from what I have said. In assigning the limits of our intuition in relation to causality and activity in themselves, [94] I said enough to show that I do not judge it possible to demonstrate metaphysically the existence of activity in the corporeal world; yet I cannot but insist that if the constant relation of phenomena in space and time, and the invariable succession of some things after others, prove any thing in favor of causality, we must admit the opinion which holds that there is true activity in bodies; that in a secondary order the reason of the changes of some is contained in others; and that consequently there is in the corporeal world a chain of second causes which reaches back to the first cause, the origin and the reason of all that is.

CHAPTER XVI
INTERNAL CAUSALITY

164. Consciousness reveals the existence of a faculty within us which produces certain internal phenomena. If we concentrate our attention by means of a free act of our will, we experience the production of images and ideas. The works of the imagination are an irrefutable proof of our internal activity. Sensations furnish the materials; but the fancy builds edifices with them. Who, if not ourselves, gave them their new form? We must confess that if we are absolutely without activity, nature completely deludes us, making us believe that we are active.

Our recollections offer another proof of true activity. We propose to think of a country which we have visited, and wish to recollect its details; at the command of the will the imagination is aroused and displays to our intuition the scenes which we once saw. But these images already existed, it will be said, and it was only necessary to awaken them; but it cannot be said that they existed in act, for we had no actual consciousness of them; and the command of our will was necessary and sufficient in order to force them to reappear. This new presence adds something to our habitual state, and is produced within us by the mere act of the will.

It is true that we do not know the manner of this production; but it is certain that consciousness assures us that it immediately follows an act of our will; and we have, to say the least, a strong proof that there is in us a force which produces the transition of these images from their habitual to an actual state. The same may be said of all recollections; and if we often find that we cannot recollect all that we wish to, this only proves that our active faculties are limited by certain conditions from which they cannot free themselves.

165. Without considering recollections, every one knows how ideas are elaborated in meditation. Our ideas are not the same when we begin to reflect on any subject, as after we have meditated for a long time on it. Sometimes without the assistance obtained by reading any new work or hearing any new observation, by the mere force of our own reflection we have made clear and distinct what was before only a confused idea. To

say that the new ideas are the result of others which already existed in our mind only proves that our understanding has a true activity; for this result, whatever its origin, is something new, it produces a new state in the soul, since it now knows perfectly what before it either knew not at all, or only in a confused manner. The relations of the sub-secant to the secant, and of the sub-tangent to the tangent, are geometrical ideas within the reach of the most ordinary intellects: so also are the similarity of the triangles which are imagined for the purpose of comparing lines with each other, and the successive approximation of the sub-secant to the sub-tangent, and of the secant to the tangent; but to reduce those elements to the point where the wonderful theory of infinitesimal calculus shines forth with the strongest light, an immense distance has to be passed over. Shall we say that those geniuses who first crossed over this distance thought nothing new, because they already had the elements from the combination of which this theory results?

166. If this productive activity is clearly seen in any phenomena, it is certainly in the acts of freewill. What becomes of freedom, if the soul does not produce its volitions? Freedom means nothing, if they are only phenomena produced by another being, in which the soul has no other part than that it is the subject in which they are produced. It is a contradiction to say that the soul is free, and at the same time deny that it is the principle of its determinations.

167. Mere intelligence, even mere sensibility, and in general, every phenomenon implying consciousness, seems to be the exercise of an activity; and in this sense I have shown [95] that we have intuition of an internal activity. If to know, to will, to have consciousness of a sensation, are not *actions*, I know not where the type of a true action can be found. To perceive a thing, to will it, the imperative act of the will which makes me seek the means of obtaining it, are undoubtedly actions; and action is the exercise of activity. The idea of life represents activity in its most perfect degree; and among the phenomena of life, the most perfect are those which imply consciousness; if we do not call these actions, we must say that we have no idea of action or of activity.

Although we do not know the manner of the production, we are conscious of it, we have intuition of the action in itself. When we see a bodily motion we behold a passive modification; but when we experience within ourselves the phenomena of consciousness, we behold an action, and consequently have an intuition of our activity.

168. Here an objection arises. If internal phenomena are truly actions, why are they so often independent of our will? We suffer despite ourselves;

ideas come upon us which we would fain cast off; thoughts arise so quickly and spontaneously as to seem rather inspirations than the fruit of labor. Where in such cases is the activity? Are we not forced to say that these phenomena are wholly passive?

169. This objection, apparently so conclusive, proves nothing against internal activity. In the first place, we might answer that the soul being passive in some cases, does not prove that it is so in all; and that in order to affirm the existence of internal activity, we require only certain phenomena to be produced by it. But it is not even necessary to admit that activity is not found in the cases proposed by the objection; for, if we carefully examine them, we shall find that even there the soul exercises a true activity.

The force of the objection rests on the appearance within us of certain phenomena without the concurrence of our will, and at times in spite of it; but this only leads us to infer that there are other functions in the soul independent of freewill without obliging us to believe that these functions are not active. With this observation the difficulty at once disappears. There are within us certain phenomena which we neither willed before nor after they appeared; so far I concede. Therefore there are within us phenomena in which the soul is purely passive; this I deny. The consequence is illegitimate; all that could logically be deduced is, that certain phenomena appear and are continued in the soul without the concurrence of our will.

The same thing happens with the body: there are functions which it exercises independently of our freewill, such as the circulation of the blood, respiration, digestion, assimilation of food, transpiration, and others; but there are others which are only performed at the command of the will, as eating, walking, and in general whatever relates to the motion and position of the members. Why may not a similar thing happen in the soul? Why may not the soul have active faculties which are developed, and produce various phenomena, without the concurrence of the will?

I do not believe any reply to this solution possible. Still I propose to strengthen it by some remarks on the character of the phenomena in which it is pretended that the soul is purely passive.

170. The objection speaks of painful sensations, in which apparently the soul has no activity. Who will say that a man to whom I apply a burning iron, and who suffers horrid pain, exercises in this the activity of his soul? Is it not more reasonable to say that the soul is here purely passive, and in a state very like that of the body when pressed down by the weight of another body? If any activity is exercised in such a case it is rather that of reaction against a painful sensation. Reflect well upon these observations, and you will find that they contain no difficulty whose solution cannot be found in

the preceding paragraph. I admit that the painful sensation does not depend on the freewill of the sufferer, and that his free action is opposed to this sensation; but despite all this, the soul may have a true activity in the mere fact of perceiving: it only shows that the exercise of this activity is subject to necessary conditions which when they exist are more powerful for its development than is our will to prevent it. Nothing is more certain than the development of certain active faculties independently of our freewill. What more active than violent passions? And yet it is often impossible for us not to feel them; and it requires all the command of our freewill to restrain them within the bounds of reason.

171. Sensation in itself cannot be all passive; and those who maintain that it is, show that they have meditated but little on the facts of consciousness. These facts are essentially individual, and inasmuch as they are facts of consciousness, absolutely incommunicable. Another may feel a pain very like, and even equal to, that which I suffer; but he cannot experience the same *numerically* considered; for my pain is so essentially mine, that if it is not mine it does not exist. Therefore pain cannot be communicated as an individual entity to me, and all that can be done to produce it in me, is to excite my sensitive power so as to experience it.

This observation shows that sensations cannot be merely passive facts. A passive modification is all *received*; the subject suffering *does* nothing. From the moment that the subject has in itself some principle of its modification, it is not purely passive. Sensation cannot be all *received*; it must be *born* in the subject under some influence or other, on this or that occasion; but the being which experiences it must contain a principle of its own experience; otherwise it would be a *lifeless* being, and could not perceive.

172. The objection speaks of painful sensations as though their necessity were an exception from the general rule; whereas all sensations, pleasant or unpleasant, are equally necessary, provided the sensitive faculties are placed in the conditions necessary for their exercise. There is the same necessity in the pain which I feel if a burning coal is placed in my hand, as in the sight of a beautiful painting placed before my eyes.

173. The spontaneousness of internal phenomena, in the pure intellectual order, or in that of imagination or sentiment, confirms the existence of an activity independent of our freewill, and by no means indicates that these phenomena are purely passive.

There is an important circumstance to be observed here. The exercise of the functions of the soul is connected with the phenomena of the organization. Experience teaches that the soul perceives with more or less activity, according to the disposition of the body; and it is a fact known from all antiquity that certain liquors have an inspiring power. The state of the digestion causes heavy dreams and torments the fancy with horrible forms; fever raises or depresses the imagination; sometimes it increases the strength of the understanding, and sometimes it produces a stupor in which intelligence is extinguished. These phenomena offer a greater field to observation when they reach a very high degree, as happens when the organic functions are greatly disturbed; but this shows that there is an immense scale passed over before arriving at the extremity; so that some phenomena, whose spontaneous appearance seems inexplicable, perhaps depend on certain unknown conditions to which our organization is subject. Whatever opinion be adopted as to the equality or inequality of human souls, no one has any doubt but that the differences of organization may have an influence on the talent or character, and that certain minds of extraordinary faculties owe a part of their endowments to a privileged organization.

Hence it may be inferred that what is called the spontaneity of the soul, and which has attracted so much attention from some modern philosophers, is a phenomenon very generally known, and one which neither destroys internal activity nor tells us any thing new as to its character.

It is certain that there are certain phenomena in our soul which are independent of our freewill; but there is no doubt that their presence is sometimes sudden and unexpected, because the conditions of our organization with which they are connected are unknown. But this is only extending to a greater number of cases what we have frequently remarked in psychological facts, the effects of disease, and what we constantly experience in sensations. What is a sensation but a sudden appearance of a phenomenon in our soul, produced by a change in the state of the organs?

174. I do not mean by this to say that all spontaneous thoughts, and in general all phenomena which suddenly appear within us without any known preparation, arise from affections of the organization; I only wished to recall a physiological and psychological fact, the neglect of which might produce useless and even dangerous speculations. In reading the works of some modern philosophers who treat this point, it seems as though their object were to prepare the way for maintaining that the individual reason is only a phenomenon of the universal and absolute reason; and that inspirations, and in general all spontaneous phenomena independent of freewill, are only indications of the absolute reason appearing to itself in the human reason; that what we call our *me* is a modification of the absolute being; and the personality of our being is only a phasis of the absolute and impersonal reason.

175. What is called spontaneity, the intuition of former times, to the eyes of reason and of criticism can only be the primitive teaching which the human race received from God: whatever some modern philosophers say to the contrary is only a partly disguised repetition of the sophisms of the incredulous of every epoch, presented in a deceitful dress by men who abuse the talents which they possess. Read with reflection the writings to which we allude, strip them of some high-sounding and enigmatical terms, and you will find in them nothing more than what Lucretius and Voltaire had already said after their own fashion.

CHAPTER XVII
REMARKS ON SPONTANEITY

176. There is nothing easier than to write a few brilliant pages on the phenomenon of spontaneity; some philosophers of our day discourse of the genius of the poets, of the artists, and of the captains of all ages, the fabulous and the heroic times, mysticism and religion, in books which are neither philosophy, nor history, nor poetry, but which can only be regarded as a flood of agreeable and harmonious words with which writers of sparkling fancy and inexhaustible eloquence deluge the overpowered intellect of the ingenuous reader. And after all, what is this spontaneity, this inspiration of which they tell us so much? Let us fix our ideas by establishing and classifying facts.

177. Reason properly so called is not developed in the human mind when completely isolated from other minds; the sight of nature is not sufficient to arouse it. The stupidity of children found in the woods and the scanty intelligence of deaf-mutes are undeniable evidence of this truth.

178. The human mind, when placed in communication with other minds, experiences a development in part direct and spontaneous, in part reflex and elaborate. This is another fact which we all perceive within ourselves. Minds are developed with greater spontaneousness in proportion as their qualities are more advanced.

179. Of the thoughts which occur to us suddenly and which seem to us purely spontaneous, not a few are reminiscences, more or less faithful, of what we have before read, heard, or thought; and consequently they proceed from a *preparatory* fact, which we do not remember. This explains how labor perfects the inventive faculty.

180. As the organization of our body exercises a powerful influence in the development of the soul's faculties, we may say that the spontaneity of some internal phenomena is connected with certain changes of our organization.

181. There is no *philosophical* difficulty in admitting an *immediate* communication of our mind with another mind of a higher order; and consequently there is none in admitting that some internal spontaneous phenomena arise from the direct influence of this higher mind upon ours.

182. The human race did not originally have a spontaneous development independent of the action of the Creator; philosophy shows us the necessity of a primitive teaching, without which the human race would have remained in a state of brute-like stupidity. This last remark requires a further explanation.

183. Religion reveals a primitive instruction and education of the human race given by God himself to the person of the first man; this is in perfect conformity with what both reason and experience assert.

Our mind possesses innumerable germs, but their growth requires an external cause. What would a man be who had been alone from his infancy? Little more than a brute: the precious stone would be covered with coarse earth which would prevent its glistening.

Language does not and cannot produce ideas; this is certain: the reason of ideas is not in language, but the reason of language is in ideas. Words are signs; and that which is not conceived can have no sign. But this sign, this instrument is of a wonderful use; words are to the understanding what wheels are to the power of a machine; the power imparts motion, but the machine would not go without wheels. The understanding might have some motion without language, but very slow, very imperfect, very heavy.

184. The Bible represents man as speaking as soon as created; language was therefore taught him by God. This is another wonderful fact which reason fully confirms. Man could not invent language. This invention surpasses all that can be imagined, and would you attribute it to beings so stupid as men without language? Better to say that a Hottentot could suddenly invent infinitesimal calculus.

185. The most ignorant man who knows a language possesses an incredible treasure of ideas. In the simplest conversation we may find many physical, metaphysical, and moral ideas. Take the following sentence, which is within the comprehension of the lowest mind: "I did not wish to pursue the beast farther for fear that, becoming irritated, he might do harm." Here are the ideas of time, act of the will, action, continuity, space, causality, analogy, end, and morality.

Time past:—I *did* not;

Act of the will:—*wish*;

Action:—to *pursue*;

Continuity and space:—*farther*;

Analogy:—*becoming irritated*; since from irritation in other instances, it is inferred in the present; and it is also known from what happens to ourselves if molested.

Motive and end:—*for fear, that irritated*, etc.;

Causality:—*he might do harm*;

Morality:—*not to harm others*.

186. Science is discovering the affinity of languages, finding them united in great centres. The dialects of savages are not elements, but fragments; they are not the lisping speech of infancy, but the torpid and extravagant jargon of degradation and ebriety.

187. Language cannot produce in the mind the idea of a sensation which it has not: all the words in the world could not give one born blind the idea of color. Still less could pure ideas, distinct from all sensation, result from language; and this is a strong argument in favor of innate ideas.

188. The ideas of unity, number, time, and causality express things which are not sensible; therefore they cannot be produced in us by any sensible representation expressed in language. Yet these ideas exist in us as germs susceptible of a great development, first by sensible experience, and then by reflection. The child who burns his hand in the fire begins to perceive the relation of causality, which he afterwards generalizes and purifies. The great ideas of Leibnitz on causality were the ideas of Leibnitz the child. The difference was in the development. Thus the organization of the giant oak is contained within the shell of the acorn.

Some have said that man's understanding is like a blank tablet on which nothing is yet written; others that it was a book which he had only to open in order to read; I believe it may be compared to a letter written in invisible ink, which looks white until rubbed with a mysterious liquid which brings out the black characters. The magic liquid is instruction and education.

189. Show me a single nation which of itself has emerged from a savage or a barbarous state. All known civilizations are subordinated one to another in an uninterrupted chain. European civilization owes much to Christianity, and something to the Roman; the Roman to the Greek; the Greek to the Egyptian; the Egyptian to the Oriental; and over the Oriental civilization hangs a veil which can be lifted only by the first chapters of Genesis. 190. In order to know the human mind it is necessary to study the history of humanity; whoever isolates objects too much runs in danger of mutilating them; hence so many ideological frivolities which have passed for profound investigations, although they were as far from true metaphysics as the art of arranging a museum symmetrically is from the science of the naturalist.

191. If innate ideas be defended, it is impossible to deny to our understanding a power to form new ideas accordingly as objects, especially language, excite it; otherwise it would be necessary to say that we do not learn any thing, and cannot learn any thing; that we have every thing beforehand in our mind, as if written in a book. Our understanding seems to resemble a case containing all kinds of types; but, in order that they may mean any thing, the hand of the compositor is necessary.

This image of printer's types reminds me of an important ideological fact: I mean the scanty number of ideas which are in our mind, and the great variety of combinations of which they are susceptible. All that is in the intellectual order, or is contained in the categories, whether we adopt those of Kant or those of Aristotle, or any others, may be reduced to a very few. Each of those ideas which we call generative is like a ray of light which, passing successively through innumerable prisms and refracted on a number of spectra, presents an infinite variety of colors, shades, and figures.

As our thought is almost entirely reduced to combination, and as this combination may be made in various ways, there is a wonderful agreement in the fundamental combinations which all minds have. In the secondary points there is divergence, but not in the principal. This proves that the human mind, in its existence and in its development, depends on an infinite intelligence, which is the cause and master of all minds.

192. Reject these doctrines so accordant with philosophy and with history, and spontaneity, whether of the individual or the race, either means nothing, or it expresses the vague and absurd theories of ideal pantheism.

CHAPTER XVIII
FINAL CAUSALITY;—MORALITY

193. Those beings which act by intelligence must have, besides their efficient activity, a moral principle of their determinations. In order to will, the faculty of willing is not alone sufficient; it is necessary to know that which is willed, for nothing is willed without being known. Hence arises *final causality*, which is essentially distinct from efficient causality, and can exist only in beings endowed with intelligence.

194. Recalling what was said in the tenth chapter of this book, we may observe that final causes form a series distinct from that of efficient causes; what in the latter is physical action, is in the former, moral influence. In a painting, the series of efficient causes is the pencil, the hand, the muscles, the animal spirits, and the command of the will. This series, which is necessary for the execution of the painting, may be combined with different series of final causes. The artist may purpose by the brilliancy of his genius to acquire renown, and by renown to enjoy the happiness of a great name. Another series may be, to please a person for whom he is working; and this in order that the person may pay him a sum of money; and the money in order to gratify the artist's wants or pleasures. A third series may be, in order to seek in painting a distraction from a grief; and this in order to preserve his health. It is evident that many series of a purely moral or intellectual influence may be imagined, and which concur in the production of the effect only, in so far as combined with the series of efficient causes, they influence the artist's determination.

195. This moral influence may be exerted in two ways: either necessarily bending the will, or leaving it free to will or not will; in the first case, there is a voluntary, but necessary spontaneousness; in the second, there is a free spontaneousness. Every free act is voluntary, but not every voluntary act is free. God freely wills the conservation of creatures; but he necessarily wills virtue, and cannot will iniquity.

196. Regarding only efficient causality, we have only the relations of cause and effect; but considering final causality, a new order of ideas and facts is presented, which is *morality*. Let us first of all establish the existence of the fact.

197. Good and evil, moral, immoral, just, unjust, right, duty, obligation, command, prohibition, lawful, unlawful, virtue, and vice, are words which we all use continually, and apply to the whole course of life, to all the relations of man with God, with himself, and with his fellow-men, without any doubt as to their true meaning, and perfectly understanding each other, just as when we speak of color, light, or other sensible objects. When the term lawful or unlawful is applied to an act, who ever asks what it means? When this man is called virtuous, that vicious, who does not know the meaning of these expressions? Is there any one who finds a difficulty in understanding the expressions which follow: he has a right to perform this act; he is obliged to comply with that circumstance; this is his duty; he has neglected his duty; this is commanded; that is prohibited; this is right; that is wrong: this is a heroic virtue; that is a crime? No ideas are more common, more ordinarily used, by the ignorant as by the learned; by barbarous as by civilized nations; in the youth of societies as in their infancy, and in their old age; in the midst of pure customs, as of the most revolting corruption; they express something primitive, innate in the human mind and indispensable to its existence, something which it cannot throw off while it retains the exercise of its faculties. There may be more or less error and extravagance in the application of these ideas to certain particular cases: but the generative ideas of good and evil, just and unjust, lawful and unlawful, are the same at all times, and in all countries; they form, as it were, an atmosphere in which the human mind lives and breathes.

198. It is remarkable that even those who deny the distinction between good and evil, are forced to admit it in practice. A philosopher, with his pen in his hand, laughs at what he calls the prejudices of the human race concerning the difference between good and evil; but say to him: "It seems to me, Sir Philosopher, that you are a detestable wretch, to spend your time in destroying that which is most holy on earth;" and you will see how soon he will forget his philosophy and all that he has said of the empty meaning of the words virtue and vice, become indignant at being thus addressed, warmly defend himself, and attempt to prove to you that he is the most virtuous man in the world, giving repeated arguments of *honesty, sincerity,* and *honor.* It matters little that in his lofty theories, honor, sincerity, and honesty, are unmeaning words, since they can have no sense unless the word order is admitted; the philosopher is not staggered by an inconsequence, or rather, he takes no notice of it; moral ideas and sentiments are awakened in his mind as soon as he hears himself called immoral, he ceases to be a sophist, and becomes a man again.

199. Can the idea of this moral order be a prejudice, which, without any thing in reality corresponding to it, or any foundation in human nature,

owes its origin to education, so that it would have been possible for men to have lived without moral ideas, or with others directly contrary to those which we now have? If it is a prejudice, how comes it that it is general to all times and countries? Who communicated it to the human race? who was strong and powerful enough to make all men adopt it? How did it happen that the passions, when in possession of their liberty, renounced it, and suffered a bridle to be put on them? Who was that extraordinary man who subdued all times and all countries, the most brutal customs, the most violent passions, the most obtuse understandings, and diffused the idea of a moral order over the whole face of the earth, notwithstanding the diversity of climates, languages, customs, and necessities, and the differences in the social condition of nations, and gave to this idea of the moral order such force and consistency that it has been preserved through the most complete revolutions, amid the ruins of empires, and the fluctuations and transmigrations of civilization, remaining firm as a rock, unmoved by the furious waves of the river of ages?

Here is not the hand of man; a phenomenon of this sort does not spring from human combinations; it is founded on nature, and it is indestructible because it is natural; thus, and thus only, is it possible to explain its universality and permanence.

200. To deny all difference between good and evil is to place one's self in open contradiction with the ideas the most deeply rooted in the human mind, with all its most profound and most powerful sentiments; all the sophisms of the world could not persuade any one, not even the sophist himself, that there is no difference between consoling one who is afflicted, and adding to his afflictions; between assisting the unfortunate, and increasing their misfortunes; between being grateful for a favor, and doing evil to the benefactor; between fulfilling a promise, and breaking it; between giving alms, and taking what belongs to another; between being faithful to a friend, and betraying him; between dying for one's country, and selling it to the enemy; between respecting the laws of modesty, and violating them without shame; between sobriety and drunkenness; between temperance and moderation in all the acts of life, and the disorder of unbridled passions. No argument, nor genius, nor cavil can destroy the dividing line. The sophist discusses, imagines, feigns, subtilizes, but in vain; nature is there; she says to senseless man: So far mayst thou go, but here shall thy pride be broken.

201. If there is no intrinsic difference between good and evil, and all that is said of the morality and immorality of actions is a collection of words which have no meaning, or only such as they have received from human convention; how is it that whilst the just man sleeps securely in his bed, the evil-doer is tossed about with a heart struggling with remorse? Whence

come those sentiments of love and respect inspired by what we call virtue, and the aversion created by what is called vice? Do not the love of children, the veneration of parents, fidelity to friends, compassion for suffering, gratitude towards benefactors, the horror which all men have for a cruel father, a parricide son, an unfaithful wife, a dishonest friend, a traitor to his country, a hand red with the blood of its victim, oppression of the weak, desertion of the orphan, do not all these sentiments show clearer than the light of day the hand of the Almighty engraving in our souls the ideas of the moral order, and strengthening us with sentiments which instinctively show us, even when we have not time to reflect, the path which we should follow?

202. I do not deny that serious difficulties are encountered in examining the grounds of morality; I admit that the analysis of the knowledge of good and evil is one of the most hidden points of philosophy; but these difficulties prove nothing against the difference we have established. No one denies the existence of a building because he cannot see how deep its foundations go: its depth is a proof of its solidity, a guaranty of its duration. The difference between good and evil demonstrated *a priori* by the interior sentiments of the heart, is strengthened with further evidence if we regard the consequences of its existence or non-existence. Let us admit the moral order, and suppose all men to regulate their conduct conformably to this *prejudice*. What will be the result? The world becomes a paradise; men live like brothers, using with moderation the gifts of nature, dividing with each other their happiness, and aiding one another to bear misfortune; the most lovely harmony reigns in the individual, the family, and society; if the moral order is a prejudice, let us confess that never did prejudice have more grand, beneficial, and delightful consequences; if virtue is a lie, never was there one more useful, fairer, or more sublime.

203. But let us make the counterproof. Let us suppose this prejudice to disappear, and all men to be convinced that the moral order is a vain illusion which they must banish from their understanding, their will, and their acts; what will be the result this time? The moral order destroyed, the physical alone remains; every one thinks and acts according to his views, passions, or caprices; man has no other guide than the blind instinct of nature or the cold speculations of egotism; the individual becomes a monster, all the ties of family are broken asunder; and society, sunk in a frightful chaos, rapidly advances to complete destruction. These are the necessary consequences of the rejection of the *prejudice*. Language would be horridly mutilated if the ideas of the moral order should disappear; good and bad conduct would be words without meaning; praise and blame would have no object; even vanity would lose a great part of its food; flattery would be forced to

confine itself to natural qualities, considered in the purely physical order; to pronounce the word merit, would be forbidden under pain of falling into absurdity.

204. See, then, if any objection could be sufficient to make such consequences admissible. Whoever, frightened at the difficulties accompanying the examination of the first principles of morality, should undertake to deny morality, would be as foolish as the husbandman who, seeing the stream which waters his fields, should insist on denying the existence of its waters because inaccessible crags prevent his approach to their source.

CHAPTER XIX
VARIOUS EXPLANATIONS OF MORALITY

205. There have been many disputes concerning the origin and character of the morality of actions; the same happening here as elsewhere, that the understanding becomes perplexed and confused whenever it attempts to penetrate into the first principles of things. As I am not going to write a treatise on morals, but only to analyze the foundations of this science, I shall confine myself to giving the character, as far as possible, of the primitive ideas and sentiments of the moral order, without descending to their application. In this I shall proceed, as usual, on the analytic method, decomposing the fact established in the preceding chapter, glancing at the various explanations which have been given of it, showing the insufficiency and inexactness of some of them, before coming to the only one which appears to me true and complete.

206. What is good? what is evil? why are things good or evil? in what does goodness or evil consist? what is their origin?

We are told that good is that which is conformed to reason, that which is in harmony with the eternal laws, that which is pleasing to God, and that evil is that which is opposed to reason, that which contradicts the eternal law, that which displeases God. This is true, but does it completely solve the question on a scientific ground?

The moral worth of the dictate of reason depends on its conformity to the eternal law; when, therefore, to found the moral order, you call in the former, you also appeal to the latter; they are not therefore two solutions of the question, but only one.

Acts cannot please or displease God, except as conformed to the eternal law; therefore, to judge of the goodness or evil of acts by their relation to the pleasure or displeasure of God, is to judge of them by their conformity to the eternal law.

From this it may be inferred that, although an act conformed to reason, one agreeing with the eternal law, and one displeasing to God, express different aspects of an idea, they all mean the same when used in explaining the foundations of the moral order.

207. The rules of the eternal law do not depend on the *free* will of God, since, in that case, God could make good evil, and evil good. The eternal law cannot be any thing else than the eternal reason, or the representation of the moral order in the divine intellect. Morality thus seems, according to our mode of conception, to precede its representation; that is to say, morality seems to be represented in the divine intellect because it is; but not that it is because it is represented. In the moral order we come to something resembling metaphysical and geometrical science. Geometrical truths are eternal, inasmuch as they are represented in the eternal reason; and this representation supposes an intrinsic and necessary truth in them, since the representation would otherwise be false. As this truth must have some eternal foundation, [96] and this foundation cannot be in any finite being, it must be sought for in the essentially infinite being, which contains the reason of all things. The infinite intellect represents the truth, and is, therefore, true; but this truth is itself founded on the essence of the infinite being which knows it.

208. Moral truths are not distinguished in this respect from metaphysical; their origin is in God, moral science cannot be atheistic. Why are some things represented in God as good and others as evil? To ask the reason of this is like asking why triangles are not represented as circles, and circles as triangles. If there is an intrinsic necessity, either we can assign no reason for it or we must at any rate come to a reason which can be explained by no other reason. It will in any case, be necessary for us to come to a point where we can only say: It is so. Any further satisfaction, which we might desire, is beyond our reach, as we do not intuitively see the infinite essence which contains the first and ultimate reason of all things.

209. It is necessary first to suppose good and evil before things can be represented as such, or even conceived as so represented. What is a good thing? If we say it is being represented as good in the divine mind, the thing defined is contained in the definition; the difficulty still remains: what is it to be represented as good?

Goodness cannot consist in the simple representation, so that whatever is represented in God is good; for then every thing would be good, as every thing is represented in God.

Therefore, in order that a thing may be good, it must not only be represented, but represented under such or such a character which makes it good; but still the difficulty remains: what is this character?

210. Let us make these ideas clearer by comparing a metaphysical with a moral truth. All the diameters of the same circle are equal; this truth does not depend on any particular circle, it is founded on the essence of all

circles; this essence is in turn represented eternally in the infinite essence, where with the plenitude of being, is contained the representation and knowledge of all the finite participations in which the wisdom and power of God may be exercised. All the participations are subject to the principle of contradiction, in none of them can being cease to exclude not-being, or not-being to exclude being; hence proceeds the necessity of all the properties and relations, without which the principle of contradiction cannot subsist; among these is the equality of all the diameters of the same circle.

211. These considerations suggest the question: is it possible to explain the moral order like the metaphysical and mathematical, by showing it contained in the principle of contradiction?

212. It is easy to see that in all metaphysical and mathematical truths, identity is expressed or denied. All formulas are reduced to A is B, or A is not B; this is the general formula of all truths of an absolute order. But it is otherwise in the moral order, where nothing is ever expressed absolutely, as is shown by the very form of the propositions. God is good, expresses a metaphysical truth, God must be loved, or in other words, we ought to love God, expresses a moral truth. Note the difference: in one case we say *is* absolutely; in the other, *must be, ought to be, there is obligation*, etc., using different expressions which all mean the same thing; but in all, the verb *to be*, as an absolute affirmation, disappears. It seems that no moral proposition could be thus expressed, if we regard the primitive elements of our moral ideas; for all these propositions express the idea of duty, which is essentially a relative idea.

213. To love God is good. This is a moral proposition whose structure seems to contradict what I have just established. Here an absolute affirmation is found expressed simply by *is*, as in metaphysical or mathematical propositions. Still, the least reflection will suffice to show that this absolute character is destroyed by the nature of the predicate. What is the meaning of *good*? Here we have an essentially relative idea which communicates this character to the proposition. To love God is good, is the same as: to love God is a thing conformed to reason, or to the eternal law, or pleasing to God, or a thing which we are under obligation to do; it is always a relative idea, and never absolute, like being, not-being, a triangle, a circle, etc.

214. Good, say some, is that which leads to the end which corresponds to intelligent beings. This explanation must not be confounded with the theory of private interest;—a theory alike rejected by religion and by the sentiments of the heart, and combated by the most profound thinkers;— here, in speaking of end, the last end is meant, which is something superior to what is understood by the expression, private interest. Without doubt,

to arrive at the last end, is a great interest of every intelligent being; but at least this interest is taken in an elevated sense, and does not promote the development of a paltry egotism.

Having thus designated the difference between these doctrines, I say that not even the latter seems to me admissible. Moral good must lead to the end; but this does not constitute the character of morality. For, what is meant by end? If God himself is meant, a moral act is that which leads to God; in which case the difficulty still remains, for we again ask, what is meant by *leading*? If it means to conduce to the happiness which consists in a union with God, *how* does it conduce to this happiness? By the performance of what God has commanded;—certainly; but then we ask: I. Why does doing what God has commanded conduce to happiness? II. Why has God commanded some things and prohibited others?—which is equivalent to putting anew the question of intrinsic morality.

215. Besides, the idea of happiness represents something very different from the idea of morality. Imagining a being which sacrifices all that it possessed for the sake of other beings, we have the idea of a highly moral being, but not a happy being. If morality consisted in happiness, the participation of happiness would be the participation of morality; every enjoyment would be a moral act; and could only be immoral because too short or feeble. In proportion as we rose to the idea of a stronger and more lasting enjoyment, we should form the idea of a more elevated morality; the enjoyment the most free from trouble would be the purest act of morality; who does not see that this overthrows all our moral ideas, and is repugnant to every sentiment of the heart?

216. It is not enough to say that a moral being will obtain happiness, and that its happiness will be great in proportion to its morality; this only proves that happiness is the reward of morality; it does not authorize us to confound the two, the guerdon with the merit.

217. To confound morality with happiness is to reduce morality to a calculation, to strip virtue of the pure lustre which charms and attracts us, and makes it appear more beautiful accordingly as it is joined with greater suffering. If we identify happiness with morality, disinterestedness becomes a calculation of interest, a sacrifice of a smaller to a greater interest, a loss for the present to gain in the future.

No! the morality of actions is not an affair of calculation: the virtuous man obtains a reward; but, in order that the act may be virtuous, something more is necessary than a combination for the purpose of obtaining it; there must be something which makes the act merit the reward; and we cannot even conceive that a reward can be reserved for any act, unless the act is in itself meritorious.

When God prepared punishment for some acts and rewards for others, he must have found an intrinsic difference in them; and therefore he gave them different destinies; but, according to the systems which we are opposing, acts could be good only inasmuch as they lead to a reward, and there would be no reason why some should lead to it rather than others. This reason must be found in an intrinsic difference in the acts themselves; or we fall into the absurdity of saying that all actions are in themselves indifferent, and the good may be evil, and the evil good.

218. To lead to the good of mankind is another incomplete character of the morality of actions. It is clear that this morality would be only human, and would not include the intrinsic morality which we consider common to all intelligent beings.

219. What, too, is the good which is spoken of? In what state are mankind considered? Do you mean a society constituted as a nation, or mankind, properly so called; one generation or many; their destiny on earth or hereafter in another life? Are you speaking of their *well-being*, or of their development and perfection abstracted from their greater or less well-being? If the morality of actions is to be placed in their *conduciveness*, so to speak, to the general good of mankind, in what does this supreme good consist? Is it the development of the understanding, of the imagination, or of the heart; or in the perfection of the arts, which secure material enjoyments? You must not, then, place moral perfection as the end; for by the supposition it is only the means; and the actions will be more moral accordingly as they are more useful means of obtaining the general good.

220. To say that morality is only the object of sentiment, and that no other mark of what is good can be given than the mysterious perfection which we find in virtue, is to banish morality as a science, and to shut the door against all investigation. I do not deny that there is in us a moral sentiment, or that our heart feels mysterious sympathy for virtue; but I believe the scientific study of the foundations of the moral order to be compatible with this fact. It is necessary to acknowledge the primitive character of some facts of our mind, and not attempt to explain every thing; but we must guard against exaggeration in this respect, which is only the more dangerous when covered with the cloak of modesty.

CHAPTER XX
FUNDAMENTAL EXPLANATION
OF THE MORAL ORDER

221. There must be something absolute in morality. It is not possible to conceive any thing all relative, without something absolute on which it is founded. Moreover, every relation implies a term to which it relates, and, consequently, though we suppose a series of relations, we must come to a last term. This shows why purely relative explanations of morality do not satisfy the understanding; reason, and even sentiment seek an absolute basis.

Besides, this purely ontological argument in favor of the absolute in morality, there are others not less conclusive, and which are within the reach of ordinary men.

222. In the infinitely perfect being we conceive infinite holiness, independently of the existence of creatures; and what is infinite holiness but *moral* perfection in an infinite degree? This argument is decisive for all the world, excepting atheists: whoso admits the existence of God must admit his holiness; the contrary is repugnant to reason, to the heart, to common sense. Therefore something absolutely moral exists; therefore morality in itself cannot be explained by any relation of creatures to end, since morality in an infinite degree would exist though there had never been any creature.

223. In conceiving a created intelligent being, we also conceive morality as an inflexible law to which the actions of this being must be subjected. It is to be observed that we conceive this morality, even supposing only one intelligent being; therefore morality cannot be explained by the relations of creatures to each other. Imagine one man all alone on the earth, can you conceive him exempt from all morality? Would he be equally beautiful in the moral order, whether he labored to perfect his intellect and develop his faculties harmoniously, or abandoned himself to his coarse instincts, lowering himself to the level of the beasts by his stupidity and debasement? Imagine the earth, the whole corporeal universe, and all created beings, except one intelligence, to disappear; can you conceive this creature wholly exempt from all moral law? Can you suppose all his thoughts and acts

of the will to be indifferent, and that morality is for him an unmeaning word? Impossible, unless you place yourself in open struggle with our primary ideas, with our profoundest sentiments, with the common sense of mankind. This, then, is another proof that in the moral order there is something absolute, an intrinsic perfection, independent of the mutual relations of creatures; that certain acts of an intelligent and free creature have a beauty of their own.

224. The imputability of actions offers another argument in confirmation of this truth. Morality is never measured by the result; its perfection is appreciated by what is *immanent*, that is, by the motives which have impelled the will, by the greater or less deliberation which preceded the act of the will, by the greater or less intensity of the act. If the result is sometimes considered, all its moral worth arises from the interior of the soul. Whether the result was foreseen or unforeseen; whether it was possible or not to foresee it; whether it was willed or not; whether it was proposed as the principal or secondary object; whether it was desired or accepted with sorrow; these and other such considerations are present when the merit or demerit of an action which has had such or such result, is weighed and appreciated. Hence this result has no weight in the moral order except in so far as it is the expression of the act of the will.

225. This character of *immanence*, which is essential to all moral acts, overthrows all the theories which found morality on external combinations; and shows that the act of a free and intelligent being is good or bad in itself, absolutely abstracted from its good or bad consequences, which were not contained in the internal act in one way or another. A man, who, by an act which he did not and could not foresee, should seriously injure the whole human race, would be innocent; and another who with an evil intention should benefit mankind, would be guilty. It is not a virtuous act to save one's country through a motive of vanity or ambition; and the unfortunate man, who with a pure and disinterested intention and with an ardent desire to save his country, should by an error produce its downfall, would not cease to be virtuous; the very act whose result is so sad, is considered an act of virtue.

226. In what, then, does absolute morality consist? Where is the hidden source of this ray of beauty which we all perceive, which penetrates every thing, making all things beautiful, and without which the world of intelligences would wither and fade away?

It seems to me that on this point, as on many others, science has not paid sufficient regard to the admirable profoundness of the Christian religion, which answers with one word, as full of tenderness as of meaning: *Love.*

I particularly call the attention of my readers to the theory which I am going to unfold. After so many difficulties as we have hitherto encountered concerning the moral order, we must try to gain some light on so important a subject. This light will more and more confirm a truth which science reveals. When we come to the principles or the last results of science, the ideas of Christianity are not useless; they throw light on the foundation and on the summit of the edifice of human knowledge.

Let not the reader imagine that instead of a scientific theory, I am going to offer him a chapter of mysticism. I am sure that in the end the reader will be convinced that, even under a purely scientific aspect, this doctrine is much more exact and profound than that of those authors who carefully avoid using the word *God*, as though this august name would be a blot on the pages of science.

227. Absolute morality is the love of God; all moral ideas and sentiments are applications and participations of this love.

Let us give a proof of this by carrying this principle to all the parts of the moral world.

What is absolute morality in God? What is the attribute of the infinite being, which we call holiness? The love of himself, of his infinite perfection. In God there is no duty, properly so called, there is an absolute necessity of being holy; for he is under the absolute necessity of loving his infinite perfection. Thus morality in its most absolute sense, in its highest degree, is infinite holiness; it is independent of all freewill. God cannot cease to be holy.

228. But it may be asked, why *must* God love himself? This question has no meaning if the matter is rightly understood; for it supposes that what is entirely absolute can be exactly expressed in relative terms. The proposition: God *must* love himself is not exact; strict exactness is expressed only in this: God loves himself; for it expresses an absolute fact in an absolute manner. If it is now asked, why God loves himself; I answer that it might as well be asked, why God knows himself, why he knows the truth, or why he exists; when we come to these questions, we have arrived at the primitive origin, at absolute, unconditioned things; therefore every *why* is absurd.

229. Morality can, therefore, be expressed in an absolute proposition. It is in itself, in an infinite degree, an absolute truth; it implies an identity whose opposite is contradictory: it is not less connected with the principle of contradiction than all metaphysical and geometrical truths. Its simplest formula is: the infinite loves itself.

230. God in his intelligence sees from all eternity an infinity of possible creatures. Containing in himself the ground of their possibility and of all their relations among themselves or to their Creator, nothing can exist independent of him; hence it is not possible for any being to cease to be directed to God. The end which God proposed in the creation can be no other than himself; since before the creation only God existed, and after the creation there were no perfections in creatures which were not contained in God in an infinite degree, either formally or virtually. Therefore this direction of all creatures to God as their last end, is a condition inseparable from them, and seen by God from eternity in all possible worlds. Whatever is created or may be created is a realization of a divine idea, of that which was represented in the infinite mind, with the absolute or relative properties which pre-existed in that representation. Therefore whatever exists or may exist must be subject to this condition, it must be directed to God, without whom its existence would be impossible.

231. Among the creatures, in which is realized the representation pre-existing in the divine mind, there are some endowed with will, which is an inclination to what is known, and, by means of an act of the understanding, becomes a principle of its own determinations. If the creature knew God intuitively, the acts of its will would be necessarily moral; for it would necessarily be an act of the love of God. The rectitude of the created will would then be a constant reflection of the infinite holiness, or of the love which God bears himself. The moral perfection of the creature would not in that case be free, though it would still be an eminent degree of moral perfection. There would be a perpetual conformity of the created will to the will of God, for the creature loving God by a happy necessity, could will nothing but what God wills. The morality of the created will would be this constant conformity to the divine will, which conformity would not be distinguished from the essentially moral and holy act, by which the creature would love the infinite being.

But since the knowledge of God is not intuitive, since the idea which the creature has of God is an incomplete conception involving many indeterminate notions, the infinite good is not loved by necessity, because it is not known in its essence. The will has an inclination to good, but to good indeterminately; and therefore it does not feel a necessary inclination to any real object. The good is presented under a general and indeterminate idea, with various applications, and to none of them is the will inclined necessarily; hence proceeds its freedom to depart from the order seen by God as conformed to his sovereign designs; when freedom, far from being a perfection, is a defect arising from the weakness of the knowledge of the being which possesses it.

232. The rational creature conforming in its acts to the will of God, realizes the order which God wills; loving this order, it loves what God loves. If, although realizing this order, the creature in its freedom does not love the order, but acts from motives independent of it, its will, performing the act materially, does not love what God loves; and here is the line which divides morality from immorality. The proper morality of an act consists in explicit or implicit conformity of the created will to the divine will; the mysterious perfections of moral acts, that loveliness in them which charms and attracts us, is nothing else than conformity to the will of God; the absolute character which we find in morality is the explicit or implicit love of God, and, consequently, a reflection of the infinite holiness, or of the love by which God loves himself.

By applying this doctrine to facts, we shall see more clearly still its perfect exactness.

233. To love God is a morally good act; to hate God is a morally evil act, and of the most detestable character. Where is the morality of the act of loving God? In the act itself, the reflection of the infinite holiness, which consists in the love which God has for his infinite perfection; here is a palpable proof of the truth of our theory. The love of the creature for the Creator has always been regarded as an essentially moral act, as the purest morality; which shows that in the secondary and finite order, this act is the purest and most faithful expression of absolute morality.

234. If we ask why we must love God, we are ordinarily reminded of the benefits which he has conferred upon us, of the love which he bears us, and even of the example of the love which we owe to our friends and benefactors, and especially our parents; these reasons are certainly very useful in order to make the morality of the act in some sense palpable, and to move our heart; but they are not completely satisfactory in the field of science. For, if we could doubt that we ought to love the infinite Being, the author of all beings, it is clear that we should also doubt that we ought to love our parents, our friends, or our benefactors. Therefore our love for them must be founded on something higher, or else, when asked why we love them, we must remain without an answer.

235. To wish to perfect the understanding is a moral act in itself. Whence proceeds the morality of this act? God, in giving us intelligence, evidently wished us to use it. Its use, therefore, enters into the order known and willed by God; in willing this order, we will what God wills; we love this order which God loved from all eternity, as a realization of his supreme designs; if, on the contrary, the creature does not perfect his intellectual faculties, and making use of his freedom leaves these faculties unexercised, he departs from the order established by God, he does not will what God wills, he does not love what God loves.

236. A man may perfect these faculties merely for the sake of obtaining the pleasure of being praised by others; in this case he realizes the order in the perfection of his understanding, but he does not do so from love of the order in itself, but from love of something distinct which does not enter into the order willed by God; for it is evident that God did not endow us with intellectual faculties for the fruitless object of obtaining each other's praise. Here, then, is the difference which we know, which we perceive between two equal actions done with different ends: the will in one perfects the understanding as a simple realization of the divine order; perhaps we may not be able to explain what there is there, but we know for certain that this will is right; in the other the will is the same, it wills the same thing, but it suffers something foreign to this order to mingle with it; and the understanding and the heart both tell us this act which does something good, is not good, it is not virtue, —it is meanness.

237. There is a person in great want, but who, nevertheless, has every probability of soon improving his fortunes, Lentulus and Julius each give him an alms. Lentulus gives his, because he hopes that when the poor man is better off he will remember his benefactor, and assist him if necessary. The action of Lentulus can have no moral value; in judging of it we see a calculation, not a virtuous act. Julius gives the alms solely in order to succor the unfortunate man, who excites his pity, without thinking of the return which may be made; the action of Julius is morally beautiful, it is virtuous. Whence this difference? Lentulus does good, assisting the needy; but not from love of the internal order of the act; he bends this order towards himself. God, willing that men should stand in need of each other, also willed that they should mutually help one another; to help one, therefore, simply in order to alleviate his wants is to realize simply the order willed by God; to help one for a particular end, is to realize this order not as it is established by God, but as combined by man. There is a *complication* of view, the *simplicity* of intention is wanting, —this simplicity so recommended by Christianity, and even in philosophy containing a profound meaning.

238. Regarding the purely natural order, we find that all moral obligations have in the last result a *useful* object; as all prohibitions are directed to prevent an injury; but it does not suffice for morality, that we will its utility, we must will the order itself from which the utility results; for the greater the reflection, and the love with which this order is willed, without any mixture of heterogeneous views, the more moral is the act.

To help the poor with the *simple* view of assisting them, out of love for them, is a virtuous act; to help them, out of this love, and with the *explicit* reflection that it is complying with a *duty* of humanity, is still more virtuous; to help them, for the thought of God, because you see in the poor man the image of God, who commands you to love him, is a still more virtuous act than either of the other two; to help them, even against the inclination of your own heart, excited by resentment against them, or moved by other passions, to subdue yourself with a firm will for the love of God, is an act of heroic virtue. Observe that the moral perfection of the act increases in proportion as the thing in itself is willed with greater reflection and love; and arrives at the highest point when, in the thing loved, it is God himself that is loved. If the views are selfish the order is perverted, and morality is banished; when there are no selfish views, but the act is prompted principally by sentiment, the action is beautiful, but belongs rather to sensibility than to morality; when the sacrifice tears the heart, but the will preceded by reflection commands the sacrifice, and the duty is performed because it is a duty; or perhaps an act not obligatory is done for the love of its moral goodness, and because it is agreeable to God, we see in the action something so fair, so lovely, so deserving of praise, that we should be confounded if asked the reason of the sentiment of respect which we feel for the person who for such noble motives sacrifices himself for his fellow-men.

Conformably to these principles we may clearly and exactly determine the ideas of morality.

239. Absolute morality, and consequently the origin and type of the moral order, is the act by which the infinite Being loves his infinite perfection. This is an absolute fact of which we can give no reason *a priori*.

In God there is, *strictly* speaking, no duty; there is the absolute necessity of being holy.

240. The act essentially moral in creatures is the love of God. It is impossible to found the morality of this act on the morality of any other act.

241. The acts of creatures are moral in so far as they participate of this love, explicitly or implicitly.

242. Creatures which see God intuitively, love him necessarily; and thus all their acts, stamped with this august mark, are necessarily moral.

243. Creatures which do not see God intuitively necessarily love good in general, or under an indeterminate idea; but they do not love necessarily any object in particular.

244. In this love of good in general, these free acts are moral, when their will wills the order which God has willed, without mingling with this order foreign or contrary combinations.

245. In order that an act may be moral, it is not necessary that the one who performs it should think explicitly of God, nor that his will should love him explicitly.

246. The act is more moral, in proportion as it is accompanied with greater reflection on its morality and its conformity to the will of God.

247. Moral sentiment was given us in order that we might perceive the beauty of the order willed by God; it is, so to speak, an *instinct* of love of God.

248. As this sentiment is innate, indelible, and independent of reflection, even atheists experience it.

249. The idea of moral obligation or duty results from two ideas: the order willed by God, and the physical freedom to depart from this order. God granting us life, wills us to try to preserve it; but man is free, and sometimes kills himself. He that preserves his life fulfils a duty; he that destroys himself, infringes it. Thus the idea of duty contains the idea of physical freedom, which cannot be exercised, in a certain sense, without departing from the order which God has established.

250. Punishment is a sanction of the moral order; it serves to supply the necessity which is impossible in free beings. Creatures that act without knowledge, fulfil their destiny by an absolute necessity; free beings do not fulfil their destiny by an absolute necessity, but by that kind of necessity produced by the sight of a painful result.

251. Here may be seen the difference between physical evil and moral evil even in the same free being; physical evil is pain; moral evil is the departure from the order willed by God.

252. Unlawful is what is contrary to a duty.

253. Lawful is what is not opposed to any duty.

254. The eternal law is the order of intelligent beings, willed by God conformably to his infinite holiness.

255. Intrinsically moral acts are those which form a part of the order which God (supposing the will to create such or such beings) has willed necessarily, by force of the love of his infinite perfection. Such actions are commanded because they are good.

256. The actions which are good because they are commanded are those which form a part of the order which God has willed freely, and of which he has given creatures knowledge.

257. The command of God is his will communicated to creatures. If this will is necessary, the precept is natural, if free, the precept is positive.

258. Regarding the natural only, the order willed by God is that which leads to the preservation and perfection of created beings. Actions are moral when conformed to this order.

259. The natural perfection of beings consists in using their faculties for the end for which their nature shows them to be destined.

260. Nature has charged each individual to take care of his own preservation and perfection.

261. The natural impossibility of man's living alone, shows that the preservation and perfection of individuals must be obtained in society.

262. The first society is the family.

263. Parents must support and educate their children; for without this the human race could not be preserved.

264. Conjugal duties arise from the order necessary for the preservation and perfection of the society of the family, which is indispensable for the preservation of the human race.

265. The more necessary the connection of an act with the preservation and perfection of the family, the more necessary is its morality, and consequently the less subject to modifications.

266. The immorality of acts contrary to chastity, and especially of those against nature, is founded on great reasons of an order indispensable for the preservation of the individual and the species.

267. Passions, because they are blind, are evidently given us as means, not as ends.

268. Therefore, when the gratification of the passions is taken, not as a means, but as the end, the act is immoral. A simple example will explain this idea. The pleasure of eating has a very useful object in the preservation of the individual; thus to eat *with* pleasure is not evil, but good; to eat *for* the pleasure of eating is to invert the order: the act is not good. The same action which in the first case is very reasonable, in the second, is an act of *gluttony*. Common sense renders any proof of this superfluous.

269. If a man lived all alone, the use of his physical freedom could never injure any one but himself; the moral limit of his freedom would be to satisfy his wants and desires in conformity to the dictates of reason. But as men live in society, the exercise of the physical freedom of one necessarily interferes with the freedom of others; to prevent disorder it is necessary that the physical freedom of each one should be restricted a little, and that all should be subjected to an order conformed to reason and conducive to the general good; hence the necessity of civil legislation. But as the legislation cannot be established or preserved by itself alone, a public power becomes necessary. The object of society is the general good, in subjection to the principles of eternal morality; the same is the object of the public power.

270. This theory explains satisfactorily the double character presented by the moral order: the absolute, and the relative. The heart, reason, and common sense force us to acknowledge in the moral order something absolute and independent of the consideration of utility; this is explained by rising to an absolute act of absolute perfection, and regarding the morality of creatures as a participation of that act. Reason and experience teach that the morality of actions has *useful* results; this is explained by observing that the absolute act includes the love of the order which must rule among created beings in order that they may fulfil their destinies. This order, then, is at the same time *willed* by God, and *conducive* to the special end of each creature; therefore it is at the same time both *moral* and *useful*.

271. But these two characters are always kept essentially distinct; the first we *perceive*; the second we *calculate*. When the first is wanting, we are *evil*; when the second fails, we are *unfortunate*. The painful result is *punishment* when our will has knowingly violated the order; otherwise, it is simply *misfortune*.

272. I hope I may flatter myself that this theory is somewhat more satisfactory than those invented by some modern philosophers for the purpose of explaining the absolute nature of morality. I had need of the idea of God, it is true; but I conceive no moral order, if God be taken from the world. Without God morality is nothing but a blind sentiment, as absurd in its object as in itself; the philosophy which does not found it on God, can never explain it scientifically; it must confine itself to establishing the fact as a necessity whose character and origin they know nothing of.

273. I shall add one observation which is an epitome of my whole theory, and will show wherein it differs from others which likewise acknowledge that the foundation of the moral order is in God, and that the love of God is the first of all duties. The systems to which I refer, suppose the idea of morality to be distinct from the idea of the love of God; but I say that the love of God is the *essence* of morality. Thus I assert that the infinite holiness is *essentially* the love with which God loves himself; that the first and essentially moral act of creatures is the love of God; that the morality of all their actions consists in explicit or implicit conformity to the will of God, which is the same as the explicit or implicit love of God.

One of the most remarkable results of this theory which places the essence of morality in the love of God, or of the infinite good, is that it destroys the difference of form of moral and metaphysical propositions, showing that the *must* and *ought* of the former is reduced to the absolute *is* of the latter. [97] The explanation of this important result is the following.

The proposition: to love God is good morally, is an absolute and identical proposition; for moral goodness is the same thing as the love of God.

The proposition: to love our neighbor is good, is reduced to the former, since to love our neighbor is, in a certain sense, to love God.

The proposition: to help our neighbor is good, is reduced to the last, for to help is to love.

The proposition: man ought to preserve his life, is explained by this absolute proposition: the preservation of man's life *is* willed by God. Thus the word *ought* expresses the necessity that man should preserve his life, if he does not mean to oppose the order willed by God.

These examples are enough to show how easily moral propositions may be reduced to an absolute form. I cannot see how this is possible, if instead of saying that the love of God is morality, we distinguish between morality and love, saying that the love of God is a moral act.

274. Whatever judgment may be formed of this explanation, it cannot be denied that by it, a profound wisdom, even in the natural and philosophical order, is recognized in that admirable doctrine of our divine Master, in which he calls the love of God the first and greatest of the commandments; and in which, when he wishes to point out the character of the moral good, he especially designates the fulfilment of the divine will.

275. If we place the essence of morality in love, that which is moral must appear beautiful, since nothing is more beautiful than love; it must be agreeable to the soul, since nothing is more pleasing than love. We see also why the ideas of disinterestednessss and sacrifice seem so beautiful in the moral order, and make us instinctively reject the theory of self-interest; nothing more disinterested than love, nothing more capable of great sacrifices.

276. Thus egotism is banished from the moral order: God loves himself, because he is infinitely perfect; outside of him there is nothing to love which he has not created. The love which he has for creatures is completely disinterested, since he can receive nothing from them. The creature loves itself and also others; but what it loves in itself and in other creatures, is the reflection of the infinite good. It desires to be united to the supreme good, and in this it places its last happiness; but this desire is united with the love of the supreme good in itself, which the creature does not love precisely for the reason that thence results its own happiness.

CHAPTER XXI
A GLANCE AT THE WORK

277. I have approached the term of my labor; and it is well to cast a glance over the long path which I have travelled.

I proposed to examine the fundamental ideas of our mind, whether considered in themselves, or in their relations to the world.

278. With regard to objects, we have found in our mind two primitive facts; the intuition of extension, and the idea of being. All objective sensibility is founded on the intuition of extension; all the pure intellectual order in what relates to indeterminate ideas, is founded on the idea of being. We have seen that from the idea of being proceed the ideas of identity, distinction, unity, number, duration, time, simplicity, composition, the finite, the infinite, the necessary, the contingent, the mutable, the immutable, substance, accident, cause, and effect.

279. We find in the subjective order, as facts of consciousness, sensibility, or sensitive being, (including, in this, sentiment as well as sensation,) intelligence, and will; whence we have intuitive ideas of determinate modes of being, distinct from extended beings.

280. Thus all the elements of our mind are reduced to the intuitive ideas of extension, sensibility, intelligence, and will, and the indeterminate ideas which are all founded on the idea of being.

281. From the idea of being, combined with not-being, springs the principle of contradiction, which of itself produces only indeterminate cognitions. In order that science should have an object that could be realized, the idea of being must be presented under some form. Our intuition gives two: extension, and consciousness.

282. Consciousness presents three modes of being: sensibility, or sensitive being; intelligence, and will.

283. Extension, considered in all its purity, as we imagine it in space, is the basis of geometry.

284. The same extension modified in various ways, and placed in relation with our sensibility, is the basis of all the natural sciences, of all those which have for their object, the corporeal universe.

285. Intelligence gives rise to ideology and psychology.

286. The will, in so far as moved by ends, gives rise to the moral sciences.

287. The idea of being begets the principle of contradiction; and, by this principle, the general and indeterminate ideas, whose combination produces ontology, which circulates, like a life-giving fluid, through all the other sciences.

288. Such I conceive the tree of human science: to examine its roots was the object of the *Fundamental Philosophy*.

NOTES TO BOOK SEVENTH

ON CHAPTER I.

There are not wanting those who have believed that time is a thing very easily explained. Such is the opinion of Buffier in his celebrated *Traité des premières verités*. [98] After explaining in his own way in what duration and time consist, he adds:

"J'admire donc que tant de philosophes aient parlé du *temps* et de la *durée* comme de choses inexplicables ou incompréhensibles: *si non rogas, intelligo*, leur fait-on dire, et selon la paraphrase de Locke, *plus je m'applique à découvrir la nature du temps, moins je la conçois. Le temps qui découvre toutes les choses ne saurait être compris lui-même.* Cependant, à quoi se réduisent tous ces mystères? A deux mots que nous venons d'exposer."

It is strange that so distinguished a writer should not have known, or should not have remembered, that the difficulty of explaining time was acknowledged not only by the philosophers of whom he speaks, but even by so eminent a man as St. Augustine. The words to which he alludes are from St. Augustine, and are found in the fourteenth chapter of the second book of his confessions:

"Quid enim est tempus, quis hoc facile, breviterque explicaverit? Quis hoc ad verbum de illo proferendum vel cognatione comprehenderit ... quid ergo est tempus? Si nemo ex me quærat scio, si quærenti explicare velim nescio."

"What is time? If no one ask me, I know, but if I wish to explain it, I know it not."

The great doctor discovered here a profound question, and like all great geniuses when they find themselves in sight of a deep abyss, he felt a strong desire to know what was hidden in its bottom. Full of a holy enthusiasm, he turns to God, and begs him to explain this mystery:

"Exarsit animus meus nosse istud implicatissimum enigma. Noli claudere, Domine Deus, bone pater; per Christum obsecro, noli claudere desiderio meo ista et usitata, et abdita, quominus in ea penetret, et dilucescant allucente misericordia tua, Domine! Quem percunctabor de his? et cui fructuosius confitebor imperitiam meam nisi tibi, cui non sunt molesta studia mea flammantia vehementer in scripturas tuas? Da quod amo; amo enim, et hoc tu dedisti. Da, pater, qui vere nosti data bona dare filiis tuis. Da, quoniam suscepi cognoscere te; et labor est ante me donec aperias.

"Per Christum obsecro, in nomine ejus sancti sanctorum nemo mihi obstrepat. Et ego credidi propter quod et loquor. Hæc est spes mea, ad hanc vivo, ut contempler delectationes Domini. Ecce veteres posuisti dies meos, et transeunt; et quomodo, nescio. Et dicimus, *Tempus et tempus, tempora et tempora. Quamdiu dixit hoc ille; quamdiu fecit hoc ille; et quam longo tempore illud non vidi; et duplum temporis habet hæc syllaba; ad illam simplam brevem.* Dicimus hæc, et audimus hæc: et intelligimur, et intelligimus. Manifestissima et usitatissima sunt, et eadem rursus nimis latent, et nova est inventio eorum. (Lib. XI., cap. xxii.)

"Video igitur tempus quamdam esse distensionem, sed video an videre mihi videor? Tu demonstrabis lux, veritas. (Cap. xxiii.)

"Et confiteor tibi (Domine) ignorare me adhuc quid sit tempus; et rursus confiteor tibi (Domine) scire me in tempore ista dicere, et diu me jam loqui de tempore, atque idipsum diu, non esse nisi moram temporis. Quomodo igitur hoc sciam, quando quid sit tempus nescio? an forte nescio quemadmodum dicam quod scio? Hei mihi qui nescio saltem quid nesciam! Ecce Deus meus coram te, quia non mentior; sicut loquor ita est cor meum. Tu illuminabis lucernam meam, Domine Deus meus; illuminabis tenebras meas." (Cap. xxv.)

To present as easy things which seemed difficult to the greatest men, is, to say the least of it, rather bold. The author flatters himself, in such instances that he has settled the question when he has not penetrated beyond its surface.

It often happens that objects seem very clear at first, and we only discover the difficulty which they present, when we examine them more closely. Ask a man unskilled in questions of philosophy, what extension is, or space, or time, and he will wonder that you find any difficulty *in things so clear*. And why? Because his first reflex act does not go beyond the ordinary idea of these objects, or rather, the use of this idea. Father Buffier says, in the chapter from which we quoted before:

"Dans toutes ces recherches de métaphysique, si embarassées en apparence, il ne faut, comme je l'ai dit d'abord, que distinguer les idées les plus simples que nous avons dans l'esprit d'avec les noms qui y sont attachés par l'usage, pour y découvrir ce qui nous doit tenir lieu de première vérité à leur sujet."

I do not deny that this observation presents a useful criterion; but I cannot see in it so simple a means of solving the most difficult questions of philosophy. For the difficulty is in distinguishing with exactness these simple ideas, which, because they constitute the foundation of our knowledge, are, for this very reason, generally placed at a greater depth, and covered over with a thousand different objects, which hinder us from perceiving them clearly and distinctly, Father Buffier was led astray by the very clearness of his explanation of time, and believed he saw the bottom of the abyss, when he only saw the reflection on its surface:

"Qu'est-ce que durer? C'est *exister sans être détruit*: voilà l'explication la plus nette qu'on puisse donner de la durée; mais le simple mot de *durée* fait comprendre la chose aussi clairement que cette explication.

"Outre l'idée de la durée, nous avons l'idée de la mesure de la durée, qui n'est pas la durée elle-même, bien que nous confondions souvent l'une avec l'autre; comme il arrive d'ordinaire de confondre nos sentiments ou avec leurs effets, ou avec leurs causes, ou avec leurs autres circonstances.

"Or, cette mesure de la durée n'est autre chose que ce que nous appelons le *temps*; et le temps n'est que *la révolution régulière de quelque chose de sensible*, comme du cours annuel du soleil, ou du cours mensuel de la lune, ou diurnal d'une aiguille sur le cadran d'une horloge.

"L'attention que nous avons à cette révolution régulière fait précisément en nous l'idée du temps. L'intervalle de cette révolution se divisant en de moindres intervalles forme l'idée des parties du temps, auxquelles nous donnons aussi le nom de *temps* plus long ou plus court, selon les divers intervalles de la révolution.

"Quand nous avons une fois acquis cette idée du temps, nous l'appliquons à toute la durée que nous concevons ou que nous supposons répondre à tel intervalle de la révolution régulière, et par là nous donnons à la durée même le nom de temps, appliquant le nom de de la mesure à la chose mesurée; mais sans que la durée qu'on mesure soit au fond le temps auquel on la mesure, et qui est une révolution. Ainsi, Dieu a duré avant le temps, c'est-à-dire *a été sans cesser d'être avant la création du monde, et avant la révolution régulière d'aucun corps.*"

Here follows the passage already quoted, where the author shows his surprise that the explanation of time has been found so difficult. After giving his rule that *the simplest ideas must be separated from the terms which custom has joined to them,* he concludes with these words:

"Par ces deux moyens nous trouvons tout d'un coup l'idée ou la notion de *durée* et de *temps*: j'ai l'idée d'un être en tant qu'il ne cesse pas d'être, c'est ce qui s'appelle *durée*; j'ai l'idée de cette durée en tant qu'elle est mesurée par la révolution régulière d'un corps ou par les intervalles de cette révolution, c'est ce que j'appelle *temps*. Il me semble que ces notions sont aussi claires qu'elles peuvent l'être, et celui qui cherche à les éclaircir davantage est à peu près aussi peu sensé que celui qui voudrait éclaircir comment deux fois deux font quatre et ne font pas cinq."

What explanation is contained in these passages? I can see none. Duration, says Buffier, is uninterrupted succession, and time is the measure of this duration. But he ought to have reflected that only what has quantity can be measured; and consequently duration cannot he measured, unless he supposes a length before the measure. This is precisely what the difficulty consists in. It is well known that time is measured by reference to the revolution of some quantity.

But what he ought to have explained was, the nature of that which is measured, of this quantity, or length, independently of the measure. Measure requires *a greater and a less*, and this *greater and less* exists independently of all measure. What, then, is the nature of this quantity, of this *greater and less*?

Father Buffier observes, that although there were no succession of thought in us, and we should have only one thought, we should still have the idea of duration as much as ever. This is true, if we make the idea of duration the same as the idea of uninterrupted existence. But on this hypothesis we could not measure this duration, and consequently could not have the idea of time.

"In God," says Buffier, "there is no succession, for, does not his being endure always?" No doubt of it; but this argument instead of confirming his doctrine, only shows its weakness. The duration of God cannot be measured unless we suppose a *greater and less* in the duration of necessary and infinite being. Therefore, the idea of duration, or uninterrupted existence, does not give us the idea of time, or of a duration that can be measured.

ON CHAPTER IV.

The denial of all succession in eternity, and making it all present, without any past or future, must not be regarded as a vain subtlety of the schools. Long before the scholastics this had been taught by the most eminent authors. St. Augustine says:

"Idipsum enim tempus tu feceras: nec præterire potuerunt tempora antequam faceres tempora. Si autem ante cœlum et terram nullum erat tempus, cur quæritur quid tunc faciebas? Non enim erat tunc, ubi non erat tempus; nec in tempore tempora præcedis; alioquin non omnia tempora præcederes.

"Sed præcedis omnia tempora præterita, celsitudine semper præsentis æternitatis: et superas omnia futura; quia et illa futura sunt; et cùm venerint præterita erunt; *tu autem idem ipse es, et anni tui non deficient.* Anni tui nec eunt, nec veniunt: isti autem nostri, et eunt, et veniunt, ut omnes veniant. Anni tui omnes simul stant, quoniam stant; nec euntes à venientibus excluduntur, quia non transeunt: isti autem nostri omnes erunt cum omnes non erunt. Anni tui dies unus: et dies tuus non quotidie, sed hodie: quia hodiernus tuus non cedit crastino neque succedit hesterno. Hodiernus tuus æternitas; ideo coæternum genuisti, cui dixisti: Ego hodie genui te. Omnia tempora tu fecisti, et ante omnia tempora tu es, nec aliquo tempore non erat tempus." (Conf. Lib. XI., cap. xiii.)

In another place we find the same doctrine in these terms:

"Anni Dei æternitas Dei est. Æternitas ipsa Dei substantia est, quæ nihil habet mutabile. Ibi nihil est præteritum, quasi jam non sit; nihil est futurum, quasi nondum sit. Non est ibi, nisi *est*. Non est ibi, *fuit* et *erit*, quia et quod fuit jam non est; et quod erit nondum est; sed quidquid ibi est, non nisi est." (In Psal. 101; Serm. 2, num. 10.)

Plato was not ignorant of this truth, and the holy fathers have constantly taught it. When the scholastics adopted the definition of Boëthius, that eternity is *interminabilis vitæ tota simul et perfecta possessio*, they only embraced a doctrine as solid as it was universal.

It is difficult to explain these sublime ideas in a more lofty or a more profound manner than Fenelon does in his *Treatise on the Existence of God*. [99]

"C'est retomber dans l'idée du temps, et confondre tout, que de vouloir imaginer en Dieu rien qui ait rapport à aucune succession. En lui rien ne dure, parce que rien ne passe: tout est fixe; tout est à la fois; tout est immobile. En Dieu rien n'a été, rien ne sera; mais tout est. Supprimons donc pour lui toutes les questions que l'habitude et la faiblesse de l'esprit fini, qui veut embrasser l'infini à sa mode étroite et raccourcie, me tenterait de faire. Dirai-je, ô mon Dieu, que vous aviez déjà une éternité d'existence en vous-même avant que vous m'eussiez créé, et qu'il vous reste encore une autre éternité, après ma création, où vous existez toujours? Ces mots de *déjà* et d'*après* sont indignes de celui qui est. Vous ne pouvez souffrir aucun passé et aucun avenir en vous. C'est une folie que de vouloir diviser votre éternité, qui est une permanence indivisible: c'est vouloir que le rivage s'enfuie, parce qu'en descendant le long d'un fleuve, je m'éloigne toujours de ce rivage qui est immobile. Insensé que je suis! Je veux, ô immobile vérité, vous attribuer l'être borné, changeant et successif de votre créature! Vous n'avez en vous aucune mesure dont on puisse mesurer votre existence; car elle n'a ni bornes ni parties; vous n'avez rien de mesurable: les mesures même qu'on peut tirer des êtres bornés, changeants, divisibles et successifs, ne peuvent servir à vous mesurer, vous qui êtes infini, indivisible, immuable et permanent. Comment dirai-je donc que la courte durée de la créature est par rapport à votre éternité? N'étiez-vous pas avant moi? Ne serez-vous pas après moi? Ces paroles tendent à signifier quelque vérité; mais elles sont à la rigueur indignes et impropres. Ce qu'elles ont de vrai, c'est que l'infini surpasse infiniment le fini; qu'ainsi votre existence infinie surpasse infiniment en tout sens mon existence, qui, étant bornée, a un commencement, un présent et un futur. Mais il est faux que la création de votre ouvrage partage votre éternité en deux éternités. Deux éternités ne feraient pas plus qu'une seule: une éternité partagée, qui aurait une partie antérieure et une partie postérieure, ne serait plus une véritable éternité: en voulant la multiplier, on la détruirait, parce qu'une partie serait nécessairement la borne de l'autre par le bout où elles se toucheraient. Qui dit éternité, s'il entend ce qu'il dit, ne dit que ce qui est, et rien au delà; car tout ce qu'on ajoute à cette infinie simplicité l'anéantit. Qui dit éternité ne souffre plus le langage du temps. Le temps et l'éternité sont incommensurables, ils ne peuvent être comparés; et on est séduit par sa propre faiblesse toutes les fois qu'on imagine quelque rapport entre des choses si disproportionnées. Vous avez néanmoins, ô mon Dieu, fait quelque chose hors de vous; car je ne suis pas vous, et il s'en faut infiniment. Quand est-ce donc que vous m'avez fait? Est-ce que vous n'étiez pas avant que de me faire? Mais que dis-je? Me voilà déjà retombé dans mon illusion et dans les questions du temps. Je parle de vous comme de moi, ou comme de quelque autre être passager que je pourrais mesurer avec moi. Ce qui passe peut être mesuré avec ce qui passe; mais ce qui ne passe point est hors de toute mesure et de toute comparaison avec ce qui passe: il n'est permis de demander ni quand il a été, ni s'il était avant ce qui n'est pas, ou qui n'est qu'en passant. Vous êtes, et c'est tout. O que j'aime cette parole, et qu'elle me remplit pour tout ce que j'ai à connaître de vous! Vous êtes *celui qui est*. Tout ce qui n'est point cette parole vous dégrade. Il n'y a qu'elle qui vous ressemble. Eu n'ajoutant rien au mot d'être, elle ne diminue rien de votre grandeur. Elle est, je l'ose dire, cette parole, infiniment parfaite comme vous. Il n'y a que vous qui puissiez parler ainsi, et renfermer votre infini dans trois mots si simples. Je ne suis pas, ô mon Dieu, ce qui est. Hélas! je suis presque ce qui n'est pas. Je me vois comme un milieu incompréhensible entre le néant et l'être. Je suis celui qui a été; je suis celui qui sera; je suis celui qui n'est plus ce qu'il a été; je suis celui qui n'est pas encore ce qu'il sera; et dans cet entre-deux que je suis, un je ne sais quoi qui ne peut s'arrêter en soi, qui n'a aucune consistance, qui s'écoule rapidement comme l'eau; un je ne sais quoi que je ne puis saisir, qui s'enfuit de mes propres mains, qui n'est plus dès que je le veux saisir ou l'apercevoir; un je ne sais quoi qui finit dans l'instant même où il commence; en sorte que je ne puis jamais un seul moment me trouver moi-même, fixe et présent à moi-même, pour dire simplement: Je suis. Ainsi, ma durée n'est qu'une défaillance perpétuelle. O que je suis loin de votre éternité qui est indivisible, infinie, et toujours présente tout entière! Que je suis même bien éloigné de la comprendre! Elle m'échappe à force d'être vraie, simple et immense; comme mon être m'échappe à force d'être composé de parties, mêlé de vérité et de mensonge, d'être et de néant. C'est trop peu que de dire de vous que vous étiez des siècles infinis avant que je fusse. J'aurais honte de parler ainsi; car c'est mesurer l'infini avec le fini qui est un demi-néant. Quand je crains de dire que vous étiez avant que je fusse, ce n'est pas pour douter que vous existant, vous ne m'ayez créé, moi qui n'existais pas: mais c'est pour éloigner de moi toutes les idées imparfaites qui sont au-dessus de vous. Dirai-je que vous étiez avant moi? Non; car voilà deux termes que je ne puis souffrir. Il ne faut pas dire, *vous étiez*; car *vous étiez* marque un temps passé et une succession. Vous êtes: et il n'y a qu'un présent, immobile, indivisible et infini que l'on puisse vous attribuer, pour parler dans la rigueur des termes. Il ne faut point dire que vous avez toujours été, il faut dire que vous êtes; et ce terme de *toujours*, qui est si fort pour la créature, est trop faible pour vous; car il marque une continuité et non une permanence. Il vaut mieux dire simplement et sans restriction, que vous êtes. O Etre! ô Etre! votre éternité, qui n'est que votre être même, m'étonne;

mais elle me console. Je me trouve devant vous comme si je n'étais pas; je m'abîme dans votre infini; et loin de mesurer votre permanence, par rapport à ma fluidité continuelle, je commence à me perdre de vue, à ne me trouver plus, et ne voir en tout que ce qui est; je veux dire vous-même. Ce que j'ai dit du passé, je le dis de même de l'avenir. On ne peut point dire que vous serez après ce qui passe; car vous ne passez point. Ainsi, vous ne serez présent en parlant de vous. On ne dit point d'un rivage immobile, qu'il devance ou qu'il suit les flots d'une rivière: il ne devance ni ne suit; car il ne marche point. Ce que je remarque de ce rivage par rapport à l'immobilité locale, je le dois dire de l'être infini par rapport à l'immobilité d'existence. Ce qui passe a été et sera, et passe du prétérit au futur par un présent imperceptible, qu'on ne peut jamais assigner. Mais ce qui ne passe point existe absolument, et n'a qu'un présent infini: il est, et c'est tout ce qu'il est permis d'en dire: il est sans temps dans tous les temps de la création. Quiconque sort de cette simplicité, tombe de l'éternité dans le temps."

NOTE TO BOOK EIGHTH

(3) Perhaps some of my readers, who are not well acquainted with the history of philosophy, may think that I have extended the explanation of the idea of the infinite to too great length, and consider these questions as serving rather to subtilize, than to acquire solid knowledge. This is a great mistake. At all times the philosophical questions of the idea of the infinite have held a prominent position, and at the present time there is scarcely any which require to be more carefully examined, if we wish to stay the progress of pantheism. I shall not cease to repeat that a great many of the most serious errors have their birth in a confusion in their fundamental ideas; if one is well grounded in these ideas, he has nothing to fear from certain works whose secret in leading one astray, consists in using incomprehensible words, or in giving a false sense to those which can be understood. However this may be, I would remind those who believe these questions mere scholastic cavils, that they must regard as cavillers the most eminent philosophers of ancient and modern times.

NOTE TO BOOK NINTH

(4) I know that some modern philosophers, and more especially M. Cousin, reject the accusation of pantheism, and explain in their own way those passages of their works in which this error is professed. As it is not possible for me to examine at any length, a question which would require the insertion of long extracts, I merely refer the reader to what I have said in the body of the work, and with respect to M. Cousin, to the extracts which I have made in my *Letters to a Skeptic in Matters of Religion, Letter I*. It is not the fault of M. Cousin's adversaries that he has used such clear expressions that no man of sound judgment can doubt that they contain a full profession of pantheism. Leaving to the philosopher the responsibility of his intentions, I shall only beg our young men not to judge lightly of the disputes of the neighboring kingdom, which are not always received here through faithful organs; and to withhold their faith from those who would attempt to persuade them that there is no ground for the alarms of men of sound philosophical doctrine.

FOOTNOTES

[1] *Traité des Sensations.* Préface.

[2] See Chap. I.

[3] Book III.

[4] *Transcendental Æsthetics*, § 1.

[5] He speaks of intuitive perception, not of perception in general.

[6] *Transcendental Logic.* Introduction.

[7] *Transc. Log. Transc. Anal.* Book I., Chap. I., Sec. I.

[8] *Transcendental Logic.* Book II., Chap. III.

[9] See what has been said concerning *representation, immediate intelligibility,* and *representation of causality and ideality,* in Chapters X., XI., XII., and XIII., of Book I. of this work.

[10] See Chap. VI.

[11] See Book I., Chs. III. and XXIII.

[12] See Bk. I., Ch. XXVI.

[13] P. I., Q. L. XXIX., A. 12.

[14] *Ib.* Q. L. XXXIV., A. 5.

[15] See Chs. XII. and XIII.

[16] See Ch. XX.

[17] See Ch. XXI.

[18] See Bk. I., Chs. XXXVI., XXVII., and XVIII.

[19] See Bk. IV., Ch. XXIII. to Ch. XXVII.

[20] Sec. 5, P. 1, C. 3, A. 1, § 2.

[21] See Book IV., Ch. XXI.

[22] See L. IV., C. XXIII. to XXVII.

[23] See L. IV., C. XXX.

[24] See L. IV., C. V.

[25] See L. V., C. X.

[26] See L. IV., C. XXVIII. and XXIX.

[27] See Lib. III., Ch. XX.

[28] See Lib. III., Chs. XII., XIII., and XIV.

[29] See Ch. III.

[30] Trans. Æsth. II., A. § 6. w. f.

[31] See Bk. IV., Chapters XIV. and XV.

[32] See Bk. I., Ch. III.

[33] See Bk. I., Ch. XX.

[34] See Bk. I., Ch. XXV.

[35] See Bk. I., Chap. III.

[36] See Book V., Ch. XI.

[37] See Book V., Chapters XIV., XV., and XVI.

[38] See Chap. V.

[39] See Bk. III., Chaps. XIX., XXI., XXIV., XXV., XXVI., XXVII. and XXVIII.

[40] I am speaking of the difference between *positive* quantities; for with regard to other quantities we may express an infinite difference algebraically. Let the two quantities be (∞ - a) and ($-a$). The difference between them will be expressed in this equation, $D=(\infty - a) - (-a) = \infty - a$ $a = \infty$.

[41] See Book III., Chapter VIII.

[42] *Lettres entre Leibnitz et Clarke*, Vième Écrit. de Leibnitz, § 73.

[43] Von den Paralogismen der reinen Vernunft, p. 297.

[44] See Bk. IV., Chs. XIII., XIV., XV., XVI., XXI., and XXII.

[45] Critik der reinen Vernunft, p. 298.

[46] Critik der reinen Vernunft, p. 299.

[47] See Book VIII., Chapters XII. and XIV.

[48] See Chaps. VI., VII., VIII., IX., and X.

[49] Non ergo per essentiam suam, sed per actum suum se cognoscit intellectus noster, et hoc dupliciter. Uno quidem modo particulariter, secundum quod Sortes, vel Plato percipit se habere animam intellectivam ex hoc,

quod percipit se intelligere. Alio modo in universali, secundum quod naturam mentis humanæ ex actu intellectus consideramus. Sed verum est quod judicium, et efficacia hujus cognitionis per quam naturam animæ cognoscimus, competit nobis secundum derivationem luminis intellectus nostri a veritate divina, in qua rationes omnium rerum continentur, sicut supra dictum est. Unde August. dicit in 9 de Trin. Intuemur inviolabilem veritatem, ex qua perfecte quantum possumus, deffinimus, non qualis sit uniuscujusque hominis mens, sed qualis esse sempiternis rationibus debeat. Est autem differentia inter has duas cognitiones; nam ad primam cognitionem de mente habendam sufficit ipsa mentis præsentia, quæ est principium actus, ex quo meus percipit seipsam: et ideo dicitur se cognoscere per suam præsentiam. Sed ad secundam cognitionem de mente habendam, non sufficit ejus præsentia: sed requiritur diligens, et subtilis inquisitio. Unde et multi naturam animæ ignorant, et multi etiam circa naturam animæ erraverunt. Propter quod August. dicit 10 de Trin. de tali inquisitione mentis, Non velut absentem se quærat mens cernere; sed præsentem quærat discernere; id est cognoscere differentiam suam ab aliis rebus, quod est cognoscere quidditatem, et naturam suam. S. Thom. *Sum. Theol.* P. I. Q., LXXXVII., A. 1.

[50] Odyss., Bk. IV.

[51] See Bk. I., Chap. VII.

[52] *Grundlage der gesammten Wissensehaftslehre.* Erst. Th. 1. § 6. b.

[53] Here, as elsewhere, in the examination of Fichte's system, I have translated the German word *setzen* and the Spanish *poner* by the verb *to suppose.* Had I known any better word I should have used it, but I think this sufficiently explains the philosopher's meaning. I have also found the French word *poser* which exactly corresponds to it, and which M. Cousin uses in his sketch of Fichte's system, translated *suppose* by Mr. Ripley, in the *Specimens of Foreign Literature.*—Translator.

[54] See Bk. IV., from Ch. I. to X.

[55] *Grundlage der gesammten Wissenschaftslehre,* I. Theil, § I., pp. 97-98.

[56] Ib., II., Th. § 4. B., p. 129.

[57] Ib., D., pp. 137-8.

[58] Ib., Deduction der Vorstellung, III., pp. 233-4.

[59] See Bk. IV., Chs. XXIII., XXIV., XXV., XXVI., and XXVII.; and Bk. V., Chs. VII. and VIII.

[60] Ib., § 3., pp. 106-7.

[61] Ib., III., Th. § 5, II., p. 256.

[62] Ib., p. 255.

[63] See Bks. II., III., and IV.

[64] See Bk. III., Ch. XVII.

[65] Kant, *Critik der reinen Vernunft, Trause. Log.*

[66] Preface of the edition of Leipsic, 1838.

[67] See Bk. V., Chs. IX. and X.

[68] See Bk. V., Ch. IX.

[69] See Bk. I., Ch. VIII. to XIV.

[70] See Bk. I., Ch. XXV.

[71] See the whole of Book VIII.

[72] See Bk. IV., Chs. XXIII., XXIV., XXV., XXVI., and XXVII.

[73] See Ch. II.

[74] See Bk. VIII., Ch. XX. to the end.

[75] See Bk. IV., Chs. XXII. to XXVIII., and Bk. V., Chs. VII. and VIII.

[76] See Bk. V., Chs. VII. and VIII.

[77] See Bk. VII.

[78] See Bk. VII., Chs. IV. and V.

[79] *Lett. filos. sulle vicissit. della filosofia*, Lettera XIV.

[80] See Book V., Chap. IX.

[81] See Bk. I., Chap. XXV.

[82] See Bk. IV., Chaps. XI., XIII., XIV., XV., XVI., XIX., XX., XXI., and XXII.

[83] See Bk. IV., Chap. XXI.

[84] Ib., § 135.

[85] Ib., § 134.

[86] Ib., § 130.

[87] Ib., Chap. XXII.

[88] Ib., § 139.

[89] See Book IV., Ch. XXII.

[90] See Bk. IX., Chs. VI., VII., IX., and XI.

[91] See Bk. IX.

[92] See Ch. XIII.

[93] See Bk. III.

[94] See Chs. XI. and XIII.

[95] See Ch. XII.

[96] See Bk. IV., Chs. XXIV., XXV., XXVI., and XXVII.

[97] See §§ 210, 211, 212, and 213.

[98] Part II., ch. xxiii. De la durée et du temps.

[99] II. part, ch. ii., § 9.